THE KOREAN PENINSULA
1950-1953

THE
GENERAL
VS. THE
PRESIDENT

Also by H. W. Brands

The Reckless Decade
T.R.
The First American
The Age of Gold
Lone Star Nation
Andrew Jackson
Traitor to His Class
American Colossus
The Murder of Jim Fisk for the Love of Josie Mansfield
The Man Who Saved the Union
Reagan

E
GENERAL
VS. THE
PRESIDENT

*MacArthur and Truman at the
Brink of Nuclear War*

H. W. Brands

DOUBLEDAY
New York   London   Toronto
Sydney   Auckland

All rights reserved. Published in the United States by Doubleday,
a division of Penguin Random House LLC, New York, and
distributed in Canada by Random House of Canada, a division
of Penguin Random House Canada Limited, Toronto.

www.doubleday.com

DOUBLEDAY and the portrayal of an anchor with a dolphin are
registered trademarks of Penguin Random House LLC.

Book design by Michael Collica
Jacket design by Michael J. Windsor

Jacket images: (left) Douglas MacArthur: US Army/The LIFE Picture
Collection/Getty Images; (right) President Harry S. Truman: George Skadding/
The LIFE Picture Collection/Getty Images (both colorized); (center) first
atomic explosion, July 16, 1945: Everett Historical/Shutterstock

Library of Congress Cataloging-in-Publication Data
Names: Brands, H. W., author.
Title: The general and the president : MacArthur and Truman
at the brink of nuclear war / H. W. Brands.
Description: First edition. | New York : Doubleday, [2016]
| Includes bibliographical references and index.
Identifiers: LCCN 2016021412 (print) | LCCN 2016028026 (ebook) |
ISBN 9780385540575 (hardcover) | ISBN 9780385540582 (ebook) |
Subjects: LCSH: Truman, Harry S., 1884–1972—Political and social views.
| MacArthur, Douglas, 1880–1964—Political and social views. | Nuclear
warfare—Government policy—United States—History—20th century. | United
States—Military policy. | Presidents—United States—Biography. | Generals—
United States—Biography. | World War, 1939–1945—Influence. | Cold
War—Political aspects—United States. | Korean War, 1950–1953—Diplomatic
history. | Korean War, 1950–1953—China. | BISAC:
HISTORY / United States / 20th Century. | HISTORY / Military / Korean
War. | BIOGRAPHY & AUTOBIOGRAPHY / Presidents & Heads of State.
Classification: LCC E814 .B73 2016 (print) |
LCC E814 (ebook) | DDC 973.918092—dc23
LC record available at +https://lccn.loc.gov/2016021412

MANUFACTURED IN THE UNITED STATES OF AMERICA

1 3 5 7 9 10 8 6 4 2

First Edition

CONTENTS

THE
GENERAL
VS. THE
PRESIDENT

December 1950

C LEMENT ATTLEE DIDN'T like appearing flustered. The British prime minister's predecessor, Winston Churchill, was the one who indulged in dramatics: the speeches about blood, sweat and tears; finest hours; Iron Curtains. Attlee had evicted Churchill from 10 Downing Street at the end of World War II in no small part because the British people wanted less drama and more predictability. Yet the sudden news from America had even Attlee sweating. The House of Commons was debating the optimal course of British foreign policy when the BBC brought word that Harry Truman was brandishing the atom bomb against China. This itself horrified the British lawmakers. The American president was the only person in history who had ordered the use of the monstrous weapon, and a man who had atom-bombed Japan might, without additional scruple, do the same to China. But there was a crucial new element, these five years after Hiroshima and Nagasaki, that made the prospect still more appalling. The Russians had the bomb, too, and were China's allies. A nuclear war in 1950 would not be one-sided.

And there was something else, something that pushed the alarm level in Britain far past that of any previous Cold War crisis. By Truman's own statement, the decision on use of the atom bomb rested with the American field commander in Korea, Douglas MacArthur. Attlee and many others in Britain could think of no one more frightening than MacArthur to have control of the bomb. MacArthur was brilliant, brave and imaginative—even his critics granted that. But the general had isolated himself so long in Asia, and surrounded himself with such sycophants, that he had lost all perspective. He suffered from an extreme version of the theater commander's habit of thinking his own region the pivot of any conflict. During World War II MacArthur had behaved as though fascism would triumph or be defeated according to the outcome of battle in the Pacific; in the Cold War he contended that communism would win or lose depending on what happened in Asia. He had chafed at the communist victory in China's civil war, now a year past. The outbreak of fighting in Korea five months ago had given him his chance to engage the communists, and the sudden entry of China into the conflict, just a week ago, had raised the stakes dramatically. MacArthur seemed to relish the opportunity to smash the communists, using whatever weapons were available. And now Truman was making the ultimate weapon available.

The House of Commons burst into an uproar on hearing the word from Washington. Members of Attlee's Labour party, already convinced that the Americans were reckless and MacArthur was a maniac, threatened a mutiny against their prime minister for his support of the American-led effort in Korea. To quell the uprising, Attlee announced that he would travel to America. He implied that he would talk sense and restraint into Truman. But he knew, and they knew, that this was more than he could guarantee. The mutiny hung fire, stemmed for the moment yet hardly vanquished.

Britain's alarm was broadly shared. None of the countries that had supported the United States in the defense of South Korea had bargained on the fighting there triggering World War III. The French distrusted MacArthur even more than the British did, and made no secret of the fact. The French National Assembly called for immediate negotiations to defuse the crisis in Korea. French premier René Pleven hastened to London to meet Attlee before the British prime minister left for Washington, and to lend his voice to those insisting that the Americans refrain from rash moves. Fear of the bomb united rightist and leftist parties in Italy, where protesters branded Truman a war criminal. West German officials, on the front line of the Cold War in Europe, refused to comment publicly but privately said America's use of the bomb against China would almost certainly compel a Russian response, probably against them. India's government, which earlier had conveyed a warning from Beijing that the Chinese would enter the Korean conflict if MacArthur insisted on sending U.S. troops to the Korean-Chinese border—a warning MacArthur had airily dismissed—now predicted that a resort to greater force would provoke a cataclysm. Pope Pius XII urged Catholics to pray that the world might be spared.

Americans shuddered as well. "Is it World War III?" asked the *New York Times*. The paper didn't say yes, but it couldn't say no. New Yorkers flooded the civil-defense offices of the city and state with demands to know where they should seek refuge when the Russian bombs began falling. The state director of civil defense tried to calm things but only made them worse when he said his office was operating "on the basis that an atomic or other attack could take place at any time." The response in other cities and states was much the same.

Members of Congress displayed caution about criticizing the president for standing up to the communists; none wanted to get into the crosshairs of Joseph McCarthy, at the peak of his red-baiting power. But several took pains to assert that the pertinent legislation gave authority over the use of the bomb to the president alone, not to any general. Nonpoliticians were less leery. Clergy and educators implored Truman to refrain from the terrible step he seemed to be contemplating. Frederick Nolde, speaking for the World Council of Churches, declared, "We would veritably be playing into the hands of those who want to pin upon us the tangible responsibility for starting a world war."

IF THE WORLD was alarmed, Harry Truman was livid. And he blamed Douglas MacArthur for getting him into this mess. In his five years as president, Truman had tolerated repeated slights and affronts from MacArthur: the general's habit of making pronouncements on matters beyond his military responsibilities, his failure to return to America to brief the government on the U.S. occupation of Japan, his campaigning for president in 1948 without bothering to resign his command. Truman had suppressed his anger, lest a public row between the president and the general threaten the precarious stability of the Far East. When MacArthur had refused to travel more than half a day from his headquarters in Tokyo to discuss the war in Korea, Truman had undertaken the long journey to Wake Island. There he heard the general state with utter self-assurance that the Chinese would never dare to enter the Korean fighting. If they did, they would be obliterated.

A month later the Chinese entered the war. And they proceeded to manhandle MacArthur's army. Truman was stunned and outraged. How could MacArthur not have seen this coming? Had his arrogance simply blinded him?

MacArthur's horrendous misjudgment had put Truman in an impossible position. Since 1945 the president had been walking a knife-edge of decision between appeasement and war: between yielding to communist pressure and tipping the planet into a new world conflict. In 1946 a stern warning had sufficed to keep the Kremlin from grabbing Iran. In 1947 a stronger dose of American power, in the form of military aid to Greece and Turkey, had preserved the Balkans from a communist takeover. A massive airlift in 1948 had kept Berlin free. The North Atlantic Treaty of 1949 made clear to Moscow that an attack on any of America's allies would be met with the full force of America's arsenal. Billions of dollars of Marshall Plan money continued to pour into Europe to bolster democracy there.

The North Korean attack on South Korea in June 1950 proved that the communists never rested. Truman had responded with measured force, enough to secure South Korea yet not so much as to bring the Soviets into the conflict. But then MacArthur's recklessness had provoked the Chinese to enter the fight. The Soviets, linked to the Chinese by a military pact, and as opportunistic as ever, wouldn't miss a chance to jump the United States where America's alliances were most vulnerable, should the Asian war escalate further. And further escalation was exactly what MacArthur was demanding.

The knife-edge that Truman had been walking suddenly terminated above an abyss. He couldn't go forward without risking a nuclear World War III. He couldn't retreat without undermining the morale of all who looked to America for leadership of the forces resisting communism. MacArthur had drastically narrowed the president's options, and the general had the gall to complain that *his* hands were being tied.

Reporters had heard of MacArthur's complaints; they knew they had a story. They asked Truman for a response. What measures would he authorize the general to employ to fend off the Chinese?

Truman didn't want to answer this question, not least because he hadn't decided. Anyway, as a poker player he knew not to tip his hand. But as a Democratic president harassed by Republicans for softness on communism, he judged he had to say something. "We will take whatever steps are necessary," he replied.

"Will that include the atomic bomb?" a reporter asked.

"That includes every weapon we have."

"Does that mean that there is active consideration of the use of the atomic bomb?"

"There has always been active consideration of its use."

This was huge news. Never had the president spoken so openly about using the bomb. Another reporter wanted to be sure he had heard Truman correctly. "Did we understand you clearly that the use of the atomic bomb is under active consideration?"

"Always has been," Truman said curtly. "It is one of our weapons."

How would the decision on use be made?

"The military commander in the field will have charge of the use of the weapons, as he always has."

This was even bigger news. MacArthur's finger was on the nuclear trigger. The reporters scrambled to file their stories. The shock waves rolled around the world.

As the extent of the alarm echoed back to Washington, Truman's advisers urged him to let the White House issue a clarification. Truman agreed, but grudgingly, for he prided himself on plain speaking. The clarification stated that use of the atom bomb had been under consideration since the start of hostilities in Korea; whenever the United States went to war, all weapons were considered. As to who would make the basic, strategic decision to use the bomb, that would be the president. Tactical choices about where and when the bomb would be used would be left to the military commander in the field.

The clarification didn't alleviate the alarm, for it didn't materially revise Truman's own words. The president was considering the use of the bomb, and MacArthur would determine the time and place.

Truman cursed his bad luck, and he cursed MacArthur. The last thing he wanted was to have to use atomic weapons. He claimed not to have lost sleep over the bombing of Hiroshima and Nagasaki, but no one takes the deaths of a hundred thousand civilians lightly. He hoped not to have to make such a decision again. And this time the consequences would be far more terrible. World War II had ended with atomic bombings; World War III would begin with them. But he couldn't back down. The Chinese were watching. The Russians were watching. Americans were watching. The world was watching.

Now Attlee was coming. Truman hated being on the spot like this: having to explain that he wasn't intending to start another world war, yet having to avoid seeming fearful or reluctant to oppose the communists.

And it was MacArthur's doing. Truman couldn't decide whether the general was the damnedest fool in the army, which had its share of fools, or the canniest political operator he had ever tangled with. Truman had to admit that MacArthur had outmaneuvered him, placing him on the brink of a broader war against China, when that was the last place he wanted to be.

DOUGLAS MACARTHUR, SITTING calmly in his office on the top floor of the Dai Ichi Building in central Tokyo, wondered what all the fuss was about. MacArthur disdained politicians as a class, whether prime ministers or presidents. He believed politicians lacked the knowledge or nerve to make the decisions national safety required. He had dealt with presidents for decades and not found one who didn't falter at the moment of truth or put partisan self-interest ahead of the country's interest. This was why he had kept his distance from Washington. His deliberate exile was in its sixteenth year; he had resisted repeated requests from the White House to come home, and he would continue to resist them as long as he could. His work was more important than what consumed the office seekers. He had guided the Philippines to independence; he had defeated imperial Japan and was building a republican Japan. For the last five months he had been holding the line against communism in Korea.

He was on the verge of doing much more. Since 1945 freedom had been in retreat; communism had captured Eastern Europe and then China. It had come close to engulfing all of Korea. But there he had made a stand and subsequently sent the communists reeling. His success was no thanks to Washington, where the president and his advisers had fretted and quavered until he—Douglas MacArthur—had taken the responsibility upon himself and plunged ahead.

In short order he accomplished what no one else—no president, no general—had accomplished during the Cold War, rolling back the red tide and reclaiming territory previously lost to communism. And once more he defied the fretters, who didn't want to upset the communists of China. He again assumed responsibility and ordered his troops to the Korean border with China.

It was then that the Chinese entered the war, causing everyone in Washington—and London and several other world capitals, apparently—to run for cover. MacArthur took the new development in stride. He admitted that he hadn't expected such large numbers of Chinese to appear in Korea. But what the politicians interpreted as a mauling he accounted the cost of springing the Chinese trap. He had foiled the communists' plan to annihilate his army; he was retreating but stretching their supply lines and rendering them vulnerable to his airpower. He now had the communists just where he wanted them.

All that was required was nerve in Washington. He didn't expect it to appear unprompted. Harry Truman was no less the political animal than Franklin Roosevelt, whom MacArthur had had to educate during World War II. Truman might be educated, too. The general took encouragement from the president's remarks about the atom bomb; maybe he *did* see what was at stake in Korea. Would he follow through? Could he stand up to Attlee and the others who would beseech him to step back? Time would tell.

Was it World War III? Not yet. But if a lifetime at arms had taught Douglas MacArthur anything, it was that an inordinate fear of war was the surest guarantor of war. Hadn't the democracies learned anything from Hitler? Appeasement of the fascists had caused World War II; appeasement of the communists would cause World War III. Only the brave deserved to live free.

MacArthur classed himself among the brave. His country had agreed with his self-assessment, having awarded him all the medals and ribbons it issued. He had risen to the challenge of battle on numerous occasions in the past half century, and, at seventy, he was not too old to rise to the challenge again. He was ready, indeed eager. He had felt this same thrill of anticipation at the crucial moments of World War II, when history had rested on his shoulders. He had delivered then. And if the politicians would get out of his way, he would deliver once more.

PART ONE

TWO ROADS UP THE MOUNTAIN

1

O F ALL THE amazing deeds of bravery of the war, I regard MacArthur's personal landing at Atsugi as the greatest of the lot," Winston Churchill wrote afterward. The former prime minister, a connoisseur of courage, was speaking of the American general's daring flight to the heart of enemy territory at the close of the Pacific war in 1945. The Japanese emperor, following the atomic bombing of Hiroshima and Nagasaki, had called on his subjects to cease fighting, yet more than twenty divisions of soldiers, who had been prepared to give their last drop of blood to keep the Americans from securing a foothold on Japan's sacred soil, retained their weapons and their positions on the Kanto Plain. Kamikaze pilots, some having already received the rites for the dead, awaited only a word to carry out their suicide missions. Squads of young civilians, outraged at the emperor's call for surrender, stormed about Tokyo and nearby Yokohama vowing to resist to the end.

Douglas MacArthur, as the commander of U.S. Army forces in the Pacific, would receive the formal Japanese surrender on board the battleship *Missouri* in Tokyo Bay. Prudence suggested he arrive with the ship, its powerful escort and the protection the vessels and their guns provided. MacArthur refused. He insisted that he would enter Japan ahead of the navy, protected only by the moral force that came with righteous victory. His aides urged him to reconsider. Who knew what some bitter-ender might do? All it took was one bullet, one grenade, and the general would be a dead man. Worse, an assassination might rekindle the Japanese war spirit. If he *must* enter ahead of the navy, he should wait for more army troops. At the very least, he should be accompanied to Atsugi, the air base for Tokyo, by a substantial guard of well-armed soldiers.

He waved aside the worries. He declared that he would travel to Atsugi alone, with only his airplane's crew and his personal staff. His courage would be all the shield he required. He knew the Asian mind. "Years of overseas duty had schooled me well in the ways of the Orient," he later wrote. The Japanese would understand his action and be more impressed by one man alone than by any number of ships or regiments.

Courtney Whitney, one of the staff who accompanied MacArthur on the historic flight, recalled never having been more nervous. "We circled the field at little more than treetop height, and as I looked out at the field and the flat stretches of Kanto Plain, I could see numerous anti-aircraft emplacements," Whitney wrote. "It was difficult not to let my mind dwell on Japan's recent performances. The war had been started without a formal declaration; nearly everywhere Japanese soldiers had refused to give up until killed; the usual laws of war had not been complied with; deadly traps had frequently been set. Here was the greatest opportunity for a final and climactic act. The anti-aircraft guns could not possibly miss at this range. Had death, the insatiable monster of the battle, passed MacArthur by on a thousand fields only to murder him at the end? I held my breath. I think the whole world was holding its breath."

The plane landed without incident. Not a gunner or an airman tried to impede the general's arrival. Only later did MacArthur learn that Japanese army commanders had sent special squads to remove the propellers from potential kamikaze planes, so worried were they about an attack.

MacArthur displayed not the slightest hesitation, not the least tremor. His plane pulled to a halt, and he emerged in the open door. He wore the same unadorned khaki shirt as always, collar open. His crumpled uniform cap was on his head, sunglasses on the bridge of his nose. His corncob pipe was in his hand. He turned to General Robert Eichelberger. "Bob," he said, "this is the payoff."

Japanese troops lined the road from the airfield, their backs to MacArthur's car. Eichelberger was puzzled. Were they protesting MacArthur's presence? Were they protecting him against attack? Eichelberger eventually realized this was a sign of utmost respect. "The turning away of faces was an obeisance which previously had been accorded only to the Emperor himself."

THE MYSTIQUE OF MacArthur was never greater than at that moment. Not everyone was taken by it; the unsmitten argued that the danger that day was less than MacArthur's acolytes, and even the experienced Churchill, judged. The U.S. Navy's presence was obvious on the ground as well as in the harbor; a marine officer remarked, "Our first wave was made up entirely of admirals trying to get ashore before MacArthur." Instead of having to contend with suicide squadrons, MacArthur faced hundreds of reporters and photographers. The army's paratroop corps had landed not just munitions but *musicians,* and the small band of players greeted MacArthur with a military march. The Japanese supplied vehicles for the drive from the air base, but because nearly everything on wheels had been destroyed in the months of American bombing, the procession was led by a charcoal-burning fire engine that started with a loud explosion and featured a siren that couldn't be shut off. Even Courtney Whitney, the most smitten of the MacArthur acolytes and one not disposed to spoil the mood of dauntless courage, likened the fire engine to the Toonerville Trolley.

Yet the Japanese were entranced by MacArthur. "He is a man of light," a Japanese diplomat, Toshikazu Kase, wrote. "Radiantly, the gathering rays of his magnanimous soul embrace the earth. . . . In the dark hour of our despair and distress, a bright light is ushered in, in the very person of General MacArthur." The Japanese had expected harsh treatment from their conquerors, not least because of the brutality their soldiers had meted out to the peoples *they* had conquered. But MacArthur made clear from the beginning that he was a different kind of conqueror. When he discovered how meager were the food supplies in Japan, he ordered American troops to stick to their rations and not feed themselves at the expense of the Japanese. This astonished the Japanese; what conquering army had ever not lived off the land? He ordered that the quarter million Japanese troops on the Kanto Plain be disarmed not by American troops but by their own officers. This astonished the Japanese even more; what conqueror had ever trusted an enemy to disarm itself? How could this American so well understand the Asian concept of face, and be so magnanimous, as to spare the soldiers the humiliation of having to turn over their weapons to an enemy? MacArthur countermanded an order by the U.S. Navy forbidding Japanese fishing vessels to venture across Tokyo Bay, lest some launch mines against the American ships there. The Japanese needed to eat, he explained matter-of-factly.

In the words he uttered at the formal surrender ceremony, MacArthur spoke not of conquest or dominion but of peace and reconciliation. Tokyo Bay bristled with American power; the greatest battle fleet in the world was gathered there. Generals and admirals lined the deck of the *Missouri*. MacArthur was conspicuous for the absence of decorations on his uniform. "Look at Mac," an American sailor whispered. "Ain't he got no ribbons?" A fellow seaman responded, "If he wore them, they'd go clear over his shoulder." The Japanese delegation came aboard, expecting to be held up to public disgrace. "A million eyes seemed to beat on us with the million shafts of a rattling storm of arrows barbed with fire," Toshikazu Kase wrote. "I felt their keenness sink into my body with a sharp physical pain." Representatives of Britain, the Soviet Union, China and several other Allied powers joined the group.

MacArthur had received no instructions from Washington on what to say or do. "I was on my own, standing on the quarterdeck with only God and my own conscience to guide me," he recalled. He found his way. "We are gathered here, representative of the major warring powers, to conclude a solemn agreement whereby peace may be restored," he declared. "The issues, involving divergent ideals and ideologies, have been determined on the battlefields of the world and hence are not for our discussion or debate. Nor is it for us here to meet, representing as we do, a majority of the peoples of the earth, in a spirit of distrust, malice or hatred. But rather it is for us, both victors and vanquished, to rise to that higher dignity which alone befits the sacred purposes we are about to serve. . . . It is my earnest hope, and indeed the hope of all mankind, that from this solemn occasion a better world shall emerge out of the blood and carnage of the past—a world founded upon faith and understanding, a world dedicated to the dignity of man and the fulfillment of his most cherished wish: for freedom, tolerance and justice."

MacArthur signed the surrender document on behalf of the United States. He invited the representatives of the other countries to do the same. After all had done so, he said, "Let us pray that peace be now restored to the world, and that God will preserve it always. These proceedings are now closed."

Toshikazu Kase could hardly believe what had happened. "For me, who expected the worst humiliation, this was a complete surprise," the diplomat recalled. "I was thrilled beyond words, spellbound, thunderstruck." MacArthur's eloquence and vision were like nothing he had ever experienced or heard of. "Here is a victor announcing the verdict to the prostrate enemy. He can exact his pound of flesh if he so chooses. He can impose a humiliating penalty if he so desires. And yet he pleads for freedom, tolerance, and justice." Kase felt a tremendous burden lift from his soul. "MacArthur's words sailed on wings," he said. "This narrow quarterdeck was transformed into an altar of peace."

MACARTHUR CONTINUED TO astonish. He took up residence, with his wife, Jean, and their seven-year-old son, Arthur, in the American embassy. For his office he chose one of the few structures in Tokyo that had survived the American firebombing, an insurance building overlooking the grounds of the imperial palace. The building soon acquired the name Dai Ichi, or "Number One." He departed the embassy at 10:30 each morning in a black Cadillac brought in from the Philippines, where it had belonged to a sugar baron grateful for MacArthur's role in liberating those islands. The car was distinctive enough, but the American flags floating above the fenders and the license plate bearing the number 1 on a field of five silver stars made unmistakable that this car was the American general's. A sergeant drove MacArthur slowly through the streets of the capital. Sometimes MacArthur read newspapers or reports; at other times he sat staring forward, contemplating or even meditating. "His white hands were smooth as wax, only blemished by the brown spots of age," wrote Faubion Bowers, a major who often rode guard in the front seat. "His fingers were exquisitely manicured, as if lacquered with polish. He held them in his lap, peacefully. His profile, which I knew better than his full face, was granitic. He was always immaculately clean-shaven, and I never saw a nick on him. He had large bones, an oversize jaw that jutted a little. From face to walk, from gesture to speech, he shone with good breeding. . . . He was really very beautiful, like fine ore, a splendid rock, a boulder."

Bowers worried that MacArthur's predictable routine and the slow pace of the car made him vulnerable to attack from a sniper or bomb thrower. Indeed, intelligence reports uncovered a plot against the general's life. MacArthur ignored the information and maintained his routine. Bowers asked if the driver might at least pick up the pace and move through the city more swiftly. MacArthur told him the pace was fine the way it was. Bowers was still uncomfortable. "Sir, may I ask another question about security?" he inquired.

MacArthur nodded.

"What does the general feel about carrying firearms?"

MacArthur appeared puzzled. "Me?"

Bowers shook his head. "No, I."

MacArthur put down the paper he was reading and pondered the matter, as though the carrying of arms by his security guard was a novelty he had never considered. Finally, taking up his paper again, he said, "Suit yourself. Just don't make a fuss."

MacArthur's blitheness about his own safety was sincere; he really did *not* worry about assassination, being too immersed in other matters. But it was also for effect. He appreciated the Japanese fascination with him and his habits, and he knew that each example of fearlessness enhanced his stature the more.

Though his office overlooked the imperial grounds—and the Imperial Plaza, where, Japanese propaganda had boasted during the war, MacArthur would be paraded in chains before being hanged—he made no effort to see the emperor. After years of demanding the unconditional surrender of Japan, the U.S. government, at the last moment, had allowed the emperor to keep his throne. The world awaited the interview between MacArthur and Hirohito. Many observers supposed the general would march to the gate of the imperial palace and compel entrance; members of his staff suggested he order the emperor to the Dai Ichi. He did neither. "I shall wait," he told his staff. "And in time the emperor will voluntarily come to see me." He knew the Oriental mind, he said again, and would turn it to his benefit. "The patience of the East rather than the haste of the West will best serve our purpose."

Events once more proved him right. At the Dai Ichi arrived a request from the emperor's staff for a meeting, at the general's convenience. MacArthur accepted the request and directed that the emperor be treated with every respect. The meeting was held in the American embassy. At the appointed time, a motorcade of black German Daimlers crossed the moat surrounding the imperial palace and drove to the embassy. The emperor, his closest minister and a translator rode in one car; numerous other officials occupied the rest. One of MacArthur's assistants greeted the emperor and explained that while the translator could accompany the emperor, everyone else had to wait outside. Panic engulfed the entourage; never had the emperor been so exposed, and to foreigners no less. But the embassy guards had their orders and barred the way.

The emperor himself was patently nervous. He entered the reception hall, where MacArthur met him. "I offered him an American cigarette, which he took with thanks," MacArthur recounted afterward. "I noticed how his hands shook as I lighted it for him. I tried to make it as easy for him as I could, but I knew how deep and dreadful must be his agony of humiliation." MacArthur's dress and demeanor signaled the new order in Tokyo. The emperor, the supplicant, came dressed in a formal Western morning coat; MacArthur received him in the casual attire he always wore. The general was nearly a foot taller than the emperor, and the official photograph of the meeting, soon transmitted to the world, showed the emperor stiffly at attention, arms straight at his sides, while MacArthur slouched a little, with arms akimbo and hands on his hips.

MacArthur initially feared, from the emperor's nervousness, that he had come to beg for his life. Many in America and the other Allied countries were calling for him to be tried as a war criminal. MacArthur had decided not to do so, estimating that he would be more useful alive than dead. But he hadn't informed the emperor, and he thought things might get awkward if the emperor began denying responsibility for Japan's actions.

The emperor did just the opposite. "I come to you, General MacArthur, to offer myself to the judgment of the powers you represent, as the one to bear sole responsibility for every political and military decision made and action taken by my people in the conduct of war," he said.

MacArthur hadn't yet formed an opinion of the emperor's character, but suddenly he knew the sort of man he was dealing with. "A tremendous impression swept me," he recalled. "This courageous assumption of a responsibility implicit with death, a responsibility clearly belied by facts of which I was fully aware, moved me to the very marrow of my bones. He was an Emperor by inherent birth, but in that instant I knew I faced the First Gentleman of Japan in his own right."

YET IT WAS MacArthur who now ruled where the emperor had only reigned. The general embarked on a project unprecedented in history:

the rapid transformation of an ancient civilization and feudal order into a modern liberal democracy. He made a checklist of objectives: "Destroy the military power. Punish war criminals. Build the structure of representative government. Modernize the constitution. Hold free elections. Enfranchise the women. Release the political prisoners. Liberate the farmers. Establish a free labor movement. Encourage a free economy. Abolish police oppression. Develop a free and responsible press. Liberalize education. Decentralize the political power. Separate church from state."

Certain changes came readily. The Japanese war machine had largely been destroyed by the war and its leaders discredited; the Japanese people were relieved to be rid of its remaining influence. Releasing political prisoners required little more than opening the doors to their cells.

Other reforms struck deeply into the structure of Japanese society. Freeing the farmers required breaking the hold of feudalism in the countryside and delivering land to those who worked it. MacArthur was never one to underestimate his own accomplishments, but in the area of land reform he believed he outdid himself. "I don't think that since the Gracchi effort of land reform in the days of the Roman Empire there has been anything quite so successful of that nature," he remarked.

Enfranchising women was no less revolutionary. MacArthur never dissolved the Japanese government, which continued to function under his supervision. But when the legislature, or diet, refused to rewrite the Japanese constitution in a manner that matched his vision of Japan's future, he assumed the job himself. On a yellow legal pad he sketched a new charter for the defeated country. Aides filled in the details. The resulting document enfranchised women, guaranteed civil liberties, secured the right of collective bargaining to workers, and demoted the emperor from divinity to mortal status. Most novel, among these headspinning innovations, was a no-war clause, by which Japan renounced war as a sovereign right.

The diet accepted the "MacArthur constitution," as it was commonly called. The general was pleased. "It is undoubtedly the most liberal constitution in history, having borrowed the best from the constitutions of many countries," he declared with pride of authorship.

In the first election under the new constitution, in April 1946, tens of millions of Japanese who had never voted went to the polls. Some thirteen million women cast their ballots alongside their husbands, fathers and sons. Dozens of women put themselves forward as candidates for the diet; thirty-eight were elected.

MacArthur was delighted with the turnout, but many Japanese traditionalists, and even some comparative liberals, were troubled by particular results. One legislator, educated at Harvard Law School, called MacArthur shortly after the winners were tallied. "I regret to say that something terrible has happened," the man said. "A prostitute, Your Excellency, has been elected to the House of Representatives."

MacArthur considered the matter. "How many votes did she receive?" he queried.

The lawmaker answered, "256,000."

MacArthur suppressed a smile. "Then I should say there must have been more than her dubious occupation involved," he said.

THE WHIRLWIND OF reform continued. MacArthur encouraged the formation of labor unions by Japanese workers, although he drew the line when leftists attempted to organize a general strike. "The persons involved in the threatened general strike are but a small minority of the Japanese people," he said in warning. "Yet this minority might well plunge the great masses into a disaster not unlike that produced in the immediate past by the minority which led Japan into the destruction of war." The masses heeded MacArthur's words, and the general strike never took place.

He refashioned the Japanese educational system and reorganized public health. When famine threatened the devastated country, he commandeered three million tons of food from U.S. Army stores. Congress conducted an inquiry, which MacArthur brushed aside. "Give me bread or give me bullets," he told the inquisitors. He curtailed the power of the *zaibatsu*, the industrial oligopolies that had underpinned the Japanese military before the war.

He jolted Japanese sensibilities by insisting on religious freedom and dismayed certain Westerners by his explanation. "Although I was brought up as a Christian and adhere entirely to its teachings, I have always had a sincere admiration for many of the basic principles underlying the Oriental faiths," he said. "Christianity does not differ from them as much as one would think."

He oversaw the trial of Japanese war criminals. The emperor was conspicuously exempted from prosecution, but other leading figures, including former prime minister Hideki Tojo, were convicted and sentenced to death. Western reporters asked to witness the executions, but MacArthur refused. Pressure was placed on his superiors, including the secretary of the army, who tried to change the general's mind. MacArthur again refused, deeming himself above such meddling. The executions went forward unobserved.

HE BECAME A Japanese institution. A hastily written biography published in Japanese sold hundreds of thousands of copies—in a country where disposable income was meager. Japanese women wrote to him imploring that he sire their children. Anecdotes of MacArthur circulated instantly. One day he was entering the elevator in the Dai Ichi. A Japanese man already inside the car, seeing the great general, bowed and started to step out. MacArthur insisted that he remain and they rode together. He afterward received a letter from the man. "I am the humble Japanese carpenter who last week you not only permitted but insisted ride with you in the same elevator," the man said. "I have reflected on this act of courtesy for a whole week, and I realize that no Japanese general would have done as you did." Japanese newspapers learned of the story and gave it full coverage. A play was written and performed about the incident, which became, as well, the subject for a painting that was reproduced and displayed in households around the country.

The general's abstemious lifestyle became part of the MacArthur legend. He ate the same thing every day: fruit, cereal, eggs and toast for breakfast, taken with coffee; soup, salad and coffee for each of lunch and dinner. The Japanese knew he worked every day, Christmas included, and that he never took vacations. He allowed himself movies in the evenings; he watched them in his rocking chair while smoking a cigar. Newsreels showing the annual Army-Navy football game would bring him to the edge of his rocker cheering for the Black Knights of West Point.

His energy seemed boundless. A reporter asked MacArthur's doctor if the general was a good patient. "I don't know," the doctor replied. "He's never sick." Another reporter, familiar with MacArthur for decades, wrote, "I first met him in 1917 when he was a young major. He oozed energy, ability and ambition from every pore. Meeting him here in Tokyo 31 years later, it amazed me to see how few changes had been wrought by time. Still arrow straight and with the same flash of eye and aquilinity of features. . . . Few members of his staff, even though many years his junior, can match his physical endurance."

Within a few years of his arrival, many Japanese couldn't imagine their country without him. He had spared them disgrace and retribution; he was guiding them to genuine self-government; he had brought them into the light of modernity. When they considered what they had suffered under his predecessors, they hoped he would never leave.

2

HARRY TRUMAN SHARED their hope. Truman was delighted with MacArthur's achievements in Japan, which freed the president to focus on parts of the world that were more troublesome and, to Truman's way of thinking, more important. The Cold War had grown out of the failure of the victors of World War II in Europe to agree on the future of Germany, which remained under the occupation of the armies that had defeated Hitler's Reich in 1945. The United States, Britain, France and the Soviet Union each held zones of Germany, and each controlled a sector of Berlin, an island within the Soviet zone. The Americans, British and French found themselves increasingly at odds with the Soviets, with the two sides gradually remaking their zones in their own images: the former democratic and more or less capitalist, the latter authoritarian and strictly socialist. Growing cooperation among the three Western powers evoked Soviet fears of a revived Germany, and Moscow registered various complaints. Failing to receive satisfaction, the Russians in June 1948 imposed a blockade of Berlin, barring access to the city from the Western zones by rail, highway, river and canal.

The Berlin blockade was the most serious crisis of the Cold War to date, and the sternest test of Harry Truman's leadership. Truman had responded to previous challenges with words and money. In 1947, when an anticommunist regime in Greece struggled to beat back a communist insurgency, Truman proclaimed a policy of American support for such regimes. The Truman Doctrine, as the policy was called, was accompanied by $400 million in aid to Greece and neighboring Turkey, and its success there caused it to be extrapolated, at least implicitly, to other countries and regions. Later that same year Truman's secretary of state, George Marshall, announced a plan for reconstruction aid for Europe. The economies of the continent had never recovered from the war; the physical destruction wreaked by bombs, artillery shells, tank treads and fire had been matched by institutional destruction inflicted on governments, banks, markets and laws; and both calamities had been aggravated by emotional destruction to souls and psyches caused by the worst cataclysm to befall any civilization in history. The Marshall Plan would rebuild Europe physically, and at the same time it would reconstruct institutions and help restore morale. This last was crucial, in that a restoration of morale was considered essential to keeping voters in France, Italy and other struggling countries from following the siren song of communism into the Russian embrace.

Yet, vital as they were, the words and money of the Truman Doctrine and the Marshall Plan weren't blood and steel. And when Soviet troops closed access to Berlin, threatening to strangle and starve the free half of the city into submission, Harry Truman had to decide whether he was willing to match military force with military force.

"DEAR MARGIE," THE president wrote as the Berlin crisis was building. Margaret Truman was the sole child of Harry and Bess Truman, and to Margaret the president often confided opinions and sentiments he shared with no one else. The letters he sent her were usually short and topical; this one was long and biographical. "I'm going to give you a record for yourself regarding these times," he explained. "You know of course what a terrible campaign the one of 1940 was. No one thought I could win, including the President." But he had won, holding his Senate seat and shortly afterward sponsoring legislation that established the Committee to Investigate the National Defense Program. The Truman Committee, as it was labeled, uncovered corruption in war spending and earned its chairman a national reputation. "Then came 1944 and that terrible Chicago Convention," Truman wrote to Margaret, referring to the national convention that nominated Franklin Roosevelt for a fourth term. The only drama involved who would be Roosevelt's vice president. "I went there to nominate Byrnes. He'd told me that Roosevelt wanted him for Vice-President, and I thought he did." But Roosevelt kept silent, and various bigwigs were skeptical about James Byrnes, currently director of war mobilization. Several said they wanted to retain Henry Wallace, the incumbent vice president, but if Wallace was unacceptable to the party—as he quickly proved to be, with Southern conservatives muttering seditiously against his unrelenting liberalism—then they backed Truman. "I said to all and sundry that I was not a candidate, would not be and that I was perfectly happy in the Senate," Truman told Margaret.

But Roosevelt decided on Truman. "On Tuesday evening Bob Hannegan came to see me at the Stephens Hotel and told me that Roosevelt wanted me to be the V.P. candidate. I said 'no' point blank, and went on working for Byrnes." For a time it seemed that Truman's wishes would be honored. But after forty-eight hours things changed. "Roosevelt was nominated on Thursday and then the real pressure began hammering me to say yes. Finally Hannegan asked me to come over to the Blackstone and listen to a conversation he was to have with Roosevelt in San Diego." Truman obliged. "Roosevelt's first question of Hannegan was 'well have you got that fellow from Missouri lined up?' Bob said no he's very contrary. Then the President said, 'Well, you tell him if he wants to take the responsibility of breaking up the Party in the middle of the war to go ahead and do it.' Well, that put a new face on things."

Truman acceded, and Roosevelt was reelected. "As you know, I was Vice-President from Jan. 20 to April 12, 1945," Truman continued. "I was at Cabinet meetings and saw Roosevelt once or twice in those months. But he never did talk to me confidentially about the war, or about foreign affairs or what he had in mind for the peace after the war." Truman remembered in detail the day everything changed. "The catastrophe we all dreaded came on April 12 at 4:35 P.M. At 7:09 I was the President." Roosevelt's sudden death left Truman with a great deal of catching up to do. "I had to start reading memorandums, briefs, and volumes of correspondence on the world situation. Too bad I hadn't been on the Foreign Affairs Committee or that F.D.R. hadn't informed me on the situation. I had to find out about the Atlantic Charter, which by the way does not exist on paper, the Casablanca meeting, the Montreal meeting, Tehran meeting, Yalta, Hull's trip to Moscow, Bretton Woods, and numerous other things too numerous to mention."

Truman also had to learn about the atom bomb project, of which he had known nothing. He received conflicting forecasts. "Adm. Leahy told me that he was an explosives expert and Roosevelt had just thrown $2,600,000,000 away for nothing. He was wrong. But his guess was as good as any." Truman learned that the bomb worked when it was successfully tested in New Mexico in July 1945. He was at Potsdam trying to get the Soviets to enter the war against Japan. "All of us wanted Russia in the Japanese War. Had we known what the atomic bomb would do, we'd have never wanted the Bear in the picture."

In the aftermath of Potsdam, Truman discovered what the Soviets were really like. "We entered into agreements for the government of Germany—not one of which Russia has kept," he wrote to Margaret. "We made agreements on China, Korea and other places, none of which Russia has kept. So that now we are faced with exactly the same situation with which Britain and France were faced in 1938/39 with Hitler. A totalitarian state is no different whether you call it Nazi, Fascist, Communist or Franco's Spain."

The tension over Germany, centering on Berlin, was greater than ever, Truman told his daughter. "Things look black." The moment of crisis was coming. "A decision will have to be made. I am going to make it." He assured Margaret he would do so with a clear conscience. "I just wanted you to know your dad as President asked for no territory, no reparations, no slave laborers—only peace in the world. We may have to fight for it. The oligarchy in Russia is no different from the Czars, Louis XIV, Napoleon, Charles I and Cromwell. It is a Frankenstein dictatorship worse than any of the others, Hitler included."

"Be a nice girl and don't worry about your dad's worries," he told Margaret in concluding. "But you'll hear all sorts of lies about the things I've told you. These are the facts. I went to Potsdam with the kindliest feeling toward Russia. In a year and a half they cured me of it."

SOME OF THE lies Truman warned his daughter about would come from the communists, but the more insidious ones—as he interpreted affairs in the summer of 1948—originated with Republicans and Democrats. Even while war loomed in Germany, Truman faced the fight of his political life in America. He hadn't wanted to be vice president, but Roosevelt had prevailed on him; he *really* hadn't wanted to be president, but Roosevelt died on him. "Boys, if you ever pray, pray for me now," he told reporters the day after Roosevelt's death. "I don't know whether you fellows ever had a load of hay fall on you, but when they told me yesterday what had happened, I felt like the moon, the stars and all the planets had fallen on me." One of the reporters replied, "Good luck, Mr. President." Truman groaned, "I wish you didn't have to call me that."

For a long time after inheriting the presidency, he wasn't sure he wanted to keep the job. He thought others were more qualified. Dwight Eisenhower was his first choice. Truman met Eisenhower during the Potsdam conference and was tremendously impressed. "General," he told Eisenhower, "there is nothing you may want that I won't try to help you get. That definitely and specifically includes the presidency in 1948." Eisenhower was startled. "Mr. President," he said, "I don't know who will be your opponent for the presidency, but it will not be I."

Truman continued to deem Eisenhower the man for the job, despite the general's giving little indication where he stood on most matters of public policy or even which party he favored. In early 1947 Truman approached Eisenhower again; again Eisenhower disavowed interest in politics.

Only after that did Truman decide to run. There was much he disliked about the presidency; in his diary he called the White House the "Great White Jail," and he bristled at the "lies" he regularly attributed to his opponents and the critical press. His first two years were a trying time for anyone to be president, in domestic affairs no less than foreign. The war had created strains in the economy but prevented their release; after the war's end the strains threatened to rupture the fabric of American life. Workers sought wage increases to catch up with price increases and staged hundreds of strikes to get them. Consumers, who had been hoping that the conversion from war production to peace production would end the wartime rationing and replenish car showrooms, appliance stores and even grocery shelves, grew angry when the strikes effectively extended the rationing. A coal strike raised the specter of a shivering winter, and a strike on the railroads portended continent-wide paralysis. Truman jawboned the union leaders, to little effect; he threatened to draft railroad workers so he could order them back to work. He brought a lawsuit against the coal miners.

His actions produced mixed results in the marketplace of business and labor and cost him dearly in the political square. Republicans and conservative Southern Democrats had nursed grievances against the New Deal for more than a decade; unable to rescind its obnoxious measures while Roosevelt lived, they saw in Truman a much weaker defender of the emerging welfare state. Truman's anti-union measures alienated many of those who should have been his stoutest supporters. The country as a whole showed weariness and exasperation with Democrats in Washington.

The dissatisfaction dragged Truman's approval ratings to depths plumbed only by Herbert Hoover amid the Great Depression, and it propelled the Republicans to victories in the 1946 elections, when they seized control of both houses of Congress for the first time since the 1920s. The Republicans assaulted what remained of the labor front of the Democrats by passing the Taft-Hartley bill, a measure that restricted the organizing rights of unions. Truman vetoed the bill, but Congress overrode the veto, making the president's weakness even more obvious. The Republicans, looking toward the 1948 presidential election, saw nothing but promise in Truman's woes.

Truman added to the ranks of his enemies, especially in the South, by endorsing civil rights reform. He considered it high time the South entered the twentieth century. "The main difficulty with the South is that they are living eighty years behind the times and the sooner they come out of it the better it will be for the country and themselves," he wrote to an old Missouri friend who had urged him to soft-pedal the race question. "I'm not asking for social equality, because no such thing exists, but I am asking for equality of opportunity for all human beings and, as long as I stay here, I am going to continue that fight." He noted recent violence. "When the mob gangs can take four people out and shoot them in the back, and everybody in the country is acquainted with who did the shooting and nothing is done about it, that country is in a pretty bad fix from a law enforcement standpoint. When a Mayor and a City Marshal can take a negro Sergeant off a bus in South Carolina, beat him up and put out one of his eyes, and nothing is done about it by State Authorities, something is radically wrong with the system." He remarked how racist violence perversely adapted to changing circumstances. "On the Louisiana and Arkansas Railway when coal burning locomotives were used, the negro firemen were the thing because it was a back-breaking job and a dirty one. As soon as they turned to oil as a fuel it became customary for people to take shots at the negro firemen and a number were murdered because it was thought that this was now a white-collar job and should go to a white man." Crimes like this couldn't be tolerated. "I can't approve of such goings on and I shall never approve it, as long as I am here," he told his friend. "I am going to try to remedy it and if that ends up in my failure to be reelected, the failure will be in a good cause."

Congress was in no mood to give Truman what he wanted on civil rights or anything else at this point, and so the president acted on his own. He issued executive orders prohibiting racial discrimination in federal hiring and directing the armed services to desegregate. The latter order posed the sterner test, pitting presidential authority against military tradition. Tradition won—for the time being. The desegregation order had no immediate positive effect on its intended beneficiaries, as the military brass, socially conservative and frequently Southern, found reasons to drag their boots. And the order had an immediate *negative* effect on Truman, by antagonizing Southern Democrats even more.

Yet the more resistance Truman encountered, the more determined he became to fight for his job. It was an uphill battle even to win the Democratic nomination. A left wing of Democratic liberals, refusing to acknowledge that 1947 wasn't 1937, berated Truman for not extending the New Deal. This group boosted Henry Wallace and loudly proclaimed that Wallace would be president already if FDR, in a moment of weakness, hadn't bumped him from the 1944 ticket. They threatened to bolt the party. Southern Democrats threatened to do the same, albeit for conservative, anti-civil-rights reasons. Many career Democrats, recognizing that the country was suffering from Democratic fatigue, believed that only a fresh face at the top of the ticket offered any hope for success in 1948.

The weight of the combined opposition might have discouraged another man, but not Truman, who simply fought harder than ever. He roundly criticized the potential defectors as "double-crossers all" and predicted, "They'll get nowhere—a double-dealer never does." He shamelessly manipulated the levers of presidential power to ensure the seating of friendly delegates at the Democratic convention, so that by the time the delegates gathered, his nomination was secure.

Yet nearly everyone thought it an empty honor. The Republican victories in the 1946 congressional elections appeared to presage a GOP capture of the White House; Democratic delegates were a dispirited group as they convened in Philadelphia. "You could cut the gloom with a corn knife," recalled Alben Barkley, who came away with the nomination for vice president. "The very air smelled of defeat." A local cabdriver remarked, "We got the wrong rigs for this convention. They shoulda given us hearses."

Truman ignored the gloom. And when he gave his acceptance speech, he injected new life into the convention and the party. The roll call had taken hours; midnight was long past by the time Truman mounted the rostrum. The delegates were exhausted, but his appearance, in a dapper white linen suit, and his defiance of what everyone else considered overwhelming odds awoke some of the party's fighting spirit. "Senator Barkley and I will win this election and make these Republicans like it— don't you forget that!" he declared. Speaking without notes, in the staccato, hand-chopping style that was his trademark, he explained, "The reason is that the people know that the Democratic Party is the people's party, and the Republican Party is the party of special interest, and it always has been and always will be." Truman lambasted the Republicans in Congress for bemoaning conditions in the country but taking no steps to change them. "The Republican platform cries about cruelly high prices. I have been trying to get them to do something about high prices ever since they met the first time." He castigated Republican tax changes, passed over his veto, as a program that "helps the rich and sticks a knife into the back of the poor." The Republican platform called for increasing Social Security benefits. "Think of that!" Truman lampooned. "Increasing Social Security benefits! Yet when they had the opportunity, they took 750,000 off the Social Security rolls! I wonder if they think they can fool the people of the United States with such poppycock as that!"

Truman jolted the convention and the country by announcing that he would summon the Eightieth Congress into special session. He had previously labeled the Eightieth Congress the worst in history; he was going to give the Republican majority a chance to prove him wrong. "What that worst 80th Congress does in this special session will be the test. The American people will not decide by listening to mere words, or by reading a mere platform. They will decide on the record."

THE POLITICAL DRAMA in America unfolded against the intensifying crisis in Europe. Truman interpreted the Soviet pressure on Berlin as a trial of democracy's willingness to defend Germany; if the Kremlin could force the Americans and their allies out of Berlin, it might drive them from Germany altogether. The challenge triggered the Midwestern stubbornness on which Truman prided himself. "We'll stay in Berlin—come what may," he wrote in his diary just days after his acceptance speech.

His advisers weren't all sure this could be done or even that it was a good idea to try. George Marshall was supportive, but James Forrestal, the secretary of defense, hesitated. "Marshall states the facts and the conditions with which we are faced," Truman wrote after a meeting with the two. "Jim wants to hedge—he always does. He's constantly sending me alibi memos which I return with directions and the facts. . . . I don't pass the buck, nor do I alibi out of any decision I make."

How to stay in Berlin became the crucial question. General Lucius Clay, the U.S. commander for Germany, advocated calling what he considered the Kremlin's bluff. An armed convoy should be sent along the autobahn toward Berlin. If the Russians wanted to stop it, they would have to fire. He didn't think they would, because he didn't think they wanted a war.

Truman judged that if the Russians wanted a war, they would find a way to start one. But he didn't wish to play into their hands. And he feared that excessive force might produce a war by accident. As he wrote later, "We had to face the possibility that Russia might deliberately choose to make Berlin the pretext for war, but a more immediate danger was the risk that a trigger-happy Russian pilot or hotheaded Communist tank commander might create an incident that could ignite the powder keg."

The president rejected the armed convoy in favor of an airlift. The communists had not closed the air lanes to Berlin, and until they did, it was just possible that West Berlin might be fed from the air. This would be a stopgap; never in history had a city of any size been supplied from the air for any length of time. The Russians had, in effect, laid siege to the city. They knew something about sieges, having endured the epic siege of Leningrad during the war. That encirclement had claimed a million Russian lives and produced gruesome scenes of hunger, disease, exposure and madness that would haunt the survivors forever. Joseph Stalin, who had been complicit in the suffering by refusing to surrender Leningrad, had good reason to doubt that any democratic government could show such resolve.

For their part, the West Berliners knew about Soviet treatment of those who fell into their orbit, especially if they resisted. As the European war had approached its climax, with the armies of Russia, America and Britain closing in on Berlin, the Germans in the capital prayed that the Americans or the British would get there first. Russian brutality was infamous. Russian soldiers shot Germans on a whim; they raped women and girls; often hungry themselves, they starved the Germans from necessity and spite. As bad as the war's aftermath was in the rest of Germany, it was worst in the Soviet zone around Berlin. While the Americans were beginning to restore the economy in the western zones of the former enemy, the Russians were bleeding the eastern zone dry. Tools, machines and whole factories were dismantled and shipped to Russia. Jobs vanished, with no sign of return. Berliners, trapped inside the Soviet zone, scurried like rats amid the urban ruins and scraped the fields outside the city seeking rotten turnips and moldy potatoes.

Stalin clearly hoped to break the West Berliners' will to resist. As tenuous as their existence was before the blockade set in, they would quickly realize it would only get worse. He offered food to those who would cross over into East Berlin. Some did. Others entered the shadowy world of the black market, trading whatever they had of value for one more meal.

But the great majority determined to stick it out. Parents went without food in order to feed their children. Nearly everyone went without nonessentials, which soon disappeared from store shelves. To ration the coal supply, the West Berlin authorities rolled electrical blackouts across the city, forcing mothers to awake in the middle of the night to cook their potatoes, which they tried to keep warm until their families arose.

Truman appreciated what the Berliners were risking, and he did everything he could to make the airlift work. It didn't start promisingly. A quick accounting estimated that the relief planes would have to deliver forty-five hundred tons of food and other essentials a day, but the first day's effort was a meager eighty tons. Reporter Marguerite Higgins of the *New York Herald Tribune* asked General Clay if the airlift could long succeed. "Absolutely impossible," he responded.

But Truman's determination helped make the impossible happen. With practice, ingenuity and courage, the pilots, crews, controllers and many others involved in the airlift dramatically increased its capacity. By the end of the summer the rescue mission was holding its own, and the West was holding its ground in Berlin.

The airlift was one of the grand spectacles of the time. Day after day, night after night, the roar of the cargo planes never ceased. The planes flew in good weather and bad; on landing they hardly turned off their engines for unloading before flying back to the western zones of Germany for another cargo. The children of Berlin, who had learned during the war to hide on hearing the sound of airplane motors, caught on that these were good planes. They crowded the space behind the fence at Tempelhof Airport hoping for something to eat. One American pilot, Gail Halvorsen, handed out candy to the kids; the response was so heartbreakingly positive that he started dropping candy from his plane. The cargoes wafted down on improvised parachutes, and Halvorsen became famous in Berlin as the Candy Bomber. American children donated sweets to keep the Candy Bomber supplied; eventually, tons of candy, chewing gum and other tasties rained down from the sky over Berlin.

Truman was pleased yet hardly reassured. He understood that the airlift proceeded on Soviet sufferance. The heavily laden cargo planes were easy targets for gunners or fighter planes. At each step of the Berlin crisis, the Russians had ratcheted things tighter. Truman wasn't sure how they could ratchet them any tighter now without triggering a war. And the air link to Berlin was a fragile skein. A single incident could set in motion a chain of escalation.

In mid-September the president met with his military advisers, who briefed him on the progress of the airlift. "I have a terrible feeling afterward that we are very close to war," he wrote in his diary.

POLITICS AT HOME made Truman's situation worse. The Republicans rallied behind New York governor Thomas Dewey, who had made a respectable showing against Roosevelt in 1944 and appeared poised to capitalize on Truman's multiple weaknesses. Meanwhile the Democrats did anything *but* rally behind Truman. Henry Wallace led the liberals out the left door of the party to regroup under the Progressive banner, while Strom Thurmond and many Southerners exited to the right, to run as States' Rights Democrats, or Dixiecrats. Numerous polls gave a big lead to Dewey, who proceeded cautiously, to preserve his advantage, and began making lists of those he would appoint to cabinet offices.

With nothing to lose, Truman campaigned furiously. He mounted a grueling whistle-stop train tour, hammering the "do-nothing" Republican Congress, which obliged in the special session by living down to his epithet. He reiterated that the Democrats stood for the honest, ordinary people while the Republicans did the bidding of the wealthy. "It will be the greatest campaign any President ever made," Truman wrote to his sister midway through the tour. "Win, lose, or draw, people will know where I stand and a record will be made for future action by the Democratic Party." Speaking of the 140 stops so far, he said, "We had tremendous crowds everywhere. From 6:30 in the morning until midnight the turnout was phenomenal. The news jerks didn't know what to make of it—so they just lied about it!"

Voters warmed to Truman's plainspoken style. "Give 'em hell, Harry!" they shouted lustily. "I don't have to give 'em hell," Truman rejoined. "It's a lot worse for me to tell the truth on 'em, because they can't stand the truth."

Polls showed the race tightening, but Truman appeared to run out of time. As late as election day the cause seemed lost. The anti-Truman *Chicago Tribune*, extrapolating from Dewey's strong showing in the East, gloatingly went to press that evening with the front-page banner "Dewey Defeats Truman."

Yet Truman had the laugh the next day. Overnight tallies revealed that the West had gone heavily Democratic, returning the president to office by a comfortable margin.

Clark Clifford, then in the early stage of a career as political guru to Democratic presidents, proclaimed the victory a personal triumph for Truman. "It wasn't, in my opinion, because he was a skilled politician that he won," Clifford said. "He was a good politician . . . a sensible politician. . . . But that wasn't why he was elected president. . . . It was the remarkable courage in the man—his refusal to be discouraged, his willingness to go through the suffering of that campaign, the fatigue, the will to fight every step of the way, the will to win. . . . It wasn't Harry Truman the politician who won; it was Harry Truman the man."

TRUMAN'S COURAGE CONTINUED to be tested in Berlin. If the president had known how long Stalin intended to apply the tourniquet to the city, he might have made a different decision at the outset. It was one thing to keep Berlin alive during the summer, when demands for fuel were comparatively modest, but as winter approached, the challenge intensified dramatically. Winter weather, moreover, complicated the choreography of getting the planes in and out of Berlin.

But Truman was as stubborn as Stalin was patient, and having inspired the West Berliners to stand against the Russians, the president determined to see the mission through. He and the Berliners knew what was at stake. "The Soviets had declared that all of Berlin was theirs, and their newspapers in German language didn't cease to foretell the realization of that claim," remembered Willy Brandt, who would become mayor of West Berlin and then chancellor of West Germany. "They spread rumors of different kinds, they didn't spare threats and intimidations. Thus, here and there, doubts arose as to whether one would be able to resist the Russian pressure in the long run. The retaliation and vengeance in case of a defeat would be terrible."

The airlift intensified as the days grew colder and shorter. The pilots and controllers grew bolder and more imaginative; the cargo crews devised methods of getting tons out of the planes in mere minutes. The people of Berlin bent their backs to rebuilding runways pounded to dust by the constant traffic.

The struggle, the privation, the shared danger, had a marvelous effect. With each week that passed that Berlin did not capitulate, the Berliners grew more self-confident. By the beginning of 1949 it was becoming clear, even to Stalin, that the blockade had backfired. Its immediate purpose had been to drive a wedge between the Berliners and the West; its result was to make the Berliners the Germans most devoted to the West. The larger Soviet aim had been to weaken the American attachment to Europe; the success of the airlift furnished the final impetus to the North Atlantic Treaty of April 1949, which bound the United States to Europe as nothing before. The ultimate retort to Stalin was the amalgamation of the western zones of Germany into the single Federal Republic of Germany, precisely the result the Berlin blockade had been initiated to prevent.

By the time the Russians dropped the blockade in May 1949, the world viewed Harry Truman with new respect. The accidental president, lately returned to office by a vote of the American people, had gone toe-to-toe with Stalin, and Stalin had yielded. Truman's combination of firmness and patience had held freedom's ground without provoking war. It was hard to imagine any chief executive doing better.

3

Y ET DOUGLAS MACARTHUR imagined just that. More precisely, MacArthur imagined himself being president. He had climbed to the pinnacle of the American military; as a five-star general, he was outranked only by George Marshall, who had preceded him to that level by two days. He could achieve nothing more at arms; the sole public office not beneath him was the presidency. Many of his correspondents and visitors told him he would be a better president than Truman; his sense of honesty compelled him to agree, usually silently.

People had told him this before. He hadn't disagreed then, either, though he now realized he should have. In 1944 he had allowed himself to be put forward as a candidate for the Republican nomination for president. He permitted a draft-MacArthur campaign to develop, and he exchanged letters with a Republican congressman, Arthur Miller of Nebraska, who denounced Franklin Roosevelt in the most vitriolic terms. "If this system of left-wingers and New Dealism is continued another four years," Miller said, "I am certain that this monarchy which is being established in America will destroy the rights of the common people."

"I appreciate very much your scholarly letter," MacArthur replied. "Your description of conditions in the United States is a sobering one indeed and is calculated to arouse the thoughtful consideration of every true patriot."

MacArthur polled strongly in parts of the Midwest before the professionals in the Republican party made clear how difficult it would be to elect a general over his commander-in-chief in the middle of a war. George McClellan had tested this route during the Civil War and failed.

The MacArthur boom fizzled, prompting MacArthur to disavow further interest. "I request that no action be taken that would link my name in any way with the nomination," he said. "I do not covet it nor would I accept it."

He received his punishment a short while later. Or so he interpreted a summons from Roosevelt to meet him in Hawaii. The stated purpose of the meeting was to decide on American strategy during the final phase of the war against Japan, but MacArthur felt he was being displayed to the press and the public like a conquered foe, a prop in Roosevelt's reelection campaign. "The humiliation of forcing me to leave my command to fly to Honolulu for a political picture-taking junket!" he expostulated aboard the *Bataan,* his personal plane, en route to Hawaii.

He did his best to resist the part. Samuel Rosenman, a Roosevelt aide and speechwriter, described Roosevelt's arrival aboard the cruiser *Baltimore.* The gangway was lowered, and Admiral Chester Nimitz and many other officers came aboard. "One officer was conspicuously absent," Rosenman recalled. "It was General Douglas MacArthur. When Roosevelt asked Nimitz where the general was, there was an embarrassed silence. We learned later that the general had arrived about an hour earlier, but instead of joining the other officers to greet the Commander-in-Chief, he had gone by himself to Fort Shafter." Roosevelt and the others waited to see if MacArthur would appear. Eventually they tired and determined to go ashore without him. A sudden commotion halted them halfway. "A terrific automobile siren was heard," Rosenman related, "and there raced onto the dock and screeched to a stop a motorcycle escort and the longest open car I have ever seen. In the front was a chauffeur in khaki, and in the back one lone figure—MacArthur."

Everyone watched Roosevelt to see his reaction. The president declined to be provoked. "Hello, Doug," he said when MacArthur arrived on deck. Noting the general's nonregulation attire, he asked, "What are you doing with that leather jacket on? It's darn hot today."

"I've just landed from Australia," MacArthur said pointedly. He looked to the sky. "It's pretty cold up there."

MacArthur joined Roosevelt and the other brass on a tour of Oahu. They returned to Honolulu and gathered in a house on Waikiki. A large map displayed the Pacific theater. Roosevelt got down to business. "Where do we go from here?" he asked MacArthur.

"Leyte, Mr. President," he said, indicating the western Philippines. "And then Luzon."

MacArthur spent the next several hours telling Roosevelt why the attack on Japan must proceed through the Philippines. He was articulate and forceful. He wore Roosevelt out. "Give me an aspirin before I go to bed," the president moaned to his doctor that evening. "In fact, give me another aspirin to take in the morning. In all my life nobody has ever talked to me the way MacArthur did."

IF MACARTHUR WAS chastened by his first attempt at presidential politics, the experience didn't prevent him from trying again in 1948. Indeed, it seemed to have whetted his ambition. And the circumstances in 1948 were much more promising for a challenge to a sitting president. The war was over, eliminating the awkwardness of a wartime run by a general. MacArthur was more famous than ever, being hailed as the hero of the Pacific war and the remarkable administrator of Japan. And Truman was far more vulnerable than Roosevelt had been.

MacArthur had reason to believe he could win. His staff made sure he saw the results of a 1945 Gallup poll in which Americans were asked to name the greatest figure in world history. Franklin Roosevelt came first, followed by Abraham Lincoln, Jesus Christ, George Washington and Douglas MacArthur. Another poll, by the American Institute of Public Opinion, in 1946 asked Americans to name the greatest person then living. MacArthur received the top listing, followed by Eisenhower and Truman.

Various Republicans read the same polls and launched a MacArthur-for-president campaign. The general encouraged them. "The need is not in the concentration of greater power in the hands of the state, but in the reservation of much more power in the people," he declared, by way of deriding the New Deal and the Democrats who had supported it, including Harry Truman. William Randolph Hearst, the media baron who despised the New Deal as much as anyone did, declared at once for MacArthur. "We must DRAFT General MacArthur for the Presidency," the Hearst press blared. "Beyond any rivalry and any partisanship . . . Douglas MacArthur is the MAN OF THE HOUR." Robert McCormick, owner of the *Chicago Tribune,* wrote to MacArthur personally, saying, "Your career has not paralleled Washington's or Lincoln's, but in its own particular sphere is as great as either of theirs."

MacArthur responded eagerly. "No man could fail to be profoundly stirred by such a public movement," he said of the efforts on his behalf. "I can say, and with due humility, that I would be recreant to all my concepts of good citizenship were I to shrink because of the hazards and responsibilities involved from accepting any public duty to which I might be called by the American people."

MacArthur's name was entered in early Republican primaries. "MacArthur sentiment is rising in Wisconsin and Illinois," asserted *U.S. News & World Report*. Yet many of MacArthur's supporters wished he would come home and campaign. As it was, the general was still playing loose with a Pentagon prohibition on active-duty officers getting involved in politics. MacArthur seemed to want to have it both ways: to keep his current job while working to win a higher one.

He couldn't pull it off. He lost the Republican primary in Wisconsin, the nearest approximation to a home state for him, to Harold Stassen, a former governor of Minnesota who wasn't at all shy about campaigning. He finished fifth in the Nebraska primary. His backers implored him to return to America and campaign. He decided Japan couldn't spare him, and he asked that his name be withdrawn from future primaries.

Yet he had won a handful of delegates, and they carried the MacArthur banner to the Republican convention in Philadelphia. His name was placed in nomination but not until the roll call of states got to Wisconsin, just before dawn on the day after the serious candidates had been put forward. The delegates had nearly all gone home, and the janitors formed the largest delegation. On the first ballot MacArthur received 8 votes, to subsequent nominee Dewey's 434.

CHASTENED A SECOND time, he turned his attention back to Japan. The occupation had accomplished much of what he hoped for it; he began to think of how it would end. There would be a peace treaty, and full sovereignty would be restored to the Japanese people. Most of the U.S. troops would go home. And their commander would retire from the army. To try politics again? Who knew? The next election was a long way off.

Yet the path to a Japanese peace treaty turned crooked almost at once.

As smooth as the postwar evolution of Japan was under MacArthur's tutelage, the affairs of China, Japan's historic rival, could not have been more turbulent. A civil war had been raging in China for decades; the war against Japan nominally brought the Chinese antagonists together, but few students of Chinese affairs and next to none of the participants were surprised that the civil war flared anew as soon as the Japanese war ceased. Chiang Kai-shek's Nationalist party controlled the government and the army and enjoyed the support of the United States, but Mao Zedong's Communists gained ground rapidly in the countryside. By the beginning of 1949 Chiang and the Nationalists were reeling. Harry Truman, after much thought and discussion, concluded that the Nationalists, demoralized by battlefield defeat and by corruption among their commanders, were a lost cause. The president declined to throw good money after bad and washed his hands of the Nationalists' fate. They were driven from the Chinese mainland to Formosa, as Taiwan was still often called, and in the autumn of 1949 the Communists proclaimed the People's Republic of China. Chiang Kai-shek impotently shook his fist from Formosa.

MacArthur watched with dismay from Japan. His peaceable kingdom, with the no-war clause of its constitution, was suddenly threatened by hordes of Chinese just across the Sea of Japan. They were technically deficient, lacking the arms and transport to project military power across the water, but their numbers were daunting. And they might well get modern arms from their co-ideologists in Russia, who would be more than happy to cause trouble for the United States in Japan. The Russians had been angling for a role in the Japanese occupation, but MacArthur until now had kept them out. Allied with China, they might force their way in.

MacArthur reflected that the communist victory in China changed the terms of the discussion about Japan's future. It complicated the security negotiations designed to ensure that Japan remain safely within the American sphere after the restoration of Japanese sovereignty. It compelled closer scrutiny of events in the region around China, lest the red virus spread. Quite possibly it would delay the signing of the peace treaty. The old soldier might not be going home as soon as he thought.

4

H ARRY TRUMAN HAD noted MacArthur's inept run for president with the scorn of the professional politician for the rank amateur—a scorn quite comparable to that which MacArthur felt toward politicians meddling in military affairs. The president was annoyed at the insubordination implicit in an electoral challenge to the commander-in-chief by an active-duty officer, but he considered MacArthur an insufficient political threat to warrant sanction at the time. Truman simply filed the matter in his mental dossier on the general.

The victory over Dewey delighted Truman; he had proved the naysayers wrong. But the thrill didn't last, and his second term wasn't six months old before he began to wonder why he had re-upped. The collapse of the anticommunist front in China was the big story of the summer of 1949, and the Republicans and no small number of Democrats laid the blame directly at Truman's feet. The end of the summer brought an even greater shock when American spy planes patrolling the Siberian coast sniffed radioactive fallout of the kind produced by an atomic explosion. Truman's scientific advisers quickly concluded that the dreaded day had come: the United States had lost its nuclear monopoly. The president weighed how to break the news to the American people; he opted for a terse written statement. "I believe the American people, to the fullest extent consistent with national security, are entitled to be informed of all developments in the field of atomic energy," the statement said. "That is my reason for making public the following information. We have evidence that within recent weeks an atomic explosion occurred in the U.S.S.R." Truman asserted that there was nothing surprising about this development. "Ever since atomic energy was first released by man, the eventual development of this new force by other nations was to be expected. This probability has always been taken into account by us." Now that the probability had become a reality, the world had to get serious about arms control. "This recent development emphasizes once again, if indeed such emphasis were needed, the necessity for that truly effective enforceable international control of atomic energy."

Truman's conclusion seemed a howling non sequitur to many in the United States. More arms, not fewer, was the necessary response to the Russian bomb, the critics said. Truman was a fool or worse not to see this. The administration had been asleep, letting the Russians acquire the bomb, if it hadn't colluded in the communists' acquisition of the monster weapon.

The collusion charge might have seemed preposterous if not for further flabbergasting news that broke a short while later. Alger Hiss, a former State Department official, had been accused of spying for the Soviets. Hiss vigorously denied the charge and was supported in his denial by members of the Truman administration, conspicuously Dean Acheson, successor to George Marshall as secretary of state. Congress investigated, and Hiss repeated his denial, yet new evidence strongly suggested he was lying. The statute of limitations prevented prosecution for espionage, but Hiss was charged with perjury for his denial. He was convicted and sentenced to five years in prison. At almost the same time, American and British intelligence services belatedly uncovered the presence of Soviet spies in the wartime atom-bomb project; one of the spies, Klaus Fuchs, was indicted, prosecuted and convicted in Britain. The Truman administration didn't announce what information Fuchs had delivered to his Soviet handlers, but Truman's critics assumed the worst and again lambasted the president for a shocking lapse in this most sensitive area of security.

Though he didn't say so in public, Truman knew that the information Fuchs had given the Russians probably included material relating to a far bigger bomb than those that destroyed Hiroshima and Nagasaki. The "super"—or thermonuclear, or hydrogen—bomb was thought to be feasible but had seemed to American planners unnecessary as long as America's monopoly on atom bombs held. The loss of the monopoly, combined with the unsettling knowledge that the Russians knew about the hydrogen bomb, prompted frantic discussions at the highest levels of the American national security apparatus. Some officials argued for greater arms-control efforts to keep the world from crossing the thermonuclear threshold. Others contended that such a course was too risky; the Russians simply couldn't be trusted.

Truman sided with the skeptics and in January 1950 announced that the United States would build the big bomb. "It is part of my responsibility as Commander in Chief of the Armed Forces to see to it that our country is able to defend itself against any possible aggressor," the president said in a written statement. The United States wasn't abandoning arms control, but until such control became real and reliable, America had to look to its own security. "Accordingly, I have directed the Atomic Energy Commission to continue its work on all forms of atomic weapons, including the so-called hydrogen or superbomb."

Truman understood the implications of his decision. He was launching the world, or at least the world's greatest powers, on an arms race into territory unimagined only a few years before. The race might have apocalyptic consequences for humanity. "The atom's power in the wrong hands can spell disaster," he declared. But this was precisely why the United States must maintain an atomic advantage. "It can be used as an overriding influence against aggression and reckless war, and for that reason I have always insisted that, within the resources of a balanced security system and a balanced economy, we stay ahead of all the world in atomic affairs."

TEN DAYS LATER Joseph McCarthy seized the national spotlight. The junior senator from Wisconsin, a Republican whom most Americans had never heard of, had pondered various issues by which he might draw attention to himself. But none seemed sufficiently galvanizing until the quadruple whammy of the communist victory in China, the Soviet atom bomb, the discovery of the Soviet spies and the race for the hydrogen bomb caused even the most phlegmatic Americans to fear that their country was in grave danger. McCarthy decided to test the fear for its political possibilities. In February 1950 he traveled to Wheeling, West Virginia, to give a speech that promised, ahead of the event, to be like scores of speeches McCarthy had given during the previous few years.

The venue was undistinguished: the Ohio County Republican Women's Club. West Virginia had voted Democratic since the 1930s, and Republicans in the state weren't exactly a force to be reckoned with. Neither was McCarthy, as far as anyone could tell, which was why he was speaking to the group this Thursday afternoon.

His remarks made headlines in the local paper, the *Wheeling Intelligencer*. "M'Carthy Charges Reds Hold U.S. Jobs," the paper declared. But what he said beyond this was hard to discern. The paper buried excerpts from McCarthy's speech on page 12, and the reporter who filed the story confessed that he worked from a text McCarthy gave him rather than from notes of what the senator actually said.

The gist of the charge was that the federal government was infested with communists. McCarthy was quoted as saying he had a list of 205 communists in the State Department alone. The figure caught the attention of other papers and was quickly repeated. The allegation was almost as quickly denied. "We know of no Communist members in the department and if we find any they will be summarily discharged," a State Department spokesman said.

The attention inspired McCarthy to amend and elaborate. He telegraphed Truman to say, "In a Lincoln Day speech at Wheeling Thursday night I stated that the State Department harbors a nest of Communists and Communist sympathizers who are helping to shape our foreign policy. I further stated that I have in my possession the names of 57 Communists who are in the State Department at present." McCarthy brushed aside the State Department's denial. "You can convince yourself of the falsity of the State Department's claim very easily," he told the president. "You will recall that you personally appointed a board to screen State Department employees for the purpose of weeding out fellow-travelers. Your board did a painstaking job and named hundreds which it listed as 'dangerous to the security of the nation' because of Communistic connections." McCarthy praised the probe, which had its roots in a 1947 order by Truman to investigate potential disloyalty in government. But the president had failed to follow up, McCarthy said. He acknowledged that he had not seen the records of the board, but he asserted that he had been told on good authority that the board had identified 300 persons who should be discharged. Yet Secretary of State Acheson had fired only around 80. McCarthy did not say that the 205 figure he had adduced in

Wheeling was roughly the difference between 300 and 80, but Truman could draw the inference, as could the millions who read McCarthy's telegram when he released it to the press.

McCarthy continued, regarding the retention of most of the allegedly disloyal individuals, "I understand that this was done after lengthy consultation with Alger Hiss." McCarthy didn't say where his new count of 57 came from. But the number, which would continue to change in further McCarthy allegations, was less important than the principle of obstruction he imputed to the administration. Acheson and the State Department were criminally culpable, yet the obstructionist-in-chief was Truman himself. "You signed an order forbidding the State Department's giving to the Congress any information in regard to the disloyalty or the Communistic connections of anyone in that department." McCarthy demanded that the president rescind the order and deliver the names of the disloyal to the appropriate congressional committees. "Failure on your part will label the Democratic party of being the bedfellow of international communism," he concluded.

TRUMAN HAD GROWN accustomed to being slandered by Republicans and other political opponents, but McCarthy, in so baldly alleging collusion with communism, crossed the line. The president responded with outrage. "This is the first time in my experience, and I was ten years in the Senate, that I ever heard of a senator trying to discredit his own government before the world," he wrote. "You know that isn't done by honest public officials. Your telegram is not only not true and an insolent approach to a situation that should have been worked out between man and man, but it shows conclusively that you are not even fit to have a hand in the operation of the government of the United States. I am very sure that the people of Wisconsin are extremely sorry that they are represented by a person who has as little sense of responsibility as you have."

Truman didn't mail this letter, though. He often vented in drafts and set his words aside until he cooled off. In this case he realized he would simply be playing into McCarthy's hands. The senator would surely share the response with the press; he might even read it aloud to the Senate. Truman didn't propose to give the Republican lowlife any more material than he was making up on his own.

F
OR THE MOMENT McCarthy was a minor irritant; Truman's
larger problem was the storm of criticism evoked by the communist victory in China. Congressional Republicans included a
powerful bloc whose members revered Chiang Kai-shek and demanded
his restoration as the leader of all of China. Robert Taft had contested
Dewey for the Republican nomination in 1948 and was judged the front-
runner for 1952; the Ohio senator now excoriated the Truman administration for having abandoned Chiang. "There is not the slightest doubt
in my mind that the proper kind of sincere aid to Nationalist China a
few years ago could have stopped communism in China," Taft declared.
Dean Acheson and his cabal at the State Department were especially
to blame. "The State Department has been guided by a left-wing group
who obviously have wanted to get rid of Chiang and were willing at least
to turn China over to the Communists for that purpose."

The Republicans insisted that Congress investigate the sordid affair,
and such was the uproar in the country that the majority Democrats felt
obliged to go along. The Senate Foreign Relations Committee called
Louis Johnson, the secretary of defense, and Omar Bradley, the chairman
of the Joint Chiefs of Staff. The Republican members of the committee
sought to reveal a rift between the diplomats of the State Department
and the military men of the Defense Department on the importance of
Formosa. They didn't get far. Chairman Tom Connally of Texas kept
reporters out of the session, but he briefed them after it ended. Johnson
and Bradley had said that Formosa should not be allowed to fall to the
communists but that it didn't warrant occupation by U.S. troops, Con-

nally related. He continued: "Secretary Johnson also strongly pointed out that there has been no rift between the Department of Defense and the Department of State with respect to our basic policy and objectives in that area."

The Republicans on the committee, unsatisfied, demanded to hear from Douglas MacArthur. General MacArthur was the American commander with greatest experience of the Far East and the one with present responsibility for the region. He must give his views.

Connally disagreed and declined to summon the general. Bringing Johnson and Bradley across the Potomac to Capitol Hill was one thing, he said; bringing MacArthur across the Pacific and North America was quite another. Besides, MacArthur didn't want to leave Japan. "General MacArthur several times has refused to come to the United States," Connally observed. "Shall we send the sheriff for him?"

MacArthur wound up testifying indirectly. One of the Republicans on the committee shared with reporters MacArthur's thinking, as explained by Bradley. "General Bradley said MacArthur's views had been fully taken into consideration. The views of MacArthur and the Joint Chiefs of Staff seem in fact to be pretty much the same about Formosa, except that MacArthur attaches more urgency to the situation. MacArthur and the Joint Chiefs agree that Formosa in hostile hands would be a menace to our lifeline."

MACARTHUR INDEED BELIEVED that a hostile Formosa would be a menace. He judged the administration's treatment of Chiang disgraceful and destructive. "The decision to withdraw previously pledged American support was one of the greatest mistakes ever made in our history," he later wrote. "At one fell blow, everything that had been so laboriously built up since the days of John Hay"—the author of America's first conscious policy toward China, in the 1890s—"was lost." With the Republican conservatives, MacArthur laid the blame at the feet of Dean Acheson. "In an address before the National Press Club in Washington, Secretary of State Acheson declared Formosa outside 'our defense perimeter.'" MacArthur tried to remedy this woeful mistake. "I felt that the Secretary of State was badly advised about the Far East, and I invited him to be my guest in Tokyo. I had never met Dean Acheson, but felt certain that his own survey of the Asiatic situation would materially alter his expressed views." Acheson refused to be educated, MacArthur recounted. "He declined the invitation, saying that the pressure of his duties prevented him from leaving Washington. He did, however, visit Europe eleven times during his stay in office."

MacArthur's Far Eastern command initially included China's neighbor Korea. His subordinate General John Hodge had led a landing of American forces at Inchon in September 1945 that shortly encountered Russian troops who had entered the northern part of the country upon Moscow's eleventh-hour declaration of war against Japan. The American and Soviet governments agreed to divide the country at the 38th parallel to facilitate the surrender of Japanese forces. The Americans would occupy the region south of the parallel, the Russians the region north. The division was a matter of convenience, with both sides assuming that a high-level peace conference would determine the fate of Korea along with the other issues outstanding from the war.

But the conference never took place, and the temporary division of Korea congealed into permanence. North of the 38th parallel Kim Il Sung imposed communist rule; south of the parallel Syngman Rhee established an anticommunist yet hardly less authoritarian regime. The United Nations General Assembly approved resolutions endorsing Korean unity, but nothing was done to implement them. Few people outside the country paid it much attention.

MacArthur visited Seoul in the summer of 1948 to congratulate Rhee on his assuming the presidency of the Republic of Korea, yet when the Soviets announced in early 1949 that they had evacuated their troops from North Korea, MacArthur recommended the removal of U.S. troops from the South. They were gone by the end of June, at which point MacArthur's responsibility for Korea ceased.

Consequently Dean Acheson's omission of Korea from America's defense perimeter, in the January 1950 National Press Club speech MacArthur cited, occasioned much less notice than his exemption of Formosa. Since the early twentieth century the National Press Club had provided a place for reporters to drink, smoke and compare notes; since the 1930s it had hosted a series of luncheons at which newsmakers broke bread with news writers and sometimes broke stories. The luncheons allowed officials like Acheson to explain policies in fuller detail and with greater nuance than they often could elsewhere, and to do so before an audience that was well informed, attentive and professionally unpartisan. Speakers' remarks were typically not recorded, encouraging the open dialogue the club members valued. Attendance at the luncheons varied; mayors drew smaller crowds than prime ministers. The Acheson lunch was a hot ticket on account of the heat Acheson and the Truman administration were feeling over China. The room was packed, and the secretary of state was given ample opportunity to defend and elucidate the administration's position.

Acheson traced the evolution of American policy toward China in general and toward Chiang in particular. "After the war Chiang Kai-shek emerged as the undisputed leader of the Chinese people," Acheson said. "Only one faction, the Communists, up in the hills, ill-equipped, ragged, a very small military force, was determinedly opposed to his position. He had overwhelming military power, greater military power than any ruler had ever had in the entire history of China. He had tremendous economic and military support and backing from the United States. He had the acceptance of all other foreign countries." And yet he had squandered those advantages, losing the support of the Chinese people through corruption and misgovernment. "What has happened, in my judgment, is that the almost inexhaustible patience of the Chinese people in their misery ended. They did not bother to overthrow this government. There was really nothing to overthrow. They simply ignored it throughout the country." No amount of American aid could have changed things.

Acheson went on to describe the defensive perimeter of the United States in the western Pacific region. It ran along the island chain that stretched from the Aleutians of Alaska south and west through Japan and the Ryukyu Islands to the Philippines. Acheson indeed omitted mention of Formosa, though many strategists considered it a crucial part of the island chain. Korea was omitted too, being part of the mainland rather than the island chain. Regarding the areas he did not include in America's defensive zone, Acheson said, "It must be clear that no person can guarantee these areas against military attack. But it must also be clear that such a guarantee is hardly sensible or necessary within the realm of practical relationship. Should such an attack occur—one hesitates to say where such an armed attack could come from—an initial reliance must be on the people attacked to resist it and then upon the commitments of the entire civilized world under the charter of the United Nations, which so far has not proved a weak reed to lean on by people who are determined to protect their independence against outside aggression."

The Republicans who pounced on Acheson for omitting Formosa said next to nothing about Korea. China was the obsession of the congressional Republicans, aided by such conservative media stalwarts as *Time* magazine's chief, Henry Luce, who had been born in China to American missionary parents; Korea was the obsession of no one in America. Truman and Acheson were roundly condemned for losing China; their concession of half of Korea elicited yawns and even, in some quarters, approval for not risking a land war in Asia. Korea was considered so unimportant that just days after Acheson's speech the House rejected the administration's request for continued aid to that country.

Nor was the South Korean government upset by Acheson's remarks. Quite the contrary. A memo of a meeting between Truman and South Korean ambassador John Myun Chang summarized: "The Ambassador expressed the appreciation of President Rhee and the National Assembly for the Secretary's remarks regarding Korea at the Press Club and the Secretary's letter of January 20 to President Truman." In the Press Club speech Acheson had supported U.S. aid to Korea, and the January 20 letter was a warning that the rejection of aid augured damage to American policy not only toward Korea but toward other parts of the world. The letter expressed a determination to get the House to reconsider. The House did so after the administration pared down the money for Korea and linked it to new aid to Chiang Kai-shek.

In Tokyo Douglas MacArthur was silent about Acheson's omission of Korea. If the general even noticed it, he kept his thoughts to himself. Like Congress, he worried far more about China and Formosa.

6

OBSERVERS OF HARRY Truman often wondered what he saw in Dean Acheson. The two men could hardly have been more dissimilar. Acheson's elegantly credentialed education—Groton, Yale, Harvard Law—contrasted starkly with the autodidactic version of Truman, whose classroom experience ended when he exited high school. Acheson oozed arrogance Truman abided in no one else. Acheson suffered fools, meaning most of those who disagreed with him, hardly at all. Truman took care with his clothing and appearance but never looked more than Main Street natty; Acheson adopted the fashions and style of Savile Row. Truman gazed out frankly on the world through plain, rimless glasses; Acheson's eyebrow was perpetually arched. Long past the time when public figures in America had abandoned facial hair, Acheson's thin mustache accentuated the curl of his lip as he sneered at his critics. Harry Truman was a man of the ordinary people of America; Dean Acheson was everything ordinary Americans loved to hate.

Even Acheson's friends thought so. Oliver Franks served as British ambassador to the United States and came to know Acheson quite well. Franks was struck at once by the contrast between Truman and Acheson. "President Truman is a rather simple and uncomplicated man," Franks said. "Acheson is considerably different. He combines an eighteenth century style of personal taste with the moral conscience and austerity of a seventeenth century Puritan. I don't mean that he doesn't drink and enjoy good living, but his life is austere." Franks continued, "Two qualities are at war in Acheson. The historical sense which he shares with Truman, and the lawyer's skill at creating the case which he must argue.

His sheer lucidness could be overwhelming and could take him out of the context in which he was arguing. Acheson also takes pride in doing hard, pioneering things. He never allows himself to forget the New England roots out of which it is all done." Acheson had reasonably good relations with a few senators and representatives who shared his seriousness of purpose. "Like himself, they were gentlemen," Franks said. "They had a code." But for the majority of legislators, Acheson felt nothing but disdain. "Acheson is incapable of entertaining intellectual shoddiness with patience. He lacks the indispensable political gift—for a long run political career—of believing that every argument has an equally legitimate intellectual background. That gift just wasn't given to Acheson. He could not tolerate entertaining trivial ideas or reasoning, however well meant, as worthy of respect. And when he chose to say what he was thinking, the words wounded and were neither forgotten nor forgiven. His unwillingness to show deference to every piece of nonsense a senator or congressman chose to utter was complete."

Acheson convicted himself out of his own mouth, once he was beyond the reach of politics. In retirement he expressed grave reservations about the fundamental principles of democracy. "You all start with the premise that democracy is some good," he told two visitors who were asking why democracies had difficulty conducting effective foreign policy. "I don't think it's worth a damn. I think Churchill is right, the only thing to be said for democracy is that there is nothing else that's any better, and therefore he used to say, 'Tyranny tempered by assassination, but lots of assassination.' People say, 'If the Congress were more representative of the people it would be better.' I say the Congress is too damn representative. It's just as stupid as the people are, just as uneducated, just as dumb, just as selfish."

Acheson conceded occasional exceptions. "Vandenberg is a typical example of somebody who got educated," he said of Republican senator Arthur Vandenberg of Michigan. "Very largely, Cordell Hull"—Franklin Roosevelt's secretary of state—"did this. He took a fellow from Grand Rapids, who was a perfect editor of the Grand Rapids newspaper. He didn't look any further than furniture"—the chief industry of Grand Rapids—"not a bit. And Hull began to tell him about the world. What you had to do to get certain results. And Van was sort of open-mouthed at this. He said, 'My God!' It was sort of like having Marco Polo come home and talk with you. 'I'll be damned. You really mean it's like that?'

'Yes, it really is.' And he said, 'Well, God, then we're going to do something about it.' Then he became a fellow who had ideas but never strolled far off first base."

Robert Taft was a harder type. "Bob was very educated on certain things," Acheson said of the Ohio senator. "Public housing he knew a lot about and was for, and was radical as hell on that; but so far as them foreigners out there are concerned, to hell with them, they didn't vote in Ohio and they were not good, and shiftless. Get a good Army, Navy and Air Force, and to hell with it."

While he served as secretary of state, Acheson held his tongue on the deficiencies of democracy, but his arrogance still showed. And it provoked the Republicans beyond endurance. "I look at that fellow," Nebraska senator Hugh Butler declared. "I watch his smart aleck manner and his British clothes and that New Dealism, everlasting New Dealism in everything he says and does, and I want to shout, Get out! Get out! You stand for everything that has been wrong with the United States for years."

AGAINST ALL ODDS, Acheson and Truman got along splendidly. They had spoken, by chance, just days before Franklin Roosevelt's death. "I had a long meeting with Mr. Truman and for the first time got a definite impression," Acheson wrote to his son. "It was a very good impression. He is straight-forward, decisive, simple, entirely honest." Acheson didn't have to add, to his son, that these traits were just the opposite of Roosevelt's, which was why Acheson and other officials of the State Department had found Roosevelt so difficult to deal with. Truman promised to be a subordinate's dream. "He, of course, has the limitations upon his judgment and wisdom that the limitations of his experience produce, but I think he will learn fast and will inspire confidence."

Acheson took pains to make himself Truman's tutor. An assistant secretary of state when Truman became president, Acheson remained a deputy during Truman's first term. But his bosses—Secretaries of State Edward Stettinius, James Byrnes and George Marshall—were, respectively, inexperienced, distracted and often ailing, allowing Acheson great leeway to shape American policy. He and Truman saw eye to eye on the need for firmness toward the Soviet Union, and a mutual admiration developed between the two men. When Marshall retired following Truman's 1948 election victory, Acheson was the obvious successor.

Acheson's elevation to the post of America's top diplomat did nothing to improve his opinion of those he considered his intellectual and moral inferiors. Nor did it moderate his arrogance. He disdained to defend himself against those he called "primitives," among whom he placed Joseph McCarthy first. Instead he defended Alger Hiss. He said he had known Hiss and his brother Donald Hiss from childhood and trusted their word implicitly. He judged that the court that convicted Hiss had got the verdict wrong. He told reporters, "I do not intend to turn my back on Alger Hiss."

He should have. Evidence released from Soviet archives many years later revealed with near conclusiveness that Hiss had indeed spied for Moscow. But Acheson considered Hiss one of his own kind, several cuts above McCarthy and the others who persecuted honest men like himself.

Acheson's defense of Hiss outraged McCarthy and the senator's Republican allies. McCarthy read to the Senate Acheson's statement of support for Hiss and wondered aloud if the secretary of state intended to "turn his back on other Communists who were associated with Hiss." Senator Homer Capehart of Indiana demanded that Truman fire Acheson for sheltering Hiss and said he was "prouder than ever" that he had voted against Acheson's confirmation as secretary of state. Senator Bourke Hickenlooper of Iowa blasted Acheson and Truman in the same breath by proclaiming that there would be a "mass revolt by the American people" if the people knew to what lengths the administration had gone in covering up for Hiss. The Senate, despite its solid Democratic majority, proceeded to vote to authorize its Foreign Relations Committee to launch an investigation of the charges leveled by McCarthy and the others about a cover-up of communists in the State Department.

Meanwhile, Acheson demanded that McCarthy produce his list of communists, whether the version with 205 or the mere 57. And Acheson's spokesman, John Peurifoy, denied the other numbers the senator slung around. The president's loyalty board had not identified 300 department employees as disloyal, and it had not fired 80, Peurifoy said. Reporters asked Peurifoy how much confidence he had in the department's ability to detect disloyalty in its ranks. Would the department's security system "screen out a Dr. Fuchs"? one inquired. The Fuchs case had nothing to do with the State Department, but the revelation that America's most closely guarded secret had been compromised lent credence to the conservative charges of laxness in matters of national security. Peurifoy made no promises. "All I can say is that our system is a continuing process," he replied. "It's a difficult job and we keep at it."

McCarthy refused to reveal his lists. He said that doing so would compromise the investigative agencies that had unearthed the identities of the people on the lists. He similarly refused to identify the agencies. He hinted at having informants inside the State Department, but he refused to identify them, saying their jobs would not be "worth a tinker's damn" if he did so.

Acheson sniffed in derision, confirmed in his dismal judgment of democracy. The American system could produce an admirable leader like Truman, but it also produced primitives like McCarthy. And the primitives appeared to be gaining ground.

7

ARTHUR MACARTHUR IV was the only child of Douglas and Jean MacArthur. He was named for Douglas MacArthur's father, Arthur MacArthur Jr., and elder brother, Arthur MacArthur III, who died of appendicitis more than a decade before Arthur IV was born. Twelve years old in early 1950, the boy had never visited America. His earliest years were passed in the Philippines, from which he escaped by PT boat with his father and mother as the Japanese were closing in on Corregidor in 1942. The boy and his mother spent the rest of the war in Australia, where he acquired a touch of an Ozzie accent, and they joined his father in Japan at the end of the war.

Living in the American embassy in the middle of bombed-out Tokyo, Arthur had few playmates. At the first birthday party he celebrated in Japan, the guests were army generals and colonels who played musical chairs and made sure the boss's kid won. Occasionally, a foreign diplomat would appear with a child around Arthur's age, but for the most part the boy dwelled in a world of adults: his father, his mother, his British governess, the household staff, his father's aides. He was often alone, reading books and comics or rowing about the embassy pond in a red, white and blue boat that bore the same name as his father's airplane, *Bataan*.

He craved his father's attention and regularly received it at one particular time of day: early morning. Douglas MacArthur allowed himself to be awakened every day at seven by Arthur, who would tear into his parents' bedroom and wrestle with his father in the big bed. The three would be joined by the family's four dogs, and father, son and canines would romp about the room making all manner of noise. Jean would retreat to another room to escape the exuberance.

The general treated his son as a genius. When the boy showed an aptitude for music, he received instruments and instruction in musical theory and practice. When Arthur painted a watercolor, MacArthur invited reporters to see it and declared the work "better than a Rembrandt."

MacArthur's father had been a distinguished general and a winner of the Medal of Honor. MacArthur himself was even more distinguished, and likewise a Medal of Honor winner. MacArthur assumed his son would continue the martial tradition. He wrote to the corps of cadets at West Point, where he had excelled as a student and later served as commandant, "I hope that God will let me live to see the day when young Arthur MacArthur is sworn in on The Plain as a plebe at West Point."

FAMILY TRADITION MEANT a great deal to Douglas MacArthur. He could recite from memory the story of his father's heroics during the American Civil War, when the senior MacArthur had been an adjutant with a Wisconsin regiment at the Battle of Missionary Ridge. "No one seems to know just what orders may have been given, but suddenly the flag of the 24th Wisconsin started forward," Douglas MacArthur would say. "With it was the color sergeant, the color guard of two corporals and the adjutant. Up they went, step by step. The enemy's fire was intense. Down went the color bearer. One of the corporals seized the colors as they fell, but was bayoneted before he could move. A shell took off the head of the other corporal, but the adjutant grasped the flag and kept on. He seemed surrounded by nothing but gray coats. A Confederate colonel thrust viciously at his throat, but even as he lunged a bullet struck and the deflected blade just ripped a shoulder strap. No movement yet from the Union lines. And then, above the roar of battle, sounded the adjutant's voice: 'On, Wisconsin!'"

MacArthur could see the fighting unfold before his mind's eye. "They come, then; they come with a rush and a roar, a blue tide of courage, a whole division of them. Shouting, cursing, struggling foot by foot, heads bent as in a gale! Gasping breath from tortured lungs! Those last few feet before the log breastworks seem interminable! Men tumble over like tenpins! The charge is losing momentum! They falter! Officers are down! Sergeants now lead! And then, suddenly, on the crest—the flag! Once again that cry: 'On, Wisconsin!' Silhouetted against the sky, the adjutant stands on the parapet waving the colors where the whole regiment can see him! Through the ragged blue line, from one end of the division to the other, comes an ugly roar, like the growl of a wounded bear! They race those last few steps, eyes blazing, lips snarling, bayonets plunging! And Missionary Ridge is won."

MacArthur could never recount the battle without hearing that primal roar of the Union soldiers, without feeling the blast of the shells and the rush of the bullets, without tasting the salt of sweat and blood. The story had become his story as much as his father's, for the MacArthurs were cut from a single cloth of Scots courage. He had since heard the roar, felt the blast, tasted the salt of his own battles. Yet it all began on Missionary Ridge.

"The adjutant suddenly falls to the ground exhausted, his body retching, racked with pain. He is a terrible sight—covered with blood and mud, hatless, his smoke-blackened face barely recognizable, his clothes torn to tatters. Sheridan, the division commander, utters not a word—he just stares at him—and then takes him in his arms. And his deep voice seems to break a little as he says: 'Take care of him. He has just won the Medal of Honor.'"

THERE WAS MORE to the MacArthur tradition than valor. There was firm adherence to military principle in the face of political meddling. Douglas MacArthur entered West Point about the time his father, by then a general in the U.S. Army, was appointed military governor of the Philippines. The son cut a swath through the academy. "Handsome as a prince he was, six feet tall and weighing about 160, with dark hair and a ruddy, outdoors look," recalled an admirer. Another contemporary described him as "brave as a lion and smart as hell." Yet some thought him too full of himself. "Arrogant from the age of eight," remarked one of the skeptics. Another classmate declared, "To know MacArthur is to love him or hate him—you can't just like him." MacArthur ranked first in his class three out of his four years, achieving in his final year the coveted rank of first captain, a distinction previously enjoyed by such academy models as Robert E. Lee and John Pershing.

His initial posting took him to the Philippines. The assignment might have been awkward under any circumstances, with his father the ranking officer in the recently acquired American colony. But it was rendered more awkward by a feud that had developed between Arthur MacArthur and William Howard Taft, the civilian governor of the Philippines. Arthur MacArthur was responsible for military security in the islands, and he blamed Taft for sacrificing security to political convenience. MacArthur's innate haughtiness didn't help matters, goading Taft beyond endurance and bringing governance of the Philippines to a standstill. Eventually President Theodore Roosevelt felt obliged to relieve MacArthur and recall him to America.

Yet he still managed to promote his son's career. The army sent Arthur MacArthur on a tour of East Asia, and he took Douglas along. They ventured to Japan after that country stunned Russia with a sneak attack against its Pacific fleet and commenced a successful war against the much larger power. Washington wanted to know how Japan had done it and what it portended for the United States. "I met all the great Japanese commanders," Douglas MacArthur remembered later: "Oyama, Kuroki, Nogi and the brilliant Admiral Heihachiro Togo—those grim, taciturn, aloof men of iron character and unshakeable purpose. It was here that I first encountered the boldness and courage of the Nipponese soldier. His almost fanatical belief in and reverence for his Emperor impressed me indelibly."

Father and son spent nine months in Asia and the surrounding waters. They visited China, Indochina, Siam, the East Indies and India, speaking to government officials, local dignitaries, military officers and ordinary men and women. Douglas MacArthur was smitten by the Orient, which he came to consider the crucible of humanity's fate and his own country's. "Here lived almost half the population of the world, with probably more than half of the raw products to sustain future generations. Here was western civilization's last earth frontier. It was crystal clear to me that the future and, indeed, the very existence of America were irrevocably entwined with Asia and its island outposts."

The Asia tour proved a last hurrah for Arthur MacArthur, who never recovered professionally from his firing in the Philippines. He was promoted to lieutenant general, the highest-ranking officer in the army, but was passed over for chief of staff, the highest post, and when his bête noire, Taft, became president, he retired, a bitter man. He regularly gathered with his comrades from the Civil War, who still revered the hero of Missionary Ridge. Their reunions gradually grew less frequent as their numbers dwindled, but they summoned the fraternal spirit for a fiftieth reunion, at which they shared the old stories, sang the old songs, toasted comrades present and gone. Arthur MacArthur rose to recognize their valor and to be recognized for his. But after a few words he collapsed. He died on the spot, surrounded by his men, who said a prayer as he left them forever.

"My whole world changed that night," Douglas MacArthur recalled. "Never have I been able to heal the wound in my heart."

FORTY YEARS LATER the wound dully ached, most days. But it sharply throbbed each time a politician put the trivialities of popularity and vote-getting ahead of the life-and-death business of war and military strategy. His father's death had redoubled Douglas MacArthur's determination to construct a career that would have made the old general proud. He fought in World War I with unsurpassed distinction. Appointed chief of staff to the commander of the famous Forty-Second, or Rainbow, Division, he delegated the paperwork of his staff job to subordinates and headed for the front. He joined a French raid into German-held territory to capture prisoners to interrogate. For his bravery he received the Croix de Guerre. A short while later he spearheaded an American attack against the German lines. He had warned his men about the dangers of poison gas and insisted that they keep their gas masks handy at all times. He ignored his own advice, advancing with neither mask nor weapon other than a riding crop. He was gassed and briefly incapacitated. Yet rather than being embarrassed, he concluded upon recovery that the fearless figure he presented was worth any added risk. To complement his riding crop he donned puttees, and to fashion a distinctive profile he removed the metal band that held the brim of his hat in place. The hat slouched in a devil-may-care manner, which drew additionally from a turtleneck sweater and a long scarf that caught the French breezes. Some of his soldiers thought him a dandy, but none required a second look to recognize him.

MacArthur carried off his pose by exhibiting courage and audacity unexcelled in the American Expeditionary Forces. Promoted to brigadier general, he led his brigade from the front. His gallantry and flair for the dramatic made him a reporter's dream. "I had never before met so vivid, so captivating, so magnetic a man," wrote journalist William Allen White. "He stood six feet, had a clean-shaven face, a clean-cut mouth, nose and chin, lots of brown hair, good eyes with a 'come hither' in them that must have played the devil with the girls, and yet he was as 'he' as Chapman's bull in the Estes Park meadow."

MacArthur's comrades were equally impressed. An officer who served with him throughout the war declared, "He has no superior as an officer in the world." His divisional commander said, "MacArthur is the bloodiest fighting man in this army. . . . There's no risk of battle that any soldier is called upon to take that he is not liable to look up and see MacArthur at his side. At every advance MacArthur, with just his cap and his riding crop, will go forward with the first line. He is the source of the greatest possible inspiration to the men of this division, who are devoted to him." The French commander in his sector called MacArthur "the most remarkable officer I have ever known." A grizzled noncommissioned officer employed more picturesque colorful language: "He's a hell-to-breakfast baby, long and lean, kind to us and tough on the enemy. He can spit nickel cigars and chase Germans as well as any doughboy in the Rainbow."

MACARTHUR RETURNED TO America after the war, and the army named him superintendent of West Point. He was the youngest officer to hold that position in generations, and he set about dragging the academy into the twentieth century. He liberalized the curriculum to inform cadets about the world beyond the military, and he substituted study of World War I for that of the Civil War. Most shocking to the faculty, he made personal visits to their classes, taking notes and afterward suggesting improvements.

His reforms aroused resistance, which he might have weathered had it been confined to the affairs of the academy. In fact his most powerful opponent was one he crossed in an affair of quite another sort. John Pershing, the commander of U.S. forces in France during the war and currently army chief of staff, had been eyeing Louise Cromwell Brooks, a wealthy young widow, for some time, as newspapers were reporting. But Louise preferred MacArthur, who was handsomer, closer to her own age and a rising rather than a setting star. The courtship hardly counted as one: MacArthur met Louise at a party and proposed to her that night.

She said yes. They were wed on Valentine's Day 1922 at her stepfather's Palm Beach estate. "Marriage of Mars and Millions," one paper cheekily observed.

Pershing had his revenge. He banished MacArthur to the Philippines. Pershing naturally denied any link between the distant posting and the intimacy between MacArthur and Louise. "It's all damn poppycock," he said of the allegations. "If I were married to all the ladies that gossips have me engaged to, I'd be a regular Brigham Young."

Pershing eventually retired and MacArthur returned from exile, to the relief of Louise, who nonetheless divorced him a few years later. He recovered sufficiently to marry Jean Faircloth, a Tennessee woman eight years younger than Louise, in 1937.

In 1925 he took part in a crucial test of the military chain of command. General Billy Mitchell was an air corps hero of World War I and a pain to his commanders. He ardently believed and loudly stated that airpower held the key to victory in the next war. He found an audience in Congress that paid heed to his theory, against the opposition of the navy and its supporters, who held that the blue-water fleet was and always must be America's first line of defense. A trial of Mitchell's theory was proposed and conducted; surplus warships, including a captured German dreadnought, were the targets. When the ships sank, Mitchell's stock rose, along with the ire of his antagonists. After further provocations—he castigated the Navy and War Departments for "incompetency, criminal negligence and almost treasonable administration of the national defense"—the anti-Mitchell group arranged his court-martial.

MacArthur received an order to join the court. He later called it "one of the most distasteful orders" he ever got, for he sided with Mitchell on the right of officers to speak their minds. "It is part of my military philosophy that a senior officer should not be silenced for being at variance with his superiors in rank and with accepted doctrine," he explained. "I have always felt that the country's interest was paramount, and that when a ranking officer, out of purely patriotic motives, risked his own personal future in such opposition, he should not be summarily suppressed." In any event, suppression would fail. "The one thing in this world that cannot be stopped is a sound idea. The individual may be martyred, but his thoughts live on."

Mitchell was martyred professionally. Conviction by the court required but a two-thirds majority, which was what the prosecution obtained. Mitchell was suspended from duty, prompting his angry resignation. He died before the next war proved him a prophet.

How MacArthur voted on the verdict forever remained a mystery. The balloting was secret, and MacArthur never said how he cast his vote. In his memoir he was evasive. "I did what I could in his behalf and I helped save him from dismissal," he declared. But he might have been referring to the sentence rather than the verdict.

THE MITCHELL CASE revived MacArthur's painful memories of his father, similarly martyred to politics. The old wound stabbed yet again when Franklin Roosevelt hauled him to Honolulu as a political trophy in 1944. And it stabbed whenever he thought of Harry Truman. Truman's early reputation as a political hack, the fair-haired boy of Boss Tom Pendergast of Kansas City, was familiar even to one who disparaged politics as much as MacArthur did. MacArthur's desire to restore honor to the White House had been a large part of his reason for running for president in 1948. Truman's performance since then had done little to improve MacArthur's opinion of him. Truman continued to obsess about Europe and ignore Asia, which was where, MacArthur was convinced, the struggle for the world would be won or lost. Truman had fiddled while China fell to the communists, and he seemed intent on undermining Chiang Kai-shek, the last hope for China, at every turn.

The one benefit of Truman's failure to focus on Asia was that it had allowed MacArthur a free hand in Japan. In the early summer of 1950, as the occupation approached its fifth anniversary, MacArthur felt pleased with what he had accomplished there. China was a new source of worry, and a serious one, but the reforms he had initiated in Japan were taking firm root, and the Japanese people were busily rebuilding their society along liberal, peaceful lines. MacArthur was confident that Japan, aided by the security alliance with America that would accompany any peace treaty, would be able to hold its own as the free world's refutation of the pernicious doctrines of the Chinese Communists.

In moments of reflection he asked himself if any other great country had ever owed more to one man. He could not think of an instance. He had done well. His father would be proud.

8

HARRY TRUMAN'S FATHER had set a different example from MacArthur's. Where military heroes ran in the MacArthur line, marginal farmers and failed businessmen characterized the Trumans. John Truman was too young to have fought in the Civil War, though if he had been older, it would have been a toss-up which side he would have fought on. John Truman's family owned slaves, but Missouri, where the family lived, stuck with the Union. Missouri sent soldiers to both sides in the war and itself experienced some of the conflict's fiercest fighting, much of it Missourian on Missourian.

John Truman married Mattie Young in 1881. Three years later they christened their first child Harry S. The *S* denoted nothing except the inability of the father and mother to agree on a middle name. The child's grandfathers had names that started with *S*, and so his parents settled for the unaccompanied sibilant. The neighbors saw little odd in the compromise, for the thrifty Scots-Irish who populated western Missouri were sometimes known to economize on orthography this way.

John and Mattie perceived promise in the boy, who read avidly, especially history, and who played the piano with gusto. On his tenth birthday Harry received a four-volume set, *Great Men and Famous Women,* in which the men, who substantially outnumbered the women, included such heroes of history as Hannibal and Andrew Jackson, Cyrus the Great and Cortés, Lafayette and Robert E. Lee. Harry's piano playing, together with the eyeglasses that corrected his badly deficient vision, made him the object of ridicule among his peers. "It's a very lonely thing being a child," he observed later.

The family moved to Independence, Missouri, when John decided to give business a try. Harry attended elementary school in Independence and graduated from Independence High School. Ever afterward he called Independence home.

It was the home, as well, to Bessie Wallace, who lived on the town's proudest street and was much admired by her classmates. Harry sat in front of her in school and dreamed of her at night. "If I succeeded in carrying her books to school and back home for her, I had a big day," he remembered.

John Truman's ventures in commerce thrived at first but failed about the time Harry finished high school. The failure put college out of the question. Harry took work as a timekeeper for the Santa Fe Railroad and then as a teller in a Kansas City bank. He grew out of his shyness and discovered in himself an ability to get along with others. But he prospered insufficiently to resist a call from his father to return to the family farm. For a decade he plowed, planted, harrowed and harvested. The labor was tiring and tedious and only intermittently profitable.

John Truman tried to supplement the family income by running for county office, giving Harry a taste of politics. He wasn't impressed. "Politics is the sure ruination of many a good man," he wrote to Bess Wallace. "Between hot air and graft he usually loses not only his head but his money and friends as well." Still, it might beat farming or business. "If I were real rich I'd just as soon spend my money buying votes and offices as yachts and autos." He couldn't decide. "To succeed financially a man can't have any heart. To succeed politically he must be an egotist or a fool or a ward boss tool."

Truman fought in World War I, though much less spectacularly than Douglas MacArthur. He had joined Missouri's national guard a decade before the war, out of the same combination of patriotism, boredom and desire for belonging that motivated militia membership for generations. He quit after a few years, deciding he wasn't cut out for the military, even as a part-timer. The onset of war pulled him back. The war touched his sense of duty; it promised to be exciting; it gave him an excuse to leave the farm. And it prompted Bess, whom he had wooed since school, to agree to marry him. But he surprised her, and perhaps himself, by withdrawing his offer. He was going off to fight, he said. He might die. He might be maimed. He couldn't bear to think of her as a widow or, worse, bound to half a man. They had waited this long. They could wait until he returned from France.

He surprised himself a second time by getting elected lieutenant of his artillery battery. He hadn't thought of himself as a leader or a vote-getter, but the men of the battery apparently did. He had never before been responsible for much beyond himself and some farm animals. Now he had his men to look after.

They shipped out in the spring of 1918 and reached France after zig-zagging through waters infested with German submarines. Paris opened his eyes, though not to Frenchwomen, he assured Bess. "Have only seen one good-looking French woman and she was married to some general or admiral or something," he wrote. "Anyway he had seven or eight yards of gold braid on him."

After training with French artillerists, he rejoined his regiment and was given charge, as captain now, of Battery D. Most of his men were Irish Catholics from Kansas City, with a rowdy reputation. They had driven off previous captains and appeared intent on doing the same to Truman. They laughed at his glasses and ignored his commands.

It was the first crisis of his public life. "I could just see my hide on the fence when I tried to run that outfit," he recalled later. "Never on the front or anywhere else have I been so nervous." But he rose to the challenge. After a barracks brawl that sent several men to the infirmary, he busted the noncommissioned officers who should have kept the men in line. "I didn't come over here to get along with you," he told the other NCOs. "You've got to get along with me. And if there are any of you who can't, speak up right now and I'll bust you."

His decisiveness got the attention and won the respect of the men. It helped matters that they soon saw battle and so could fight Germans instead of one another. Artillery batteries were positioned behind the trenches, and most escaped the horrors of machine gun fire and hand-to-hand combat. But they paid for their dispensation by being targeted by enemy artillery.

Battery D's heaviest action came in September 1918. Truman's unit took part in one of the most savage outpourings of high explosives in history, at the opening of the Meuse-Argonne offensive. Thousands of American guns pounded the Germans and were pounded in return. Truman's battery did its brutal part, the gun barrels growing so hot that they sizzled the soaked gunnysacks laid over them for cooling.

After three hours the American artillery stopped firing, to let the infantry charge forward against the softened German defenses. The artillery followed. Horses and men dragged the guns across the shattered landscape, sinking every few feet in the cratered mud. German shells and rifle fire rendered the going deadly. Reports circulated of an imminent German counterattack. Truman and his men would be ordered either to retreat across the broken terrain or to stand their ground and die firing.

Things never reached this point. The Germans did not counterattack. The offensive continued, ultimately claiming more than a hundred thousand Americans killed, wounded, captured or missing. The greatest losses were among the infantry. Yet Truman and his gunners received their baptism by fire. "It isn't as bad as I thought it would be," he wrote to Bess. "But it's bad enough."

The war ended a month later. Truman's battery fired right up to the hour of the armistice. At eleven o'clock in the morning of November 11, all the guns fell silent. Truman was stunned by the sudden absence of their roar. "It made me feel as if I'd suddenly been deprived of my ability to hear," he wrote. "The men at the guns, the captain, the lieutenants, the sergeants and corporals looked at each other for some time, and then a great cheer arose all along the line. We could hear the men in the infantry a thousand meters in front raising holy hell. The French battery behind our position were dancing, shouting and waving bottles of wine." The celebration continued throughout the day and into the evening. "I went to bed about 10 p.m. but the members of the French battery insisted on marching around my cot and shaking hands. They'd shout, 'Vive le Capitaine Américain, vive le Président Wilson,' take another swig from their wine bottles and do it over. It was 2 a.m. before I could sleep at all."

KANSAS CITY GAVE its soldiers a grateful welcome on their return from France, and Truman's battery boys swore eternal loyalty and friendship to their captain. They promised their business as well. Tired of farming, Truman opened a haberdashery with Eddie Jacobson, a buddy from the war. The shop, on a bustling street in Kansas City, became a reunion ground for Battery D. At first the business flourished. The returning soldiers had wads of money they hadn't been able to spend in the service, and civilians joined the reconversion from wartime production to peacetime consumption. Truman's boys would drop by to see Captain Harry and stay to purchase a tie, a shirt, a belt or a pair of gloves.

But the economy hit a bump and the country pitched into recession. Sales at Truman & Jacobson slid, then plunged. Less than three years after it opened, the store closed, leaving the partners deeply in debt.

Truman, determined to pay the debt, reconsidered his opposition to politics. Tom Pendergast was the local Democratic boss, head of the political machine that ran Kansas City the way Tammany Hall ran New York and comparable machines ran other cities. Pendergast bought votes with favors financed by kickbacks from city contractors and levies on officeholders. Like the head of any large enterprise, Pendergast was always on the lookout for fresh talent, and in Truman he thought he detected it. Truman was smart, hardworking and apparently honest. This last trait might have seemed, to the uninitiated, unimportant or even counterproductive in a system dependent on the bending and breaking of laws. But in fact it was crucial. Pendergast cheated taxpayers, but he didn't want his subordinates cheating *him*. The fact that Truman could rely on the loyalty of the Battery D boys counted strongly in his favor, for each of those boys was worth up to several votes, depending on how many relatives he had.

Pendergast offered Truman a nomination for county judge. This was an administrative post rather than a judicial one, but it sounded impressive and its holder, with the other two judges on the court, controlled spending on roads and bridges. Kickbacks from construction were a major source of revenue to the Pendergast machine.

Truman accepted the offer. He discovered during the campaign that he liked the give-and-take of politics. His plainspoken style appealed to Missourians, and the support of his battery mates suggested he was the kind of man his constituents could count on. The race was closer than comfort allowed, but in the end he eked to victory. Captain Harry became Judge Truman.

Yet he remained Tom Pendergast's protégé. And when Pendergast requested favors, Truman was expected to deliver. Small requests, of the sort one friend did for another, came easily. But a larger imposition evoked a bout of angst. "The Boss wanted me to give a lot of crooked contractors the inside," Truman wrote afterward. He wrestled with the matter. He couldn't deny Pendergast without jeopardizing his job. He had a family to consider, for he had married Bess and they had a small daughter, Margaret. Yet he had to live with himself. "Since childhood at my mother's knee, I have believed in honor, ethics and right living."

He met with Pendergast, who was flanked by the expectant contractors. "These boys tell me that you won't give them contracts," the boss said.

"They can get them if they are the low bidders," Truman replied. "But they won't get paid for them unless they come up to specifications."

He held his breath, his future passing before his eyes.

Pendergast shook his head. Truman anticipated an explosion. Instead he got mere exasperation. "Didn't I tell you boys?" the boss said to the contractors. "He's the contrariest cuss in Missouri."

For reasons best known to himself, Pendergast allowed Truman to indulge his conscience. Possibly he reckoned the political value of being seen as tolerating independence on the county board. Certainly he reasoned that with the other two judges in his pocket, he could still get what he wanted. Maybe something in Truman appealed to a hidden streak of honor in Pendergast.

Truman had no further trouble with Pendergast until he decided to seek a promotion. Pendergast had less control over nominations to Congress than in local elections, but Truman applied for his support in preparing to make a bid for the House of Representatives. Pendergast refused. Truman, stung, abandoned hopes of advancement to Washington.

But then, without warning, Pendergast offered him something better: a nomination to the Senate. Truman guessed he wasn't the boss's first choice, but he was in no position to look this gift horse in the mouth.

He campaigned vigorously and won narrowly. Most observers credited Pendergast. The boss sent him off to Washington with simple advice: "Work hard, keep your mouth shut and answer your mail."

He did all that. And he supported Franklin Roosevelt, author of the most ambitious reform program in American history. "I was a New Dealer from the start," Truman explained decades later, still proud of his Roosevelt connection. Truman's humble Missouri Valley background could hardly have been more different from Roosevelt's patrician Hudson Valley upbringing, yet the two shared a belief that America owed the support of government to people who suffered distress and privation through no fault of their own, as millions were suffering in the depths of the Great Depression.

Truman's support for Roosevelt transcended conviction, though. Truman had discovered in himself a desire to make a mark on the world. He saw Roosevelt as a ticket to influence, even power. He had valued the loyalty of his men during the war, and he had given loyalty, if not obedience, to Tom Pendergast. In both cases loyalty had served him well. He would give loyalty to Roosevelt. "I am hoping to make a reputation as a Senator," he explained to Bess.

A critical test came when Roosevelt sought to expand the Supreme Court and appoint friendly justices. Roosevelt's advisers warned him against the attempt, editorialists decried it, and even ardent New Dealers thought it risky. But Roosevelt pressed ahead. And Truman backed him.

Roosevelt lost. He had pushed too far. The failure cost the president badly, depriving him of the aura of inevitability that had cloaked him from the start of the New Deal. With three years left in his second and presumably final term, he appeared the lamest of political ducks.

But then a new war erupted. The fighting began in Asia, where Japan attacked China. It spread to Europe when Germany invaded Poland. Americans didn't want to get involved, but many heeded arguments floated tentatively at first, then with greater conviction, that the danger abroad warranted lifting the hoary but never formalized ban on presidential third terms. Roosevelt's experience might be just what was needed to keep America safe. The Democrats obligingly nominated him again, and voters reelected him.

Missouri voters simultaneously reelected Truman. His Pendergast connection had become a liability when the boss was convicted of tax evasion, yet Truman campaigned as hard as ever, and his constituents continued to admire his forthrightness and pluck. He won by the narrowest of margins.

As Roosevelt surveyed the capital after the elections, he could see that the ranks of his loyalists had thinned. Yet there in the Senate sat the most loyal of all, Harry Truman.

That loyalty was repaid when Roosevelt needed a replacement for Henry Wallace in 1944. And it made Truman president when Roosevelt died.

FIVE YEARS LATER Truman still marveled at the train of events that got him to where he was. And he still wondered, at times, if the prize was worth the winning. His victory in 1948 had been satisfying, but the troubles that followed had left him no respite. He looked forward to the first full weekend of the 1950 summer. He would be going home: to Independence, to the family farm, to the people who had known him before he was president and, he hoped, would still claim him after his presidency ended. He had one official chore on the morning of Saturday, June 24: the dedication of a new airport in Baltimore. But after that he would be off duty for the rest of the weekend. He would board the presidential DC-6, the *Independence*, and fly to Kansas City. He would spend a quiet Saturday afternoon and evening with Bess and Margaret, who had preceded him west. On Sunday he would visit his brother and sister and inspect the family farm. He would return to Washington on Monday. Like the farm boy he often still felt himself to be, he checked the weather forecast and recalled why corn liked the Missouri Valley: ninety degrees, humid, chance of thundershowers.

Saturday morning and afternoon unfolded as planned. The dedication went smoothly, the flight was uneventful, and the thunderstorms stayed away. Dinner was served at 6:30, and the open windows caught the first stirrings of cooling air. Until dark the Trumans sat on a screened porch in the old house, talking everything but politics. They moved indoors to the library, mentally preparing for bed. An easy day for the president was ending on a quiet note.

Then, jarringly, the telephone in the hallway rang. It was Dean Acheson, who had taken the president's absence from Washington as occasion to have a holiday of his own, at his house in Maryland.

"Mr. President, I have very serious news," Acheson said. "The North Koreans have invaded South Korea."

PART TWO

TEST OF NERVE

ONE OF US got much sleep that night," Margaret Truman remembered. "My father made it clear, from the moment he heard the news, that he feared this was the opening round in World War III."

The president's instinct was to return to Washington at once. Dean Acheson persuaded him otherwise. The country was still adjusting to air travel, for presidents no less than for anyone else. An unscheduled night flight would signal alarm, besides being risky, Acheson said. Better to wait until the following day. Meanwhile, the secretary of state would do what could be done for South Korea from the distance of America. He had already directed the American representative at the United Nations to request an emergency meeting of the Security Council for the next morning. And he was talking to the Pentagon about options to present to the president on his return.

On Sunday morning the Truman family behaved as though it were any other Sunday. Bess and Margaret went to church at Trinity Episcopal in Independence. Truman skipped his morning walk in favor of an early start to Grandview, where the family farm was located. He spoke for an hour and a half with his younger brother, Vivian, and Vivian's two sons and five grandchildren. He inspected a new milking machine and nodded approval of a recently purchased horse. He proceeded to the nearby home of his younger sister, Mary Jane, who had never married. By now radio and wire service reports were full of the news of the North Korean invasion, but Truman appeared oblivious to it and spoke to no one from the media.

Only when he got back to Independence did he address the matter. A copy of a telegram from the U.S. ambassador in Seoul, John Muccio, to the State Department awaited him. "It would appear from nature of attack and manner in which it was launched that it constitutes all out offensive against ROK," Muccio summarized, employing the shorthand for the Republic of Korea, or South Korea. Truman read the message with a grim face, then stepped outside to meet the reporters who clamored for a statement. "Don't make it alarmist," the president said, despite feeling no little alarm himself. "It could be a dangerous situation, but I hope it isn't." The reporters wanted more, but Truman demurred. "I can't answer any questions until I get all the facts."

"Has there been a formal declaration of war by North Korea?" a reporter shouted.

"No, there is no formal declaration of war," Truman said. "That I know."

Truman's aides announced that the president was cutting short his visit. "The President talked to Secretary Acheson and has three or four important decisions to make," said Eben Ayers, the assistant press secretary. "He feels he should go back to Washington right away."

Bess and Margaret chose to remain in Missouri, but they saw Truman off. Neither spoke to the press, yet reporters read in their faces the strain they felt. "Mrs. Truman was calm but serious," a regular on the White House beat recorded. "She looked much as she appeared on the fateful evening of the late President Roosevelt's death, when her husband took the oath of office." Margaret Truman watched the departure from the edge of the runway. "She stood staring up, absorbed, at her father's big plane, her hands clasped under her chin in a subconscious, prayerful attitude."

Truman arrived at Washington's National Airport a bit past seven in the evening. Acheson met him, accompanied by Louis Johnson, the secretary of defense. Johnson's presence wasn't Acheson's idea; the secretary of state judged Johnson more devoted to his own career than to the interests of the administration or the country. But Johnson insisted, as the president's right hand for defense. The three men were driven to Blair House, across Pennsylvania Avenue from the White House, which was under renovation.

They were joined by the president's top military advisers. The three service secretaries were there: Frank Pace of the army, Francis Matthews of the navy and Thomas Finletter of the air force. The Joint Chiefs of Staff came: Chairman General Omar Bradley, General J. Lawton Collins for the army, Admiral Forrest Sherman for the navy and General Hoyt Vandenberg for the air force.

They all sat down to dinner. Despite the pressing nature of the business at hand, the president insisted that they eat before they talk. He was hungry, and he didn't want the wait staff to hear what was being said.

When the last dishes were cleared and the staff had retired to the kitchen, the discussion began. Acheson led off. The secretary of state understood the dynamics of meetings, and at this early moment he judged that this meeting might define the Truman presidency, not to mention preventing or precipitating World War III. He had told Truman to stay in Missouri in part so he could prepare. "During the afternoon I had everyone and all messages kept out of my room for an hour or two while I ruminated about the situation," he recalled later. "'Thought' would suggest too orderly and purposeful a process. It was rather to let various possibilities, like glass fragments in a kaleidoscope, form a series of patterns of action and then draw conclusions from them." Acheson asked himself what role the Soviet Union had played in the North Korean attack. "It seemed close to certain that the attack had been mounted, supplied, and instigated by the Soviet Union and that it would not be stopped by anything short of force." But whose force? And how much? "If Korean force proved unequal to the job, as seemed probable, only American military intervention could do it. Troops from other sources would be helpful politically and psychologically but unimportant militarily." What did the North Korean attack mean for the larger Cold War? What did Moscow want out of it? How forceful should be the American response? "Plainly, this attack did not amount to a *casus belli* against the Soviet Union. Equally plainly, it was an open, undisguised challenge to our internationally accepted position as the protector of South Korea, an area of great importance to the security of American-occupied Japan."

Acheson now made this last case to Truman and the president's other advisers. The president himself had declared in the case of Greece and Turkey that aggression must not go unanswered; Korea was no less vital to American security than Greece and Turkey had been. If anything, it was *more* vital, Acheson said. American credibility was no less at stake in Asia than it was in Europe. As an immediate first step toward stemming the North Korean aggression, the secretary of state urged the president to authorize General MacArthur to send weapons from American stores in Japan to the army of South Korea.

A stroke of sheer luck, involving the United Nations, facilitated the decision for Truman. The president had signed the UN charter in 1945 with great hopes that the international body could be a significant force for peace. Conventional wisdom held that World War II had been the result of the failure of the democracies to stand up to fascism when that ideology first reared its head in Germany and Japan. Americans understood that their country had been the principal laggard, not even deigning to join the interwar League of Nations. Pearl Harbor jolted the isolationism out of the American system, and Franklin Roosevelt and then Harry Truman made the United Nations a priority in their planning for the postwar period. Yet Americans, still worried about being dragged into other countries' quarrels and sitting atop the pyramid of world power, insisted on a veto of substantive actions by the UN. America's principal wartime allies, Britain and the Soviet Union, demanded no less for themselves, and so the Security Council procedures specified that each of its five permanent members—France and China were added to the initial three—possess a veto over the decisions of the council and therefore over the important actions of the United Nations as a whole.

Had the spirit of cooperation of the war years persisted, the veto rule might have been no more than a sporadic inconvenience. But amid the emerging Cold War the cooperation vanished, and the Soviet veto, actual or merely threatened, largely paralyzed the Security Council and the UN. The point of the Security Council was to provide for the collective security of the peace-loving nations of the world against occasional and would-be aggressors, who would be punished or deterred by the law-abiding majority. The paralysis of the Security Council compelled the Truman administration to look elsewhere for partners in maintaining international order. The North Atlantic Treaty of 1949 bound its dozen members to a form of collective security less comprehensive than that envisioned by the founders of the United Nations, but better than nothing. Or so hoped Truman and his advisers in the summer of 1950, when the Atlantic alliance was scarcely a year old and quite untested.

But they hadn't given up on the UN, and the stroke of luck made them think there was life in the international body yet. Following the communist victory in China, the United States had refused to recognize the new government in Beijing or to allow the envoy Beijing sent to the

United Nations to assume China's seat there. The Soviet delegate to the UN, protesting the American veto of Beijing's seating, boycotted the sessions of the Security Council. He was absent at the time of the North Korean invasion and therefore unable to cast a Russian veto against a measure demanding that North Korea cease its aggression and withdraw its forces from South Korea and calling on UN member states to aid South Korea in repelling the North Korean invasion. The result was that Truman, by saying yes to weapons for South Korea, could promote two objectives at once: opposing communist aggression and reviving the ideal of comprehensive collective security through the United Nations.

Acheson had further recommendations. MacArthur should order American warplanes from Japan to provide cover for the evacuation of American nationals from South Korea. More controversially—or at least it would become controversial once the Republicans got wind of it— Acheson urged a strong effort to keep the fighting confined to Korea. The secretary feared that the Korean troubles might trigger a renewal of China's civil war. To forestall this, he recommended that the president order the American Seventh Fleet to patrol the Formosa Strait and prevent any attack by Chinese forces against Chiang's troops and position; at the same time, the fleet should prevent Chinese Nationalist forces from attacking the Chinese mainland. Acheson judged it imperative to keep the Korea question separate from the China question, which was vexing enough on its own.

Omar Bradley seconded Acheson's call for a vigorous response. Bradley brought to the discussion of Korea an experience of large-scale warfare surpassed by no officer in American history; his command of the Twelfth Army Group in Europe during World War II had placed more than a million men under his orders. He was known as a soldier's general, leaving the politics of command to the likes of Dwight Eisenhower, with whom he had been sharing quarters when news arrived that Franklin Roosevelt had died and Harry Truman become president. George Patton was the one who brought the news. "The three of us were saddened and depressed," Bradley remembered. "We talked for nearly three hours. It seemed an irreplaceable loss." Bradley, like the others, expected little from Truman. "He had had no experience in dealing with Churchill and Stalin. . . . None of us knew Truman or much about him. He came from my home state, Missouri, but I had to confess almost complete ignorance. I knew only that he had served in the Army in World War I and had risen to political prominence through the ranks of what I regarded as a somewhat unsavory political machine in Kansas City, Missouri. From our distance, Truman did not appear at all qualified to fill Roosevelt's large shoes." Bradley didn't dispute a comment by Patton: "It seems very unfortunate that in order to secure political preference, people are made Vice President who were never intended, neither by party nor by the Lord, to be President."

Bradley improved his knowledge of Truman four months later when the new president traveled to defeated Germany for the Potsdam conference. "I liked what I saw," Bradley recollected. "He was direct, unpretentious, clear-thinking and forceful. His knowledge of American history, particularly U.S. military history, was astonishing. I found him to be extremely well informed about the battles we had fought in Africa, Sicily, Italy and on the Continent."

Truman appointed Bradley head of the Veterans Administration after the war, a post that cemented Bradley's reputation as the "GI's general." He became army chief of staff in 1948 and then the first chairman of the Joint Chiefs of Staff. As chairman he encountered Douglas MacArthur, whom he had not seen since his time at West Point, when Bradley had been a cadet and MacArthur superintendent. Bradley arrived in Japan just days after MacArthur's seventieth birthday. "Even so," Bradley recounted, "he was remarkably vigorous and keen and could not have been a more gracious host. For the first time I had an opportunity to take the measure of the man. He was awesomely brilliant; but as a leader he had several major flaws: an obsession for self-glorification, almost no consideration for other men with whom he served, and a contempt for the judgment of his superiors. Like Patton and Monty"—British field marshal Bernard Montgomery—"MacArthur was a megalomaniac."

Bradley's confidence in Truman and his skepticism of MacArthur would inform his counsel to the former and his orders to the latter. In the initial Blair House meeting on June 25, Bradley was battling an illness recently contracted on another trip to Japan. Bradley arrived with the group from the Pentagon. He wasn't impressed with Louis Johnson, whom he called "erratic." He didn't expect much from the service secretaries. Francis Matthews was "earnest but discredited"—by some statements that, to Bradley, showed woeful lack of experience and judgment. Frank Pace and Thomas Finletter were new and untested. "Only the JCS had substantial military expertise," Bradley said of the Defense contingent: "Hoyt Vandenberg, steady and cool; Forrest Sherman, emerging as a gifted strategist; Joe Collins, a 'can-do' administrator and advocate, and I." Yet he himself was far from full strength. "On this historic night I was so ill that all I wanted to do was crawl in bed."

But he soldiered on. In response to Acheson's remarks, Bradley said he interpreted the North Korean attack in the context of actions by communist groups and forces since the end of the war. Russia and its allies had been probing the West, seeking and exploiting weakness. "We must draw the line somewhere," Bradley said. The Russians weren't ready for war, he asserted, and so the risk of escalation was modest. Korea offered "as good an occasion for action in drawing the line as anywhere else." He endorsed the use of American warplanes, which would have a "great morale effect" on the South Koreans even if they didn't destroy any North Korean tanks or other assets. He added that American warships might provide artillery support on South Korea's eastern coast. Yet Bradley questioned the value of sending much American matériel to the South Koreans, who weren't trained to use some of the equipment, especially F-51 fighter planes. And though Acheson hadn't recommended it, Bradley doubted the advisability of sending American ground forces to South Korea in any large numbers. American troop strength had been drastically reduced after the war, and the United States did not have troops to spare. If America was going to fight the communists, there were more important places to do so than the Korean peninsula.

Lawton Collins—called Joe by most who knew him—reported that he had been in communication with MacArthur in Tokyo. The army chief reported that MacArthur, without waiting for authorization from Washington, was already shipping mortars, artillery and other equipment to South Korea, and he was making F-51s available for South Korean pilots to fly from Japan back to South Korea.

No one at the meeting seemed surprised that MacArthur had acted without orders. The military men knew MacArthur, and they knew that he heeded his own counsel on what a military situation required. Truman had heard enough about MacArthur to be coming to the same conclusion. The president, already inclined to approve the dispatch of weapons to Korea, saw no reason to stickle about the timing.

Forrest Sherman was more eager than Bradley or Collins to jump into Korea in force. The chief of naval operations didn't think the Russians wanted war. "But if they do, they will have it," he said. "The present situation in Korea offers a valuable opportunity for us to act." The United States could not allow Korea to fall to the communists. "Korea is a strategic threat to Japan." Yet Sherman agreed with Acheson and Bradley on the need to keep the Korean and Chinese questions separate. Chiang had to be prevented from attacking the Chinese mainland. "We must apply our guarantees against military action both ways," he said. "We could not otherwise justify our action."

Hoyt Vandenberg joined the others in saying America must stop the North Koreans. Yet the air force chief wasn't so sure the Russians wouldn't fight. He said his planes could knock out North Korea's tanks with little trouble if the only cover the tanks received was from the North Korean air force. But if Russian jets joined the fight, that would be a different matter. They would fly from bases much closer to the action than the American bases in Japan.

Truman asked if American planes could knock out the Russian bases.

"It could be done if we used A-bombs," Vandenberg replied.

Atomic weapons had never been used tactically—against specific military targets rather than strategically against cities—but the American military was developing plans for doing so. Experts and laypersons alike debated whether a meaningful distinction between tactical and strategic use actually existed, especially now that the Soviets had atomic weapons, too. Would the Kremlin consider *any* American use of such weapons an affront requiring a nuclear response? Would tactical use inevitably escalate to strategic use? No one could say, and no one at the Blair House meeting chose to pursue the matter.

Frank Pace seconded Omar Bradley's doubts about committing American ground forces to Korea. The army secretary hoped MacArthur's swift action in supporting the South Koreans would make that unnecessary.

Thomas Finletter asserted that MacArthur was the man of the hour. "General MacArthur should be authorized to go beyond mere evacuation," the air force secretary said. He drew an analogy to the period before World War II, when the democratic powers had refused to stand up to German and Japanese aggression. "We should take calculated risks, hoping that our action will keep the peace."

Louis Johnson disagreed. The defense secretary wanted to hold MacArthur on a short leash. "The instructions should be detailed so as not to give him too much discretion," Johnson said. "There should not be a real delegation of presidential authority to General MacArthur." He concurred with the army men about the inadvisability of sending U.S. troops to Korea unless absolutely necessary.

Truman listened, then made his decisions. He authorized the weapons shipments MacArthur had already begun. He directed that the general dispatch a survey group to Korea, to see what else might be needed. He approved the repositioning of the Seventh Fleet to keep Chiang and the Chinese Communists apart. Preparing for the worst, he ordered the air force to draw up plans "to wipe out all Soviet air bases in the Far East." He emphasized, however, that this was an order for planning, not for action. The State and Defense Departments should calculate where the Soviet Union might move next. The president stressed the role of the United Nations. "We are working entirely for the United Nations," he told the group.

As the meeting ended, Truman swore all present to secrecy. No one was to speak to the press, even on background, without clearance from him.

On Monday morning the White House released a statement condemning the "unprovoked aggression against the Republic of Korea." The statement reflected Truman's decision to act under the auspices of the UN. "In accordance with the resolution of the Security Council, the United States will vigorously support the effort of the Council to terminate this serious breach of the peace," it said. "Those responsible for this act of aggression must realize how seriously the Government of the United States views such threats to the peace of the world. Willful disregard of the obligation to keep the peace cannot be tolerated by nations that support the United Nations Charter."

As the president's statement was being distributed, Truman spoke privately with George Elsey about the situation in Korea. Elsey had served in the White House Map Room under Franklin Roosevelt and had accompanied Truman to Potsdam; he subsequently became a confidant and sounding board for Truman in matters of foreign and military policy. On this occasion Elsey initiated the conversation. "I stayed behind to chat with the President about the significance of Korea," Elsey recorded. "I expressed my very grave concern about Formosa. I said it seemed to me this was the perfect course for the Chinese communists to take." The North Korean invasion might well be a distraction to cover a Chinese attack on Formosa.

Truman's concerns were broader. "The President walked over to the globe standing in front of the fireplace and said he was more worried about other parts of the world. He said he had ordered MacArthur to give ammunition to the Koreans, that the Air Force and the Navy were to protect the evacuation of Americans. That much was easy and clear. But what he was worried about, the President said, was the Middle East. He put his finger on Iran and said: 'Here is where they will start trouble if we aren't careful.' 'Korea,' he said, 'is the Greece of the Far East. If we are tough enough now, if we stand up to them like we did in Greece three years ago, they won't take any next steps. But if we just stand by, they'll move into Iran and they'll take over the whole Middle East. There's no telling what they'll do, if we don't put up a fight now.' The President appeared sincerely determined to go very much further than the initial orders that he had approved for General MacArthur the evening before."

10

Truman initially hoped the display of American resolve would suffice to hold the line in Korea. The president continued to keep his top advisers publicly quiet, but he allowed Dean Acheson to brief a few congressional leaders privately. Acheson called Republican senator Alexander Wiley of Wisconsin, a frequent thorn in the administration's side, to say that the situation in Korea was "in pretty good shape." The South Koreans had suffered from the surprise of the first assault but were now "in pretty good fighting shape." Wiley wanted more information. He asked what General MacArthur was doing. Acheson said MacArthur had things well in hand and it was MacArthur's judgment the president was relying on. Wiley asked if the United States would send in its own troops. Acheson said the president was considering the matter but no American troops had been committed as yet. In another conversation, with Democrat John Kee of West Virginia, the chairman of the House Committee on Foreign Affairs, Acheson said he thought the South Koreans could defend themselves unless outside forces—Soviet or Chinese, presumably—entered the war.

Events in Korea soon dispelled the optimism in Washington. North Korean tanks reached Seoul on the second day of fighting. Syngman Rhee's government fled the capital, which appeared on the verge of falling. Truman tried to buck up the ROK leadership. He summoned the South Korean ambassador to the White House. A memo of the meeting captured Truman's message: "The President said that he had already issued orders to General MacArthur to supply all items of ammunition and equipment which, in General MacArthur's opinion, the Korean army was trained to use, and that the Koreans must now continue to fight effectively so that help from the United States could strengthen them. He pointed out that the battle had been going on for only forty-eight hours, and that other men and other countries had defended their liberties under much more discouraging situations through to ultimate victory." The ambassador replied that his country's soldiers were brave but lacked the necessary equipment. Truman reiterated his encouragement. "The President again said that help was on the way and that the Koreans must develop the steadfast leadership which would carry them through this crisis."

On Monday evening Truman gathered his national security team again. Acheson recommended lifting restrictions on the use of American airpower, which until now had been confined to protecting the evacuation of American nationals. Acheson urged the president to order American planes to "offer the fullest possible support to the South Korean forces, attacking tanks, guns, columns, etc. of the North Korean forces in order to give a chance to the South Koreans to re-form."

This much was easy. Truman approved the request at once.

Frank Pace asked whether Acheson's recommendation applied only to areas south of the 38th parallel. Acheson said yes: no action north of the parallel.

Truman nodded, adding, "Not yet."

Acheson then recommended continued efforts to ensure that the question of China—which was to say, Formosa—not become entangled in the Korean question. The president's decision to interpose the Seventh Fleet between Chiang and mainland China was a crucial step in the right direction.

Truman allowed himself to muse on the future of Formosa. He said he wished that consideration be given to "taking Formosa back as part of Japan and putting it under MacArthur's command."

Acheson didn't think this wise at all. The secretary of state could only imagine what MacArthur might try to do with Formosa. But he deflected the president's request. The Formosa issue, he said, should be deferred to a later day.

Truman continued to muse. He said he had received a letter from Chiang some weeks earlier in which the generalissimo had hinted at resigning his office if this would facilitate a constructive solution to the Formosa question. The letter was a private one, Truman said, and he had kept it secret. But the offer was worth considering. "We might want to proceed along those lines in order to get the Chinese forces helping us," Truman said. "The Generalissimo might step out if MacArthur were put in."

Again Acheson discouraged the president. Chiang was unpredictable, he said. "He might resist and throw the ball game." Better to wait. Acheson added that the United States should not get mixed up in the politics of Formosa.

Truman now granted that Acheson was probably right. He said he wouldn't give Chiang a nickel after the millions he had squandered. "All the money we have given them is now invested in United States real estate," he said.

Joe Collins returned the discussion to the prospects for South Korea. The army chief said the situation there was bad. The ROK army was dispirited. "The Korean chief of staff has no fight left in him."

Acheson contended that the United States needed to fight, even if the cause were doomed. America's allies demanded nothing less. They might forgive defeat, but they could never forgive refusal to fight.

Truman reflected that he had done everything he could since becoming president to forestall this kind of situation. "Now the situation is here and we must do what we can to meet it." He wondered whether he ought to mobilize the national guard. He asked Omar Bradley if this was necessary. If so, he—the president—would have to go to Congress to ask for money to pay for the mobilization. He reiterated that the United States must do everything it could for Korea.

Bradley replied that mobilizing the guard might be necessary. If the president committed ground forces to Korea, the guard would be needed to fill in elsewhere. But a decision wasn't immediately required.

Truman told Bradley and the chiefs to weigh the matter. Yet he added, "I don't want to go to war."

NEITHER DID THE members of Congress the president brought to the White House the next morning. Truman didn't intend to involve them in the decision process, but as a former senator he knew he had to keep them informed. He praised the prompt action of the UN Security Council in condemning the North Korean invasion, without dwelling on the fortuitous absence of the Soviet delegate that made the pertinent resolution possible. He read to the senators and representatives a statement his press secretary, Charlie Ross, was about to release. The statement summarized the events of the preceding forty-eight hours: the North Korean invasion, the Security Council resolution, the North Korean refusal to heed the resolution, the council's call to member states to render assistance in executing the resolution. "In these circumstances," Truman read, "I have ordered United States air and sea forces to give the Korean Government troops cover and support." More than Korea was at stake, the president asserted. "The attack upon Korea makes it plain beyond all doubt that communism has passed beyond the use of subversion to conquer independent nations and will now use armed invasion and war." The aggression must not be allowed to spread, as to Formosa. "Accordingly I have ordered the 7th Fleet to prevent any attack on Formosa." Yet the United States was not willing to reopen the Chinese civil war. "I am calling upon the Chinese Government on Formosa to cease all air and sea operations against the mainland. The 7th Fleet will see that this is done." Truman reiterated that the United States was acting at the behest of the United Nations. "I know that all members of the United Nations will consider carefully the consequences of this latest aggression in Korea in defiance of the Charter of the United Nations. A return to the rule of force in international affairs would have far-reaching effects. The United States will continue to uphold the rule of law."

When he finished reading the statement, Truman extemporized. The communist aggression in Korea could not be tolerated, he said. "This act was very obviously inspired by the Soviet Union. If we let Korea down, the Soviets will keep right on going and swallow up one piece of Asia after another. We have to make a stand some time or else let all of Asia go. If we were to let Asia go, the Near East would collapse and no telling what would happen in Europe. Therefore I have ordered our forces to support Korea as long as we can—or as long as the Koreans put up a fight and give us something we *can* support."

Truman spoke a mouthful here, anticipating the next quarter century of American policy toward Asia. His claim that the Kremlin was behind the North Korean attack—that world communism was, in effect, a monolith—rendered the fighting in Korea a test of America's global resolve. His prediction that a failure to resist aggression in Korea would lead to the collapse of one country and region after another—that the countries and regions were dominoes waiting to fall—made a forceful response all the more imperative. Skeptics at the time challenged both of Truman's assertions, and historians would debate them. The evidence was mixed. In the early 1950s communists in other countries looked to Moscow for leadership, not to mention material support. But Mao Zedong and the Chinese Communists had their own agenda, as events of the 1960s would demonstrate. And Kim Il Sung had sufficient reasons of *his* own for wanting to reunify Korea; he evidently received Stalin's approval for the attack on South Korea but didn't require Stalin's inspiration. As for the domino theory, it was never really tested. The United States *did* fight in Korea—and then in Vietnam. The American defeat in Vietnam didn't disprove the theory, which was more about America's willingness to fight than about the outcome of any particular conflict.

Truman's auditors on this day were not among the skeptics. The lawmakers were sobered into silence by the president's remarks. After several moments Alexander Wiley asked whether Truman's orders to General MacArthur were pursuant to the Security Council resolution. Truman said they most certainly were. Wiley then asked if MacArthur had sufficient military resources to give adequate aid to South Korea. What kinds of planes could he send, for example?

Hoyt Vandenberg started to answer, but Louis Johnson interrupted the air force chief to say this was highly sensitive information. Until all at the meeting promised secrecy, Johnson explained, General Vandenberg must say no more. The lawmakers gave the required pledge. Wiley thereupon withdrew his question. It sufficed, he said, to know that America was providing what the president deemed sufficient force.

After Frank Pace volunteered that no American ground troops were being sent to Korea, Senator Millard Tydings reported that conferees from the Senate and the House had that very morning come to an agreement to extend the military draft. Tydings made clear that the Korean crisis had strongly influenced the decision. Truman offered his thanks, calling the extension "vitally essential."

Several of the lawmakers wanted to know about the connection between the administration's actions toward Korea and those toward Formosa. Truman explained that his policy toward Korea was in support of the United Nations, while policy toward Formosa was wholly American.

Tom Connally asserted that the present moment was a crucial test of the United Nations. "If the United Nations is ever going to do anything, this is the time," the Texas Democrat said. "If the United Nations cannot bring the crisis in Korea to an end, then we might just as well wash up the United Nations and forget it." Connally's statement evoked general assent, and Truman repeated that what the United States did in Korea would be in support of and in conformity with the decisions of the Security Council.

Dean Acheson noted that the president's public statement conspicuously avoided mention of the Soviet Union. It referred simply to "communism." The administration knew that Moscow was behind the attack in Korea, Acheson said, but proclaiming as much in public could be counterproductive. "This government is doing its best to leave a door wide open for the Soviet Union to back down without losing too much face." The secretary of state added that it would be helpful if the members of Congress would similarly eschew reference to the Soviet Union. "If we publicly say that the Soviets are responsible for the actions of the communists in North Korea, then, as a matter of prestige, the Soviet government will be forced to continue supporting the North Korean forces and we will find ourselves with a really tough scrap on our hands. If, however, we leave the door open, the Soviet Union may well back down and call off the North Koreans."

The lawmakers nodded. The Republicans doubtless considered how they might eventually use the president's words and actions against him, but for the moment, with communist forces on the rampage, they were willing to fall in line.

THE NORTH KOREAN attack on South Korea took Douglas MacArthur quite by surprise. Only days before the attack, MacArthur had met with Louis Johnson and Omar Bradley, who had traveled to Tokyo to talk about the defense of Asia. MacArthur handed them a memo conveying his assessment of the threats to the American position in the Far East. The memo focused almost exclusively on Formosa. "The strategic interests of the United States will be in serious jeopardy if Formosa is allowed to be dominated by a power hostile to the United States," MacArthur asserted. "Formosa in the hands of the Communists can be compared to an unsinkable aircraft carrier and submarine tender ideally located to accomplish Soviet offensive strategy and at the same time checkmate counteroffensive operations by United States Forces based on Okinawa and the Philippines." Communist control of Formosa would threaten to outflank anticommunist positions in Indochina and the Indonesian archipelago. "Historically Formosa has been used as a springboard for military aggression directed against areas to the south." The loss of Formosa would echo across Asia and beyond. "The future status of Formosa can well be an important factor in determining the political alignment of those national groups who have or must soon make a choice between Communism and the West." MacArthur understood that his views on Formosa differed from those of some in Washington, which was why he was making such an impassioned case. He meanwhile gave scarcely a thought to Korea, with the result that the North Korean attack caught him flat-footed and unprepared.

It wasn't MacArthur's first such failure, and it followed a personal history of believing he knew better than his civilian superiors what the American interest required. Following the Billy Mitchell trial, MacArthur had been appointed army chief of staff, and in this position, during the Great Depression summer of 1932, he watched with growing concern the arrival in Washington of thousands of unemployed veterans of World War I come to petition Congress for early payment of bonuses promised to them for 1945. The vets called themselves the Bonus Expeditionary Force, or Bonus Army, and many brought wives and children. Some members of Congress sympathized, but President Herbert Hoover did not. He said the federal budget couldn't bear the expense. He urged the vets to go home.

But many had no homes to go to. They bivouacked on the south bank of the Anacostia River, two miles from the Capitol. They policed themselves well, yet their lingering alarmed Hoover, who knew that disgruntled European veterans of the war had helped overturn democracy in Italy and were threatening to do so in Germany. When some communists attached themselves to the Bonus Army, Hoover caught a stronger whiff of revolution.

MacArthur did too. He declared that many of those passing themselves off as veterans were phonies and that a large portion of these were reds. As the summer dragged on and some of the discouraged veterans departed the capital, the radical ratio increased. "Not more than one in ten of those who stayed was a veteran," he later asserted. He told his adjutant, Major Dwight Eisenhower, that there was "incipient revolution in the air."

MacArthur responded with alacrity when Hoover ordered the regular army to move against the Bonus Army. MacArthur often wore a business suit to work, but for this occasion he changed into full uniform. Eisenhower urged him to assign the operation to a subordinate, saying it was beneath the dignity of the chief of staff to engage in crowd control. MacArthur ignored the advice and took personal command.

The petitioners retreated before MacArthur's column of several hundred fully equipped troops. Hoover, pleased with the success of the operation, had the secretary of war, Patrick Hurley, send a messenger directing MacArthur not to cross the Anacostia River into the Bonus Army's camp. MacArthur refused to receive the messenger or the message. Hurley sent another messenger. Again MacArthur refused to listen. Eisenhower, who accompanied MacArthur, recalled, "He said he was too busy and did not want either himself or his staff bothered by people coming down and pretending to bring orders."

MacArthur's column crossed the river and entered the camp. The troops set fire to the tents, shacks and lean-tos, depriving the residents of such homes as they had cobbled together and destroying their meager possessions. One infant died from tear gas, and a small boy was bayoneted while trying to save his pet rabbit. Photographers recorded the destruction and its human cost.

MacArthur was unrepentant. He called a press conference to proclaim the victory. Yet perhaps worrying that he might be seen as having gone too far, he credited Hoover rather than himself. "Had he waited another week, I believe the institutions of our government would have been threatened," he said.

Neither Hoover nor Hurley mentioned that MacArthur had rebuffed the president. Hurley publicly offered praise. "Mac did a great job," Hurley said. "He's the man of the hour."

Another observer was more insightful. Franklin Roosevelt, the Democratic nominee for president, was preparing his campaign against Hoover. As he read the accounts of what was already being derided as the "Battle of Anacostia Flats," he turned to adviser Felix Frankfurter. "Well, Felix," Roosevelt said, "this will elect me."

After Roosevelt was indeed elected, he kept a close eye on MacArthur, whom he considered a threat to democracy. Rexford Tugwell, another Roosevelt adviser, overheard Roosevelt speaking on the telephone to Huey Long, the Louisiana senator and demagogue. Roosevelt remarked, after he put down the phone, that Long was the second most dangerous man in America. Tugwell inquired who was the first. "Douglas MacArthur," Roosevelt replied.

The new president arranged for MacArthur to take charge of the creation of an army for the Philippines, which Congress had slated for independence in a decade's time. The perquisites of the job included the rank and salary of a Philippine field marshal. To encourage MacArthur to accept the offer, Roosevelt allowed him to retain his rank and salary in the U.S. Army.

No American had ever been a field marshal before, and MacArthur liked the distinction. Dwight Eisenhower, who was assigned to assist MacArthur in the Philippines, thought it was silly. "General," he told MacArthur, "you have been a four-star general. This is a proud thing.

There's only been a few who had it. Why in the hell do you want a banana country giving you a field-marshalship?"

MacArthur waved aside the criticism. He told Eisenhower that Asians were impressed with rank and title. He accepted the field marshalship and designed his own uniform: black and white sharkskin, with stars and braid. Eisenhower concluded that MacArthur was becoming too political. MacArthur thought he had no choice. Not for the last time, and hardly alone among military commanders, MacArthur judged his theater preeminently vital to his nation's security. He continually importuned Washington to increase spending for the Philippine military, arguing that Japan posed the greatest threat to America and that the Philippines constituted America's first line of defense.

But during the 1930s Congress and the American people preferred pretending that the oceans were as wide as ever, and the lawmakers ignored his pleas for funding. The result was that when war came to America at Pearl Harbor, the Philippines were indefensible. For this MacArthur could blame Washington, and he did. Less plausible was his explanation as to why he allowed his airplanes to remain on the ground, easy targets for Japanese bombers, nine hours after his signalmen received reports of the Pearl Harbor attack. He blamed his subordinates and miscommunications. The consequence was the destruction of half of MacArthur's air force, and with it such slim hope as had existed for preventing a Japanese landing in the Philippines. Once the enemy established a beachhead, the loss of the islands was inevitable.

MacArthur called on Washington to strike back hard. "The time is ripe for a brilliant thrust with air carriers," he declared. He demanded that the U.S. government press the Soviet Union to attack Japan from the north. "Entry of Russia is enemy's greatest fear," he cabled.

Roosevelt and the War Department ignored his pleas. Finding itself, after Germany's declaration of war against the United States, in a two-theater war, the administration in Washington made a fundamental decision to focus on defeating Hitler. The Pacific would have to wait. As for Russia, Stalin's regime was fighting for its life against the Nazis in Europe. It was not at war against Japan and was not about to go to war against Japan, despite anything Washington might say.

When MacArthur realized he was on his own, he did an extraordinary thing. He endorsed a request by Philippine president Manuel Quezon to Roosevelt to allow the Philippines to seek a separate peace with Japan. Such a deal might be the only way to avert a "disastrous debacle," MacArthur wrote to Roosevelt. Contradicting his earlier statements about the indispensability of the Philippines to American defense, he now declared that the Philippines mattered little to the larger balance of the war.

Dwight Eisenhower, at this point assistant to Chief of Staff George Marshall, read MacArthur's proposal and concluded that his old boss was "losing his nerve." Roosevelt rejected the request out of hand. "American forces will continue to keep our flag flying in the Philippines so long as there remains any possibility of resistance," the president ordered MacArthur. "It is mandatory that there be established once and for all in the minds of all peoples complete evidence that the American determination and indomitable will to win carries on down to the last unit."

But the last unit did not mean the last man. MacArthur directed a fighting retreat to the Bataan peninsula and Corregidor Island. American and Philippine troops on Bataan suffered grievously from lack of food and other supplies. MacArthur and his staff on Corregidor endured repeated bombardment from Japanese planes and guns. MacArthur tried to lift his men's spirits. "Help is on the way from the United States," he declared. "Thousands of troops and hundreds of planes are being dispatched." The statement was not true, and MacArthur knew it was not true. Perhaps he hoped to make it true by shaming Washington. If so, he failed. His men held the false promise against him.

As the Japanese closed in, Roosevelt ordered MacArthur to leave. It was one thing to lose a garrison, but to lose a general of MacArthur's stature, just months into the war, was too much for the president to risk. MacArthur should depart Corregidor and proceed to Australia, where he would assume command of combined Allied forces in the southwestern Pacific.

MacArthur made a show of resisting. "These people are depending on me now," he said of the Filipinos. "Any idea that I was being withdrawn for any other purpose than to bring them immediate relief could not be explained."

Roosevelt reiterated his order. And so MacArthur slipped off Corregidor aboard a PT boat and escaped to the southern Philippines. There he boarded a plane to Australia. On arrival he explained that the president had ordered him to break through the Japanese lines and go to Australia to organize a counteroffensive against Japan and for the relief of the Philippines. "I came through," he said, "and I shall return."

Roosevelt chose to treat MacArthur's flight from the Philippines as an act of great courage and insisted that the general receive the Medal of Honor. America needed heroes, the president judged, and MacArthur was the closest approximation at the moment. Three years later, MacArthur did return to the Philippines, en route to Japan. In the excitement of the victory in the Pacific war, the general's failure to anticipate the Japanese attack in 1941 was largely forgotten—though not by the American soldiers MacArthur left behind after his escape from Corregidor, who suffered some of the worst brutality the Japanese meted out anywhere.

MACARTHUR'S FAILURE TO anticipate the North Korean attack in 1950 did less immediate damage to American forces than the surprise he suffered in 1941; it was the South Koreans who bore the initial weight of the North Korean onslaught. MacArthur, disguising any discomposure, moved at once to parry the communist blow. Without awaiting orders from Washington, he dispatched a cargo ship filled with ammunition to South Korea. He ordered American warships and planes based in Japan to escort the cargo vessel. Only the next day, following Truman's Blair House meeting with Acheson and the other advisers, did MacArthur receive authorization for these actions, as well as instructions to provide naval support and air cover for the evacuation of American dependents from Korea.

His mission soon escalated. As ROK defenses crumbled before the communist advance, Truman approved the offensive use of American air and naval power against the North Koreans in South Korea. MacArthur sent his planes and ships into action. Within hours American warplanes were engaging North Korean planes, and within days they had shot down dozens.

Again per instructions from Washington, MacArthur sent a survey group to South Korea. The group had no sooner reached the battle zone than its leader cabled MacArthur declaring that the ROK forces, even aided by American air and naval units, were utterly inadequate to withstand the communist pressure. To prevent the overrunning of South Korea, American ground troops were necessary.

MacArthur decided to see for himself. His plane, the *Bataan,* took off in a rainstorm and landed in the wake of a North Korean attack near the spot where South Korean president Rhee now stood to meet him. MacArthur listened to Rhee boast of the numbers of men he could have under arms shortly. He heard less optimistic comments from American ambassador Muccio. MacArthur then insisted on being driven to the battlefront. He and his entourage piled into three old cars and headed toward the sound of fire. Mortar shells began falling around them, but MacArthur demanded that they press on. He observed South Korean soldiers streaming away from the fighting. He took mental notes before turning to one of his aides and remarking, "It is a strange thing to me that all these men have their rifles and ammunition, they all know how to salute, they all seem to be more or less happy, but I haven't seen a wounded man yet." He concluded that they hadn't actually fought and probably would not fight, absent a major shift in the balance of forces.

En route back to Japan, MacArthur told a reporter, "The moment I reach Tokyo, I shall send President Truman my recommendation for the immediate dispatch of American divisions to Korea." In the event, it was the next day before he got the message off, but his counsel was stark. "The Korean army and coastal forces are in confusion, have not seriously fought, and lack leadership through their own means," he wrote. "Organized and equipped as a light force for maintenance of interior order, they were unprepared for attack by armor and air. Conversely, they are incapable of gaining the initiative over such a force as that embodied in the North Korean army." Yet the country could be saved. "The civilian populace is tranquil, orderly and prosperous according to their scale of living. They have retained a high national spirit and firm belief in the Americans. The roads leading south from Seoul are crowded with refugees refusing to accept the Communist rule." But they could retreat only so far. "It is essential that the enemy advance be held or its impetus will threaten the overrunning of all Korea. . . . The Korean army is entirely incapable of counter action and there is grave danger of a further breakthrough. If the enemy advance continues much further it will seriously threaten the fall of the Republic." The conclusion was unavoidable. "The only assurance for the holding of the present line, and the ability to regain later the lost ground, is through the introduction of U.S. ground combat forces into the Korean battle area."

12

TRUMAN DID NOT want to send ground troops to Korea. He did not want to go to war. He didn't like the sound of the word, and he liked the reality even less. "Mr. President," a reporter inquired of him while MacArthur was in Korea, "everybody is asking in this country, are we or are we not at war?"

"We are not at war," Truman declared.

"Are we going to use ground troops in Korea?"

Truman hoped not, but he wasn't prepared to say so. "No comment on that," he said.

"Mr. President, in that connection it has been asked whether there might be any possibility of having to use the atomic bomb?"

"No comment."

A reporter returned to Truman's first answer. Reporters were not automatically allowed to quote from Truman's news conferences, and this reporter wanted to get the president on record. "Mr. President, could you elaborate on this statement that—I believe the direct quote was, 'We are not at war.' Could we use that quote in quotes?"

"Yes, I will allow you to use that," Truman said. "We are not at war."

The reporter followed up. "Could you elaborate, sir, a little more on the reason for this move, and the peace angle on it?"

"The Republic of Korea was set up with the United Nations' help," Truman said. "It is a recognized government by the members of the United Nations. It was unlawfully attacked by a bunch of bandits." The UN Security Council had called on the world community to aid the South Koreans in resisting the aggression. "The members of the United Nations are going to the relief of the Korean Republic to suppress a bandit raid on the Republic of Korea."

A reporter gave Truman the label he was looking for. "Mr. President," he said, "would it be correct, against your explanation, to call this a police action under the United Nations?"

"Yes," Truman said. "That is exactly what it amounts to."

THE TERM HAD been used before, often by colonial powers attempting to impose their will on unruly locals. The term claimed a legitimacy for the imposition, with the policing powers asserting their own definition of order and good government. Truman, in the middle of his press conference, didn't parse the phrase and its use; he was searching for an alternative label to war, and he clutched the one the reporter offered. But neither did he disavow it afterward, and the label stuck.

MacArthur sneered when he heard the phrase. He was a soldier, not a policeman. And war was war, not a police action. "Even then, it was evident that this was far more than a 'police action,'" he wrote later. "In Korea, Communism had hurled its first challenge to war against the free world. Now was the time for decision. Now it was as clear as it would ever be that this was a battle against imperialistic Communism. Now was the time to recognize what the history of the world has taught from the beginning of time: that timidity breeds conflict, and courage often prevents it."

TRUMAN WASN'T TIMID, but neither did he wish to be rash. He knew he had to respond to the communist challenge in Korea; lack of response to fascist aggression in the 1930s had invited World War II, and he wasn't going to repeat the mistake. Yet he didn't want to widen the conflict unnecessarily. Korea was no more vital, per se, to American national security than it had been when Dean Acheson omitted it from America's defensive perimeter. What *was* vital was the support of America's allies and the United Nations for the overall concept of collective security. The UN had ordered the defense of South Korea, and America's allies and other member states were rallying to the call. Truman didn't want to have to choose between Korea and collective security, but if forced, he would take the latter over the former. The United States could survive without Korea; it could not survive without allies.

The Joint Chiefs of Staff, even before receiving MacArthur's demand for combat troops, had proposed to enlarge the general's authority to use American force in Korea. In a June 29 meeting with the president, Louis Johnson read a draft of a letter the chiefs wished to send to MacArthur. The letter allowed U.S. troops to defend themselves if they encountered Soviet troops in Korea.

Truman interrupted. "I do not want any implication in the letter that we are going to war with Russia at this time," he said. "We must be damn careful. We must not say that we are anticipating a war with the Soviet Union. We want to take any steps we have to to push the North Koreans behind the line"—the 38th parallel—"but I don't want to get overcommitted to a whole lot of other things that could mean war."

Johnson nodded and kept reading, but Frank Pace dissented. The army secretary said he had "considerable reservations" about limiting MacArthur in any way.

Truman stood firm. The president said he was willing for MacArthur to destroy air bases and ammunition depots above the 38th parallel, in order to reduce the North Koreans' ability to sustain their invasion of South Korea. But there must be no use of ground forces against North Korea proper. "He is not to go north of the 38th parallel," Truman said.

The president turned to Dean Acheson and asked if he had heard anything from the American ambassador in Moscow. Acheson deferred the question to discuss the scope of MacArthur's instructions. He said the State Department accepted that American warplanes should be free to attack North Korean air bases. And he had no objection to American planes firing on North Korean army units. "If, for example, an American plane sees Communist tanks coming down the road, it should attack those tanks without much concern as to which side of the 38th parallel they happen to be on." But Acheson had to insist that American planes *not* go outside North Korea to China or the Soviet Union. "No one would be able to foresee the consequences if one of our planes got over into Manchuria," he said, referring to the region of China adjacent to North Korea.

As for ground troops, Acheson was willing to see them sent to South Korea. "It would be a great disaster if we were to lose now," he said.

"And it is essential to give the commander on the spot whatever he needs to stop the disaster." In the event American troops encountered Soviet troops, they should treat them as any other enemy. "If an American unit found Soviet forces, in Soviet uniforms, attacking them, they naturally had to have the right to defend themselves," Acheson said.

Truman apparently thought the letter to MacArthur was to be made public, and he didn't want to go on record as saying he was ready for Americans to fight Soviet forces. Johnson and Acheson assured him that the letter would be kept secret. Truman dropped his objection, and a consensus emerged, as the notes of the meeting recorded: "Everybody agreed that if General MacArthur's men met Soviet troops they should defend themselves even if that meant actual engagement between United States and Soviet forces."

Truman returned to his question about the news from Moscow. Acheson read a letter from the American ambassador, Alan Kirk, recounting an interview with Soviet deputy foreign minister Andrei Gromyko. In the interview Gromyko took what had been the Kremlin's position from the outset regarding the fighting in Korea: that it had been provoked by the South Koreans. "Therefore the responsibility for these events rests upon the South Korean authorities and upon those who stand behind their back." More interesting was Gromyko's next remark: "As is known, the Soviet Government withdrew its troops from Korea earlier than the Government of the United States and thereby confirmed its traditional principle of noninterference in the internal affairs of other states. And now as well the Soviet Government adheres to the principle of the impermissibility of interference by foreign powers in the internal affairs of Korea."

Acheson said he and the State Department interpreted Gromyko's remarks as evidence that the Soviets did not intend to intervene openly in Korea. Yet he cautioned that statements from Communist China, warning of retaliation in the event of American attacks on Manchuria, suggested a strategy of preparing an entrée for the Chinese into the fighting.

"That means the Russians are going to let the Chinese do the fighting for them," Truman said.

The conversation turned to offers, from other members of the UN, of ships and naval facilities to aid in the defense of South Korea. Truman was eager to accept. "Take everything," he said. "We may need them." He added, though, "Everything should be accepted as a contribution to the work which General MacArthur is doing for the *United Nations*. No offers of armed resistance should be accepted as contributions to United States efforts, but only as contributions in support of the resolutions of the United Nations Security Council."

Acheson observed that it would be helpful if the administration knew more about what was happening in the field. He asked Louis Johnson whether the Defense Department and the joint chiefs could get MacArthur to report in a timely and regular manner.

Before Johnson could answer, Truman cut in. "Order General MacArthur, in the name of the President, to submit complete daily reports," he told the defense secretary.

Yet Truman guessed that giving MacArthur an order and having it followed might be two separate things. He knew enough of MacArthur's history to realize that the general often acted as an authority unto himself. "It is just as hard to get information out of MacArthur now as it was during the war," he grumbled. The president closed the meeting by saying he had no quarrel with the general or anyone else. "I just want to know the facts."

13

THE FACTS WERE bad enough. Within hours, before dawn on June 30, MacArthur's cable describing the collapse of the South Korean army and calling for U.S. ground troops reached Washington. The joint chiefs immediately arranged a teleconference with Tokyo. The chiefs to this point had authorized MacArthur to employ U.S. ground forces to secure a port and an air base near Pusan on the southeastern coast. They now asked the general if this would be sufficient.

He declared emphatically that it would not. "Your authorization, while establishing basic principle that United States ground combat troops may be used in Korea, does not give sufficient latitude for efficient operation in present situation," he telegraphed. He needed more, and he needed it at once. He proposed to send a regimental combat team immediately and to reinforce it with two divisions as soon as possible. "Time is of the essence, and a clear-cut decision without delay is imperative," he said.

THE CHIEFS CALLED Frank Pace, who called Truman. The president's rural habits died hard, and though it was still very early, he was awake. When Pace recounted the teleconference with MacArthur, Truman approved the dispatch of the regimental team. But he wanted to talk with his advisers before going further. He met with Louis Johnson, the three service secretaries and the joint chiefs at 8:30 that morning. The group reviewed MacArthur's request for the two divisions, as well as an offer by Chiang Kai-shek of thirty-three thousand Chinese Nationalist troops for use in Korea.

Truman was initially inclined to accept Chiang's offer. MacArthur would require weeks to gather and transport the American divisions to Korea, while Chiang said his troops could sail within days. "Time was all-important," Truman remarked later.

Dean Acheson demurred. Acheson distrusted Chiang as much as ever, and he feared that Chinese Nationalist entry into the Korea fighting would simply invite Chinese Communist entry. It might also prompt a Chinese attack against Formosa. "The net result might well be the reverse of helpful," Acheson said.

The joint chiefs agreed. They noted that Chiang's army was poorly equipped and might be as helpless against North Korean tanks as the South Koreans were. Besides, Chiang's troops would require American transport from Formosa to Korea, and that transport would be better employed ferrying American men and matériel.

Truman dropped the idea, and discussion turned to how the Chinese and Soviets might respond to the introduction of U.S. troops into Korea. Would the Chinese enter the war? Would the Soviets move in the Middle East or Europe? No one had any firm answers, and Truman didn't expect them. But the questions had to be raised. The president wanted all to remember that much more was at stake than Korea. The United States had global responsibilities.

After all this, approval of MacArthur's request for two divisions was nearly a foregone conclusion. The general in the field was saying, in no unmistakable terms, that they were necessary. Their deployment fell fully within the scope of the United Nations resolution authorizing the defense of South Korea. The action would demonstrate America's commitment to collective security against communist aggression.

Truman gave the okay. And the United States went to war in Korea.

IT WASN'T LOST on Truman, though the matter hardly arose in the discussions among his advisers, that he was breaking constitutional ground with this decision. The Constitution clearly assigns to Congress the authority to declare war; for a president to take the country to war without congressional approval was novel if not downright unconstitutional. To be sure, the United States had at times past engaged in armed conflict without congressional declaration of war. American ships had exchanged fire with French ships in the late 1790s, and American ships and marines had tangled with the Barbary pirates in the early nineteenth century. Franklin Roosevelt had bent the rules of neutrality in ordering the navy to cooperate with the British against Germany ahead of American entry into World War II. In the early twentieth century U.S. marines had been deployed in various countries of Central America. But these episodes were fleeting or minor in scope, and the principle remained that for anything serious in the way of armed combat, congressional approval was required.

Truman, apt student of history that he was, understood this even as he pioneered a new principle. He didn't know what a precedent he was setting in ordering combat troops to Korea—that wars waged on presidential authority would become the rule rather than the exception—but he knew he was treading on what had been congressional turf, and he summoned seventeen leading members of Congress to explain. He said he had been meeting with his top advisers and had just reached some important decisions. He read a statement, which was released to the press during the meeting, summarizing these decisions. "The President announced that he had authorized the United States Air Force to conduct missions on specific military targets in Northern Korea where militarily necessary, and had ordered a naval blockade of the entire Korean coast," Truman read. "General MacArthur has been authorized to use certain supporting ground units." Truman stressed that these actions were being taken under the auspices of the United Nations. He noted that several other countries were joining the UN effort.

Tom Connally inquired where the American troops that were being sent to Korea were coming from. Omar Bradley answered for the president, saying they were from MacArthur's command in Japan. Connally asked if the UN forces in Korea would be under a unified command. Truman assured him that all military forces would be under MacArthur. Connally nodded approval, saying he wanted every other nation to understand clearly that MacArthur was "the boss."

Senator Millard Tydings of Maryland, another Democrat, asked for details about the contributions of other nations. He wished to make sure the other countries sent ground forces to fight beside the Americans.

This would be very important for American morale, once the casualty lists started growing. The senator didn't want anyone to think the fight in Korea was a "private American war."

Truman interjected that he hadn't committed troops to actual combat yet. In fact he had, but he hadn't announced it. So far as the public—and the lawmakers present—knew, the troops were simply supposed to keep communications and supply lines open.

Tydings answered that he was thinking ahead. He reiterated that foreign troops would be essential to American morale.

Louis Johnson volunteered vaguely that one nation had offered ground troops. Some of the lawmakers doubtless guessed he was speaking of Nationalist China, but he didn't confirm it.

Alexander Wiley wondered if American forces around the world had been placed on alert. Berlin was a chronically sensitive spot. The Russians had just announced the closure of some power plants in Germany; in conjunction with the fighting in Korea, should this be interpreted as an ominous sign?

"I don't interpret," Truman answered. "I am just waiting to see what will happen."

Wiley asked about the Red Chinese. Were they going to help the North Koreans?

Truman said he had no information on the subject. He acknowledged that rumors were swirling. "But they are just rumors, and we will have to wait and see."

Republican congressman John Vorys returned to the issue of allied troops. "It would be a fine thing if we could get some Asiatic peoples in the fighting to help us, not just other white people," he said. "If we got a few Asiatics into the fighting, it wouldn't look so much like 'white man's imperialism.'"

Truman reflected that this was a difficult matter. Tipping the hand Johnson had held close, he said, "If we got some Asiatics—like Chiang's men on Formosa, for example—we would have to be awfully careful of the Chinese Communists."

Republican Kenneth Wherry, the Senate minority leader, was the first to raise the constitutional question. Was the president going to consult Congress before sending troops to Korea?

Truman said some troops had already been ordered to Korea. But if there were a real emergency, he would "advise Congress."

Wherry wanted more. "The Congress ought to be consulted," he said.

Truman replied that he had responded to an emergency. "There was no time for lots of talk. There had been a weekend crisis, and I had to act. I just had to act as commander-in-chief, and I did. I told MacArthur to go to the relief of the Koreans and to carry out the instructions of the United Nations Security Council."

"I understand action all right," Wherry countered. "But I do feel the Congress ought to be consulted before any large-scale actions are taken again."

Truman promised that if large-scale actions were to take place, he would "tell the Congress about it."

Vice President Alben Barkley tried to change the subject. He asked about ships the British government had offered for use in the waters around Korea.

But Wherry would not be distracted. He stood up and demanded the floor. The president simply must consult Congress before taking drastic steps, he said.

Truman still refused to utter the word "consult." He promised that as further intelligence arrived, he would "inform" the members of Congress. He added, unhelpfully, "If there is any necessity for congressional action, I will come to you." But this might not be necessary. "I hope we can get those bandits in Korea suppressed without that."

Wherry objected to the imprecision of part of Truman's press release. He wanted more details about the orders sent to MacArthur. Congress and the American people required full knowledge of what was being done in America's name.

Alben Barkley agreed that the last sentence ought to be modified. But the vice president thought it should state more explicitly that the president, rather than General MacArthur, would be the one making the decisions on troop use. "The statement ought to say that the President is in control of the forces and is issuing the orders to them."

Truman had deliberately directed that the statement be released during the meeting. It was too late to make changes, he told the group. In any event, he had to disagree with the vice president. "This is all very delicate," he said. "I don't want it stated any place that I am telling MacArthur what to do. He is not an American general now, he is acting for the United Nations. It would spoil everything if we said he was just doing what we tell him to do." Truman added that of course MacArthur *was* obeying orders from Washington. But the administration couldn't say that. "We must be very careful not to let ourselves be put in that light to the rest of the world."

WHEN TRUMAN ASSURED the lawmakers at the meeting that MacArthur was obeying orders, he didn't know something he soon discovered: that MacArthur had ordered bombing of North Korea and the dispatch of ground troops to Korea without awaiting approval from Washington. The president received a copy of an order MacArthur had sent to the commanding general of his Eighth Army, Walton Walker. "Move the 24th Division at once to Pusan by air and water," MacArthur wrote. "The 24th Division will establish a base at Pusan with a view to early offensive operations." MacArthur made clear that the Twenty-Fourth would be under his direct control. "Upon arrival Pusan Commanding Gen 24th Division will operate under instructions from this Hq."

"I don't understand this order of MacA's," Truman scribbled beside the copy the Defense Department forwarded to the White House. "Why was this given *before* he had received full authorization in response to his telegram and the telecom of early hours of the 30th?" Truman was discovering more about MacArthur's concept of command each day, and he didn't like what he learned. But amid the crisis in Korea he saw no alternative to accepting the general's fait accompli.

Truman appreciated the momentous nature of the decisions made that day—whether by himself or by MacArthur. Perhaps sensing he might benefit from a paper trail, he recorded his recollection of the chronology of the previous several hours. The document revealed both what the president had decided and what he remained undecided about. "Frank Pace called at 5 A.M. E.D.T.," Truman wrote. "I was already up and shaved. Said MacArthur wanted two divisions of ground troops. Authorized a regiment to be used in addition to the authorizations of yesterday, to be used at Mac's discretion. . . . Called Pace and Louis Johnson and told them to consider giving MacArthur the two divisions he asked for and also to consider the advisability of accepting the two divisions offered by the Chinese Nationalist Government. That Government is still recognized as the 5th permanent member of the Security Council U.N. Since Britain, Australia, Canada and the Netherlands have come in with ships and planes we probably should use the Chinese ground forces." Though Truman had deferred a decision on Chiang's offer, he hadn't ruled out accepting it. Yet he appreciated how acceptance might complicate matters that were complicated enough already. "What will that do to Mau Tze Tung we don't know. Must be careful not to cause a general Asiatic war." Always in Truman's mind was the broader struggle against the Soviet Union, the only enemy that could do real damage to the United States. "Russia is figuring on an attack in the Black Sea and toward the Persian Gulf. Both prizes Moscow has wanted since Ivan the Terrible who is now their hero with Stalin and Lenin."

14

MARGUERITE HIGGINS WASN'T yet thirty when the Korean War began, but she was already a veteran war reporter. Born in Hong Kong, where her father worked in international trade, she had covered the final campaigns of World War II in Europe for the *New York Herald Tribune,* which sent her to Germany for the postwar Nuremberg trials. She observed the Berlin airlift, about which she quizzed Lucius Clay. The *Herald Tribune* subsequently dispatched her to Japan to report on the MacArthur occupation.

Maggie Higgins was blond and attractive and determined not to let those attributes keep her from getting the stories she sought. She was in Tokyo watching MacArthur when the fighting in Korea began. "The Red invasion of South Korea on Sunday, June 25, 1950, exploded in Tokyo like a delayed-action bomb," she wrote. "The first reports of the dawn attack were nonchalantly received by the duty officer at the Dai Ichi building. He didn't even bother to wake General MacArthur and tell him. But within a few hours the swift advance warned us of the power of the attackers. South Korea, the last non-Communist outpost in North Asia, was crumbling. America had to decide at once whether to lend fighting support to its South Korean protégé or cede it outright to the Reds."

The decision hadn't been made when Higgins reached the front lines of the fighting. She and three other reporters hitched a ride on an American transport plane sent to evacuate American civilians from Seoul, and they arrived amid the chaos of the South Korean retreat. "There were hundreds of Korean women with babies bound papoose-style to their backs and huge bundles on their heads," she recounted. "There were scores of trucks, elaborately camouflaged with branches. South Korean soldiers in jeeps and on horses were streaming in both directions." She spoke to an American colonel attached to the Korean Military Advisory Group, or KMAG, about why the South Koreans weren't making a better show of things. "The South Koreans have a pathological fear of tanks," the colonel said. "That is part of the reason for all this retreating. They could handle them if they would only use the weapons we have given them properly." Higgins later had reason to doubt the colonel's explanation, but for the moment it seemed to explain what she saw.

The same American officer blamed the South Koreans for botching the retreat. Higgins was riding in a U.S. Army jeep with an American lieutenant toward a bridge over the Han River—"the only escape route," she wrote. "As we raced through the rainy darkness a sheet of orange flame tore the sky. 'Good God, there goes the bridge,' said the lieutenant." Their escape route blocked, the lieutenant and Higgins turned back toward the city, where the colonel regathered the three score members of his staff. "The South Koreans blew up that bridge without even bothering to give us warning, and they blew it much too soon," he said. "Most of the town is still in their hands. They blew that bridge with truckloads of their own troops on the main span. They've killed hundreds of their own men."

Higgins eventually found an alternate route across the Han River, where she encountered MacArthur, on his first visit to the battle zone. She needed to get back to Japan so she could file her story for the *Herald Tribune,* and the general offered her a lift on the *Bataan.* The plane had just taken off when MacArthur's aide, Courtney Whitney, told her the general would like to see her in his cabin. She gladly accepted the offer and found herself charmed. "In personal conversation General MacArthur is a man of graciousness and great lucidity," she recorded later. "So far as I am concerned, he is without the poseur traits of which I have heard him accused. It has always seemed to me most unfortunate that the general held himself so aloof from most of the newspapermen in Tokyo. I am convinced that if he would spare the time, even once a month, to see correspondents, he would dissolve most of the hostility felt toward his command and toward him personally."

Higgins was impressed by MacArthur's decisiveness and confidence. In a voice that exuded self-assurance, he told her, "It is certain that the

South Koreans badly need an injection of ordered American strength. The South Koreans are in good physical condition and could be rallied with example and leadership. Give me two American divisions and I can hold Korea." The general wasn't sure Washington shared his confidence. "The moment I reach Tokyo, I shall send President Truman my recommendation for the immediate dispatch of American divisions to Korea," he said. "But I have no idea whether he will accept my recommendation."

While MacArthur made his recommendation to Washington, Higgins sent her story to New York. She caught the next plane back to Korea to gather more material. This time she rode on an American transport hauling supplies to Suwon, to which the South Korean army had retreated. "As our heavy, unarmed ammunition ship rumbled off the runway the crew was in a fine state of nerves," she recorded. "For the past two days Yak fighters"—Communist warplanes—"had been spurting bullets at the Suwon strip. The day before a transport had been shot down going into the same field." The transport pilot was a veteran of the Pacific war and took his new job matter-of-factly. "In a few minutes we reach hot weather," he said as they approached the war zone. "Put on your chutes and grab a helmet." Then he glanced back at the cargo he was carrying: 155-millimeter artillery shells. "Though I don't know what in Christ good a chute will do if we do get hit."

They dodged the incoming fire and landed heavily. The pilot had to brake hard to stop short of wrecked planes piled at the end of the runway. Higgins climbed out and immediately faced a familiar challenge. "I was greeted by a dour army colonel," she wrote. "He was the nervous, officious type that the Army seems to have a talent for producing. 'You'll have to go back, young lady,' the colonel said. 'You can't stay here. There may be trouble.' Somewhat wearily, I brought out my stock answer to this solicitude. 'I wouldn't be here if there were no trouble. Trouble is news, and the gathering of news is my job.'"

While the colonel was beginning to reiterate his prohibition, Higgins spied a jeep approaching, driven by the lieutenant she had met before. "Hey, Lieutenant!" she shouted. "How about a ride back to headquarters?" The lieutenant, unaware of the colonel's comments and pleased to chauffeur a pretty woman, nodded assent. "As the jeep swept by I jumped aboard and we were off before the colonel could do anything but sputter," Higgins recalled.

American officers flown in from Japan had reinforced the existing advisory group, but their numbers and influence were too small to stem the ROK retreat. "The moment the jeep rattled into the pine-dotted Suwon headquarters I sensed another crisis," Higgins recounted. "It was 6 P.M. In the main wooden building little knots of officers were talking in low voices. Major Greenwood of KMAG spotted me as I got out of the jeep, walked over with elaborate casualness, and said, 'Don't go far away from headquarters. It looks bad again.'" His advice was prescient, as Higgins soon discovered. "The events of that evening provided the most appalling example of panic that I have ever seen."

The panic began when the temporary headquarters received reports that North Korean tank units had somehow crossed the Han River and were rapidly approaching Suwon. Higgins and two other reporters were eavesdropping outside a conference room where American officers were consulting their South Korean counterparts. "Suddenly the doors of the conference room scraped open. We heard the thump of running feet and a piercing voice, addressed to the officers within the room: 'Head for the airfield!'"

Higgins pushed her way into the conference room to find out what was going on. She was abruptly told she wasn't allowed in the room. But she blocked an American colonel who was trying to get out. She demanded to know why the warning said to go to the airfield. "Why, if there is something wrong, don't we all take the road south to Taejon?"

"We're surrounded," the colonel said. "We're surrounded." He pushed past her, evidently intending to reach the airfield as soon as possible.

"The panic of the next few minutes jumbled events and emotions so wildly that I can remember only episodic flashes," Higgins recalled. "I remember a furious sergeant stalking out of the Signal Corps room and saying to Keyes"—Keyes Beech of the *Chicago Daily News*—"'Those sons of bitches are trying to save their own hides. There are planes coming, but the brass won't talk. They're afraid there won't be room for everybody.'" The sergeant's suspicions spread rapidly. "The rumor that the officers were trying to escape without the rest swirled around the camp like a dust storm. From then on every mess sergeant, jeep driver, code clerk, and correspondent had just one idea—to get hold of every and any vehicle around. Any South Korean who owned four wheels and was unlucky enough to be near headquarters that night was on foot from that second forward. That was the fastest convoy ever formed, and probably the most disheveled."

The convoy headed out. "The first jeeps started bouncing toward the airfield without orders or direction," Higgins wrote later. "They were filled with infuriated GIs determined not to be left behind by the brass. Correspondents and photographers, hitching rides as best they could, joined the race." Major Walter Greenwood began to organize a perimeter defense. "Mines were laid, machine guns entrenched, small-arms ammunition distributed. It began to look to me like a fair start toward a Korean Corregidor."

No one knew when or if the rescue planes would arrive. But it was hard to imagine there would be enough to ferry everyone to safety. The anger among the enlisted men grew.

Suddenly the defense of the airfield seemed to lose its urgency. The officers' attention was drawn elsewhere. They began piling back into their jeeps and driving away. Gradually Higgins and the others learned that an escape route had been discovered—a road not interdicted by the North Koreans. "So we were not surrounded after all," Higgins muttered to Keyes Beech. "This is a fine way to find out."

This new exodus, commenced in the dark, was even more chaotic than what had preceded it. "About 11 P.M. we decided to follow the crowd of Americans unhappily bumping southward on the rutted dirt road," Higgins wrote. "Then the torrential Korean rains started. Korean nights are cool even in the summer, and with this pitiless downpour the temperature was like a foggy winter's day in San Francisco. None of the men were wearing more than shirts and slacks, and I was still in my blouse and skirt. There had been no time to buy or scrounge a khaki shirt and pants. The rain pounded down without letup during the seven miserable hours in our completely open jeep. The blankets we put over us soon were soaked through, and we just sat helplessly, as drenched as if we had gone swimming with our clothes on."

At dawn Higgins's part of the column reached Taejon, where they learned that American relief troops were on their way from Japan. MacArthur's recommendation had been accepted. An American general Higgins buttonholed said, "Two companies of American troops were airlifted into southern Korea this morning."

Reflecting on what she had seen, she asked the general, "Don't you think it's too late?"

"Certainly not," he said. "It will be different when the Americans get here. We'll have people we can rely on. To tell you the truth, we've been having a pretty rough time with the South Koreans. We can't put backbone into them. What are you going to do with troops who won't stay where they're put? We have no way of knowing whether the South Korean reports are accurate or just wild rumor. It will be better when we have our own organization. It may take one or two divisions."

Speaking with hindsight, Higgins later reflected on this conversation. "None of us, military or civilian, had the remotest idea of what we were really up against: a total of thirteen to fifteen enemy divisions. This meant approximately one hundred and fifty thousand well-armed, hard fighting Reds, equipped with the only heavy tanks in that part of the world."

Realization would come presently. For the moment, Higgins's interlocutor exuded confidence. She asked the general, "How long will it be before we can mount an offensive?"

"Oh, two weeks or so—maybe a month."

"But suppose the Russkies intervene?" Keyes Beech inquired.

"We'll hurl them back too."

15

THE PANIC IN Korea caused even Truman's harshest critics to hold their political fire at home. The senators and representatives who met with the president in the Cabinet Room returned to the Capitol, where none expressed more than modest reservations about Truman's handling of the emergency. Kenneth Wherry declined to tell reporters he had hectored Truman about consulting Congress; rather he praised the president for having drawn a firm line against communist aggression—although he couldn't resist adding, "At long last." Robert Taft had been sharply critical of Truman for circumventing Congress. "We are now actually engaged in a de facto war with the North Korean Communists," the Ohio Republican had complained two days earlier. "It is a complete usurpation by the President of authority to use the armed forces of this country." But he supported the principle of bold action and on this day declared, "When you are in, you've got to go all out." Harry Byrd of Virginia was a Democrat but more conservative than many Republicans. Yet Byrd backed Truman without reservation. "The President will have my full and unqualified support in all measures that are necessary to drive the North Koreans out of South Korea," he said. "This is a time for unity, as we must win." William Knowland of California would come to be called the "Senator from Formosa" for his admiration for Chiang Kai-shek, but at present he was willing to focus on Korea and accept Truman's formulation of the American role in that country. "There is no necessity of a declaration of war," Knowland said. "This is more of a police action." Congressman Charles Eaton of New Jersey came from the White House meeting to make a statement that perhaps surprised some members of the flock of this former minister. "We've got a rattlesnake by the tail," Eaton said, "and the sooner we pound its damn head in, the better."

For the moment the president appeared to have neutralized even Joseph McCarthy. Amid the concern over Korea, the Senate closed its investigation into McCarthy's allegations of communists in government. McCarthy blasted the move as part of a "whitewash" and swore to carry on. "My own investigation will continue," he said. "I have now got five investigators working round the clock." But many in the capital sighed relief. "There is in Washington tonight a spirit of far greater cooperation than at any time in the last few years," veteran reporter James Reston observed. "Moreover, the somber spectacle of American planes engaged against a Communist aggressor 7,000 miles away from home, long before the United States is ready for a major war, has finally overwhelmed the spirit of McCarthyism that has pervaded this city for months."

YET FOR ALL the nods in Truman's direction, Douglas MacArthur was the man of the hour. "As the American people watch eagerly for news from Korea," the *New York Times* editorialized, "one constantly recurring cause of satisfaction and assurance is surely to be found in the fact that it is Douglas MacArthur who directs this effort in the field. Fate could not have chosen a man better qualified to command the unreserved confidence of the people of this country. Here is a superb strategist and an inspired leader; a man of infinite patience and quiet stability under adverse pressure; a man equally capable of bold and decisive action. His long years of experience in the Orient, his thorough grasp of the fundamentals of organization and supply, the immense prestige which he enjoys not only in this country but throughout the whole Pacific world, all these are assets of immeasurable value."

MacArthur needed every talent attributed to him. The North Koreans captured Seoul and drove far into South Korea as the South Koreans continued to flee before them. The American troops thrown into the battle weren't much help at first. Maggie Higgins described the disadvantages the inexperienced and ill-equipped GIs labored under during the early weeks of the war. "When orders to attack first went out to the fifty-odd youngsters in our bazooka team," she said of a unit assigned to keep a column of North Korean armor from passing down a road, "they gazed at the tanks as if they were watching a newsreel. It took prodding from their officers to make them realize that this was it—that it was up to them to attack. Slowly, small groups of them left their foxholes, creeping low through the wheat field toward the tanks. The first swoosh from a bazooka flared out when they were nearly five hundred yards away from the tanks. But the aim was good and it looked like a direct hit." Yet it didn't please the lieutenant commanding the unit. "Damn!" he said. "Those kids are scared. They've got to get close to the tanks to do any damage."

The North Koreans didn't wait for the Americans; their lead tank closed in on the Americans' foxholes. Its turret gun blazed and machine guns wielded by its crew strafed the American positions. "Through my field glasses I could see a blond American head poke up out of the grass," Higgins wrote. "The young soldier was trying to adjust his aim. Flashes from the tank flicked horribly close, and I thought I saw him fall. It was so murky I wasn't sure. But in a few minutes I heard a soldier shout, 'They got Shadrick, right in the chest. He's dead, I guess.'"

The American soldiers gamely kept firing at the enemy tanks but did little damage. The tanks rumbled right past them. The Americans fell back, despondent. "My God, they look as if the ball game was over and it's time to go home," a journalist colleague of Higgins's remarked. Higgins approached a sergeant. "What's going on?" she asked. The sergeant replied bitterly, "We ran out of ammo. And the enemy infantry moving up way outnumbers us. Besides, these damn bazookas don't do any good against those heavy tanks—they bounce right off."

The story was similar all along the front. A lieutenant colonel staggered into his general's field headquarters. He was exhausted and had a shrapnel wound in his leg. "I'm sorry, sir," the colonel told the general. "We couldn't stop them. They came at us from all sides. We fired until we ran out of ammo." The colonel paused. "We lost a lot of men."

"The wounded?" the general asked.

"The litter cases were abandoned, sir."

The general winced. "Let's hear it from the beginning," he said.

"Right, sir. As you know, we were dug in north of the town of Osan on ridges on either side of the main road. We had some recoilless 75s, some mortars and other artillery. About eight-thirty in the morning those heavy tanks started rolling in on us. We took them under fire at about fifteen hundred yards and hit four or five. But we couldn't stop them. They rolled right by our positions. We sent the bazooka boys down, but their fire couldn't hurt that armor. Pretty soon the tanks got around to our rear and were shooting at our positions from behind. Then the infantry came in with automatic weapons and rifles. Some were dressed like farmers, in whites, and the rest had on mustard-colored uniforms. They came in like flies, all around us. We had no way of protecting ourselves from encirclement. We didn't have enough men to deploy. Then we got caught in the cross fire of the tanks and infantry."

A captain whose company was assigned to defend the town of Chonan had a similar experience. "The gooks really trapped us," he told Higgins. "They let us through the town, then came at us from the hills and from the rear. Those tanks must have been there all the time, hidden behind those deserted-looking houses. We got lots of them"—the North Korean soldiers—"but you can't get a tank with a carbine."

Even after American tanks arrived, they often proved no match for the heavier Russian tanks the North Koreans used. An infantry sergeant complained bitterly after trying to lead a counterattack: "Them American tanks run out on us the minute they heard the Russian babies coming round the corner. I asked the tank commander where the hell he thought he was going. He had the nerve to tell me he was heading back because his tank was at an unfair disadvantage against Russian armor. I asked that slob what sort of armor he thought I had on my back."

The soldiers' anger grew. Early efforts by American fighter planes to lend support to ground operations often did as much damage to the Americans as to the enemy. Higgins overheard a GI complain, after one close call from friendly fire, "Why don't those jet guys either stay at thirty thousand feet or go back to the officers' club?" A lieutenant who barely survived a firefight accosted Higgins demanding to know what she was writing for the home audience. "Are you correspondents telling the people back home the truth? Are you telling them that out of one platoon of twenty men, we have three left? Are you telling them that we have nothing to fight with, and that it is an utterly useless war?"

WHAT MACARTHUR NEEDED was more U.S. troops; what he got first was command of a UN coalition. Negotiations between the Truman administration and the UN led to a Security Council resolution authorizing the United States to direct a unified command and the American president to name the commander, who would report to the UN through the U.S. chain of command.

Truman never considered anyone except MacArthur, who was officially apprised of his appointment by the joint chiefs. MacArthur responded directly to Truman. His words, soon made public, could not have seemed warmer. "I recall so vividly and with such gratitude that this is the second time you have so signally honored me," he radiogrammed the president. "Your personal choice five years ago as Supreme Commander for the Allied Powers in Japan placed me under an intimate obligation which would be difficult for me ever to repay, and you have now added to my debt. I can only repeat the pledge of my complete personal loyalty to you as well as an absolute devotion to your monumental struggle for peace and good will throughout the world. I hope I will not fail you."

Truman responded in like manner, also for the benefit of the American people and the world. "I deeply appreciate the letter and the spirit of your message," the president wrote to the general. "Your words confirm me—if any confirmation were needed—in my full belief in the wisdom of your selection. With my warm regards and all good wishes, I am sincerely yours, Harry S. Truman."

EVEN MORE WELCOME was the first good news from the front. The arrival of additional American troops slowed the North Korean advance and stemmed the panic that had gripped South Korea. The prospect of the imminent conquest of the entire country by the North Koreans was dispelled. "This chance he has now lost through the extraordinary speed with which the 8th Army has been employed from Japan to stem his rush," MacArthur wrote from Tokyo. Truman would tire of the self-congratulatory tone of MacArthur's missives, but for now the president was simply relieved that South Korea wouldn't be overrun by the communists. He forgave more of MacArthur's grandiloquence as the general sketched a strategy for the weeks and months ahead. "Over a broad front involving continuous local struggles, there are bound to be ups and downs, losses as well as successes," MacArthur wrote. "But the issue of battle is now fully joined and will proceed along lines of action in which we will not be without choice. . . . We are now in Korea in force, and with God's help we are there to stay until the constitutional authority of the Republic is fully restored."

MacArthur likely guessed that Truman would quote him, as the president indeed did in a radio address to the American people. "The issue of battle is now fully joined," Truman repeated. "We are now in Korea in force, and with God's help we are there to stay." Truman also quoted Joe Collins, who had just returned from a trip to Korea and Japan, where he had given MacArthur a United Nations flag to fly over his headquarters. The army chief of staff praised "General MacArthur's magnificent leadership," which had inspired him to declare, "The task that confronts us is not an easy one, but I am confident of the outcome."

The good feeling of the moment prompted Truman to pay MacArthur the courtesy of giving him an advance look at a message he was preparing to send to Congress about the conflict in Korea. The message was the administration's first serious accounting of what had happened in Korea, and it included a request for new funding that proved to be the administration's closest approximation to a request for a war declaration. "To meet the situation in Korea, we shall need to send additional men, equipment and supplies to General MacArthur's command as rapidly as possible," the president told the legislators. "The hard facts of the present situation require relentless determination and firm action. The course of the fighting thus far in Korea shows that we can expect no easy solution to the conflict there. We are confronted in Korea with well-supplied, well-led forces which have been long trained for aggressive action. We and the other members of the United Nations who have joined in the effort to restore peace in Korea must expect a hard and costly military operation."

MacArthur responded as effusively as before. "It is a great state paper, in ultimate effect perhaps the most significant of modern times, for it means that the United States has determined that the Pacific areas shall be free," the general wrote to Truman. "I am sure that the historian of the future will regard it as the focal and turning point of this era's struggle for civilization. I am proud and honored to serve under your leadership at so vital a moment. That God will preserve and protect you in your monumental task is the fervent prayer of every member of this command."

16

YET THE MUTUAL admiration was for appearances only. James Reston was one of the most distinguished journalists in America and perhaps the best-connected member of the Washington press corps. Capital insiders fed Reston information even as they read his articles and columns to see if he was treating them as well as they were treating him. When Reston wrote about MacArthur, his words spoke as much for off-the-record Washington as they did for the *New York Times*, which paid his salary. Following MacArthur's appointment as UN commander, Reston reflected on the challenges the new position held. "General Douglas MacArthur, at 70, is now entering upon the most delicate political mission of his illustrious career," Reston wrote. "As Commander in Chief of United Nations forces in defense of South Korea, he is asked to be not only a great soldier but a great statesman; not only to direct the battle, but to satisfy the Pentagon, the State Department and the United Nations in the process." Reston wondered—which was to say, important figures in Washington wondered—if MacArthur was up to the job. "He has in the past had much larger forces under his control, and on many occasions he has had to act for other nations besides his own; but never before has he been asked to display political qualities so foreign to his own nature." Reston, with many others, compared MacArthur with Dwight Eisenhower, who had led the Allied armies to victory in Europe. The comparison did not work to MacArthur's advantage. "Eisenhower had a genius for international teamwork," Reston said. "Like most great soldiers, General MacArthur is a sovereign power in his own right, with stubborn confidence in his own judgment. Diplomacy and a vast concern for the opinions and sensitivities of others are the political qualities essential to this new assignment, and these are precisely the qualities General MacArthur has been accused of lacking in the past. Not even the General's detractors, who are many in this city, question his ability to handle the military side of the battle; but even in the present developing crisis he has demonstrated his old habit of doing things in his own way, without too much concern about waiting for orders from Washington." Reston's sources had provided particulars. "His instructions in the first few days of the Korean operation were to restrict his attacks to the area of Korea south of the Thirty-eighth Parallel, but despite official denials, responsible officials here still insist that his planes attacked the North Korean capital before President Truman authorized any such action." MacArthur's high-handedness had prompted stronger orders from Washington. "Since then, he has been instructed in specific terms to stay out of the area of the Soviet Union's main Far Eastern port of Vladivostok, and to keep his planes and ships away from the territory and territorial waters of the Soviet Union and Communist China."

MacArthur's political sense became an issue in late July when he traveled to Formosa. Louis Johnson and the joint chiefs had grown worried by signs that the Chinese might be preparing an invasion of Formosa; they recommended to Truman that MacArthur be sent to the island to survey the situation there. Truman approved the recommendation.

He soon wished he hadn't. MacArthur met with Chiang Kai-shek for two days, at the end of which Chiang pronounced his delight at the decisions he and the American general had made. "An agreement was reached between General MacArthur and myself on all the problems discussed," Chiang said. "The foundation for a joint defense of Formosa and for Sino-American military cooperation has thus been laid. It is our conviction that our struggle against Communist aggression will certainly result in final victory."

Truman offered no public response to Chiang's statement, which seriously misrepresented American policy toward the Chinese Nationalists. Truman was still trying to disentangle the United States from

Chiang and the Nationalists; there was no plan for a joint defense of Formosa. At the very least the president insisted that any decision about future relations with Formosa be *his* decision and not Chiang's.

And not MacArthur's. Truman couldn't tell from Chiang's statement where the misrepresentation had arisen: with Chiang or with MacArthur. MacArthur didn't dispute Chiang's claim about a military agreement, but neither did he confirm it. In fact, he hadn't even filed a report of the trip to the joint chiefs, under whose direction he had gone to Formosa.

Truman dispatched Averell Harriman to Tokyo to get to the bottom of things. Harriman was a son of railroad magnate E. H. Harriman who had gone into banking and then diplomatic troubleshooting. He conducted delicate missions for Franklin Roosevelt during World War II, and Truman concluded that if Harriman could handle Stalin and Churchill, he might be a match for MacArthur.

The general made a show of welcoming his visitor. "Harriman and I were friends of long standing," he remarked later. "While superintendent of West Point I had hunted ducks on his preserve near Tuxedo." He brought Harriman into his confidence. "We discussed fully global conditions." Yet beneath the amicable aspect of the conversations, each man was probing the other. MacArthur didn't like what he discovered. "I found him careful and cautious in what he said, but gained these very definite impressions: that there was no fixed and comprehensive United States policy for the Far East; that foreign influences, especially those of Great Britain, were very powerful in Washington; that there was no apparent interest in mounting an offensive against the Communists; that we were content to attempt to block their moves, but not to initiate any counter-moves; that we would defend Formosa if attacked, just as we had done in Korea; that President Truman had conceived a violent animosity toward Chiang Kai-shek; and that anyone who favored the Generalissimo might well arouse the President's disfavor." MacArthur concluded, "He left me with a feeling of concern and uneasiness that the situation in the Far East was little understood and mistakenly downgraded in high circles in Washington."

Harriman was no less worried by what he gleaned from MacArthur. "General MacArthur met me at Haneda Airport," Harriman reported to Truman after the visit. "He drove me to the guest house at the Embassy. As the window between the driver and his aide, and ourselves, was open, our conversation was general." MacArthur described the tremendous progress the Japanese had made since the war. "He spoke of the great quality of the Japanese; his desire to work, the satisfaction of the Japanese in work, his respect for the dignity of work. He compared it unfavorably to the desire in the United States for more luxury and less work." MacArthur said the Japanese had been heartened by America's strong reaction to the North Korean invasion of South Korea. "They interpreted it to mean that we would vigorously defend them against Russian invasion. They were not disturbed by our temporary difficulties, since they understood the military difficulties caused by the surprise attack. Their pride had been aroused by 'his' confidence in them, shown by the withdrawal of most of the American troops. He could withdraw them all without any danger of disorder in Japan."

When they could speak more freely, MacArthur and Harriman broached more-sensitive topics. They started with Korea. "He did not believe that the Russians had any present intention of intervening directly, or becoming involved in a general war," Harriman told Truman. "He believed the same was true of the Chinese Communists." Yet the Russians and the Chinese were helping the North Koreans, supplying military training and volunteers. MacArthur evinced respect for the North Koreans as fighters. "Their tactics had been skillful, and they were as capable and tough as any army in his military experience." This reflected their Asian heritage, MacArthur told Harriman. "He described the difference between the attitude towards death of Westerners and Orientals. We hate to die; only face danger out of a sense of duty and through moral issues; whereas with Orientals, life begins with death. They die quietly, 'folding their arms as a dove folding his wings, relaxing, and dying.'"

Harriman raised the issue of Formosa. "I told him the President wanted me to tell him he must not permit Chiang to be the cause of starting a war with the Chinese communists on the mainland, the effect of which might be to drag us into a world war. He answered that he would, as a soldier, obey any orders he received from the President. He said that he had discussed only military matters with the Generalissimo on his trip to Formosa. He had refused to discuss any political subjects when the Generalissimo attempted to do so. The Generalissimo had offered him command of the Chinese National troops. MacArthur had replied that that was not appropriate, but that he would be willing to give military advice if requested by the Generalissimo to do so."

Harriman suspected MacArthur wasn't telling him the complete story. "For reasons which are rather difficult to explain," Harriman wrote to Truman, "I did not feel that we came to a full agreement on the way we believed things should be handled on Formosa and with the Generalissimo. He accepted the President's position and will act accordingly, but without full conviction. He has a strange idea that we should back anybody who will fight communism, even though he could not give an argument why the Generalissimo's fighting communists would be a contribution towards the effective dealing with the communists in China. I pointed out to him the basic conflict of interest between the U.S. and the Generalissimo's position as to the future of Formosa, namely the preventing of Formosa's falling into hostile hands. Perhaps the best way would be through the medium of the UN to establish an independent government. Chiang, on the other hand, had only the burning ambition to use Formosa as a stepping-stone for his re-entry to the mainland. MacArthur recognized that this ambition could not be fulfilled, and yet thought it might be a good idea to let him land and get rid of him that way. He did not seem to consider the liability that our support of Chiang on such a move would be to us in the East. I explained in great detail why Chiang was a liability, and the great danger of a split in the unity of the United Nations on the Chinese-Communist-Formosa policies; the attitude of the British, Nehru and such countries as Norway, who, although stalwart in their determination to resist Russian aggression, do not want to stir up trouble elsewhere. I pointed out the great importance of maintaining UN unity among the friendly countries, and the complications that might result from any missteps in dealing with China and Formosa."

Harriman was a cogent and compelling explainer in most circumstances, which was why Roosevelt and Truman entrusted him with sensitive missions. But he didn't think he got through to MacArthur. "In all, I cannot say that he recognizes fully the difficulties, both within the world and within the East, of whatever moves we make within China in our position with the Generalissimo in Formosa. He believes that our policies undermine the Generalissimo. He has confidence that he can get the Generalissimo to do whatever he is asked to undertake."

MacArthur was less evasive about Chiang and Formosa when speaking to those he considered his friends and allies. William Sebald was a graduate of the U.S. Naval Academy, an international lawyer, a diplomat and the chief political adviser to MacArthur in Japan. Sebald met with MacArthur regularly, and though he reported to the State Department, his sympathies were with the general. MacArthur reciprocated by speaking candidly to Sebald about Chiang—and about the State Department. The general dismissed as strategically immaterial all criticism of Chiang as less than the perfect democrat. "If he has horns and a tail, so long as he is anti-Communist, we should help him," MacArthur told Sebald, per Sebald's diary. "It is time that the State Department forgets its vendetta against Chiang and assists him in the fight against the communists. We can try to reform him later."

MacArthur's self-congratulation upon the deployment of the Eighth Army was premature; for another two weeks the American troops continued to retreat. The general countenanced the withdrawal as unavoidable, but he balked when the Eighth Army commander, Walton Walker, proposed to relocate his headquarters to Pusan, the port city on the southeast tip of the Korean peninsula. Whether or not Walker intended this as a prelude to evacuation, MacArthur knew many observers would draw that conclusion. He flew to Korea at once. "Walker," he said, "you can make all the reconnaissance you want. You can put your engineers to work if you like preparing intermediate trenches. But *I* will give the order to retire from this position. There will be no Dunkirk in this command. To retire to Pusan is unacceptable."

Walton "Johnnie" Walker—who liked his whiskey—had fought under George Patton in Europe during World War II, and he exhibited Patton's stubbornness without the melodrama. Yet he seemed almost melodramatic as he relayed to his subordinates what MacArthur had told him. "General MacArthur was over here two days ago," Walker said. "He is thoroughly conversant with the situation. He knows where we are and what we have to fight with. He knows our needs and where the enemy is hitting the hardest. General MacArthur is doing everything possible to send reinforcements. A Marine unit and two regiments are expected in the next few days to reinforce us. Additional units are being sent over as quickly as possible. We are fighting a battle against time. There will be no more retreating, withdrawal, or readjustment of the lines, or any other term you choose. There is no line behind us to which we can retreat. Every unit must counterattack to keep the enemy in a state of confusion and off balance. There will be no Dunkirk, there will be no Bataan. A retreat to Pusan would be one of the great butcheries in history. We must fight until the end. Capture by these people is worse than death itself. We will fight as a team. If some of us must die, we will die fighting together. Any man who gives ground may be personally responsible for the death of thousands of his comrades. I want you to put this out to all the men in the division. I want everybody to understand that we are going to hold this line. We are going to win."

Headline writers soon shortened Walker's message to "Stand or die." And stand was what the Eighth Army did. At the Naktong River they dug in and held on. Maggie Higgins witnessed the change of fortunes and the transformation in morale it effected. Walker was sufficiently traditional to think women had no place in a war zone; he ordered Higgins out of Korea. She retreated to Japan, where she appealed her expulsion to MacArthur. She pointed out that she expected no special treatment as a woman; she endured the same hardships as the male reporters. She added that singling her out injured her paper, the *Herald Tribune*, which was left without a correspondent. She started a backfire against the order, appealing to GIs and junior officers who had witnessed her courage and perseverance in the worst of the retreat south. "We hope you can talk the general out of this," more than one soldier told her. Her bosses appealed to the Defense Department. The efforts paid off. MacArthur valued good press more than most generals, and he decided he'd rather have Higgins and the *Herald Tribune* happy than angry. "Ban on women in Korea being lifted," his headquarters telegraphed to Walker and the other field commanders. "Marguerite Higgins held in highest professional esteem by everyone."

She arrived in time for one of the first major battles after Walker's stand-or-die order. The Twenty-Seventh Infantry Regiment, called the Wolfhound Regiment, was commanded by John Michaelis, a former aide to Dwight Eisenhower. Michaelis's professionalism and fighting spirit inspired his men, and he accepted with aplomb the challenge Walker had given them. Higgins overheard a midnight message from a forward battalion that had been contending with North Korean tanks all day. The message conveyed the current situation and the attitude of the battalion: "Five tanks within our position. Situation vague. No sweat. We are holding."

Higgins heard another account from a different regiment. "Antitank guns caught us on a curve several miles short of our objective," an infantry officer told her. "Troops riding on the tanks yelled when they saw the flash, but they were too late. The tanks caught partially afire and the crews were wounded. But three of the tanks were still operable. I was damned if I was going to let several hundred thousand dollars' worth of American equipment sit back there on the road. I yelled, 'Who around here thinks he can drive a tank?' A couple of ex-bulldozer operators and an ex-mason volunteered. They got about three minutes' checking out and off they went." The new men guided the tanks to safety, carrying wounded troops on their decks. Higgins found one of the drivers, who had operated bulldozers. "It's really easier to drive than a bulldozer," he said dismissively. "You just feel sort of funny lookin' in that darn periscope all the time." Later the driver sought her out. "Ma'am," he said, "if you happen to think of it, you might tell the colonel that we're hoping he won't take that tank away from us. We're plannin' to git ordnance to help us fix it up in the mornin'." The officer who told Higgins the story concluded that it had been a good day. They had lost thirty men but killed nearly three hundred. "We counted them when we fought our way up to the high ground where they had been dug in. And earlier we caught a whole platoon napping by the roadside. We killed them all."

Higgins met Colonel Michaelis after the battle. He seemed pleased. She asked him if he had any message for his division commander. He said he did. "Tell him that we will damn well hold."

18

THEY DID HOLD, and the stabilization of the Pusan perimeter allowed MacArthur to begin planning a counteroffensive that would reverse the gains the North Koreans had achieved. In Washington, Truman hoped for just such a reversal, and he looked to the general as the one person with sufficient experience, acumen and self-confidence to make it happen. Yet looking to MacArthur required the president to look past the trouble MacArthur was causing for American diplomacy.

MacArthur, meanwhile, thought *he* was the one beset. "General burst into a long tirade about a State Department clique attempting to undermine his position," William Sebald wrote in his diary after a session with MacArthur. "He said that John Allison"—another foreign service officer—"was sneaking around behind his back to get information." Sebald defended Allison, causing MacArthur to modify his charge. "The General said he didn't mean to imply that John A. was not *acting* in good faith." But Allison, like the other diplomats, knew nothing about the Asian mind, MacArthur said. Discussion moved to matters of protocol. "He turned down my suggestion that he meet with various Chiefs of Mission," Sebald recorded, "on the ground that they had no responsibility for Korea, and besides, as a 'sovereign,' why should he?—President Truman didn't do so, nor does the King of England or any other head of a state!" (The exclamation point was one of Sebald's occasional comments on MacArthur's elevated sense of self. Similar eye rolling had followed word from MacArthur's headquarters that the general didn't take kindly to the fact that addresses on letters to him from the United Nations habitually included his middle initial. "The General feels that his name should be well enough known by now," Sebald was told.) MacArthur revisited the ignorance, if not perfidy, of the diplomats. "He pilloried the State Department and said that one of these days he intends to 'blast them wide open,'" Sebald wrote. "Apparently someone is feeding him stuff from Washington which makes him very suspicious." Sebald added, "With me personally, the General is always friendly—I refuse to allow him to make me angry, despite some of his rather extravagant charges against 'Washington interference headed by the State Department crowd.'"

Occasionally, MacArthur went public with his accusations. A week after his return from Formosa, and about the time Averell Harriman got back to America from Japan, MacArthur issued a statement denying any difference between himself and the president regarding Formosa or anything else, yet alleging malign influence and motives to unnamed people who sought to create such a difference. "This visit has been maliciously misrepresented to the public by those who in the past have propagandized a policy of defeatism and appeasement in the Pacific," MacArthur said of his Formosa trip. "I hope the American people will not be misled by sly insinuations, brash speculations and bold misstatements, invariably attributed to anonymous sources, so insidiously fed them both nationally and internationally by persons 10,000 miles away from the actual events which tend, if they are not indeed designed, to promote disunity and destroy faith and confidence in American purposes and institutions and American representatives at this time of great world peril."

Truman couldn't tell what game MacArthur was playing, but he refused to take part. A reporter probed him at a news conference. "General MacArthur says there are defeatists and appeasers who are working against him," the reporter said. "Is anybody trying to set you against General MacArthur?"

"I haven't met anybody yet," Truman replied.

Another reporter couldn't hear the answer and said so.

"I haven't met anybody of that sort yet," Truman repeated. "General MacArthur and I are in perfect agreement, and have been ever since he has been in the job he is now. I put him there, and I also appointed him Commander in Chief of American and Allied Forces, at the suggestion of the United Nations. I am satisfied with what he is doing."

So, PRESUMABLY, WERE readers of much of the reporting on MacArthur and the Korean fighting. Lindesay Parrott had covered MacArthur during World War II and recounted his rebuilding of Japan afterward. Parrott was happy to follow the general into a war zone once again. "Look at him now," he quoted a MacArthur aide from aboard the *Bataan* on an August trip to the front. "Just look at him. He'll walk half the way there before we set down." The aide was referring to MacArthur's habit of pacing while he thought, even ten thousand feet above the Yellow Sea. "The General paced up and down the aisle, hands behind his back," Parrott wrote in his own voice. "His gold-laced hat had been set aside for the moment, and he wore the faded, almost white suntans he affected in the Southwest Pacific. MacArthur was crackling with energy—as he has been from the moment that hostilities began in Korea—fuller than ever of ideas, ready to drive himself and his subordinates to the utmost limits of their abilities even if he has to 'walk halfway there' in person." Parrott added, "The outcome in Asia may well depend on the result of General MacArthur's nervous walks and the ideas he coins while making them."

Parrott observed that the fighting in Korea had changed MacArthur's daily routine only modestly. "His long, black sedan with its constellation of five silver stars on red plates at the front and rear draws up as usual about 11 o'clock in the morning in front of the white-columned former insurance company building, which the Supreme Commander has used as headquarters almost since the Japanese surrender. He leaves about 2:30 for lunch at his home in the American Embassy building and returns about 4 o'clock to work until 10 or 11, rather than to 8, as he formerly did. Just why the General keeps these particular hours has never been successfully explained. Someone asked him once, so the story goes, and he replied, 'I like them.'"

Out of sight, however, MacArthur carried a much greater burden than before, Parrott explained. The blue flag of the United Nations, flying beside the Stars and Stripes at MacArthur's headquarters, betokened his obligation to the world community. Powerful and important visitors came and went, the latest being Averell Harriman. MacArthur traveled repeatedly to Korea, where he assessed the fighting and plotted the shift from defense to counterattack, and he had gone to Formosa. Yet the general was undaunted. "MacArthur has been meeting his difficulties with the same confidence which characterized his attitude even during the worst days of the South Pacific war. In his mind ultimate victory was never in doubt then—and isn't today. The Supreme Commander has an optimism which has sometimes caused even his closest staff members to cock questioning eyebrows."

Parrott described how MacArthur had drafted his first report to the joint chiefs from the front. "Routine communiqués noting the day's fighting usually are composed by various members of the staff," Parrott wrote. "Important messages, however, are scrawled by MacArthur himself on a yellow scratchpad in soft pencil, then sent to stenographers to type and mimeograph. This was one of these." Parrott was referring to the report in which MacArthur predicted ultimate victory. "There have been advances and retreats since then," Parrott continued, "but General MacArthur's assessment is that we will win. Nobody thinks the process will be a fast one. The United Nations troops have a long way to go before they battle back to the Thirty-eighth Parallel—let alone the Yalu River, the frontier between Korea and Manchuria, which may be the ultimate objective."

PERHAPS PARROTT, WHO knew MacArthur as well as any reporter, was repeating something the general had told him about ultimate objectives. MacArthur tested the bounds of policy by various means, including unattributed statements to reporters. His official brief was to repel the North Korean invasion; no one in Washington in a position of authority was saying anything about driving to the Yalu. MacArthur thought they should be *thinking* about it, even if they weren't talking about it, and he hoped to stimulate the thought processes.

He employed other methods as well. The Veterans of Foreign Wars asked him to address their national meeting, by written statement since he couldn't be spared from the theater of the war. He responded with a message that he sent to the veterans' group and to American news organizations—but not to the administration in Washington. The general thanked the veterans for their support and praised their successors, the Americans fighting in Korea, for their continued sacrifice. "From senior commanders through all ranks, their tactical skill, their invincible determination and their fighting qualities against a fanatical foe, well trained, expertly directed and heavily armed, have upheld our country's finest traditions," he said.

This was patriotic standard and doubtless the sum of what the veterans expected. But MacArthur surprised them by going much further. "In view of misconceptions currently being voiced concerning the relationship of Formosa to our strategic potential in the Pacific, I believe it in the public interest to avail myself of this opportunity to state my views thereon to you, all of whom having fought overseas understand broad strategic concepts." MacArthur proceeded to sketch a breathtaking vision of American hegemony over the world's greatest ocean. Prior to World War II, the Pacific had been an avenue of weakness for the United States, he said, as evidenced by the attacks on Pearl Harbor and the Philippines. The American victory changed this. "Our strategic frontier then shifted to embrace the entire Pacific Ocean, which has become a vast moat to protect us as long as we hold it. Indeed, it acts as a protective shield to all of the Americas and all free lands of the Pacific Ocean area we control to the shores of Asia, by a chain of islands extending in an arc from the Aleutians to the Marianas, held by us and our free allies. From this island chain we can dominate with air power every Asiatic port from Vladivostok to Singapore and prevent any hostile movement into the Pacific. Any predatory attack from Asia must be an amphibious one. No amphibious force can be successful with our control of the sea lanes and the air over these lanes in its avenue of advance. With naval and air supremacy and modern ground elements to defend bases, any major attack from continental Asia toward us or our friends of the Pacific would come to failure. Under such conditions the Pacific no longer represents menacing avenues of approach for a prospective invader; it assumes instead the friendly aspect of a peaceful lake." All that was required was for America to take measures to keep it thus. "Our line of defense is a natural one and can be maintained with a minimum of military effort and expense. It envisions no attack against anyone nor does it provide the bastions essential for offensive operations, but properly maintained would be an invincible defense against aggression. If we hold this line we may have peace; lose it and war is inevitable."

Formosa figured centrally in MacArthur's vision. Employing the imagery he had shared with the joint chiefs two months earlier, he declared, "As a result of its geographic location and base potential, utilization of Formosa by a military power hostile to the United States may either counter-balance or overshadow the strategic importance of the central and southern flank of the U.S. front line position. Formosa in the hands of such an hostile power could be compared to an unsinkable air-craft carrier and submarine tender ideally located to accomplish offensive strategy and at the same time checkmate defensive or counter-offensive operations by friendly forces based on Okinawa and the Philippines." Recent history, with which some of the veterans were personally familiar, showed that Formosa could readily be used as a springboard for aggres-sion to the south. "Should Formosa fall into the hands of an hostile power, history would repeat itself. Its military potential would again be fully exploited as the means to breach and neutralize our western Pacific defense system and mount a war of conquest against the free nations of the Pacific basin."

Taking dead aim at Dean Acheson and the State Department, MacArthur decried diplomacy as a means of determining Formosa's fate. "Nothing could be more fallacious than the threadbare argument by those who advocate appeasement and defeatism in the Pacific that if we defend Formosa we alienate continental Asia. Those who speak thus do not understand the Orient. They do not understand that it is in the pat-tern of the Oriental psychology to respect and follow aggressive, resolute and dynamic leadership—to quickly turn on a leadership characterized by timidity or vacillation—and they underestimate the Oriental men-tality. Nothing in the last five years has so inspired the Far East as the American determination to preserve the bulwarks of our Pacific Ocean strategic position from future encroachment, for few of its peoples fail accurately to appraise the safeguard such determination brings to their free institutions." Any other course would undo the good work done so far at such great cost. "It would shift any future battle area five thousand miles eastward to the coasts of the American continents, our home coast; it would completely expose our friends in the Philippines, our friends in Australia and New Zealand, our friends in Indonesia, our friends in Japan, and other areas, to the lustful thrusts of those who stand for slav-ery as against liberty, for atheism as against God."

MacArthur praised President Truman even as he warned him against the unfolding folly of his diplomatic advisers. "The decision of President Truman on June 27"—the decision to defend Korea—"lighted into flame a lamp of hope throughout Asia that was burning dimly toward extinc-tion. It marked for the Far East the focal and turning point in this area's struggle for freedom. It swept aside in one great monumental stroke all of the hypocrisy and the sophistry which has confused and deluded so many people distant from the actual scene." MacArthur wanted the vets to know *he* was the lamp keeper now, battling the hypocrites and sophists even as he fought the communists.

19

"WHEN WE FILED into the Oval Office, the President, with lips white and compressed, dispensed with the usual greetings," Dean Acheson recalled of the meeting that followed Truman's learning of MacArthur's message. The secretary of state had never seen the president so angry. MacArthur's leak of the message to the press guaranteed its publication in all the major papers ahead of the meeting by the Veterans of Foreign Wars and appeared designed to preempt any effort to suppress it.

What infuriated Truman was not so much what MacArthur said but rather that he arrogated to himself the right to say it. Truman was trying to finesse the issue of Formosa; no more than MacArthur did he wish to see it fall to the communists, yet neither did he want to provoke the Chinese by proclaiming an American protectorate over the island. He guessed he would lose the British if he did so, for they held Hong Kong only on the sufferance of the Chinese. Britain was worth far more to the United States than Formosa would ever be. Nor did Truman intend to give Chiang Kai-shek the carte blanche MacArthur's statement effectively implied. Further, the president had been struggling to keep the Formosa question separate from the Korea question; MacArthur's statement, coming from the commander of UN and U.S. forces in Korea, obliterated the separation. And in doing so, it risked blowing up the UN coalition in Korea, for none of the other members had anything like the attachment to the Chinese Nationalists that MacArthur professed. Finally, Truman insisted on the principle that major statements on American foreign policy come from the White House, not from the Dai Ichi Building in Tokyo.

He looked coldly about the room. He inquired whether any of those present—Louis Johnson, the joint chiefs and Averell Harriman, besides Acheson and members of Truman's staff—had known of MacArthur's message in advance. Heads shook all around. Still struggling to keep his temper, Truman declared that MacArthur must be ordered to withdraw his message.

Johnson nervously objected. The defense secretary judged the general too strong politically to be so publicly reprimanded. MacArthur must be treated with delicacy. "In obvious consternation, Secretary Johnson rose to his feet and stated that he had had no previous knowledge of the MacArthur statement and that he would call MacArthur immediately and request him to cancel the statement in question," George Elsey recorded.

Truman's anger now focused on Johnson. The president refused to "request" anything of MacArthur. But he wanted to make sure others in the Pentagon, namely the joint chiefs, hadn't known about this. Was Johnson covering for them? "The President swung his chair around, and facing General Collins directly, he asked the General if he had had any knowledge of MacArthur's statements," Elsey continued. "General Collins replied that he had not."

When none of the other chiefs volunteered, Truman accepted Collins's statement on behalf of the chiefs as a group.

Now Averell Harriman, whose opinion of MacArthur's integrity was declining rapidly, weighed in. "Harriman spoke up in emphatic tones about the catastrophe that would attend the release of MacArthur's statement," Elsey wrote. "The President concurred."

Acheson took the same view. The secretary of state said that MacArthur's message was at "complete variance" with the position of the American government. The message must be withdrawn. Again Truman agreed.

That seemed to settle the matter. "The meeting broke up with the promise by Secretary Johnson that he would instruct MacArthur to cancel the message," Elsey recorded.

———

CHARLIE ROSS, TRUMAN'S press secretary, didn't think this sufficient. Ross had been around Washington and around the Pentagon, and he trusted Johnson hardly more than he trusted MacArthur. He returned to the president's office half an hour later to say that MacArthur should be ordered in writing to withdraw the message, and not merely instructed orally, as he suspected Johnson would try to do. There must be a paper trail, Ross said. Truman approved the recommendation.

But the order took shape only slowly. Ross was right; Johnson didn't agree with Truman's decision and sought to circumvent it. He started by working on Acheson. Johnson called the secretary of state to express his concern. He said an order to MacArthur to withdraw the message would cause "a great deal of embarrassment." He said he and the joint chiefs preferred telling MacArthur that if he went ahead with the message, the administration would have to release a separate statement declaring that "it is one man's opinion and is not the official policy of the Government."

Acheson judged this grossly insufficient and told Johnson so. "Secretary Acheson said he thought that the matter raised the issue as to who is the President of the United States," Lucius Battle, Acheson's aide, recorded. "MacArthur had made a statement contrary to what the President and Austin"—Warren Austin, the U.S. representative at the United Nations—"have stated was our position on Formosa. Simply to say that the statement is one man's views gets the President and the Government into complete confusion as to what parts of the statement are not the Government's policy; as to whether the Government knew about the statement before it became public; why it is not our policy, etc., etc. The Secretary said he thought there was nothing to do but for the President to assert his authority, and in this way make it clear that the President's stated position on Formosa stood."

Johnson was still nervous. "Secretary Johnson at this point asked Secretary Acheson if he thought 'we dare send him a message that the President directs him to withdraw his statement,'" Battle wrote.

Acheson judged they had better dare. "Secretary Acheson said he saw nothing else to do."

Johnson claimed that his memory of the morning meeting was that the president had not definitively decided to order MacArthur to withdraw the message.

Acheson asserted positively that the president indeed decided. He said Averell Harriman had made the recommendation and Truman had accepted it. Acheson said he would call Harriman and settle the matter.

Harriman remembered things the way Acheson did. But this didn't end the debate. Steve Early had been Roosevelt's press secretary and was currently deputy secretary of defense. Besides owing his job to Johnson, Early considered himself an authority on the dissemination of news. He contended that it was too late to have MacArthur withdraw his message. The major newspapers had received copies, either directly from MacArthur or from the Veterans of Foreign Wars, whose leadership was known to favor the general over the president. Early got on the telephone with Acheson and said that the secretary's recommendation was too far behind the event. "It seemed to him that the directive of the President asked the impossible," Lucius Battle recalled Early saying. "It was not mechanically possible to withdraw the statement, because it had been received by the VFW, which is a hostile group; it has been given worldwide distribution by them. Its withdrawal would never, in his opinion, prevent its publication or answer the issue. A directive to MacArthur to withdraw the statement, not being possible of accomplishment, would add fuel to the fire, when the statement is issued." Better to stick with the explanation that MacArthur spoke only for himself and that in America everyone was allowed his opinion.

Acheson disagreed strongly. He understood that the president couldn't stop MacArthur's statement from becoming public. The question was: How would it be interpreted? "The Secretary again outlined the confused position we would be in if there was simply a repudiation of the statement if made by MacArthur, with no directive not to do so; whereas if it comes out after the order to withdraw has been sent, the President has asserted his authority, and the position of the U.S. in relation to other governments will be maintained."

Early still thought his approach would risk less trouble. He wondered if Truman could talk on the phone with MacArthur.

Acheson rejected this idea at once. "This would put the President in the position of a supplicant," he said.

Most of the debate took place out of Truman's earshot. After Charlie Ross learned that Johnson was dragging his feet, he called Early to ask if the order to MacArthur had been sent. Early said it had not and that he and Johnson were working on a statement to the effect that if questions arose in Washington about MacArthur's message to the VFW, the White House would say that the administration had no previous knowledge of it.

"Ross told Early that was emphatically not enough," George Elsey recorded, "and that it was not in accord with what Johnson had promised the President to do." Ross resolved to make the order happen. "Ross sent out an alarm for Averell Harriman, and Harriman and Ross together went in to see the President. Ross told the President that Defense seemed to be weak and indecisive."

Truman listened to their story and agreed. He at once called Johnson and told him he wanted MacArthur commanded, in no uncertain terms, to withdraw the message. He proceeded to dictate what he wanted Johnson to say.

Johnson had no choice. He cabled MacArthur: "The President of the United States directs that you withdraw your message for National Encampment of Veterans of Foreign Wars, because various features with respect to Formosa are in conflict with the policy of the United States and its position in the United Nations."

20

MACARTHUR PROFESSED ASTONISHMENT. He had never intended to cause the president any trouble, he replied to Johnson. Quite the contrary. "My message was most carefully prepared to fully support the President's policy decision of 27 June 1950, reading in part as follows: 'The occupation of Formosa by Communist Forces would be a direct threat to the security of the Pacific area and to United States forces performing their lawful and necessary functions in that area.'" MacArthur said he had simply aimed to be helpful. "My remarks were calculated solely to support and I am unable to see wherein they might be interpreted otherwise. The views were purely my personal ones and the subject had been freely discussed in all circles, Governmental and private, both at home and abroad."

Yet implicitly acknowledging that his message to the veterans had boxed the president in, the general continued, "The message has undoubtedly been incorporated in the printed agenda for the Encampment and advance press releases thereof have already reached world-wide centers of circulation. Under these circumstances I am sure that it would be mechanically impossible to suppress the same at this late date, and I believe to attempt it under such conditions would be a grave mistake." MacArthur asked Johnson to take the matter to the president again. "Please therefore present my most earnest request to the President for reconsideration of the order given me in your message, as I believe that repercussions resulting in compliance therewith would be destructive and most harmful to the National Interest."

Should the president insist on withdrawal, however, MacArthur said, he would of course accede. But he would make clear that the decision was not his. He asked Johnson, in the event the president did not change his mind, to tell the head of the VFW, "I regret to inform you that I have been directed to withdraw my message."

Johnson declined to approach Truman again, and he relayed MacArthur's statement to the VFW.

The result was an immediate clamor. No one could recall a time when the president of the United States and his commanding general had been so publicly at odds over a critical matter of policy. Editorial pages sizzled with opinions on what this meant for American policy and for future relations between the president and the general.

Truman and MacArthur, for their own separate reasons, initially refused to say *who* had directed MacArthur to withdraw the message. Truman didn't want to reveal that he couldn't rely on his own secretary of defense, and MacArthur didn't want to admit that he had been reprimanded by the president.

Yet reporters soon discovered that the reprimand came from Truman himself, and the revelation encouraged Truman's critics, quiet since the start of the Korean fighting, to tear into the president again. The VFW registered its strong preference for MacArthur by voting loudly and unanimously to affirm its "complete confidence in his integrity and ability." Congressional Republicans immortalized MacArthur's provocative message by inserting it into the *Congressional Record*. Joseph Martin, the Republican leader in the House, called Truman's decision "another flagrant example of the incredible bungling by the administration over the past five years, bungling which delivered Manchuria and most of China to the Communists and which culminated in the Korean conflict."

Reporters pressed the White House regarding the rift between the president and the general. One asked Charlie Ross if MacArthur was going to be fired.

"The President regards the incident as closed," Ross replied.

"Isn't it a fact that General MacArthur has disregarded instructions and policy a number of times since the outbreak of aggression in Korea?"

The questioner was fishing. Rumors had been circulating of tension between Truman and MacArthur, but nothing of substance had surfaced until now. Ross refused the bait. "No comment on that."

So what *was* going on? the reporters demanded.

A White House spokesman who declined to be named—quite

possibly Ross—tried to tamp down the furor. "The President's action in directing the withdrawal of General MacArthur's message was an effort to preserve the clarity of the position of the United States," he said blandly.

"THAT'S THE DAY I should have fired him," Truman later declared of MacArthur's VFW message. The president said he told Acheson, Johnson and the joint chiefs he wanted to fire MacArthur and replace him with Omar Bradley. "But they talked me out of it. They said it would cause too much of an uproar, and so I didn't do it."

Truman remembered too much. No one at the meeting recalled the president's speaking of firing MacArthur. Yet his anger had been evident enough. And some of those present might well have concluded what Truman subsequently put into words: "After that day, I knew it was only a matter of time before there'd be a showdown."

21

MEANWHILE HE HAD another problem. Several months earlier Truman had appointed Francis Matthews secretary of the navy. The appointment filled certain political needs, in that Matthews was a high-profile Irish Catholic and Irish Catholics, long stalwarts of the Democratic party, were being lured to the Republicans by Joseph McCarthy. Matthews, moreover, hailed from Nebraska and tugged back at Midwesterners drawn to the Wisconsinite McCarthy. Matthews knew Washington from service in and around government during the 1930s and 1940s. But he didn't know foreign policy, and he didn't know how to keep his foot out of his mouth.

In late August 1950 he spoke at a celebration of the sesquicentennial of the Boston Naval Shipyard. Much of his address was ordinary boilerplate for a navy secretary, especially one speaking where for generations actual boiler plate had been made into boilers. "We have no choice other than to build our military power to the strength which will make it impossible for any enemy to overcome us," Matthews said. "To reach that position all the resources of the nation should be dedicated." But America must do more than build weapons. It must be willing to use them. "We should boldly proclaim our undeniable objective to be a world at peace. To have peace we should be willing, and declare our intention, to pay any price, even the price of instituting a war to compel cooperation for peace." Faint hearts would complain, Matthews said. "They would brand our program as imperialistic aggression." Let them do so. "We could accept that slander with complacency, for in the implementation of a strong, affirmative, peace-seeking policy, though it cast us in a character new to a true democracy—an initiator of a war of aggression—it would win for us a proud and popular title—we would become the first aggressors for peace."

The concept and wording were provocative enough. Preventive war and "aggressors for peace" elicited instant headlines. But the timing made Matthews's remarks much worse. The United States was racing Russia to build superbombs, and it was easy to infer that Matthews was saying that if America got there first, it should use the monster weapons against the Russians. The sobering corollary was that if the *Russians* got there first, America—or at least Matthews—would have no moral ground for opposing a Russian preventive strike.

The MacArthur angle simply added to the Matthews problem. MacArthur was saying the United States should defend Formosa against the Chinese. Matthews was claiming the right for the United States to shoot first. One didn't have to be a logician or, if Chinese, a paranoid to conclude that together they seemed to be making the case for preemptive nuclear war against China.

At the very least, the Matthews speech, coming amid the ruckus about the MacArthur message, raised serious questions about who spoke for the American government. The White House quickly distanced the president from Matthews's remarks. But the echoes persisted, and like those of MacArthur's message to the veterans they gave America's enemies and even some of its friends reason to worry that Washington was getting trigger-happy.

TRUMAN TRIED TO clear things up in a radio and television address at the beginning of September. Truman hadn't asked Congress for a declaration of war, and so he hadn't felt obliged to specify America's war aims. But given the confusion caused by the MacArthur and Matthews statements, the president decided he'd better make clear how the U.S. government viewed the conflict in Korea and what it intended there.

He began with the importance of collective action in Korea. "For the first time in all history, men of many nations are fighting under a single banner to uphold the rule of law in the world," he said. "This is an inspiring fact. If the rule of law is not upheld we can look forward only to the horror of another war and ultimate chaos. For our part, we do not intend to let that happen." Since World War II the communists had engaged in subversion; in Korea they had turned to brutal aggression. The United States had no choice other than to act swiftly and boldly. "If the history of the 1930s teaches us anything, it is that appeasement of dictators is the sure road to world war. If aggression were allowed to succeed in Korea, it would be an open invitation to new acts of aggression elsewhere." American leadership was crucial, but so was the cooperation of other free countries. "The United Nations was able to act as it did in Korea because the free nations in the years since World War II have created a common determination to work together for peace and freedom." Fifty-three of the fifty-nine members of the UN were cooperating to oppose the challenge to peace; thirty had provided or pledged material support, including troops and weapons. Truman said that he had just received word that Greece was the latest country to offer troops. "This is welcome news. All of these troops will serve under the flag of the United Nations and under the United Nations commander, General MacArthur." The forces of freedom were still gathering; the UN troops were still outnumbered. "But their hard and valiant fight is bringing results. We hold a firm base of about 3,500 square miles. For weeks the enemy has been hammering, now at one spot, now at another, sometimes at many points at once. He has been beaten back each time with heavy loss. The enemy is spending his strength recklessly in desperate attacks. We believe the invasion has reached its peak. The task remaining is to crush it."

Several considerations guided American policy for the months ahead, Truman continued. First, the United States believed in the United Nations. "When we ratified its charter, we pledged ourselves to seek peace and security through this world organization. We kept our word when we went to the support of the United Nations in Korea two months ago. We shall never go back on that pledge." Second, the United States believed that the Koreans had a right to be free and united. "Under the direction and guidance of the United Nations, we, with others, will do our part to help them enjoy that right. The United States has no other aim in Korea." Third, the United States sought to contain the violence. "We do not want the fighting in Korea to expand into a general war. It will not spread unless Communist imperialism draws other armies and governments into the fight of the aggressors against the United Nations." Fourth, the United States particularly wanted to keep China out of the Korean conflict. "The Communist imperialists are the only ones who can gain if China moves into this fight."

Truman's fifth point took importance from the recent controversy with MacArthur. "We do not want Formosa or any part of Asia for ourselves. We believe that the future of Formosa, like that of every other territory in dispute, should be settled peacefully. We believe that it should be settled by international action, and not by the decision of the United States or any other state alone." American naval vessels patrolled off Formosa simply to deter new aggression. "The mission of the 7th Fleet is to keep Formosa out of the conflict. Our purpose is peace, not conquest."

Sixth, the United States sought freedom for all the countries of Asia. It had delivered freedom to the Philippines and was fighting for the freedom of Korea. The Soviet Union, by contrast, sought the opposite. "Russia has never voluntarily given up any territory it has acquired in the Far East; it has never given independence to any people who have fallen under its control."

Truman's seventh point addressed the Matthews flap. "We do not believe in aggressive or preventive war," Truman said. "Such war is the weapon of dictators, not of free democratic countries like the United States. We are arming only for the defense against aggression."

The corollary of this was Truman's final point. "We want peace and we shall achieve it." But peace required effort and sacrifice. "Our men are fighting for peace today in Korea. We are working for peace constantly in the United Nations and in all the capitals of the world. Our workers, our farmers, our businessmen, all our vast resources, are helping now to create the strength which will make peace secure." The world, through the United Nations, had called on the United States to lead the way to peace. "We have responded to that call. We will not fail."

TRUMAN'S SPEECH WAS for public consumption; in private the president and his most senior advisers pondered what would happen in Korea as the tide of fighting turned. In September 1950 the staff of Truman's National Security Council produced a blueprint for American policy in Korea. NSC 81 started with the past and worked to the present and future. "The political objective of the United Nations in Korea is to bring about the complete independence and unity of Korea in accordance with the General Assembly resolutions of November 14, 1947, December 12, 1948, and October 21, 1949," the paper said. "The United States has strongly supported this political objective." But no objective could be considered apart from the costs of achieving it. "If the present United Nations action in Korea can accomplish this objective without substantial risk of general war with the Soviet Union or Communist China, it would be in our interest to advocate the pressing of the United Nations action to this conclusion. It would not be in our national interest, however, nor presumably would other friendly members of the United Nations regard it as being in their interest, to take action in Korea which would involve a substantial risk of general war."

The president had to balance America's interest in unifying Korea against its interest in avoiding general war. The former would require sending UN forces across the 38th parallel and toward Korea's borders with the Soviet Union and Chinese Manchuria; the latter suggested doing so in a way that minimized the threat felt by the Russians and Chinese. The NSC authors thought it imperative that only ROK forces be employed in this sensitive task.

The authors could not stress this point too strongly. "In no circumstances should other U.N. forces"—particularly U.S. forces—"be used in the north-eastern province bordering the Soviet Union or in the area along the Manchurian border," they said.

22

Truman's public troubles with MacArthur and Matthews were still occasioning comment when another personnel matter exploded. Truman was not given to second-guessing himself, but he often regretted having chosen Louis Johnson for secretary of defense, and he sometimes wondered whether the legislation that had created the position, along with the rest of the modern American national security apparatus, was a good idea.

Since the eighteenth century American defense had rested upon a War Department and a separate Navy Department. The separation reflected America's distinctive approach to war and the country's peculiar position in the world. America's founders believed war would be an occasional endeavor best conducted by part-time soldiers: citizens called to arms on the rare occasions when geographically isolated America was attacked from abroad. Between wars they would be farmers, blacksmiths, merchants and the many other types of productive individuals a peaceful, prospering country required. Their model was Cincinnatus, the Roman hero who returned to his farm upon the defeat of Rome's enemies. Americans feared standing armies, which corrupted republics and tempted generals to seize political power; the negative example against which the Constitution and American practice were designed was Julius Caesar, the general who made himself dictator. The Constitution guarded against Caesarism by designating the president of the United States the commander-in-chief of America's armed forces; no general, however popular or ambitious, must overrule the president. American practice hedged against Caesarism by hollowing out the army between wars; the citizen-soldiers were sent home, leaving potential Caesars no one to command.

Americans worried much less about admirals seizing power. Ships were confined to the sea and to rivers, leaving the landed area of the country unthreatened. For this reason, and because navies took longer to build than armies, Americans who rejected the idea of a permanent army tolerated a permanent navy. It was small, and in wartime it was complemented by privateers—the marine equivalent of citizen-soldiers—but it was allowed a Navy Department of its own.

America's War and Navy Departments proceeded in comparative isolation from each other until the end of the nineteenth century. The U.S. navy assisted in the transport of army troops to foreign shores during the war with Mexico in the 1840s and the Spanish-American War of 1898. Navy warships convoyed army transports to Europe during World War I. But sustained joint combat operations awaited World War II, when they were most conspicuous in the Pacific theater. Douglas MacArthur, as Supreme Commander of Allied Forces in the Southwest Pacific Area, employed large elements of both the U.S. army and the U.S. navy (and elements of the armies and navies of America's allies) in the campaign against Japan. Coordinating the two services, with their separate bureaucracies, wasn't easy, and the friction, combined with an appreciation that future wars would require continued coordination, provided a strong argument for uniting the two services in a single executive department.

Yet unification might not have come without the Cold War. Had the years after World War II followed the pattern of earlier postwar eras, the army would have melted away and defense issues would have faded from the minds of voters and legislators. But the troubles with the Soviet Union caused the American government to remain focused on national security. Consequently Congress in 1947 approved the National Security Act, which placed the War and Navy Departments within a single Defense Department, which also included a new Department of the Air Force. The same act formally established the Joint Chiefs of Staff, the group of top officers that had come into being during World War II. The act created the National Security Council, a body of cabinet secretaries and other officials given the special charge of advising the president on national security policy. Finally, the 1947 act established the Central

Intelligence Agency, responsible for furnishing the president with information important to the conduct of American foreign policy.

The National Security Act stood as a lonely bright spot in Harry Truman's dealings that session with Congress, which trampled his veto of the Taft-Hartley Act just as it was approving the security act. Republicans were pleased with the efficiencies service unification promised, and they weren't especially bothered by the augmentation of presidential power implicit in unification and in the creation of the NSC and the CIA, for they expected to claim the presidency in the 1948 election.

Yet if approval of the act was straightforward, implementing it was not. Truman's first secretary of defense, James Forrestal, lasted a year and a half, making enemies in the uniformed services, in Congress and in the other executive departments before resigning under the strain of ill health. Truman's second try was Louis Johnson. "A big 250-pound bear, whose major goal was to work a miracle in the Pentagon—that is, bash heads, cut budgets, stop the interminable wrangling and truly unify the services," Omar Bradley said of Johnson and his agenda. The joint chiefs chairman added, "Johnson was flamboyant, outspoken and, rumor had it, had his eyes on the White House." Johnson's political ambitions were mentioned so often he felt obliged to deny them publicly, thereby fueling the rumor mills further.

Truman might have overlooked Johnson's ambitions, but he couldn't tolerate the disruption Johnson caused in the administration. "Louis began to show an inordinate egotistical desire to run the whole government," Truman recalled later. "He offended every member of the cabinet. We never had a cabinet meeting that he did not show plainly that he knew more about the problems of the Treasury, Commerce, Labor, Agriculture than did the Secretaries of those Departments." Truman didn't want to have to find a third defense secretary in less than three years, but by September 1950 he concluded that Johnson was more trouble than he was worth. "I made up my mind he had to go."

He knew just the man to replace Johnson, the man he would have chosen for defense secretary in the first place if he hadn't been serving already as secretary of state. George Marshall was Truman's ideal of the soldier as public servant, an officer who put the national interest above personal interest and definitely above any party interest. Marshall had stepped down from the State Department to enjoy a well-earned retirement. Truman felt badly about recalling him to service, but there was no one of comparable stature and experience he could turn to. The unified Defense Department *had* to be made to work, the president judged; the nation's security demanded it. Forrestal and Johnson had failed to accomplish the feat. Marshall was his last hope. If Marshall couldn't do the job, no one could. A bonus for Truman was that Marshall's military stature would lend authority to the president in case of a showdown with Douglas MacArthur.

Truman sought to handle the transition with delicacy. "Tomorrow I have to break the bad news to Louis Johnson," he wrote to Bess on September 7. "I think I have a way to do it that will not be too hard on him. General Marshall came to see me yesterday. I told him what I had in mind. He said, 'Mr. President, you have only to tell me what you want, and I'll do it. But I want you to think about the fact that my appointment may reflect upon you and your administration. They are still charging me with the downfall of Chiang's government in China. I want to help, not to hurt you.'" Truman concluded the story to Bess in a tone of the deepest admiration: "Can you think of anyone else saying that? I can't." Truman hoped Johnson would yield to Marshall quietly. "He can make himself a hero if he'll do that. If he doesn't, I shall simply fire him."

Johnson declined the hero role, and Truman fired him. The president immediately announced the nomination of Marshall. Ordinarily only the Senate would have had to approve the nomination, but the National Security Act prohibited the appointment of any person as secretary of defense who had been on active service in the military within ten years of the appointment. A special bill would have to be introduced and passed by both houses of Congress, waiving the ten-year rule. Truman didn't think this would be a problem, and in fact it proved not to be. Some congressional Republicans greeted the Marshall nomination as Marshall had warned: by raising the China issue again. But large majorities in both houses held Marshall in the same esteem Truman did, and the waiver bill passed each house by a margin of more than two to one. The confirmation hearing in the Senate lasted less than an hour; the upper house then confirmed Marshall's nomination by a vote of 57 to 11.

23

MacArthur probably never read NSC 81, and if he did he apparently took as mere advice its admonitions to avoid the risk of general war and to keep U.S. troops away from the border of China. MacArthur had his own ideas of how war should be waged, and he was sure they were better than those of armchair strategists thousands of miles from the theater of combat.

He knew that Korea was his final campaign. At seventy he was already far past the age when most soldiers had entered retirement or Valhalla. He intended to crown his career with his most brilliant operation. The plan had been forming in his mind since the retreat from the Han River in the war's first weeks. His ships controlled the seas around Korea, his planes the air above the peninsula. Johnnie Walker's Eighth Army had stabilized the front outside Pusan. "I was now finally ready for the last great stroke to bring my plan into fruition," he recalled later. "My Han River dream as a possibility had begun to assume the certainties of reality—a turning movement deep into the flank and rear of the enemy that would sever his supply lines and encircle all his forces south of Seoul." MacArthur conceived of military command as a genre of art; this would be his pièce de résistance. "I had made similar decisions in past campaigns, but none more fraught with danger, none that promised to be more vitally conclusive if successful."

He selected Inchon, the port city west of Seoul, as his target. Few enemy forces defended Inchon, for nature had done so itself. Tides that were among the highest in the world drained the harbor twice a day, exposing broad mudflats that mired hapless vessels. Only on the highest tides would a landing by a large military force be even conceivable. The next such tide would occur in the middle of September. MacArthur cabled the joint chiefs what he had in mind. "Operation planned mid-September is amphibious landing of two division corps in rear of enemy lines for purpose of enveloping and destroying enemy forces in conjunction with attack from south by Eighth Army," he said. "I am firmly convinced that early and strong effort behind his front will sever his main lines of communication and enable us to deliver a decisive and crushing blow."

The chiefs were skeptical. Omar Bradley was on record as saying advances in weaponry had rendered amphibious operations obsolete. MacArthur's operation would be spearheaded by marines, and the chiefs knew that Truman, an old army man, didn't like marines. In response to a recommendation by a member of Congress that the marines be granted recognition as a full-fledged service and represented on the Joint Chiefs of Staff, Truman had replied, "For your information the Marine Corps is the Navy's police force and as long as I am President that is what it will remain. They have a propaganda machine that is almost equal to Stalin's."

The chiefs, with Truman's approval, tried to talk MacArthur out of his Inchon plan. Joe Collins and Forrest Sherman flew to Tokyo. MacArthur summoned the officers who had been assigned to formulate the several aspects of the plan. They briefed him and Collins and Sherman and displayed varying degrees of confidence. Admiral James Doyle had examined the amphibious part of the attack; he declared to MacArthur and the others, "General, I have not been asked nor have I volunteered my opinion about this landing. If I were asked, however, the best I can say is that Inchon is not impossible."

MacArthur listened, smoking his pipe. When the briefers finished, Collins and Sherman expected him to respond. He took his time, apparently weighing the remarks just made. In fact he was preparing the stage for his entrance. "I could feel the tension rising in the room," he recounted afterward. "If ever a silence was pregnant, this one was." He sensed a comforting spirit from his past. "I could almost hear my father's voice telling me as he had so many years ago, 'Doug, councils of war breed timidity and defeatism.'"

He stood and started pacing. After several steps he began speaking. "The bulk of the Reds are committed around Walker's defense perimeter," he said. "The enemy, I am convinced, has failed to prepare Inchon properly for defense. The very arguments you have made as to the impracticalities involved will tend to ensure for me the element of surprise, for the enemy commander will reason that no one would be so brash as to make such an attempt. Surprise is the most vital element for success in war. As an example, the Marquis de Montcalm believed in 1759 that it was impossible for an armed force to scale the precipitous river banks south of the then walled city of Quebec, and therefore concentrated his formidable defenses along the more vulnerable banks north of the city. But General James Wolfe and a small force did indeed come up the St. Lawrence River and scale those heights. On the Plains of Abraham, Wolfe won a stunning victory that was made possible almost entirely by surprise. Thus he captured Quebec and in effect ended the French and Indian War. Like Montcalm, the North Koreans would regard an Inchon landing as impossible. Like Wolfe, I could take them by surprise."

MacArthur acknowledged that the objections the navy had made to the operation were germane and important. "But they are not insuperable," he said. "My confidence in the Navy is complete, and in fact I seem to have more confidence in the Navy than the Navy has in itself. The Navy's rich experience in staging the numerous amphibious landings under my command in the Pacific during the late war, frequently under somewhat similar difficulties, leaves me with little doubt on that score."

Collins and the army were urging a landing at Kunsan, on the west coast. "It would indeed eliminate many of the hazards of Inchon," MacArthur conceded, "but it would be largely ineffective and indecisive. It would be an attempted envelopment which would not envelop. It would not sever or destroy the enemy's supply lines or distribution center, and would therefore serve little purpose. It would be a short envelopment, and nothing in war is more futile. Better no flank movement than one such as this." Better, too, simply to send the troops to Walker outside Pusan. But neither would this meet the requirements of the hour. "To fight frontally in a breakthrough from Pusan will be bloody and indecisive. The enemy will merely roll back on his lines of supply and communication."

The only way forward was Inchon, MacArthur said. "Seizure of Inchon and Seoul will cut the enemy's supply line and seal off the entire southern peninsula. The vulnerability of the enemy is his supply position. Every step southward extends his transport lines and renders them more frail and subject to dislocation. The several major lines of enemy supply from the north converge on Seoul, and from Seoul they radiate to the several sectors of the front. By seizing Seoul I would completely paralyze the enemy's supply system—coming and going. This in turn will paralyze the fighting power of the troops that now face Walker. Without munitions and food they will soon be helpless and disorganized, and can easily be overpowered by our smaller but well-supplied forces."

MacArthur moved to his peroration. "The only alternative to a stroke such as I propose will be the continuation of the savage sacrifice we are making at Pusan, with no hope of relief in sight. Are you content to let our troops stay in that bloody perimeter like beef cattle in the slaughter-house? Who will take the responsibility of such a tragedy? Certainly not I." The consequences of the decision at hand would be felt far and long. "The prestige of the Western world hangs in the balance. Oriental millions are watching the outcome. It is plainly apparent that here in Asia is where the Communist conspirators have elected to make their play for global conquest. The test is not in Berlin or Vienna, in London, Paris or Washington. It is here and now—it is along the Naktong River in South Korea. We have joined the issue on the battlefield." This was more than the free world was doing in Europe. "We here fight Europe's war with arms, while there it is still confined to words. If we lose the war to communism in Asia, the fate of Europe will be gravely jeopardized. Win it, and Europe will probably be saved from war and stay free. Make the wrong decision here—the fatal decision of inertia—and we will be done. I can almost hear the ticking of the second hand of destiny. We must act now or we will die."

MacArthur volunteered to take full responsibility for whatever happened. "If my estimate is inaccurate and should I run into a defense with which I cannot cope, I will be there personally and will immediately withdraw our forces before they are committed to a bloody setback. The only loss then will be my personal reputation." But this would not happen. "Inchon will not fail. Inchon will succeed. And it will save 100,000 lives."

IN A LIFETIME of dramatic performances, MacArthur had never been more persuasive. It helped that he outranked everyone in the room, but he also outmaneuvered them, and the president in Washington as well. Neither the joint chiefs nor Truman could reject his promise to save 100,000 lives, given before witnesses who could be counted on to remember and testify if called upon to do so. He knew he had friends in Congress who were blaming the president for the loss of China and would be quick to blame him for the loss of Korea. He raised the stakes in saying that much more hinged on the pending decision: all of Asia, even Europe. The timing was perfect, too. The president had just slapped him publicly over Formosa, for striving too hard to defend freedom from godless communism. The president couldn't afford to slap him again. The president couldn't say no to Inchon.

The president didn't say no. Collins and Sherman reported MacArthur's bravura performance to Washington. The joint chiefs let themselves be persuaded, and Truman accepted their decision. The landing was scheduled for the highest tide of September, on the fifteenth.

THE PREPARATIONS WERE made, the troops and ships gathered and positioned. MacArthur felt the surge of excitement he had felt before every major challenge. All boded well, he thought, for the conclusive operation of his final campaign.

And then: "It was at this eleventh hour that I received a message from the Joint Chiefs of Staff which chilled me to the marrow of my bones." A decade later he still felt the shock. "The message expressed doubt of success and implied the whole movement should be abandoned. It read in part: 'We have noted with considerable concern the recent trend of events in Korea. In the light of the commitment of all the reserves available to the Eighth Army, we desire your estimate as to the feasibility and chance of success of projected operation if initiated on planned schedule.'" MacArthur sensed the stifling timidity of Washington. "What could have given rise to such a query at such an hour?" he asked himself. "Had someone in Washington lost his nerve? Could it be the President? Or Marshall, who had just become Secretary of Defense? Or Bradley? Or was it merely an anticipating alibi if the operation should run into trouble?"

MacArthur reacted at once. "I regard the chance of success as excellent," he scribbled in reply. "I go further in belief that it represents the only hope of wresting the initiative from the enemy and thereby presenting the opportunity for a decisive blow. To do otherwise is to commit us to a war of indefinite duration, of gradual attrition and of doubtful result." MacArthur wanted this on the record in writing: that the blood of American soldiers in a prolonged Asian war would be on those who denied him his chance at Inchon. "The embarkation of the troops and preliminary air and naval preparations are proceeding according to schedule," he told the chiefs. "I repeat that I and all of my commanders and staff officers, without exception, are enthusiastic for and confident of the success of the enveloping movement."

He sent the message and awaited an answer. "Was it possible, I asked myself, that even now, when it was all but impossible to bring this great movement grinding to a halt, timidity in an office thousands of miles away, even if by a President himself, could stop the golden opportunity to turn defeat into victory?" When the answer arrived, it corroborated his suspicion of the source of the hesitancy. The joint chiefs said they approved the operation and had "so informed the President." MacArthur thought the language odd but significant. "I interpreted this to mean that it had been the President who had threatened to interfere and overrule, on a professional military problem, his military advisers."

MACARTHUR READ TOO much into the message. The joint chiefs were the ones with the second thoughts. Omar Bradley knew from his own sources that MacArthur exaggerated the enthusiasm of his lieutenants for the Inchon operation. "A majority of MacArthur's staff—especially the naval and Marine officers—held gravest reservations about Inchon," Bradley recalled. "It was the wildest kind of military plan—Pattonesque."

Yet Bradley and the others deferred to MacArthur. If a commander of his stature and record expressed such confidence, they weren't going to hold him back. At the very least, they had his assurance of success on the record. If something went wrong, the blame would be his.

24

MAGGIE HIGGINS WASN'T surprised that she had to talk her way onto one of the assault ships for the Inchon invasion. The navy was even more gynephobic than the army; women on ships taunted Neptune in ways that made admirals and captains very nervous. She was told there weren't facilities for women. She was directed to a hospital ship. But her reputation apparently preceded her, and a last-minute change of orders allowed her to board one of the assault transports.

The briefings she attended revealed what the invaders were up against. "Our assault was to be made on 'Red Beach,' which wasn't really a beach at all but a rough sea wall of big boulders," she wrote. "At the moment of the first landing, the wall would tower twelve feet above the water line. Engineers had improvised wooden ladders with big steel hooks on top to enable the first wave of troops to scramble over the wall. Aerial photographs showed deep trenches dug on the inland side of the wall. If any enemy guard was still on the wall when we struck, it would be murder. The channel approaching Inchon Harbor was so narrow that the transports would have to anchor at least nine miles away from the assault beaches. Space in the harbor was reserved for warships."

The invasion fleet comprised 260 vessels. Sixty armored warships went first; these included destroyers that deliberately steamed within range of the North Korean shore batteries to draw their fire and reveal the batteries' location. The maneuver worked, and naval artillery and warplanes pounded the discovered guns.

After forty-eight hours of bombardment, the initial wave of landings hit Wolmi Island at dawn on September 15. Wolmi sat in Inchon's harbor and controlled the approaches. The operation proceeded well, and Higgins's transport, scheduled for the second assault wave, moved into position. A final briefing underscored the need for everything to happen on schedule. "The tide would be at the right height for only four hours," Higgins recorded. "We would strike at five-thirty, half an hour before dead high. Assault waves, consisting of six landing craft lined up abreast, would hit the beach at two-minute intervals. This part of the operation had to be completed within an hour in order to permit the approach of larger landing ship tanks (LSTs), which would supply us with all our heavy equipment. The LSTs would hit the beach at high tide and then, as the waters ebbed away, be stranded helplessly on the mud flats. After eight o'clock, sea approaches to the assaulting marines would be cut off until the next high tide."

Higgins and the marines she accompanied awaited their turn. "Wave Number Five," came the shout. "We threaded our way through the confusion on deck to our prearranged position," Higgins wrote. "Our wave commander, Lieutenant R. J. Shening, yelled at us to be careful climbing down the cargo nets into our craft. The cargo nets were made of huge, rough ropes. The trick was to hang onto the big knots with all your strength while you groped with your feet for the swaying rungs below. I dropped last into the boat, which was now packed with thirty-eight heavily laden marines, ponchos on their backs and rifles on their shoulders. As we shoved away from the transport sheets of spray were flung back upon us by the wind."

Their boat circled to gather with the other craft in Wave Five. Some of the marines showed their excitement; others affected nonchalance. Two played gin rummy on the engine cover, apparently oblivious to all but their cards. After picking up the other craft, Wave Five headed through the channel. "It was an ear-shattering experience," Higgins wrote. "We had to thread our way past the carriers and cruisers that were booming away at the beach, giving it a deadly final pounding. The quake and roar of the rocket ships was almost unendurable."

They circled past Wolmi, which showed the effects of the bombardment. What wasn't wrecked was burning. H hour approached and the seawall came into view. "Suddenly the great naval barrage lifted and there was gigantic silence." But only briefly. "The sky began to roar and the planes zoomed in, bombing and strafing the sea wall. It didn't seem possible that anything could survive the terrific hail of explosives."

Then silence again. This was the moment. The control ship signaled their craft's turn. "Here we go—keep your heads down!" Lieutenant Shening yelled. His warning came just in time. "Brightly colored tracer bullets cut across our bow and across the open top of our boat," Higgins recorded. The artillery and air barrage hadn't silenced all the defenders. "Somehow the enemy had survived the terrible pounding they'd been getting. No matter what had happened to the first four waves, the Reds had sighted us and their aim was excellent. We all hunched deep into the boat." Higgins noticed that the nonchalance had vanished; even the gin rummy players were edgy.

The boat ran hard into a low spot in the seawall. Still under machine gun fire, the marines were slow to debark. "Come on, you big brave marines!" Lieutenant Shening shouted. "Let's get the hell out of here!"

The marines jumped over the side and into three feet of water. Higgins followed, carrying her typewriter. They scrambled onto the seawall and flattened in the low spot, trying to stay beneath the bullets whistling overhead. "Suddenly there was a great surge of water," Higgins recounted. "A huge LST was bearing down on us, its plank door halfway down. A few more feet and we would be smashed. Everyone started shouting and, tracer bullets or no, we got out of there." But not all of them. Two marines had their feet crushed by the LST.

The marines and Higgins ran across what passed for the beach and huddled behind a mound of dirt. The marines kept moving, toward a cliff farther inland. Several were mowed down by the enemy fire. Several more were hit by friendly fire when an LST mistook them for the enemy.

Eventually the mass and power of the invading force overwhelmed the remaining defenders. Red Beach was secured. Blue Beach, the third objective after Red and Wolmi, was similarly captured. The counter-offensive was well begun.

25

H IGGINS AND THE other frontline reporters disdained the "headquarters correspondents" who followed the generals around. But MacArthur insisted on his entourage, whose members were suitably impressed. "Today, as on eleven previous landings he personally led during World War II, General MacArthur had no qualms about exposing himself to enemy fire," one related. "Wearing his familiar sweat-stained, braided campaign cap and crisp sun-tans, he watched the first phase of the joint sea and land operation open at dawn. Seated in the lookout chair aboard the flagship of Rear Adm. James H. Doyle, commander of the assault force, General MacArthur watched the beaches tremble under the bombardment of United States and British warships. Then, three and one-half hours after Marine units seized little Wolmi Island, in Inchon Harbor, General MacArthur and his staff boarded a launch. They cruised within rifle range of the North Koreans off a second beach on the edge of Inchon. Shells thundered over the launch as Allied warcraft bombarded the beach. There was no return fire."

During the weeks of preparation for the Inchon operation, even casual observers in Japan had realized something was afoot. The official name of the operation was Chromite, but reporters referred to it as Operation Common Knowledge. The North Koreans doubtless concluded that an attack was coming. Yet MacArthur contrived to keep them guessing where it would occur. His ships and planes misleadingly pounded Kunsan, which seemed the likelier target anyway.

And so when his real attack occurred at Inchon, the surprise was effectively complete. The North Koreans had failed to mine most of the Inchon harbor, apparently discounting the possibility of attack, as MacArthur assumed they would. His naval arm justified his confidence in its ability to handle the tides, and after his ship-mounted guns and Japan-based warplanes softened the shore defenses, his marines secured a beachhead and then the city with but modest casualties.

They were followed shortly by army units that complemented the marines to form X Corps, which drove swiftly inland toward Seoul and Kimpo airfield, the most important air facility in Korea. Kimpo fell first; Seoul held out for ten days. But by the month's end the North Korean garrison there had been killed, captured or dispersed.

Meanwhile Johnnie Walker's Eighth Army broke out of the Pusan perimeter and pressed hard to the north. The North Koreans, with X Corps cutting off their line of retreat, broke and ran. The enemy was trapped, MacArthur told reporters, and would soon be deprived of supplies. "If that can be accomplished, these forces will sooner or later disintegrate and cease to be a coordinated fighting enemy." Long experience decreed the outcome. "The history of war proves that nine times out of ten an army has been destroyed because its supply lines have been cut off. That's what we are trying to do."

Events unfolded as MacArthur predicted. The pincers of X Corps and the Eighth Army closed upon the North Koreans, who surrendered by the tens of thousands. Johnnie Walker proclaimed victory. "As far as we are concerned, the war is over," he said on September 25. "The enemy's army has disintegrated into ineffective pockets which have no real offensive power."

MacArthur agreed. "While mopping-up fighting is still in progress in this area," he declared on September 27, "all effective escape routes are closed and the fate of the North Korean forces caught in this pocket is sealed."

HE PREPARED TO reinstall Syngman Rhee in Seoul. The ceremony, he judged, suited the Oriental mind, which placed great store in such gestures. "But at this juncture I received an astonishing message from Washington," he recalled. "In an order, undoubtedly instigated by the

State Department, and reflecting its antagonism toward President Rhee, the Joint Chiefs of Staff admonished me that any plan for the restoration of his government 'must have the approval of higher authority.'"

In fact the chiefs were simply taking care not to cross the line from military affairs into politics, but MacArthur responded as vehemently as he had to their eleventh-hour questioning of the Inchon attack. "Your message is not understood," he wrote. "I have no plan whatsoever except scrupulously to implement the directives I have received. These directives envision support of the resolutions of the United Nations Security Council of 25 and 27 June, calling upon member governments to furnish 'such assistance to the Republic of Korea as may be necessary to repel the armed attacks and to restore international peace and security in the area.'" The existing government of South Korea was the only government recognized by the United States and the United Nations. It had never ceased to function but had simply been driven from its lawful capital by communist bandits. Now that the bandits had been defeated, it was returning to the capital. "This of course involves no reestablishment of government, nor indeed any change in government, but merely a restoration of the existing government to its constitutional seat."

Without awaiting a reply, MacArthur proceeded with his plan. He brought Walker and X Corps commander Ned Almond to Seoul to receive the Distinguished Service Cross. He addressed Rhee and other officials of the Korean government, and implicitly the world at large. "By the grace of merciful Providence," he said, "our forces fighting under the standard of that greatest hope and inspiration of mankind, the United Nations, have liberated this ancient capital city of Korea. It has been freed from the despotism of Communist rule and its citizens once more have the opportunity for that immutable concept of life which holds invincibly to the primacy of individual liberty and personal dignity."

Flouting his order from Washington, MacArthur continued, "In behalf of the United Nations, I am happy to restore to you, Mr. President, the seat of your Government, that from it you may the better fulfill your constitutional responsibility."

He thereupon sought a higher endorsement than any that could come from Washington. "In humble and devout manifestation of gratitude to the Almighty God for bringing this decisive victory to our arms, I ask that all present rise and join me in reciting the Lord's Prayer." His audience did as he bade. "Our Father, which art in heaven," they said as one. They proceeded to the end: "For Thine is the kingdom and the power and the glory forever. Amen."

MacArthur closed in his own words. "Mr. President," he said, again addressing Rhee, "my officers and I will now resume our military duties and leave you and your government to the discharge of civil responsibility."

He later recalled Rhee's response. "'We admire you,' he said with tears flowing down his cheeks. 'We love you as the savior of our race.'" MacArthur added, "And when the ceremony was over the people of Seoul lined the streets and clapped and waved their little paper flags."

"INCHON PROVED TO be the luckiest military operation in history," Omar Bradley remarked. The surprise of the North Koreans was "astonishing," he said; the whole affair was a "military miracle." And it cemented MacArthur's ascendancy over the joint chiefs and all the other critics, Bradley admitted. "The swiftness and magnitude of the victory were mind-boggling. We had been on the point of despair, bracing for a 'Dunkirk' at Pusan and/or a disaster at Inchon. A mere two weeks later the North Korean Army had been routed and all South Korea had been regained. MacArthur was deservedly canonized as a 'military genius.' Inchon was his boldest and most dazzling victory. In hindsight, the JCS seemed like a bunch of Nervous Nellies to have doubted."

The administration had no choice but to offer congratulations. George Marshall cabled MacArthur, "Accept my personal tribute to the courageous campaign you directed in Korea and the daring and perfect strategical operation which virtually terminated the struggle."

To which MacArthur replied, "Thanks, George, for your fine message. It brings back vividly the memories of past wars and the complete coordination and perfect unity of cooperation which has always existed in our mutual relationship and martial endeavors."

Truman was happy to join the cheering, despite his previous misgivings about MacArthur, for the war seemed all but over. MacArthur's Eighth Army and X Corps were closing in on the North Korean army. More than a hundred thousand of the enemy had been captured already; seizing the rest appeared a matter of time. The United Nations, with America's strong assistance and MacArthur's inspired leadership, had fulfilled its mission of restoring peace and order to Korea and destroying the army that had broken the peace and subverted order. MacArthur had been insolent, even insubordinate, but he had come through magnificently in the end. He might retire now or very shortly. Truman could afford to be generous.

So the president was. "I know that I speak for the entire American people when I send you my warmest congratulations on the victory which has been achieved under your leadership in Korea," he cabled MacArthur. "Few operations in military history can match either the delaying action where you traded space for time in which to build up your forces, or the brilliant maneuver which has now resulted in the liberation of Seoul." Truman asked MacArthur to convey congratulations to the officers and men of the services under his command. "My thanks and the thanks of the people of all the free nations go out to your gallant forces—soldiers, sailors, marines and air men from the United States and the other countries fighting for freedom under the United Nations banner. I salute you all, and say to all of you from all of us at home, 'Well and nobly done.'"

26

Y ET THE WAR wasn't quite over. Some loose ends remained. "Mr. President, have you decided what our troops will do when they reach the 38th parallel in Korea?" a reporter inquired at Truman's first news conference after the Inchon landing.

"No, I have not," Truman answered. The decision, he explained, was not his to make. "That is a matter for the United Nations to decide. That is a United Nations force, and we are one of the many who are interested in that situation. It will be worked out by the United Nations and I will abide by the decision that the United Nations makes."

But the United Nations offered no clear guidance. The decision-making process there had been complicated by the return of the Soviet delegate, and the sudden reversal of fortunes on the battlefield outpaced the ability of the members of the anti–North Korean coalition to decide what their war aims were.

MacArthur's troops got closer to the North Korean border. Again Truman faced questions. "Mr. President," a reporter asked at the next news conference, "has this government given General MacArthur specific authority to cross the 38th parallel?"

Truman still dodged. "That is a matter I can't answer publicly now." The president paused. "I will give you the answer at the proper time. We haven't reached the 38th parallel yet."

"I wonder if I could ask you this question," the reporter persisted. "Do you consider that he has implied authority to cross—"

Truman interrupted the question. "General MacArthur is under direct orders of the president and the chief of staff, and he will follow those orders," he said.

"Do those orders imply, sir, the crossing of the 38th parallel?"

"I can't answer the question."

The reporters moved briefly to other subjects before returning. "Mr. President, you said a week or so ago that the matter of crossing the 38th parallel was a United Nations decision?"

"That is correct."

"And you said today that General MacArthur is under your direct orders?"

"That is correct, but the United Nations will have to act on it first. I appointed General MacArthur as the Supreme Commander, at the request of the United Nations. They have certainly requested—will make a request of me, if they want further orders issued to General MacArthur."

"Mr. President, there was an interpretation at the State Department today that the original United Nations resolution gave General MacArthur the right to go over the 38th parallel if he deemed it necessary. Do you—"

"The original United Nations resolution was very broad," Truman said.

"In connection with the Korean situation, sir, American authorities in the United Nations have given out a six-point program for a settlement of the Korean situation. Have you seen it and would you care to comment on it?"

"You mean the broadcast asking them to surrender?"

"No sir. What I was thinking of was a plan for the settlement of the Korean situation based on our point of view."

"It hasn't been taken up with me."

Truman suddenly realized he had said too much. There had been no broadcast asking for surrender. The president fumbled as he tried to step back. "The broadcast of General MacArthur—I think made today—was taken up with me, inviting them to surrender. I think he is making that broadcast today. You will have to consider that off the record, however, until General MacArthur makes the broadcast."

Reporters agreed, yet kept asking. "Mr. President, is that a demand for unconditional surrender?"

"You will have to wait for General MacArthur's broadcast, and then I will comment on that and answer your question."

"Could you tell us when you expect him to make it?"

Truman turned to his press secretary. "I think some time today, isn't it, Charlie?"

"I think it is today," Charlie Ross replied.

"I think it is today," Truman repeated. "I think he is going to make it today, and then you can get the release of it from the State Department."

In FACT IT wasn't until two days later that MacArthur issued his surrender demand. Truman couldn't decide if the general was trying to make him look bad or if there was a more innocent explanation. MacArthur didn't enlighten him.

"The early and total defeat and complete destruction of your armed forces and war-making potential is now inevitable," MacArthur declared, when he finally issued his statement. He was addressing the commander of North Korean forces, in words that were translated into Korean and disseminated by radio from Seoul and Tokyo and in leaflets dropped from airplanes over North Korea. "In order that the decisions of the United Nations may be carried out with a minimum of further loss of life and destruction of property, I, as the United Nations Commander in Chief, call upon you and the forces under your command, in whatever part of Korea situated, forthwith to lay down your arms and cease hostilities under such military supervisions as I may direct." MacArthur also demanded the immediate release of all UN prisoners of war. "I shall anticipate your early decision upon this opportunity to avoid the further useless shedding of blood and destruction of property."

HAD THE NORTH Koreans accepted MacArthur's surrender demand, the question of the 38th parallel would have been rendered militarily moot; when they rejected it, the issue became acute. The crux of the matter was that the UN resolutions authorizing the war were vague as to how far the UN commander's authority ran, while MacArthur's military needs were specific. He wanted to exploit the disorder among the North Koreans and destroy their army, even if this required crossing into North Korea. His planes had been penetrating North Korean airspace for months; he saw no reason his troops shouldn't enter North Korea on the ground. By doing so, they could shorten the war and save many lives. But the politics of crossing were murky. MacArthur might end up occupying North Korea, which was more than Washington had bargained for when the fighting began, and definitely more than most of the countries that backed the UN mission had expected. An incursion into North Korea, moreover, might provoke a response from the Soviet Union or China and thereby risk widening the war.

In the glow of Inchon, the Truman administration decided to take a risk. The president approved instructions from the Joint Chiefs of Staff to MacArthur that were based on NSC 81 and strove to balance opportunity against risk. "Your military objective is the destruction of the North Korean armed forces," the chiefs declared on September 27. "In attaining this objective you are authorized to conduct military operations, including amphibious and airborne landings or ground operations north of the 38th Parallel in Korea, provided that at the time of such operation there has been no entry into North Korea by major Soviet or Chinese Communist forces, no announcement of intended entry, nor a threat to counter our operations militarily in North Korea." In other words, MacArthur could cross the 38th parallel as long as his only foe was the North Koreans.

Yet he must do everything he could to make sure the North Koreans *remained* his only foe. "Under no circumstances," the order continued, "will your forces cross the Manchurian or USSR borders of Korea and, as a matter of policy, no non-Korean ground forces will be used in the northeast provinces bordering the Soviet Union or in the area along the Manchurian border. Furthermore, support of your operations north or south of the 38th parallel will not include air or naval action against Manchuria or against USSR territory."

MACARTHUR MADE NO objection. He responded to the joint chiefs with an outline of his military plans. If the North Koreans rejected his surrender demand, the Eighth Army would cross the 38th parallel and drive to Pyongyang. X Corps would make an amphibious landing at Wonsan, on the east coast one hundred miles north of the 38th parallel, with the goal of effecting a juncture with the Eighth Army and cutting

North Korea in two. Operations in the northern part of North Korea would be reserved to ROK forces. MacArthur added, "There is no indication at present of entry into North Korea by major Soviet or Chinese Communist forces."

The chiefs approved MacArthur's plan. George Marshall attached a personal note. "We want you to feel unhampered tactically and strategically to proceed north of 38th parallel," the defense secretary told MacArthur.

All the same, Marshall suggested that MacArthur not make a public announcement on the subject. He should simply act. In this Marshall was relating the administration's reading of the politics of the United Nations. "Evident desire is not to be confronted with necessity of a vote on passage of 38th parallel," Marshall said of the international body. "Rather to find you have found it militarily necessary to do so."

MacArthur accepted and confirmed the authorization. "Parallel 38 is not a factor in the military employment of our forces," he replied. "Unless and until the enemy capitulates, I regard all of Korea open for our military operations."

27

T RUMAN HAD NEVER met MacArthur, and with the fighting in Korea approaching a successful conclusion, he judged it was about time. "We had never had any personal contacts at all," he remembered, "and I thought that he ought to know his Commander in Chief and that I ought to know the senior field commander in the Far East."

He tested the idea of a meeting with MacArthur on George Marshall, who approved, and then Acheson. "The President did not wish to do this if we had any doubts about it," Acheson recorded. Truman told Acheson what he had in mind. "He would like to review with General MacArthur the situation in Korea, the probable future developments and the length of time necessary for the maintenance of American forces there. He would also like to appraise the possibilities of possible Chinese interference in Korea, which the President thought was not likely, and also possible Chinese interference in Indochina."

Acheson endorsed the idea of a meeting. "I said to the President that we had been giving the matter a good deal of thought in the Department and were prepared to agree with his judgment and that of General Marshall in favor of the trip." Yet Acheson had one worry. "I hoped strongly that the policy in regard to Formosa would not become unsettled because I thought this was critical in our relations with China, and that we had made a good deal of progress with other members of the United Nations by advocating a United Nations commission and UN consideration of the future of Formosa along with a UN resolution against any military action either way."

Truman said all would be well. "The President assured me that I need not have any worries on this account."

Even so, Acheson didn't want to take chances. Truman cabled MacArthur suggesting a meeting either in Hawaii or on Wake Island. MacArthur said he couldn't possibly travel farther than Wake Island, two thousand miles from Tokyo (and seven thousand miles from Washington). Truman accepted MacArthur's preference. They agreed on Sunday, October 15, as the day of the meeting. Acheson thereupon wrote a script for a full day of talks. The president and the general would devote the morning to Korea, covering military operations and the reconstruction of the country after the fighting ended. They would lunch together. In the afternoon they would speak of "Japan, Philippines, others," Acheson wrote. He took care to leave Formosa off the list. Later in the afternoon the president and the general would meet alone, away from their staffs. Dinner would follow. After dinner a press release would be issued and any loose ends from the day tied up.

The Acheson script included talking points for Truman. "General MacArthur should be complimented for the splendid way in which he and his command have responded to the United Nations aspects of the Korean problem; he should be given the full flavor of United States public and Congressional opinion on the United Nations side." MacArthur bore primary responsibility for military matters, but he must be reminded to defer to the UN on anything political. "In working out political questions such as unification, we shall be able to influence the situation greatly, but our influence must be exercised through the United Nations and to the general satisfaction of the United Nations."

Above all, MacArthur should be made to understand that it was essential that the Korean fighting not spread. "We must do everything we can to localize the conflict in Korea," Acheson declared. "Politically, we must assure the Chinese and the Soviets that they are not being threatened militarily in Korea but we must also keep before them the recklessness of active intervention on their part. Militarily, we must use extreme measures to prevent incidents involving United Nations forces and Chinese or Soviet forces or territory."

Acheson couched several points as questions the president might put to the general. "How feasible is it to consider the use of only Korean forces in the extreme north of Korea and Asiatic forces (Indian, Pakistani, Filipino, Turkish, etc.) in the general area of the 39th–40th parallel, with United States forces more generally in the south? Should we make a strong effort to find Asiatic troops as a 'buffer' between United States forces and the Manchurian and Siberian borders?" Most crucially: "What are General MacArthur's own views about Soviet and Chinese intentions re Korea?"

Acheson didn't want Truman to raise the Formosa issue, but he supposed MacArthur might. He prepped the president accordingly. "We have full appreciation of the strategic position of Formosa and of General MacArthur's views on this subject. But we also have very much in mind the general international situation and the moral and practical value of keeping the support of an overwhelming majority of the United Nations for our action in the Far East. Our present tactic is directed toward getting international support for the military neutralization of Formosa and for an international determination that the problem of Formosa must be settled by peaceful means."

Acheson's advice and other briefings for the trip were closely held. The trip itself was not announced until the day before the president left. "General MacArthur and I are making a quick trip over the coming weekend to meet in the Pacific," Truman explained in a written statement. For reasons of security he declined to specify where in the Pacific they would meet. He said he would convey to the general the appreciation of the American people for his service on behalf of the United States and the United Nations. "He is carrying out his mission with the imagination, courage and effectiveness which have marked his entire service as one of our greatest military leaders." Truman added that they would be discussing the final phase of the war and the withdrawal of American troops. "We should like to get our armed forces out and back to their other duties at the earliest moment consistent with the fulfillment of our obligations as a member of the United Nations."

MacArthur smelled a partisan rat in the Wake Island planning. He still resented having been used by Roosevelt in 1944, and he suspected Truman of trying to steal some of his Inchon-burnished glory just weeks ahead of the 1950 midterm elections. The general complained to William Sebald that the Wake Island meeting was a "political junket." His suspicions deepened as he prepared his traveling party. American reporters in Japan asked to accompany him to Wake Island. He was inclined to say yes but thought he should check with the Pentagon. "In view of the number of Washington correspondents announced as coming, I assumed that the Tokyo representatives would be permitted to attend also, especially as my plane could accommodate a large representation," MacArthur wrote later. "I passed their requests along to the Pentagon, recommending approval, and was surprised when the request was promptly and curtly disapproved."

Things might not have happened just as MacArthur recalled. He told Sebald at the time that he liked traveling to Wake with a very small party. "The idea of the General appears to be that President Truman will arrive with a powerful staff of advisers (Gen. Bradley, Harriman, Jessup, Rusk, Pace) and a plane-load of newspapermen and photographers, while he, the General, will be alone and without advisers," Sebald wrote in his diary. "Hence, a tremendous contrast of the simple soldier who knows everything himself and does not need advisers!"

MacArthur was wary of what awaited him. The announcement of the Wake Island meeting prompted a flurry of telegrams to his headquarters from Americans offering encouragement and telling him to be on his guard. "For heaven's sake please talk some sense into Truman," one said. Another pleaded, "We urge you to use every means in your power to frustrate the plot to give Formosa and eventually the rest of Asia to the communists." Yet another made the same point more succinctly: "Do not give in on Formosa."

MacArthur was impressed by the support for himself and the animus toward Truman, and he thought Sebald should be impressed too. "He read me a sheaf of telegrams from people all over the U.S. warning him about the State Department, Truman, Communists, etc.," Sebald recorded. "They were obviously from well-wishers who telegraphed such sentiments as 'Keep a stiff upper lip'; 'Be on your guard against the evil people still in control'; etc."

John Muccio, as American ambassador, was allowed to ride in MacArthur's plane to Wake Island. "MacArthur sat down beside me and very clearly reflected his disgust at being summoned for political reasons when the front and active military operations had so many calls on his time," Muccio afterward remembered. "He was mad as hell." Courtney Whitney, also aboard, elaborated on MacArthur's mistrust. "It is an eight-hour flight from Tokyo to Wake," Whitney wrote. "And during almost all of that time MacArthur paced restlessly up and down the aisle of the plane. He talked little, but it was easy to see that his mind was alternately on what lay in store for him at Wake Island and on the war he temporarily had to leave behind. MacArthur, more than most commanders, believes in keeping in the closest personal touch with events on the battlefield—as witness his countless and hazardous trips to the front. So, more than to most commanders, the prospect of traveling two thousand miles from Korea for a conference that could be held by telecom or even telephone was most distasteful to him."

TRUMAN WAS NO less wary than MacArthur. The president recalled how the general had kept Roosevelt waiting for the meeting in Hawaii, and he determined not to suffer similar treatment. "I've a whale of a job before me," he wrote to an old friend. "Have to talk to God's righthand man." Truman's journey west occupied three days. On the afternoon of Wednesday, October 11, he flew from Washington to St. Louis, where he spent the night and the next morning. He proceeded to Fairfield-Suisun Air Force Base near San Francisco, arriving on the evening of Thursday. Just after midnight he left for Hawaii. He slept during the first part of the flight, then took the co-pilot's seat. "It was still dark, but at regular intervals the lights of ships could be seen below," he recounted later. The vessels were U.S. destroyers, positioned to lend aid in case the *Independence* encountered trouble. Truman remained up front as the plane approached Hawaii. "I had a breath-taking view of the entire chain of islands rising slowly out of the western sky, tiny little dark points in a vastness of blue that I would not have believed if I had not seen it myself. Then slowly the specks of land took shape and were distinct islands. At last the plane passed Diamond Head, circled low over Pearl Harbor, and came in for a landing at Hickam Air Force Base."

Truman spent the day touring Oahu. He met with the Hawaiian territorial governor and with Admiral Arthur Radford, commander of the U.S. Pacific fleet. He visited a military hospital and shook hands with soldiers wounded in Korea. Shortly after midnight, in the early hours of Saturday, he took off for Wake Island. He slept across the international date line, awakening on Sunday morning. Flying conditions were favorable—*too* favorable, in fact. "The pilot had to cut speed in order not to get to Wake Island before the prearranged arrival time," Truman recalled. He was not going to be kept waiting by MacArthur.

The *Independence* rolled to a stop at 6:30, just as the sky was getting light. MacArthur stood at the foot of the ramp while the president deplaned. "His shirt was unbuttoned, and he was wearing a cap that had evidently seen a good deal of use," Truman recounted in his memoir. In a note to himself written several weeks after the meeting, the president was less circumspect: "General MacArthur was at the airport with his shirt unbuttoned, wearing a greasy ham and eggs cap that evidently had been in use for twenty years."

"I have been a long time meeting you, General," the president said pointedly.

MacArthur dodged the jab. "I hope it won't be so long next time, Mr. President," he replied.

AFTERWARD MACARTHUR THREW some jabs of his own. "I had been warned about Mr. Truman's quick and violent temper and prejudices," the general wrote in his memoir. In person he concluded that the president possessed wit but lacked depth. "He seemed to take great pride in his historical knowledge, but, it seemed to me that in spite of his having read much, it was of a superficial character, encompassing facts without the logic and reasoning dictating those facts. Of the Far East he knew little, presenting a strange combination of distorted history and vague hopes that somehow, some way, we could do something to help those struggling against Communism."

At the Wake Island meeting, MacArthur kept his assessment of Truman's intellect to himself. He exuded courtesy. "Do you mind if I smoke, Mr. President?" he asked, producing a new briar pipe.

"No," Truman replied. "I suppose I've had more smoke blown in my face than any other man alive." MacArthur later recalled, "He seemed to enjoy the laugh that followed."

The two men spoke privately for an hour. Truman thought the session went well. "The general seemed genuinely pleased at this opportunity to talk with me, and I found him a most stimulating and interesting person," he recalled in his memoir. "Our conversation was very friendly—I might say much more so than I had expected." They spoke of the war in Korea, which MacArthur again said was nearly over, and of the future of Japan. MacArthur apologized for any embarrassment his message to the Veterans of Foreign Wars had caused. Truman said he considered the matter closed. MacArthur assured Truman he was not interested in politics. He had allowed the politicians to make a "chump" of him in 1948, he said, and he would not let it happen again.

No contemporary record was made of this private session. Several weeks later Truman summarized his recollection of what MacArthur had said: "The General assured the President that the victory was won in Korea, that Japan was ready for a peace treaty and that the Chinese Communists would not attack."

THE LARGER MEETING, with the rest of the military and civilian officials, followed. "The building where the conference was held was a small wooden one, freshly painted green, with two entrances," Vernice Anderson recalled. Anderson was secretary to the State Department's Philip Jessup, and she expected to type up the communiqué that would be issued at the end of the conference. "The single medium-sized room had been cleared out or was new. It also had been freshly painted. Five small folding tables had been pushed together to form a long oblong conference table surrounded, I believe, by folding chairs. These represented the sole furniture in the room. Off this room was a small bathroom and at the rear exit a small porch area separated from the main room by a swinging half door. On this porch area, which was about the size of a small closet, were a few chairs and two small tables on which we happily found cold fruit juices, water, and fresh fruit."

Truman and MacArthur arrived from their private meeting. "There was a flurry of confusion as to who was to sit where," Anderson recalled. "Since no one instructed me where to sit, I simply receded into the background into the small rear anteroom where the refreshments were and where the gentlemen had earlier taken my typewriter on which the communiqué was to be typed. Mr. Ross had announced earlier that immediately after the conclusion of the meeting we would prepare the communiqué at that site, he would then secure the approval of the President and the General, and then he would go to the press headquarters in one of the hangars and would read it to the press corps. I assumed the small anteroom was where I was to work later, so I simply sat down awaiting my next assignment."

She had hoped to stretch her legs after the flight from Hawaii, but was disappointed. "I looked out the door with the naive notion of taking a stroll on the coral reef, only to find Marine MP's with carbines and walkie-talkies posted every six feet around the building as well as Secret Service men stationed at strategic points. Then I knew I could not escape for even a short walk, although it would indeed have been welcome after our long journey. So I sat down on one of the three chairs in the small anteroom. With my secretarial training and experience, the most normal and logical thing for me to do to pass the time was to record what I heard."

WHAT SHE HEARD and recorded included MacArthur expatiating with his customary self-confidence. "I believe that formal resistance will end throughout North and South Korea by Thanksgiving," the general said. "There is little resistance left in South Korea—only about 15,000 men—and those we do not destroy, the winter will." MacArthur's intelligence units estimated that there were 100,000 North Korean soldiers in North Korea, of inferior quality but stubborn spirit. "They are poorly trained, led and equipped, but they are obstinate." MacArthur wasn't sure what he would do with them. "It goes against my grain to have to destroy them. They are only fighting to save face. Orientals prefer to die rather than to lose face." Yet their end was near, one way or the other. "It is my hope to be able to withdraw the Eighth Army to Japan by Christmas," he said. Units of X Corps would stay until the United Nations held elections for the whole of Korea, preferably by the first of the year. After that, they too would be evacuated. He recommended the creation of a new and more efficient Korean military. "If we do that, it will not only secure Korea but it will be a tremendous deterrent to the Chinese Communists moving south"—to Indochina, perhaps. "This is a threat that cannot be laughed off."

Frank Pace asked MacArthur if he was getting the cooperation from Washington he needed.

"No commander in the history of war ever had more complete and adequate support from all agencies in Washington than I have," MacArthur replied.

Truman wanted to hear MacArthur's estimate of the likelihood of outside communist involvement in Korea. "What are the chances for Chinese or Soviet interference?" the president asked.

"Very little," MacArthur answered. The Soviets and Chinese had missed their opportunity. "Had they interfered in the first or second months it would have been decisive." But not now. "We are no longer fearful of their intervention." He elaborated about the Chinese: "The Chinese have 300,000 men in Manchuria. Of these probably not more than 100 to 125 thousand are distributed along the Yalu River. Only 50 to 60 thousand could be gotten across the Yalu River. They have no air force. Now that we have bases for our air force in Korea, if the Chinese tried to get down to Pyongyang there would be the greatest slaughter."

The situation with the Russians was a bit different, MacArthur said. "They have an air force in Siberia and a fairly good one, with excellent pilots equipped with some jets and B-25 and B-29 type planes. They can put 1,000 planes in the air with some 200 to 300 more from the Fifth and Seventh Soviet fleets." Yet he wasn't worried. "They are probably no match for our air force." Soviet ground troops were not a concern. "The Russians have no ground troops available for North Korea. They would have difficulty in putting troops into the field. It would take six weeks to get a division across, and six weeks brings the winter."

A combination of Chinese ground troops and Soviet air support was not impossible, but neither was it particularly worrisome. "Russian air is deployed in a semi-circle through Mukden and Harbin, but the coordination between the Russian air and the Chinese ground would be so flimsy that I believe Russian air would bomb the Chinese as often as they would bomb us." Air support of ground troops was complicated. "Our marines do it perfectly. They have been trained for it. Our own air and ground forces are not as good as the marines, but they are effective." The communists couldn't measure up. "Between untrained air and ground forces an air umbrella is impossible without a lot of joint training. I believe it just wouldn't work with Chinese Communist ground and Russian air."

THE DISCUSSION TURNED to the Japanese peace treaty then being negotiated and whether the Soviet Union and China, as co-belligerents in the war against Japan, could be excluded from negotiations. Truman solicited MacArthur's opinion. The general suggested inviting the communists to a peace conference. "If they don't come in, go ahead," he said. "After the treaty is drawn up, submit to them a draft of the treaty and if they don't sign, go ahead with the treaty. The Japanese deserve a treaty."

Dean Rusk of the State Department said he and his diplomatic colleagues hoped to wrap up a peace treaty with Japan before the Eighth Army was withdrawn from Korea. "But your operations in Korea are going faster than the diplomats can go in getting a treaty," he told MacArthur.

"I hope to get the Eighth Army back by Christmas," MacArthur repeated.

Truman raised the question of a Pacific security alliance, comparable to the North Atlantic alliance. He asked for MacArthur's view.

"A Pacific pact would be tremendous, but due to the lack of homogeneity of the Pacific nations, it would be very difficult to put into effect," MacArthur said. "They have no military forces." He suggested instead a statement like the Truman Doctrine, promising American protection to countries battling communism. "All they want is the assurance of security from the United States. The President should follow up this conference with a ringing pronouncement. I believe that at this time, after the military successes and the President's trip, it would have more success than a Pacific pact."

Truman and MacArthur spoke of the Philippines, which seemed on the right track, and French Indochina, which did not. MacArthur expressed puzzlement at the inability of France to stem the communist insurgency in northern Vietnam. "The French have 150,000 of their best troops there with an officer of the highest reputation in command. Their forces are twice what we had in the perimeter"—around Pusan—"and they are opposed by half of what the North Koreans had. I cannot understand why they do not clean it up."

"I cannot understand it either," Truman said.

Truman dealt summarily with another country. "General MacArthur and I have talked fully about Formosa," he told the group. "There is no need to cover that subject again. The General and I are in complete agreement."

Dean Rusk mentioned a plan floated by India to put Indian and Pakistani forces on the North Korean border with China and the Soviet Union. They would act as a buffer between American forces and the Chinese and Soviets. Rusk asked MacArthur's opinion.

"It would be indefensible from a military point of view," MacArthur said. "I am going to put South Korean troops up there. They will be the buffer. The other troops will be pulled back south of a line from 20 miles north of Pyongyang to Hamhung. I want to take all non-Korean troops out of Korea as soon as possible. They ought to move out soon after the elections. The ROK troops can handle the situation." The last thing Korea needed was more foreign troops; what it needed instead was firm American support for the government of Syngman Rhee. MacArthur asserted that the United Nations was overstepping politically on the subject of the Korean government. "I have been shaking in my boots ever since I saw the UN resolution which would treat them on exactly the same basis as the North Koreans," he said. "We have supported this government and suffered 27,000 casualties in doing so. They are a government duly elected under United Nations auspices and should not be let down."

Truman agreed. "This cannot be done and should not be done," he said. "We must insist on supporting this government."

Rusk pointed out that propaganda against Rhee at the United Nations, by allies of China and the Soviet Union, was causing some coalition countries to waver in their commitment to Korea.

"Propaganda can go to hell," Truman said. "We are supporting the Rhee government."

TRUMAN HAD BEEN mentally checking items off his written agenda for the meeting. He saw they had reached the end. "No one who was not here would believe we have covered so much ground as we have been actually able to cover," he told the group. He checked his watch, which read 9:10. A luncheon had been scheduled for noon. He suggested regathering at that hour. "In the meantime a communiqué can be prepared and talks among the members of the staff can be carried on. Then I want to award a couple of medals to a couple of people and we can all leave after luncheon."

MacArthur demurred. "If it's all right, I am anxious to get back as soon as possible and would like to leave before luncheon, if that is convenient," he told the president.

Truman didn't bat an eye. "I believe this covers the main topics," he said. "Secretary Pace, did you have anything else to take up?"

"Yes, sir," Pace said, "but I can take them up separately with General MacArthur. And I imagine General Bradley has some also."

Truman nodded. "The communiqué should be submitted as soon as it is ready," he said. "And General MacArthur can return immediately. This has been a most satisfactory conference."

HE DIDN'T BELIEVE it. He had to bite his tongue to keep from saying what he *did* believe: that after he, the president of the United States, had flown seven thousand miles, it was incredibly arrogant of MacArthur to insist on leaving before lunch. A conference with the commander-in-chief didn't end until the commander-in-chief said it ended.

Truman kept his temper in check. He chatted with MacArthur while the staff was producing the communiqué. MacArthur asked if Truman intended to run for president in 1952. Truman's antennae quivered; he responded by inquiring whether MacArthur had any political plans. "None whatsoever," MacArthur replied. "If you have any general running against you, his name will be Eisenhower, not MacArthur."

Truman laughed. His personal experience of the demands of the presidency had tempered his previous enthusiasm for Eisenhower. He told MacArthur he respected Eisenhower as a general. "But he doesn't know the first thing about politics. Why, if Eisenhower should become president, his administration would make Grant's look like a model of perfection."

Truman smiled for the photographers at the Wake Island airfield as he awarded MacArthur a fourth oak leaf cluster for his Distinguished Service Medal. He shook hands with MacArthur before boarding the *Independence,* having decided that if MacArthur wouldn't stay for lunch, neither would he, and that the president must depart before the general.

The communiqué—in fact a statement issued in Truman's name, but one that MacArthur read and approved—cast the best possible light on the brevity of the meeting. "The very complete unanimity of views which prevailed enabled us to finish our discussions rapidly, in order to meet General MacArthur's desire to return at the earliest possible moment," the president's statement said. "It was apparent that the excellent coordination which has existed between Washington and the field, to which General MacArthur paid tribute, greatly facilitated the discussion." As to the substance of the talks, the president spoke in positive generalities. "Primarily we talked about the problems in Korea which are General MacArthur's most pressing responsibilities. I asked him for information on the military aspects. I got from him a clear picture of the heroism and high capacity of the United Nations forces under his command. We also discussed the steps necessary to bring peace and security to the area as rapidly as possible in accordance with the intent of the resolution of the United Nations General Assembly and in order to get our armed forces out of Korea as soon as their United Nations mission is completed."

28

TRUMAN WAS STILL putting the best face on things when he reached San Francisco en route home. "I have just returned from Wake Island, where I had a very satisfactory conference with General Douglas MacArthur," he said. Truman's critics were shouting what MacArthur had muttered under his breath: that the Wake Island meeting was a political show for a beleaguered president. Truman answered the critics obliquely. "I understand that there has been speculation about why I made this trip," he said. "There is really no mystery about it. I went because I wanted to see and talk to General MacArthur. The best way to see him and talk to him is to meet him somewhere and talk to him." As to why he had traveled such a long distance and MacArthur a much shorter one: "I went out to Wake Island to see General MacArthur because I did not want to take him far away from Korea, where he is conducting very important operations with great success. Events are moving swiftly over there now, and I did not feel that he should be away from his post too long." Truman reiterated that he and MacArthur agreed on all the important issues. "There is complete unity in the aims and conduct of our foreign policy." He relayed MacArthur's message that the war was nearly over. "General MacArthur told me about the fighting in Korea. He described the magnificent achievements of all the United Nations forces serving under his command. Along with the soldiers of the Republic of Korea these forces have now turned back the tide of aggression." America and the world could take comfort, as he himself did. "I am confident that these forces will soon restore peace to the whole of Korea."

ALMOST NO ONE in the United States bought the White House explanation of the Wake Island conference. Republicans continued to claim that it was politically motivated and were tickled that MacArthur had cut it short. Some said so outright; others were a bit more subtle. Former Minnesota governor and past and presumptively future Republican presidential candidate Harold Stassen said he applauded the president for traveling to Wake Island. "I am glad he went," Stassen said. "I am glad the conference took place." It was about time the president met the general, Stassen said, and he hoped Truman had learned something from the experience. "Any impartial observer must agree that General MacArthur is the best informed American with regard to the entire Asiatic situation." It was a tragedy of American policy and of Asian affairs that Truman had not heeded MacArthur's counsel at critical moments in the recent past. "If President Truman had asked and accepted General MacArthur's advice five years ago, China would not today be under Communist leadership," Stassen said. "If the president had asked and accepted General MacArthur's advice two years ago, the United States would not today be reading casualty lists of the youth of our nation killed and wounded in Korea. If the president had asked and accepted General MacArthur's advice one year ago the United Nations would not now be concerned about what to do next in Formosa." Perhaps a change was coming; perhaps Truman had seen the light. He could demonstrate this by deferring to MacArthur on Asian affairs. "If the President will now appoint him Supreme Commander of American military interests in all of the Asiatic-Pacific area, we will acclaim the president for that action." Stassen hoped the president would do this right thing. But if he didn't, if the president by failing to hand control of America's Asian policy to MacArthur proved that the whole Wake Island affair was a political show, then he would rightly incur the wrath of the American people. "The nation will say to its president: For shame!"

TRUMAN STILL FELT the sting of MacArthur's disrespect when he faced reporters two days after his return to Washington. "Mr. President," one asked, "are you now in complete agreement with General MacArthur on Formosa?"

Truman typically liked news conferences and the banter with reporters. But he was in a foul mood this day. His back stiffened and his mouth grew tight as he lit into the questioner. "Let me tell you something that will be good for your soul," he said. "It's a pity that you columnists and reporters that represent a certain press service can't understand the ideas of two intellectually honest men when they meet." Truman didn't identify the press service, and the reporters present couldn't figure out which one he was talking about, not least because the reporter who asked the question was from the friendly *St. Louis Post-Dispatch*. But Truman evidently had prepared his answer, and he had more to say. "General MacArthur is the commander in chief of the Far East. He is a member of the government of the United States. He is loyal to that government. He is loyal to the president. He is loyal to the president in his foreign policy, which I hope a lot of your papers were—wish a lot of your papers were. There is no disagreement between General MacArthur and myself. It was a most successful conference. Formosa was settled a month ago, or five weeks, I think it was. And there was nothing about Formosa to be settled with General MacArthur. I went out there to get General MacArthur's viewpoint on Japan and the Japanese treaty, to find out if he had any suggestions to make to the treaty which we had drawn and sent around for discussion. I went out there to find out about the rehabilitation of Korea, and I found out about it. And we have made a decision on what we are going to do about it. We talked about all the rest of the Asiatic continent and the Far East, and when General MacArthur went to leave, he said that it was one of the most successful conferences he had ever attended. And I said the same thing. There's your answer."

"Thank you, Mr. President."

"You understand now, don't you?"

"Yes, sir." Several reporters laughed at their colleague's chastening.

Truman joined the laughter, but he wasn't happy. When another reporter, several questions later, said, "Mr. President, I hate to bring up Formosa again," Truman cut him off. "Formosa is answered, and I have nothing to say further on it," he said.

"No more comment?"

"No more comment whatever. I answered you on that."

But the reporters weren't done. "Mr. President, did any question of General MacArthur's resignation arise?"

"No," Truman said. "He did not want to come back before the job is finished, he said. I imagine he meant the Japanese peace treaty, when he said that."

"Do you know how long that might be?"

"No."

Truman's demeanor at this press conference made as much news as his remarks. "Rarely has the President appeared as furious as he was today," the White House reporter for the *New York Times* observed. "He was aroused so much that the words seemed to trip over each other." A correspondent for the *Washington Post* described Truman as "very angry," with "eyes blazing." The *Post* reporter suggested that Truman realized he had lost the battle over the meaning of Wake Island. "The president's touchiness on the subject of Formosa was presumably heightened yesterday by a spate of newspaper speculation to the effect that he had won MacArthur to his way of thinking, or that it had been the other way around, in regard to the controversial island, the Nationalist Chinese government's last refuge. The implication, naturally offensive to Mr. Truman, was either that he was in a position of having to persuade a subordinate around to his viewpoint, or that a subordinate had persuaded him."

WITH AN EFFORT, Truman calmed himself, trusting that the imminent end of the war would put his MacArthur troubles behind him. American and ROK forces swept north according to MacArthur's plan, with the political significance of the 38th parallel lost in the excitement of military success. MacArthur's offensive carried the endorsement of the UN General Assembly, to which the U.S. mission in New York had appealed following the return of the Soviet delegate to UN deliberations. Resolutions of the General Assembly lacked the weight of Security Council resolutions, but the Soviet veto in the Security Council left the assembly as America's only alternative venue. On October 7 the General Assembly endorsed the goal of "the establishment of a unified, independent and democratic government in the sovereign State of Korea."

MacArthur's Eighth Army took a big step toward this end when it captured Pyongyang on October 19. The fact of the capture was important to Syngman Rhee, who accompanied MacArthur to Pyongyang and prepared to incorporate it and the rest of North Korea into the republic he headed. The symbolism was important to MacArthur and everyone else opposed to communism, for it marked the first time a communist capital had been liberated since the start of the Cold War.

The liberation of the rest of North Korea appeared likely to require but days more. MacArthur told reporters, after a visit to a zone where army paratroopers were being dropped, "I didn't see any opposition. It looks like it was a complete surprise. It looks like we closed the trap. Closing that trap should be the end of all organized resistance. The war is very definitely coming to an end." On the same day, MacArthur, speaking as UN commander, declared, "The enemy is thoroughly shattered."

Truman sent congratulations. "The progress the forces under your command have made since we met at Wake continues to be most remarkable, and once again I offer you my hearty congratulations," he said. "The military operations in Korea under your command will have a most profound influence for peace in the world."

MacArthur reciprocated with comparable feigned warmth. "I left the Wake Island conference with a distinct sense of satisfaction that the country's interests had been well served through the better mutual understanding and exchange of views which it afforded," he replied. "I hope that it will result in building a strong defense against future efforts of those who seek for one reason or another (none of them worthy) to breach the understanding between us."

In this letter MacArthur reported that victory was nearer than ever. "Operations in Korea are proceeding according to plan, and while as we draw close to the Manchurian border enemy resistance has somewhat stiffened, I do not think this represents a strong defense in depth such as would materially retard the achievement of our border objective." A week, or two at the most, would see his forces securely established along the Chinese border. The mopping up could be left to the Koreans. "It shall be my purpose, as I outlined during the Wake Island conference, to withdraw American troops as rapidly as possible."

PART THREE

AN ENTIRELY
NEW WAR

29

I T MIGHT HAVE been a result of MacArthur's excessive confidence in his knowledge of the Asian mind; it probably involved some blinding effect of his own brilliance at Inchon; it doubtless reflected his deep hostility toward communism and his accompanying scorn for all the adherents of that ideology; it certainly showed his dismissal of the integrity and capacity of State Department and other administration officials he deemed dangerously leftist; it possibly indicated aspects of advancing age; it indisputably revealed the hubris that tempts all heroes. But whatever the precise admixture of influences, MacArthur missed crucial signals that should have provoked second thoughts about the war's imminent end.

He wasn't alone. Nearly everyone else in the American chain of command missed the same signals. No sooner had the Inchon success placed American troops close to the 38th parallel than the Chinese government began to indicate that it would respond if the Americans crossed into North Korea. China and the United States lacked diplomatic relations, so the Chinese relayed their messages through India. In late September the chief of staff of the Chinese People's Liberation Army told the Indian ambassador to China, K. M. Panikkar, that China's military would not remain idle if the Americans approached the Yalu River. "They may even drop atom bombs on us," the staff chief said, according to Panikkar. "What then? They may kill a few million people." China would fight anyway. "Without sacrifice a nation's independence cannot be upheld."

The warning grew louder. On October 1, the one-year anniversary of the establishment of the People's Republic, Chinese premier and foreign minister Zhou Enlai gave a speech in which he asserted that the Chinese people wanted peace but would take up arms if threatened. "They will not be afraid to fight aggression in defense of peace," he said. "They will not tolerate foreign aggression and will not stand aside should the imperialists wantonly invade the territory of their neighbor." Zhou shortly summoned Panikkar to the foreign ministry to elaborate. He said he was talking about the Americans in Korea. If the Americans crossed into North Korea, China would enter the war. As Panikkar related afterward, "He was emphatic: 'The South Koreans did not matter but American intrusion into North Korea would encounter Chinese resistance.'"

American officials read Zhou's speech, and through the Indian government they learned of the messages given to Panikkar. But they discounted it all as a bluff. Noting that China had been declaring the defense of South Korea illegitimate from the start, one senior but anonymous American diplomat responded to the latest warning with a question: "Why didn't they get into it then"—at the beginning—"if they were going to? Why would they suddenly consider crossing the 38th parallel an invasion if they labeled the whole South Korean defense an invasion all along?" This source told the *New York Times* that the warning was "just a continuation of the Red propaganda line." He thought the Chinese would know better than to get involved in Korea's troubles. "I don't think that China wants to be chopped up."

The CIA weighed the prospects of Chinese intervention and concluded that it wasn't likely. "The Chinese Communists undoubtedly fear the consequences of war with the U.S.," the agency asserted in a memo for the president. "Their domestic problems are of such magnitude that the regime's entire domestic program and economy would be jeopardized by the strains and material damage which would be sustained in war with the U.S. Anti-Communist forces would be encouraged and the regime's very existence would be endangered." China, the CIA concluded, would likely confine itself to covert assistance to the North Koreans.

Dean Acheson agreed that the Chinese warnings were a bluff. Referencing simultaneous diplomatic actions by the Soviet Union on North Korea's behalf, Acheson later explained, "It was obvious that a combined Sino-Soviet effort was being made to save the North Korean regime. Chou's"—Zhou's—"words were a warning, not to be disregarded, but, on the other hand, not an authoritative statement of policy."

Truman said much the same thing. He considered the Indian connection dubious. "Mr. Panikkar had in the past played the game of the
Chinese Communists fairly regularly, so that his statement could not be
taken as that of an impartial observer," Truman recounted. "It might very
well be no more than a relay of Communist propaganda." Truman noted
that the warning came amid consideration of the General Assembly vote
to authorize the invasion of North Korea. "The key vote on the resolution was due the following day, and it appeared quite likely that Chou
En-lai's 'message' was a bald attempt to blackmail the United Nations by
threats of intervention in Korea."

All the same, Truman thought it necessary to modify the orders
under which MacArthur was operating. On October 8 he approved a
message sent by the joint chiefs the following day to the general: "In
light of the possible intervention of Chinese Communist forces in North
Korea, the following amplification of our directive"—the directive of
September 27 authorizing MacArthur to cross the 38th parallel but telling him to refrain from attacking Chinese territory and to keep U.S.
troops away from the Chinese border—"is forwarded for your direction:
Hereafter in the event of the open or covert employment anywhere in
Korea of major Chinese Communist units, without prior announcement,
you should continue the action as long as, in your judgment, action by
forces now under your control offers a reasonable chance of success. In
any case you will obtain authorization from Washington prior to taking
any military action against objectives in Chinese territory."

MacArthur didn't believe the Chinese would enter the war, as he
told Truman emphatically at Wake Island a week later. But the admonitions from the joint chiefs, and the president's demeanor at the meeting,
caused him to think Truman was losing his nerve. "The conference at
Wake Island made me realize that a curious, and sinister, change was
taking place in Washington," he wrote afterward. "The defiant, rallying figure that had been Franklin Roosevelt was gone. Instead, there
was a tendency toward temporizing rather than fighting it through. The
original courageous decision of Harry Truman to boldly meet and defeat
Communism in Asia was apparently being chipped away by the constant
pounding whispers of timidity and cynicism. The President seemed to
be swayed by the blandishments of some of the more selfish politicians
of the United Nations. He seemed to be in the anomalous position of

openly expressing fears of overcalculated risks that he had fearlessly taken only a few months before."

Perhaps to preempt the timidity and cynicism, MacArthur unleashed his troops. On October 24, in clear violation of the policy in place since September 27, he issued an order to Johnnie Walker and Ned Almond removing the restraint that had kept them away from the Yalu River. They were, MacArthur said, "to drive forward with all speed and with the full utilization of their force" to secure "all of North Korea."

Washington at once took notice. "Up to this point, MacArthur had not actually violated or ignored standing orders or suggested policy," Omar Bradley recalled. "His trip to Formosa and his message to the VFW had been ill-advised and unfortunate, creating needless head-aches for the administration. His decision to keep the JCS in the dark about Inchon plans was an act of arrogance. But his October 24 order"—sending U.S. troops to the borders of Korea with China and the Soviet Union—"while not technically insubordinate, came very close." The technicality was that the stricture on U.S. troops near the border was a "matter of policy" rather than a straightforward order. Nonetheless, MacArthur's move showed disturbing disregard for the chain of command. "Owing to the extreme delicacy of the issue, the use of non-ROK forces in the Northeast Provinces should have been cleared in Washington."

Yet Bradley and the chiefs declined to call MacArthur to account. Deferring to the judgment of the commander in the field, they told him they assumed he had reasons for his violation of the September 27 policy. Still, they asked him to specify what those reasons were, as his departure from the agreed-upon approach was "a matter of some concern here."

MacArthur simply denied that anything had changed. He said that the ROK forces were unable to finish off the enemy on their own. He pointed out that language of the September 27 directive barred non-ROK forces from the border provinces "as a matter of policy" only. He quoted the subsequent assurance from George Marshall that he was to feel "unhampered tactically and strategically" as he crossed the 38th par-allel. All the same, he assured the chiefs he had the spirit of the September 27 directive in mind and would not take unnecessary risks. He added, as if to close the matter, "This entire subject was covered in my conference at Wake Island."

In fact the subject had not been covered at Wake Island. But the chiefs let MacArthur's misremembering or misrepresentation pass. The aura of Inchon still surrounded him, and total victory appeared at hand. There was nothing to be gained by bickering with the commander on the ground.

30

MACARTHUR'S SELF-ASSURANCE HAD never been greater, and it never served him so ill. During the last week of October the Chinese revealed that they had not been bluffing about entering the war. "On 26 October Eighth Army was advancing on a broad front in widely separated columns in pursuit of defeated North Korean forces," Johnnie Walker reported. The troops were following MacArthur's orders to advance with all speed to the border and hence were lightly equipped, supplied chiefly by airdrops. "Supplies available were sufficient for bare maintenance of combat operations of one reinforced American division and four ROK divisions with no possibility of accumulating reserves to meet heavier opposition." That was when they had the shock of their lives. "An ambush and surprise attack by fresh, well-organized and well-trained units, some of which were Chinese Communist forces, began a sequence of events leading to complete collapse and disintegration of ROK II Corps of three divisions."

The appearance of the Chinese triggered an abrupt shift in the balance of morale, especially among the Korean troops. "Contributing factors were intense psychological fear of Chinese intervention and previous complacency and overconfidence in all ROK ranks," Walker said. He was doing everything to hold his front together. "By intense effort, progress is being made in reorganization and stabilization of II ROK Corps; however, it is at most only fifty percent effective at present. The 2d US Division has been brought up in a position to take over in the event of collapse by ROK forces."

The situation grew worse. "Chinese Communist hordes, attacking on horse and on foot to the sound of bugle calls, cut up Americans and South Koreans at Unsan today in an Indian-style massacre that may prove to be the costliest of the Korean war," the United Press reported on November 3. "Two combat regiments were badly chewed up and hundreds of civilians—men, women and children—who tried to escape along the roads leading from Unsan were killed by enemy machine-gun and mortar fire. The Communists charged in the frosty early morning hours in an attack so vicious it left the surprised and confused Americans no choice but to run. Many did not escape."

The wire service correspondent interviewed American survivors who testified to the surprise of the assault and the chaos it produced. "I woke up when they started shooting the fellows in the foxholes around me," a GI from Virginia said. "I couldn't see anything until a tank came along. I climbed on and fell off three times or was pulled off by others trying to get on. Then the tank burst into flames and we all started running." An infantryman from North Carolina said, "Someone woke me up and asked if I could hear a bunch of horses on the gallop. I couldn't hear anything. Then bugles started playing taps, but far away. Someone blew a whistle and our area was shot to hell in a matter of minutes. I'm not too sure how it all happened right now, but I know we lost more of our outfit there than got out." A corporal from Minnesota explained that he had been awakened by hand grenades. "The lieutenant tried to get us organized, but those Chinese had every man spotted and they killed every man they wanted to." A lieutenant from Washington state said, "There was no such thing as fighting back. The chances were greatest that you would hit one of your own men rather than the enemy."

MacArthur prided himself on not overreacting to bad news. He maintained his composure now, despite this stunning evidence that he had been wrong in dismissing the chance of Chinese intervention. On October 31 he forwarded to Washington without comment a report from Ned Almond describing some Chinese troops captured in X Corps' sector. "Prisoners averaged 28–30 years of age with approximately 2 year military service," the report stated. "Prisoners had not eaten in 3 days, but had new cotton quilted uniforms, winter headgear, and greenish canvas shoes with crepe rubber soles." The prisoners revealed that they had fought with the Chinese Nationalist army before their unit had been absorbed into the Communist People's Liberation Army. The artillery of their regiment was transported by horses and by the soldiers themselves.

During the next four days MacArthur pondered what the presence of the Chinese troops meant. Finally he shared his musings with the joint chiefs. "Various possibilities exist based upon the battle intelligence coming in from the front," he cabled on November 4. "First, that the Chinese Communist government proposes to intervene with its full potential military forces, openly proclaiming such course at what it might determine as an appropriate time; second, that it will covertly render military assistance but will, so far as possible, conceal the fact for diplomatic reasons; third, that it is permitting and abetting a flow of more or less voluntary personnel across the border to strengthen and assist the North Korean remnants in their struggle to retain a nominal foothold in Korea; fourth, that such intervention as exists has been in the belief that no UN forces would be committed in the extreme northern reaches of Korea except those of South Korea."

MacArthur weighed the probabilities of the scenarios he described. "The first contingency would represent a momentous decision of the gravest international importance," he said. He thought it the least likely. "While it is a distinct possibility, and many foreign experts predict such action, there are many fundamental logical reasons against it, and sufficient evidence has not yet come to hand to warrant its immediate acceptance." That left the others. "The last three contingencies or a combination thereof seem to be most likely condition at the present moment." In any event, there should be no rush to judgment. "I recommend against hasty conclusions which might be premature and believe that a final appraisement should await a more complete accumulation of military facts."

TRUMAN TOOK HIS cue from MacArthur. If the general wasn't worried, the president wouldn't worry either, at least not yet. There were other things to worry about, as Truman discovered personally on November 1. The president liked to nap after lunch when his schedule permitted, and he was snoozing in his upstairs bedroom at Blair House when two men armed with automatic weapons began firing on the guards posted at the front of the house. The authorities shortly discovered that they were Puerto Rican nationalists who hoped to kill the president to draw attention to the struggle for Puerto Rican independence. "We came here with the express purpose of shooting the president," one of the gunmen told police. The guards returned the fire, killing one of the gunmen and wounding the other. Three of the guards were wounded, one fatally.

The gunmen never got inside the house, but several bullets smashed windows and a door. The noise of the shooting drew Truman, clad in his underwear, to the window above the street, from where he looked down on the bloody confusion. A guard saw him and shouted, "Get back! Get back!" As Truman realized what was going on, he took the advice and stepped away from the window.

He dressed and went downstairs. He was scheduled to dedicate a monument at Arlington Cemetery to British field marshal John Dill, who had helped cement the military side of the Anglo-American alliance during World War II. Asked by press secretary Charlie Ross if he intended to keep the appointment, Truman said, "Why certainly." Ross later told reporters, "I never saw a calmer man in my life."

31

A FEW DAYS LATER Truman, still calm, traveled to Independence to vote. He was in Missouri when he received an alarming call from Dean Acheson in Washington. The secretary of state reported, rather breathlessly, that MacArthur was again stretching his orders. The general had directed his air force to bomb bridges over the Yalu River linking China to North Korea, to interdict Chinese transport and reinforcement, and had done so without informing the joint chiefs or anyone else in Washington. Acheson had learned of the order only because MacArthur's air commander, George Stratemeyer, had notified his service superior, Hoyt Vandenberg, who relayed the message to Robert Lovett, the undersecretary of defense, who sent word to Acheson.

The secretary of state thought the bombing a terrible idea. Bombing was a very inexact science, Acheson pointed out; some of the bombs might well go astray and hit the Chinese side of the river. Already American planes had inadvertently fired on an airfield in Soviet territory, compelling Washington to apologize. Fortunately, Moscow had accepted the apology. China was unlikely to be so forgiving. Even if the bombing did not provoke a major Chinese response, the escalation would strain the UN coalition, which sternly resisted a wider war. The bombing would antagonize the British, who remained on tenterhooks about Hong Kong; they might well feel double-crossed by this unannounced escalation. The bombing was a terrible idea, Acheson repeated. MacArthur must be stopped.

Truman gritted his teeth as he considered the matter. He didn't disagree with Acheson, but he knew what MacArthur and the general's supporters would say if the order were countermanded: that MacArthur was being denied the ability to defend American troops against the communist enemy, that Truman again was quailing before the Red Chinese, that MacArthur was strong and Truman weak.

He grudgingly conceded that MacArthur had him in a bad spot. The general was canny if nothing else. Truman grimly told Acheson to let MacArthur's bombing order stand. As Acheson recorded the conversation a short while later, "The President said that he would approve the action if it was necessary because of an immediate and serious threat to the security of his own troops."

Acheson objected. The secretary said MacArthur had not made the case that the threat was, in fact, immediate and serious.

Truman suggested that Acheson call MacArthur and let him make the case.

Acheson said he thought the communication should go through military channels.

Truman often boasted of his willingness to make difficult decisions, but in this case he passed the buck. He instructed Acheson to deal with it. "The President told me to handle the matter until his return in the way Mr. Lovett and I thought best, adding that he would be available on the telephone if necessary and that the security of our troops should not be jeopardized."

Acheson thereupon scribbled a summary for Lovett to take to the joint chiefs. "The President recognizes the great international complications which may follow the proposed bombing of the Yalu River bridge," Acheson wrote. "He is willing to face these complications if the step is immediately necessary to protect our forces. He believes under the circumstances that the joint chiefs should know from General MacArthur what the pressing reasons are for the operation. If the operation can wait until our international commitments are fulfilled, that would put us in the best position."

The chiefs took their cue. Scarcely an hour before the bombing campaign was to begin, they ordered MacArthur to stand down. He must not target anything within five miles of the Chinese border pending new authorization, toward which he was invited to supply additional justification.

MacArthur gave them an earful. Outraged at being second-guessed, particularly by Acheson, the general sent the chiefs a blistering statement of military necessity. "Men and material in large forces are pouring across all bridges over the Yalu from Manchuria," he declared. "This movement not only jeopardizes but threatens the ultimate destruction of the forces under my command. The actual movement across the river can be accomplished under cover of darkness and the distance between the river and our lines is so short that the forces can be deployed against our troops without being seriously subjected to air interdiction. The only way to stop this reinforcement of the enemy is the destruction of these bridges and the subjection of all installations in the North area supporting the enemy advance to the maximum of our air destruction. Every hour that this is postponed will be paid for dearly in American and other United Nations blood."

He said that he had been in the process of taking the steps necessary to protect his men when the suspension order arrived. "The main crossing at Sinuiju was to be hit within the next few hours, and the mission is actually already being mounted. Under the gravest protest that I can make, I am suspending this strike and carrying out your instructions. What I had ordered is entirely within the scope of the rules of war and the resolutions and directions which I have received from the United Nations and constitute no slightest act of belligerency against Chinese territory, in spite of the outrageous international lawlessness emanating therefrom. I cannot overemphasize the disastrous effect, both physical and psychological, that will result from the restrictions which you are imposing."

In what the chiefs must have read as a threat to go over their heads, MacArthur continued, "I trust that the matter be immediately brought to the attention of the President, as I believe your instructions may well result in a calamity of major proportion for which I cannot accept the responsibility without his personal and direct understanding of the situation. Time is so essential that I request immediate reconsideration of your decision pending which complete compliance will of course be given to your order."

THE JOINT CHIEFS were dumbfounded by MacArthur's response. "Neither I nor anyone else in Washington was in any way prepared for the ferocity of the blast," Omar Bradley recounted. "The first two sentences of his message amounted to a complete about-face of his forces-estimate of November 4 and caused the most profound shock in Washington." The concluding sentences added insult to the astonishment produced by the opening. "Apart from the shocking news that his complete command might now be destroyed by Chinese communists, this message said, in effect, that the JCS were a bunch of nitwits and that MacArthur would not accept orders from anyone but the President on this matter. The way the message was phrased, it was not insubordinate, but it was a grave insult to men who were his legal superiors, including George Marshall."

Yet the chiefs did as MacArthur demanded. "General Bradley read me this message over the phone," Truman recalled later, referring to MacArthur's cable. The president now realized that this buck could not be passed. He mentally recited the risks of giving the general what he wanted. "There were grave dangers involved in a mass bombing attack on a target so close to Manchuria and to Soviet soil. An overly eager pilot might easily bring about retaliatory moves; damaged planes might be forced to land in territory beyond our control." But because MacArthur was on the spot and made such an urgent case for the bombing, Truman wasn't going to override him. "I told Bradley to give him the 'go-ahead.'"

The chiefs sent MacArthur new orders. Noting pointedly that the situation reported in MacArthur's latest was "considerably changed" from his previous message, they reminded him that there were broader questions than he seemed to be considering. "We agree that the destruction of the Yalu bridges would contribute materially to the security of the forces under your command, unless this action resulted in increased Chinese Communist effort and even Soviet contribution in response to what they might well construe as an attack on Manchuria. Such a result would not only endanger your forces but would enlarge the area of conflict and U.S. involvement to a most dangerous degree." Yet they granted permission. "In view of your first sentence"—about the Chinese pouring across the Yalu—"you are authorized to go ahead with your planned bombing in Korea near the frontier including targets at Sinuiju and Korean end of Yalu bridges, provided that at time of receipt of this message you still find such action essential to safety of your forces."

But he must keep clear of Chinese territory. "It is important that extreme care be taken to avoid violation of Manchurian territory and airspace." And he must stay in touch. "It is essential that we be kept informed of important changes in situation as they occur."

32

I T WASN'T LOST on Truman that MacArthur's demand for permission to bomb the Yalu bridges arrived mere hours before the midterm elections. During the summer of 1950 the Democrats hadn't been expecting to prosper at the polls that fall. Recurring troubles in the economy had voters in a surly mood, and the communist advances overseas, combined with the charges about communists in the American government, made the president's party fear the worst. But the stunning victory at Inchon and the confident reports from MacArthur that the war was all but over and would certainly be won gave the Democrats cause for hope. Then came the shocking news of Chinese intervention. The war wasn't over at all, and it might not be won. The Democrats' hopes slumped again. MacArthur's demand to unleash his bombers could hardly have caught Truman at a more vulnerable time.

The country went to the polls on November 7 and punished Truman and the Democrats. The president's party lost five seats in the Senate and twenty-eight in the House. Though the Democrats still held majorities in both houses, Truman could expect little cooperation from Congress, since conservative Southern Democrats opposed the president as often and stoutly as many Republicans did.

He tried to put the best face on things. Aides described him to reporters as "very cheerful," albeit disappointed that several allies in the Senate had lost their seats. Yet the Washington press corps wasn't fooled. One reporter characterized Truman's present and future: "The President is taking a short vacation cruise on Chesapeake Bay aboard the presidential yacht Williamsburg before returning to Washington and a series of inevitable clashes with Congress, where Republicans and Southern Democrats will be able to dictate legislation."

AND THEN, AS abruptly as the Chinese had appeared in Korea, they disappeared. Or at least they disappeared from MacArthur's reports. The joint chiefs had followed up their permission to bomb the Yalu bridges with a message explaining that the Chinese intervention in the massive numbers MacArthur described mandated a reconsideration of the primary objective delineated in their message of September 27. "This new situation indicates your objective as stated in that message—'the destruction of North Korean armed forces'—may have to be reexamined," the chiefs said.

MacArthur wouldn't hear of it. "I cannot agree," he declared flatly. "It would be fatal to weaken the fundamental and basic policy of the United Nations to destroy all resisting armed forces in Korea and bring that country into a united and free nation." Without admitting to having exaggerated the danger from the Chinese, he said he currently had things well under control. His airpower was crucial. "I can deny reinforcements coming across the Yalu in sufficient strength to prevent the destruction of those forces now arrayed against me in North Korea." He was eager to resume the offensive and finish the job. "I plan to launch my attack for this purpose on or about November 15 with the mission of driving to the border and securing all of North Korea." Now was no time to hesitate or falter. "Any program short of this would completely destroy the morale of my forces and its psychological consequences would be inestimable. It would condemn us to an indefinite retention of our military forces along difficult defense lines in North Korea and would unquestionably arouse such resentment among the South Koreans that their forces would collapse or might even turn against us."

Lest the chiefs or the president miss his point, MacArthur made it perfectly clear. "To give up any portion of North Korea to the aggression of the Chinese Communists would be the greatest defeat of the free world in recent times. Indeed, to yield to so immoral a proposition would bankrupt our leadership in Asia and render untenable our position both politically and militarily. . . . It would not curb deterioration of the present situation into the possibility of general war but would impose upon us the disadvantage of having inevitably to fight such a war if it occurs bereft of the support of countless Asiatics who now believe in us and are eager to fight with us."

MacArthur's change of heart flabbergasted the administration in Washington. Only days earlier he had declared that the Chinese were about to overrun his army, and now he appeared not worried in the slightest. Acheson couldn't decide whether the general was being cynically manipulative or becoming unhinged. The secretary didn't dismiss the former possibility but saw strong hints of the latter. "The forces that had struck the Eighth Army during the last days of October and the opening days of November had been powerful, fully equipped, and competent— and yet they seemed to have vanished from the earth," Acheson wrote. "The five days from November 4 to 9 give an excellent example of General MacArthur's mercurial temperament. In this period he went from calm confidence, warning against hasty judgment until all the facts were in, through ringing the tocsin on the sixth to proclaim that hordes of men were pouring into Korea and threatening to overwhelm his command, to confidence again on the ninth that he could deny the enemy reinforcement and destroy him."

YET MACARTHUR WANTED still more. His bombing campaign proceeded but achieved only modest success. His planes knocked out some of the bridges, but the Chinese were quick to replace them with pontoon bridges. And in any case the Yalu was freezing with the onset of winter, rendering bridges redundant.

At the same time, MacArthur's fliers labored under severe and sometimes deadly restraint. They encountered Soviet MiG-15s piloted by Chinese airmen based in Manchuria. The Chinese quickly realized that the Americans wouldn't bomb their bases or even pursue them back over Manchuria. Accordingly they gained a great advantage in their air combat with the Americans, making the bombing of the Yalu bridges nearly impossible. General Emmett O'Donnell, the head of MacArthur's bomber command, later explained what it meant for his pilots to be forbidden to violate Chinese territory. "By violation of territory I mean we were not allowed to fly over an inch of it," O'Donnell said. "For instance the Yalu has several very pronounced bends, like most rivers, before getting to the town of Antung, and the main bridges at Antung we had to attack in only one manner. There was only one manner you could attack the bridge and not violate Manchurian territory, and that was a course tangential to the southernmost bend of the river. As you draw a line from the southernmost bend of the river to the bridge, that is your course. These people on the other side of the river knew that and put up their batteries right along the line, and they peppered us right down the line all the way. We had to take it, of course, and couldn't fight back. In addition to that, they had their fighters come up alongside and join our formation about two miles to the lee and fly along at the same speed on the other side of the river while we were making our approach. And just before we got to the bomb-away position, they would veer off to the north and climb up to about 30,000 feet and then make a frontal quarter on the bombers just about at the time of the bomb-away in a turn. So they would be coming from Manchuria in a turn, swoop down, fire their cannons at the formation and turn back into sanctuary." O'Donnell concluded with an understatement: "And the boys didn't like it."

MacArthur later supplied a more graphic version of the pilots' response to the restrictions. "One of those bomber pilots, wounded unto death, the stump of an arm dangling by his side, gasped at me through the bubbles of blood he spat out, 'General, which side are Washington and the United Nations on?'" MacArthur had no answer. "It seared my very soul," he said.

Throughout November, MacArthur battled Washington over the restrictions. He demanded at least the right of "hot pursuit": to chase attacking Chinese fighters into Chinese and Soviet territory if necessary. Truman refused, fearing an escalation of the war. MacArthur sought permission to bomb power plants on the Yalu that contributed to the North Korean war effort. Truman again refused, on grounds that the power plants supplied Manchuria and might provoke a general Chinese response. "I felt that step-by-step my weapons were being taken away from me," MacArthur lamented later.

He considered his options. "I could go forward, remain immobile, or withdraw. If I went forward, there was the chance that China might not intervene in force and the war would be over." He was willing to take the chance, though the timid in Washington were opposed. The second choice was distasteful and dangerous. "If I remained immobile and waited, it would be necessary to select a defense line and dig in." MacArthur had never liked sitting still, and he didn't like it now. "With my scant forces it would be impossible to establish a defense in depth against the overwhelming numbers of Chinese." The third choice, withdrawal, was dishonorable and defeatist. "It would be in contradiction of my orders and would destroy any opportunity to bring the Korean War to a successful end."

33

A ND SO HE went forward. On November 24 he issued a communiqué announcing an offensive he proclaimed would end the war. "The United Nations massive compression envelopment in North Korea against the new Red armies operating there is now approaching its decisive effort," he declared. His air wing had interdicted enemy lines from the north, he said, without mentioning China specifically. "Further reinforcement therefrom has been sharply curtailed and essential supplies markedly limited." He described how the eastern and western components of his pincers were closing in on the enemy. "If successful, this should for all practical purposes end the war, restore peace and unity to Korea, enable the prompt withdrawal of United Nations military forces, and permit the complete assumption by the Korean people and nation of full sovereignty and international equality." To reporters who accompanied him to the front, MacArthur declared, "I hope to keep my promise to the G.I.'s to have them home by Christmas."

John Muccio later had a distinct memory of MacArthur at this moment. The general was characterizing the offensive as a mop-up operation, and he dismissed concerns about large-scale Chinese intervention. "His exact words as I remember them were, 'There may have been twenty-five thousand Chinese cross the Yalu, but there cannot be more than thirty thousand, otherwise my intelligence would know about it.'" Muccio continued, "I can still picture him posturing with his corncob pipe. The two of us were alone at the time. MacArthur was a very theatrical personality. I think that John and Lionel Barrymore were theatrical amateurs compared to MacArthur." Muccio reflected a bit more. "I don't think MacArthur even blinked his eyes without considering whether it was to his advantage to have his eye blink or not. Everything was thought through, but it became so a part of his nature, and his personality, that it seemed to be automatic."

The end-the-war offensive began with great promise. Seven divisions of American Eighth Army and ROK troops, with a brigade of British troops, advanced on a sixty-mile front in northwestern Korea, crossing frozen rivers and encountering minimal resistance. American B-29 bombers pounded rail lines and depots, drawing only sporadic and ineffectual anti-aircraft fire. MacArthur's forces gained eight, ten, as many as fifteen miles in mere hours. "The giant U. N. pincer moved according to schedule," he announced after flying over the front and along the Yalu, where he instructed his pilot to dip the wings to salute the first American troops to reach the river. "Our losses were extraordinarily light," he told reporters. "The logistic situation is fully geared to sustained offensive operations. The justice of our cause and the promise of early completion of our mission is reflected in the morale of the troops and commanders alike."

And then, on the night of November 25, the offensive hit a hidden wall. The Chinese troops had not gone away; they had gone to ground. And they were augmented by many more of their comrades, who had slipped into Korea undetected by MacArthur's reconnaissance and intelligence. They appeared as if from nowhere and slammed into Johnnie Walker's right flank. More than 100,000 Chinese troops surged at the American and ROK units from the front, the flank and soon the rear. Another 100,000 assaulted Ned Almond's X Corps farther east. The surprise and ferocity of the Chinese attack resulted in heavy casualties, compelling Walker and Almond to pull back—in some cases to fight their way back.

The extent and nature of the Chinese offensive took time to sink in. The first reports of Chinese contact put MacArthur in mind of the engagements of late October, which had come to seem mere warnings, followed by withdrawal. But by the third day of the new offensive, the general was willing to acknowledge that things had changed dramatically. "The developments resulting from our assault movements have now assumed a clear definition," he wrote to the joint chiefs. "All hopes of localization of the Korean conflict to enemy forces composed of North Korean troops with alien token elements can now be completely abandoned. The Chinese military forces are committed in North Korea in great and ever increasing strength." Intelligence and the interrogation of prisoners caused MacArthur to estimate the number of Chinese he opposed at 200,000. "No pretext of minor support under the guise of volunteerism or other subterfuge now has the slightest validity. We face an entirely new war."

MacArthur almost never admitted that a military situation was beyond his control. But the Chinese attack jolted him into doing so. His air force couldn't interdict the Chinese columns crossing the frozen Yalu. The enemy outnumbered him and grew stronger by the day. He threw the matter back on Washington. "The resulting situation presents an entire new picture which broadens the potentialities to world-embracing considerations beyond the sphere of decision by the theater commander. This command has done everything humanly possible within its capabilities but is now faced with conditions beyond its control and its strength."

CHINA'S SURPRISE OFFENSIVE stunned Truman as much as it did MacArthur. The president had been counting the days until the war's end—until Christmas, when MacArthur would start withdrawing the American troops and the president could salute the season of peace and goodwill by claiming America's first victory over communism. Now Truman felt that all that had been done since June was for nothing— indeed for worse than nothing. American troops were being mauled, and the mauling would likely get worse, because there appeared no limit to the reinforcements China could put into the fight. Truman cursed as he asked himself how he had got into this mess.

In search of answers, and options, the president convened the National Security Council. Omar Bradley produced a map and sketched the disposition of forces in northern Korea. The joint chiefs chairman explained that MacArthur's offensive had begun a week before but had been cut short by the sudden and unexpected appearance of the 200,000 Chinese troops. Referring to MacArthur's cable declaring that the conflict had become an "entirely new war," Bradley said that this had caused the chiefs to consider whether to send MacArthur a new directive to guide him. They had debated the question at length before reaching a conclusion. "No new directive should be issued for the time being, certainly not until the military situation clarifies," Bradley said.

Douglas MacArthur at the height of his powers, in the moment of victory over Japan.

The surrender ceremony aboard the U.S.S. *Missouri*, where the Japanese answered to MacArthur and MacArthur answered to God.

This former insurance building became MacArthur's headquarters during the Japanese occupation and the Korean War.

Where MacArthur lived longer than anywhere else during his professional life: the American Embassy in Tokyo.

Victor and vanquished: MacArthur and Hirohito.

Harry Truman as vice-president elect. Henry Wallace (right), whom Truman was replacing, didn't appreciate Truman's coming between him and the ailing Franklin Roosevelt (left). Wallace would create problems for Truman in due course.

The family man, with Bess (left) and Margaret (right).

The Berlin airlift kept these children fed and West Berlin free and gave the world a new appreciation for Harry Truman.

The ones he trusted most: Secretary of State Dean Acheson (left) and General (and serially Secretary of State and Secretary of Defense) George Marshall (center).

Joint Chiefs of Staff Chairman Omar Bradley (far left) served Truman well, but Defense Secretary Louis Johnson (between Bradley and Truman) caused no end of trouble.

Truman's press conferences were crowded and informal. He liked them that way, but sometimes he said too much.

The North Korean attack on South Korea in June 1950 rapidly led to the fall of Seoul and the flight of many thousands of refugees.

U.S. troops thrown into the breach had serious difficulty finding their footing.

Journalist Maggie Higgins fought her way to the front to get the story of what was happening there.

At MacArthur's insistence, the Eighth Army dug in and held at the Naktong River.

MacArthur launched his great September counteroffensive at Inchon, in the face of resistance from the North Korean army and skepticism from Washington.

The surprise landings succeeded splendidly, as MacArthur learned in detail at this briefing on the third day of the offensive.

From Inchon the Eighth Army raced north to cut off and destroy the fleeing enemy.

North Korean troops surrendered in large numbers, and MacArthur had a look.

MacArthur's forces recrossed the Han River en route to liberating Seoul.

Waving aside Washington's objections, MacArthur personally reinstalled South Korean president Syngman Rhee in Seoul.

From Seoul to Pyongyang required but three weeks. MacArthur joined General Walton "Johnnie" Walker to celebrate the capture of the North Korean capital.

Hoping to hear how the war would end, Truman undertook the seven-thousand-mile journey to Wake Island to meet MacArthur. Omar Bradley traveled with the president and renewed his acquaintance with the general.

The fateful meeting on October 15 began with a private session, where each man took the measure of the other.

The conference facilities on Wake Island were spartan.

Vernice Anderson (center) recorded the discussions at Wake Island. She would become the most famous stenographer in America, to MacArthur's embarrassment.

Truman was tempted to tell MacArthur to straighten up in the presence of the commander in chief, but with victory seemingly near, he held his tongue.

MacArthur's offensive continued, and in November U.S. troops reached the Chinese border. Truman and the Joint Chiefs of Staff worried that China would be provoked by the proximity of the Americans, but MacArthur again ignored the naysaying.

Suddenly the Chinese entered the war in daunting strength. U.S. troops retreated through the frozen mountains.

Though U.S. tanks briefly held their ground here, MacArthur's forces were thrown back across the 38th parallel.

MacArthur's increasingly public dissatisfaction with the restraints on his war effort eventually caused Truman to relieve him. Army Secretary Frank Pace, here with MacArthur in Tokyo, was supposed to deliver the news in person, but fear of a news leak prompted Truman to fire MacArthur via a White House statement.

General Matthew Ridgway (right) *did* get the news from Frank Pace (far left). Ridgway succeeded to MacArthur's command.

On his return to America, with wife Jean and son Arthur, MacArthur was hailed as a hero. He concluded he might become president.

He held forth at length at Senate hearings, at which he was treated with pomp and deference. He never understood how the hearings proved his undoing.

Truman had the last laugh.

"The reports coming in over the press and radio about the strength and momentum of the Chinese communist offensive might well be exaggerated." He doubted that American lines had been breached as spectacularly as the reports were saying. "It is entirely possible that the Chinese offensive might not go very far because of the extremely difficult terrain, which we would find advantageous from the defensive point of view, and because the Chinese communists have a difficult supply situation." Even so, the chiefs were watching the situation closely and might feel it desirable to issue a new directive in forty-eight or seventy-two hours.

Bradley raised a second issue, which he considered more immediately serious than the situation on the ground. This was the balance of airpower over the battlefield. American intelligence revealed that the Chinese had or could have at least three hundred bombers based at fields in Manchuria. "These bombers could seriously curtail our air lift, and our planes are jammed so closely on the fields in Korea that surprise raids could do us very great damage," Bradley said. Yet despite this vulnerability, the chiefs did not recommend that MacArthur receive authorization to bomb the Manchurian bases.

Truman interrupted to ask if there was anything that could be done to mitigate the vulnerability of the American aircraft.

"There is not, short of moving many of our planes back to Japan," Hoyt Vandenberg replied. "This would, of course, mean a considerable slowing up of our operations."

Truman turned to George Marshall. The defense secretary said he had consulted with the joint chiefs and the service secretaries, asking each for their views, which he proceeded to summarize. "We are engaged with other members of the UN in suppressing a Korean aggression," he said. "We are now faced by a new Chinese aggression." The United States should maintain the UN coalition at almost all costs. And it should resolutely resist broadening the war, which would play into Moscow's hands by weakening the United States elsewhere. "We should use all available political, economic and psychological action to limit the war," Marshall said. "We should not go into Chinese Communist territory and we should not use Chinese Nationalist forces. To do either of these things would increase the danger of war with the Chinese Communists." Marshall repeated, "We should not get into a general war with the Chinese Communists."

Marshall spoke of the situation on the ground in Korea. He noted that American forces in northeastern Korea were widely scattered. "There is a big gap in our lines, and I don't know what MacArthur intends to do about that," he said. But he added, "It is *his* problem. I won't even ask MacArthur what he is going to do. We have no business, here in Washington, 8,000 miles away, asking the local commander what his tactical plans are. General Collins here, and General Smith"—Walter Bedell Smith, currently director of the CIA, formerly Dwight Eisenhower's chief of staff—"know that all during the Battle of the Bulge the War Department did not ask them one single question. We let them do the fighting. It's the same way now. We *must* follow hour by hour any developments pertaining to our getting further involved with the Chinese Communists, but we *won't* ask MacArthur his tactical plans."

Marshall commanded the respect of any gathering he addressed. The members of Truman's NSC sat silent and attentive to this point in the defense secretary's presentation. But Alben Barkley thought he owed it to Truman and the administration to interrupt and relate what he was hearing on Capitol Hill, where the vice president retained close contacts. Democratic members of Congress were outraged at MacArthur's boastfulness, which now seemed not just empty but insane. "Did General MacArthur make the statement attributed to him a week ago that the boys in Korea would be home by Christmas?" Barkley asked. "Did he know what was going on? If he did know, why did he say it? How in the world could a man in his position be guilty of such an indiscretion?"

Truman answered the question. "He made the statement," the president said. "You will have to draw your own conclusions as to why he did it."

Barkley shook his head. "He couldn't have known about the Chinese Communists if he made the statement in good faith," he said. Barkley thought it was a stupid statement if sincere. "He couldn't have gotten the boys home anyway." Again he shook his head. "I can't comprehend why the statement was made."

Omar Bradley, perhaps inclined to defend a fellow officer, proposed what he called a personal theory of MacArthur's prediction. Bradley suggested that the general's boast that American troops would be home by Christmas was a statement for Chinese consumption, a way of reassuring the Chinese that the United States had no permanent designs on Korea and were no threat to Manchuria. Yet Bradley acknowledged that even if this had been MacArthur's thinking, he should have thought more carefully. "It was still a rash statement."

Truman didn't disagree, but he cautioned against any sign from the administration that would suggest displeasure with MacArthur's performance. "No matter what we might think about MacArthur's statement, we have to be very careful not to pull the rug out from under him," Truman said. "We cannot afford to damage MacArthur's prestige at this point."

Marshall said the administration would simply have to deal with MacArthur's statement. "We regard it as an embarrassment we just have to get around in some manner." Marshall continued, "In defense of what Bradley says, MacArthur thought he had only 100,000 Chinese communists to deal with." The 200,000 he now faced were a huge surprise. Yet the surprise was understandable. "They are skillful in concealing themselves in that terrain," Marshall said.

Barkley was far from mollified. "How can we have any confidence in MacArthur's estimate that there are 200,000 Chinese communists facing us now?" the vice president demanded. "A week ago he thought there only 100,000. Maybe there aren't 200,000; maybe there are 300,000 facing us. We can't hold on if the Chinese communists go in for an all-out offensive. What do we do?"

"I can't give an immediate answer," Marshall replied. "I will say that we can't get completely sewed up in Korea. We can't tie up everything we have there." Marshall said that until very recently all the nation's defense planning had been based on the assumption that MacArthur would succeed in Korea. Now the administration had to consider what to do if MacArthur failed. "This is a gloomy possibility," he said. And it potentially presented a hard question: "How can we get out with honor?"

Joe Collins informed the group that there were no fresh units to send to reinforce MacArthur. And there would not be any until March 1951. Individual soldiers might be sent as replacements after January 1, but full units would take longer.

Marshall observed that the individual replacements wouldn't do much good. MacArthur was already short of American troops by about 30 percent. Many American divisions had large numbers of ROK troops filling in.

Collins nonetheless thought the situation was manageable. American forces could retreat to the narrow neck of the Korean peninsula and dig in there. "Despite the shortages, and unless the Tenth Corps really gets cut off, MacArthur can hold a line," Collins said.

Truman agreed, perhaps more hopefully than confidently. "MacArthur can hold a line," the president said.

Truman asked Dean Acheson to address the diplomatic issues the current crisis raised.

The secretary of state was blunt. "The events of the last few hours have moved us very much closer to a general war," he said. "There has always been some Chinese involvement in the fighting in Korea. First, the Chinese let the Koreans in Manchuria go back home to fight in Korea. Then they let a few 'volunteers' go into Korea. Now there is a mass movement of Chinese forces into Korea. What has happened is that the cloak of Chinese neutrality has been lifted gradually, and we have an open, powerful offensive attack." But the conflict was bigger than Korea or even China. "We must all think about what happens in Korea as a world matter. We must think about it all around the world at the same time because we face the Soviet Union around the world. Whatever we think of current happenings in Korea must be in the light of world events." Acheson strongly endorsed the view put forward by Marshall about limiting the Korean conflict. "We must not, under any circumstances, become involved in a general war with China," he said.

Acheson stepped conceptually back. "We must ask ourselves: What do we want in Korea?" He looked around the room. "The answer is easy," he said. "We want to terminate it. We don't want to beat China in Korea—we can't. We don't want to beat China any place—we can't. They can put in more than we can." American policy in Korea must keep the broader challenge in mind. "Our great objective must be to hold an area, to terminate the fighting, to turn over some area to the Republic of Korea, and to *get out* so that we can get ahead with building up our own strength, and building up the strength of Europe." Europe was where the Cold War would be won or lost. The administration must never forget this essential point.

Truman nodded agreement with what Acheson and the others had said. The Soviet Union, not China, was America's principal enemy; Europe was the heart of America's forward defense; Korea was symbolically important but not strategically vital; America must not alienate its allies. The president was pleased at the consensus in the highest councils of the administration.

He left the meeting satisfied—but still uncertain. He knew that MacArthur had his own ideas about American strategy and that the general, by a single command, might put the administration's consensus at naught.

34

TRUMAN HAD REFRAINED from speaking publicly about the rapidly shifting events in Korea, hoping time would make things clearer. When it didn't, he decided he had to say something, so he called a news conference, which he opened with a prepared statement. "Recent developments in Korea confront the world with a serious crisis," Truman said. "The Chinese Communist leaders have sent their troops from Manchuria to launch a strong and well-organized attack against the United Nations forces in North Korea. This has been done despite prolonged and earnest efforts to bring home to the Communist leaders of China the plain fact that neither the United Nations nor the United States has any aggressive intentions toward China." Truman couldn't predict with confidence what the immediate future would yield. "The Chinese attack was made in great force, and it still continues. It has resulted in the forced withdrawal of large parts of the United Nations command. The battlefield situation is uncertain at this time. We may suffer reverses as we have suffered them before." But the resolve of the United States and the United Nations was as firm as ever. "The forces of the United Nations have no intention of abandoning their mission in Korea." What happened in Korea mattered for the whole world, Truman said. "If the United Nations yields to the forces of aggression, no nation will be safe or secure. If aggression is successful in Korea, we can expect it to spread throughout Asia and Europe."

Truman said his administration would respond to the new situation by redoubling its diplomatic efforts at the United Nations and by accelerating the rearmament of America and America's allies. The latter action was particularly crucial, Truman said. "Because this new act of aggression in Korea is only a part of a worldwide pattern of danger to all the free nations of the world, it is more necessary than ever before for us to increase at a very rapid rate the combined military strength of the free nations." He pledged to work toward an integrated military command for the North Atlantic alliance, and he said he would be sending a supplemental defense request to Congress within days. He hoped the legislature and the American people would respond quickly. "This is a time for all our citizens to lay aside differences and unite in firmness and mutual determination to do what is best for our country and the cause of freedom throughout the world."

When Truman took questions, reporters clamored to know what the president was hearing from MacArthur. "In what detail were you informed about these MacArthur moves?" one asked, apparently referring to the win-the-war offensive.

"Every detail," Truman replied.

"Did you or the State Department raise the question of whether this offensive would affect the chances of a negotiated settlement with the Peiping government?"

"The whole matter was clearly discussed with General MacArthur every day."

"Mr. President, there has been some criticism of General MacArthur in the European press—"

"Some in the American press, too, if I'm not mistaken," Truman said.

"Particularly in the British press—"

"They are always for a man when he is winning, but when he is in a little trouble, they all jump on him with what ought to be done, which they didn't tell him before. He has done a good job, and he is continuing to do a good job. Go ahead with your question."

"The particular criticism is that he exceeded his authority and went beyond the point he was supposed to go."

"He did nothing of the kind."

"Mr. President, a few months ago this government declined the offer of Chinese Nationalist troops. Has that been up for reconsideration, in view—"

"The offer of Nationalist Chinese troops was refused for the reason that we hoped not to be involved in a world war. That situation still continues."

"Mr. President, will the United Nations troops be allowed to bomb across the Manchurian border?"

"I can't answer that question this morning," Truman said.

"Mr. President, will attacks in Manchuria depend on action in the United Nations?"

"Yes, entirely."

"In other words, if the United Nations resolution should authorize General MacArthur to go further than he has, he will—"

"We will take whatever steps are necessary to meet the military situation, just as we always have," Truman said.

"Will that include the atomic bomb?"

The president hadn't seen this coming, though he quickly realized he should have. He didn't have an answer ready. He could have declined to comment, but he had never liked that dodge. It made him appear indecisive. And indecisive was not how he wished to appear now.

"That includes every weapon that we have," he said.

This answer got the reporters' attention. One immediately followed up. "Mr. President, you said, 'Every weapon that we have.' Does that mean that there is active consideration of the use of the atomic bomb?"

Truman realized he was in trouble. He had wanted to calm the situation, and he found himself inflaming it. But he saw no way back, and so he pressed forward. "There has always been active consideration of its use," he said. Yet he immediately qualified his statement. "I don't want to see it used. It is a terrible weapon, and it should not be used on innocent men, women, and children who have nothing whatever to do with this military aggression. That happens when it is used."

After an unrelated question, the reporters returned to the issue they all knew would headline their stories. "Did we understand you clearly that the use of the atomic bomb is under active consideration?"

Truman thought he saw a way out. "Always has been. It is one of our weapons."

"Does that mean, Mr. President, use against military objectives, or civilian—"

He tried to close the discussion. "It's a matter that the military people will have to decide. I'm not a military authority that passes on those things."

These were still the days when reporters required permission to quote the president from news conferences. "Mr. President, perhaps it would be better if we are allowed to quote your remarks on that directly?"

"I don't think that is necessary," Truman said.

"Mr. President, you said this depends on United Nations action. Does that mean that we wouldn't use the atomic bomb except on a United Nations authorization?"

"No, it doesn't mean that at all. The action against Communist China depends on the action of the United Nations. The military commander in the field will have charge of the use of the weapons, as he always has."

Truman saw he was simply getting in deeper. He certainly hadn't given MacArthur authority to use atomic weapons, and he didn't intend to. He sought shallower water. "We have exerted every effort possible to prevent a third world war," he said. "Every maneuver that has been made since June 25th has had in mind not to create a situation which would cause another terrible war. We are still trying to prevent that war from happening, and I hope we may be able to prevent it."

He changed the subject by accusing his critics of sowing misunderstanding. "All these attacks and speculations and lies that have been told on the members of this government have not helped that situation one little bit. There's a big one on the front page of the paper this morning, about Acheson having interfered with the command in the Far East. There isn't one word of truth in that, and never has been. Acheson has attended strictly to his business as secretary of state, and he has done a good job. I am getting tired of all this foolishness and I'm going to bust loose on you one of these days."

He spoke the last line with what might have been a twinkle in his eye. Several reporters laughed, perhaps to ease the tension. The interview ended moments later.

Truman knew he had bungled horribly. He had sought to allay fears that the Korean conflict would become a world war, but the story that led the day's news was his threat to use atomic weapons against China. His suggestion that the choice of weapons was up to the theater commander—MacArthur—merely made things worse.

The White House quickly released an explanatory statement. "The President wants to make it certain that there is no misinterpretation of his answers to questions at his press conference today about the use of the atom bomb," the White House statement said. "Naturally, there has been consideration of this subject since the outbreak of the hostilities in Korea, just as there is consideration of the use of all military weapons whenever our forces are in combat. Consideration of the use of any weapon is always implicit in the very possession of that weapon. However, it should be emphasized, that, by law, only the President can authorize the use of the atom bomb, and no such authorization has been given. If and when such authorization should be given, the military commander in the field would have charge of the tactical delivery of the weapon. In brief, the replies to the questions at today's press conference do not represent any change in this situation."

35

T RUMAN'S STATEMENT THAT the bomb was in play in Korea outdistanced the White House clarification, and it triggered a furor across America and around the world. Nearly everyone had thought the war almost over; hadn't General MacArthur promised as much? But suddenly the planet was on the brink of World War III, which might pick up where World War II had left off, with the use of the most terrible weapons ever invented. Americans shuddered; the governments of America's allies strove to distance themselves from Washington. Clement Attlee of Britain hastily arranged a trip to America; René Pleven of France counseled him on what to tell Truman to avert the cataclysm.

Within Washington, Congress stirred into action. The legislature had never liked having its war-making authority usurped by Truman on the Korean question, but the majority Democrats had declined to challenge a president of their own party and the minority Republicans couldn't muster the votes to force the issue. Anyway, after Inchon, with victory on UN terms imminent, the president's characterization of the conflict as a police action didn't seem outlandish. The Chinese offensive changed the political calculations for both parties. Democrats worried about being dragged into a larger war; Republicans sought to blame the president for the abrupt reversal of fortunes.

Truman addressed the lawmakers' concerns and complaints in a December 1 meeting with the leaders of the two parties. Omar Bradley provided a briefing on the situation in Korea, where American and UN forces continued to reel before the Chinese onslaught. At the close of

Bradley's remarks the president inquired if the lawmakers had questions. Tom Connally asked why MacArthur's force was split into two wings, one in the east and the other in the west. Bradley pointed to the map he had brought and explained that a range of mountains separated the two wings. Communications and transport across the mountains were very difficult. Moreover, MacArthur had been trying to fulfill the UN directive to pacify and occupy as much of Korea as possible, toward the goal of holding all-country elections.

Alexander Wiley asked about the adequacy of MacArthur's intelligence. Bradley had been expecting the question, which was the one nearly all of America and much of the world was asking. He didn't wish to assign blame but couldn't dodge the obvious. "Undoubtedly General MacArthur was unaware of the size of the concentration of enemy forces," Bradley said, "or he would not have undertaken exactly the kind of operations that he did and he would have been better prepared to meet the attack."

Democratic congressman John McCormack asked how MacArthur had been caught so off guard. Wasn't it well known that there were large numbers of Chinese troops in Manchuria?

"Yes," Bradley replied.

"Isn't there a command intelligence at MacArthur's headquarters?" McCormack asked.

"Yes, there is field intelligence in Korea," Bradley replied. He said he assumed the congressman wanted to know why MacArthur wasn't aware of all the Chinese in Korea until they attacked. "The point is that the Chinese come across the Yalu River at night in small numbers, and they march down through Korea in short columns, also at night. It is very difficult to pick up these columns by air reconnaissance, and since they move in such small groups it is difficult even for our intelligence on the ground to make an accurate estimate of communist strength."

Kenneth Wherry asked if MacArthur could hold a line in Korea.

Bradley said he didn't know.

This produced a sobered pause. Truman let the message sink in before turning to Walter Bedell Smith to make the administration's larger point about Korea. The CIA director set up a new map, this one centered on Europe and the Soviet Union. He said that what was happening in Korea was closely connected to what was happening in Europe. The Soviet-controlled areas of Europe had been very quiet during the last ten days. "This in itself is a disquieting fact." But the Soviet army had been busy. "The Russians appear to have completed very large scale maneuvers in which some 500,000 men took part. Their maneuvers were concentrated on airborne troops and river crossings."

John McCormack asked Smith why the Soviets were training so many men for airlift.

"Undoubtedly the Soviets are training their airborne troops for European operations," Smith said.

McCormack asked whether, if World War III began, a bridgehead on the European continent would be important to the United States.

"An American bridgehead would certainly be important," Smith said.

Truman took over. Once again the president cast the Korean issue in global context. The administration, he said, had been working hard to build up American defenses. He had sent one supplemental budget request to Congress in September and was about to send another. The current request, for $17 billion, had been in preparation for months, he said. But it had been increased in the last few days because of the escalation of the fighting in Korea. "I hope you can consider this carefully, and act fast," he told the lawmakers. "I have been anxious for you to get all the facts about the situation with which we are faced. That is why I have had General Smith and General Bradley here to talk with you today. I want you to know the facts on which these estimates are based."

He said he and the members of his administration had been working "day and night" to keep the conflict in Korea from spreading. Congress could help by providing the funding he was requesting. The better America was armed, the less likely it would be attacked. Truman repeated that time was of the essence, in light of the recent events. The administration had accelerated its rearming timetable. "We are trying to get ready by mid-'52 what we wanted for mid-'53," he said.

As the session ended, the president urged all present to keep to themselves what they had heard there. "Don't tell anybody, not even your wives," he said. "What you heard here today is something even I don't hear unless I push these people into telling me."

36

J AMES RESTON WAS not at the meeting between Truman and the congressional leaders, yet the *New York Times* reporter evidently heard from one or more of those who had been. Washington had never been good with secrets, but the dismaying reversal in Korea, following months of tension between Truman and MacArthur, caused tongues to wag all over the capital. "Outwardly there is a new unity in Washington in the face of the crisis, but behind the scenes the atmosphere here is one of gravity and considerable bitterness," Reston wrote. "There is no doubt that confidence in Gen. Douglas MacArthur, even on Capitol Hill, has been badly shaken as a result of the events of the last few days. Similarly, there is no doubt that United States leadership in the Western world has been damaged by President Truman's acceptance of the bold MacArthur offensive and the President's rejection of the more cautious British strategy." Reston, whose sources clearly included administration officials, continued, "Ever since the Inchon landing, which was praised world-wide as one of the most adroit military operations in modern history, various suggestions have been made to the State Department and, through it and the President to General MacArthur, of the necessity for caution in approaching the Manchurian and Soviet frontiers." The British, preoccupied with the safety of Hong Kong, had argued most strongly for staying away from China's borders. But MacArthur repeatedly resisted restraint. "In each case," Reston wrote, again following his administration sources, "General MacArthur took the view that these suggestions were jeopardizing the victories he had won. Moreover, he indicated that he could not be responsible for the security of his troops—a phrase he used on several occasions—if any such policy of cautious waiting were adopted." Truman had let himself be persuaded by MacArthur, overriding his own judgment that caution was necessary.

Reston's sources explained why this was so. "First, General MacArthur was on the ground. It was assumed that his intelligence had been right about the numbers of Chinese that opposed him before the United Nations attack. It was also assumed that he had been right in his estimate that the Chinese Communists were not preparing for a counteroffensive." Events, of course, had proved these assumptions wrong. Reston added a political factor to the error equation. "From the time of the Inchon landing to the opening of last week's 'end-the-war' offensive, General MacArthur was riding high. He was supported strongly on Capitol Hill and in the country, and any open break with him certainly could not have done President Truman any good in the election."

The Chinese offensive had changed things dramatically. MacArthur wasn't riding so high, and the administration appeared less reluctant to challenge him. Reston expected the tension to grow. Meanwhile the Korean conflict was further from resolution than ever. "Nobody available here today seemed to see any honorable policy between the unacceptable extremes of appeasement and an Asiatic war."

MACARTHUR READ RESTON and other critics and grew angrier and angrier. It was bad enough, he believed, to have his hands tied by the lack of nerve of the diplomats and politicians. But to be blamed for the consequences of that hand tying was intolerable. He invited an interview with the weekly *U.S. News & World Report* and delivered his riposte. The interview took place in writing; the editors of the magazine cabled their questions to the general, who cabled his reply. The editors admired MacArthur, so much so that their questions seemed as though they had been written by him, which some might well have been.

"Were there any warnings from the U.N. or otherwise about the dangers of a winter offensive?" the editors asked.

"There were no warnings," MacArthur answered predictably. "Nor were any warnings necessary," he continued, more surprisingly. MacArthur elaborated, unveiling the argument that would become his defense against the charges of recklessness: namely, that his offensive had produced a *positive* outcome. "A winter offensive is as hard on the enemy as upon friendly forces," he said. "To have assumed defensive positions awaiting spring would not have avoided the rigors of the winter climate, for to hold these positions would require constant fighting during the winter months and it would have given the enemy an opportunity to mass his forces for a demolishing attack—with every assurance that he would jump off just as soon as a satisfactory military balance had been achieved." In other words, MacArthur had surprised the Chinese and spoiled *their* plans, rather than vice versa.

"Was there adequate knowledge of Chinese strength?" the editors asked.

MacArthur's answer implied that such knowledge was impossible, given the constraints placed upon him. "When the line of battle moved northward following the Inchon landing, the area of possible detection and interdiction of enemy movements contracted until there was left but a night's march from the border sanctuary for Chinese Communist forces to the area of hostilities. This provided means for Chinese Communist authorities to move troops forward under cover of darkness and rugged terrain with little possibility of detection." He added significantly, "Air reconnaissance across the border is prohibited."

The editors asked if major operations like the recent offensive were planned in consultation with Washington and the UN or by the theater commander alone.

"Major operations are all reported and approved prior to being launched," MacArthur said.

"Did you expect the winter offensive to be lengthy or a pushover?" the editors asked.

MacArthur granted that he had hoped the offensive would be decisive. But he reiterated that the way things had turned out was all to the good. "Had we failed to assault and uncover enemy strength and intentions, the opportunity secretly to build up from available resources of all China would inevitably encompass our destruction."

"Was this estimate based on the belief that Chinese strength was not more than 60,000?" the editors asked, citing a figure that had been widely reported.

MacArthur responded, in effect, that the number was immaterial. "The tactical course taken was the only one which the situation permitted."

"Would you describe the present situation as 'critical and serious, but not hopeless'?"

MacArthur acknowledged the gravity of the situation. But it was not hopeless, he said, "unless one completely discounts the combined resources of the free nations engaged in the Korean conflict."

"Are the Chinese supply lines vulnerable to air attack?"

MacArthur returned to the handicaps under which he operated. "Within Manchuria the Chinese supply lines are protected from our air attack." And it was only in Manchuria where they might be reasonably interdicted. "South of the border for many miles along the river line, they can enter trails leading up through rugged terrain. Under the worst conditions, troops and supplies could be moved forward under cover of night with little possibility of air detection, an essential to air interdiction."

The editors asked the question MacArthur most urgently wanted to answer on the record: "Are the limitations which prevent unlimited pursuit of Chinese large forces and unlimited attack on their bases regarded by you as a handicap to effective military operations?"

"An enormous handicap without precedent in military history," MacArthur said.

The editors asked a corollary question, the one MacArthur thought Truman and the administration were obsessing over needlessly: "Are there any signs of Russian divisions being mobilized on their border?"

"No detection of such mobilization," he said.

The editors teed MacArthur up for another swing at the constraints on his war fighting. "What accounts for the fact that an enemy without air power can make effective progress against forces possessing considerable air power?"

"The limitations aforementioned," he said, "plus the type of maneuver which renders air support of ground operations extremely difficult, and the curtailment of the strategic potentiality of the air because of the sanctuary of neutrality immediately behind the battle area."

"Is there a significant lesson in this for U.S. planning?" the editors asked, lest MacArthur's superiors fail to miss the message.

"Yes," he said simply. His previous answers had provided the details.

The editors asked MacArthur about atomic weapons. "Can anything be said as to the effectiveness or ineffectiveness of the bomb in the type of operations in which you are now engaged?"

MacArthur had learned from Truman's fumbles at the recent press conference. "My comment would be inappropriate at this time," he said.

TRUMAN GREW LIVID as he read MacArthur's interview. *U.S. News & World Report* scooped itself—and promoted the issue containing the MacArthur interview—by releasing the general's comments ahead of publication. "Tell General MacArthur we regarded his statement as so important and opportune that we gave it in full text to all the press associations for immediate publication," David Lawrence of the magazine explained by radiogram to MacArthur's headquarters.

Truman read the interview with the rest of America and could hardly contain himself. "I should have relieved General MacArthur then and there," he wrote later. He thought MacArthur's statements dishonest and entirely out of line. He bridled at the general's assertions and implications that all would have been well if only the president and the joint chiefs had listened to him. "In the first place, of course, he was wrong," Truman said. "If his advice had been taken, then or later, and if we had gone ahead and bombed the Manchurian bases, we would have been openly at war with Red China and, not improbably, with Russia. World War III might very well have been upon us. In the second place, General MacArthur himself had been the one who had said there was no danger of Chinese intervention. At Wake Island he had told me categorically that he had no evidence that a massed intervention was threatening. More important still, he had told me that he could easily cope with the Chinese Communists if they actually came in. He had said that if the Communists from China tried to retake Pyongyang they would be inviting mass slaughter. Even before he started his ill-fated offensive of November 24, he still talked as if he had the answer to all the questions. But when it turned out that it was not so, he let all the world know that he would have won except for the fact that we would not let him have his way."

Truman recalled from his army days the prerogative of subordinates to complain at the stupidity of their superiors. "Of course every second lieutenant knows best what his platoon ought to be given to do, and he always thinks that the higher-ups are just blind when they don't see his way." The difference was that second lieutenants didn't air their grievances for the world to hear. "General MacArthur—and rightly, too—would have court-martialed any second lieutenant who gave press interviews to express his disagreement."

Truman was tempted to fire MacArthur, but didn't. "The reason I did not was that I did not wish to have it appear as if he were being relieved because the offensive failed. I have never believed in going back on people when luck is against them, and I did not intend to do it now. Nor did I want to reprimand the general, but he had to be told that the kinds of public statements which he had been making were out of order."

Truman's action was less decisive than his later remarks let on. He sent no message to MacArthur specifically, on the matter of public statements and interviews. Instead he issued a gag order binding all officials of the executive branch, civilian and military. They must clear statements on foreign policy with their superiors. And American officials overseas, including diplomats and military officers, must refrain from speaking directly to reporters on foreign or military policy.

ANOTHER REASON TRUMAN didn't fire MacArthur was that he had cause to believe Korea was about to become the least of America's problems. On December 2 the CIA delivered a sobering assessment of what the full-blown Chinese intervention in Korea portended. "The attitude of the Chinese Communist regime and urgent defensive preparations in China show that this intervention was undertaken with appreciation of the risk of general war between the United States and Communist China and perhaps in expectation of such a development," the CIA authors said. They continued, and this was the main point, "It is highly improbable that the Chinese Communist regime would have accepted this risk without explicit assurance of effective Soviet support."

The Kremlin's likely course of action seemed clear to the CIA. It would back China with material support, technical personnel and perhaps "volunteers." In particular it would provide warplanes, pilots, anti-aircraft artillery and gunners to defend Chinese targets against air attack. And it would probably go to the open and forceful aid of China, under the terms of the Sino-Soviet treaty, in the event of major American or UN operations against Chinese territory. Moscow apparently had made its decision with its eyes open. "The Soviet rulers, in directing or sanctioning the Chinese Communist intervention in Korea, must have appreciated the increased risk of global war and have felt ready to accept such a development."

The CIA didn't conjecture whether the Soviets hoped for a global war at the present time. But whether they did or not, embroiling the United States in a war with China suited their aims. "If the Soviet rulers do now intend to bring on such a war, they might well prefer that it should develop from the situation in East Asia. On the other hand, even if they do not intend to precipitate a global war, they must estimate that a broadening of the Korean war into a general war between the United States and China would be advantageous to the U.S.S.R." A general war between the United States and China would slow the arming of the Atlantic alliance. It would foster dissension among the allies. It would fracture the UN coalition on Korea and weaken the international organization.

And it would hearten communist movements elsewhere in Asia. In sum, though the CIA authors didn't put it quite this way, a broader war between the United States and China would be about the best Christmas present the Kremlin could receive.

MACARTHUR WASN'T THINKING about Russia. He was worried about China and about holding his forces together in the face of the Chinese onslaught. The optimism of November wholly vanished by the first week of December. "The X Corps is being withdrawn into the Hamhung area as rapidly as possible," he wrote to the joint chiefs on December 3. "The situation within the Eighth Army becomes increasingly critical. General Walker reports, and I agree with his estimate, that he cannot hold the Pyongyang area and under enemy pressure, when exerted, will unquestionably be forced to withdraw to the Seoul area." The chiefs had urged MacArthur to link X Corps and the Eighth Army, the better to fend off the Chinese. MacArthur pronounced this impracticable and counterproductive. "Both forces are completely outnumbered and their junction would, therefore, not only not produce added strength but actually jeopardize the free flow of movement that arises from the two separate logistical lines of naval supply and maneuver."

The chiefs had also recommended a retreat to the narrow waist of the Korean peninsula, above the 38th parallel. MacArthur rejected this advice as well. "The development of a defense line across the waist of Korea is not feasible because of the numerical weakness of our forces as considered in connection with the distances involved; by the necessity of supplying the two parts of the line from ports within each area; and by the division of the area into two compartments by the rugged mountainous terrain running north and south." The line proposed was some 120 miles long, by air, and 150 miles by road. "If the entire United States force of seven divisions at my disposal were placed along this defensive line it would mean that a division would be forced to protect a front of approximately 20 miles against greatly superior numbers of an enemy whose greatest strength is a potential for night infiltration through rugged terrain. Such a line with no depth would have little strength, and as a defensive concept would invite penetration with resultant envelopment and piecemeal destruction."

MacArthur thought the chiefs—and the president—failed to understand the meaning of China's open entry into the war. "Already Chinese troops to the estimated strength of approximately 26 divisions are in line of battle with an additional minimum of 200,000 to the enemy rear and now in process of being committed to action. In addition to this, remnants of the North Korean Army are being reorganized in the rear and there stands, of course, behind all this the entire military potential of Communist China." The Chinese action was no limited incursion but a full-scale war against the United States.

MacArthur complained again at the limitations imposed on him by the chiefs and the president. The artificial sanctity of the international boundary effectively neutralized his air force, reducing the battle to an unwinnable contest of ground troops. "It is clearly evident, therefore, that unless ground reinforcements of the greatest magnitude are promptly supplied, this command will be either forced into successive withdrawals with diminished powers of resistance after each such move, or will be forced to take up beachhead bastion positions which, while insuring a degree of prolonged resistance, would afford little hope of anything beyond defense."

MacArthur stated things as starkly as he could. "The general evaluation of the situation here must be viewed on the basis of an entirely new war against an entirely new power of great military strength and under entirely new conditions." The U.S. government was asking too much of its soldiers in Korea. "This small command actually under present conditions is facing the entire Chinese nation in an undeclared war," he said. "And unless some positive and immediate action is taken, hope for success cannot be justified and steady attrition leading to final destruction can reasonably be contemplated."

He insisted on receiving new orders. "The directives under which I am operating based upon the North Korean forces as an enemy are completely outmoded by events. The fact must be clearly understood that our relatively small force now faces the full offensive power of the Chinese Communist nation augmented by extensive supply of Soviet materiel." Washington decreed disaster for America's troops if it did not recognize the new reality and act accordingly. "Time is of the essence, as every hour sees the enemy power increase and ours decline."

MACARTHUR DIDN'T GET new orders. All he got were recommendations from the joint chiefs, who couldn't bring themselves to issue a direct order. Matthew Ridgway was Joe Collins's deputy and a tough-minded fighting general. Military service ran in Ridgway's family, and he had followed his father from one army base to another while a boy. Yet he was an indifferent cadet at West Point, hardly registering in the consciousness of Commandant MacArthur, and he first won notice, during World War II, only as commander of a novelty in the U.S. Army, an airborne division. The Eighty-Second Airborne fought well in Italy and France, and an enlarged Ridgway command helped turn the tide in the Battle of the Bulge. By war's end Ridgway had earned a reputation as a commander with a knack for reversing bad situations.

He also was known for having little tolerance for nonsense from either subordinates or superiors. Ridgway sat in on the meetings of the joint chiefs at which the dire condition of MacArthur's command was reviewed, and he thought the chiefs were engaged in nonsense with

MacArthur by not issuing him an order. After one meeting he asked Hoyt Vandenberg about their diffidence. "Why don't the chiefs send orders to MacArthur and tell him what to do?" Ridgway inquired.

Vandenberg shook his head. "What good would that do? He wouldn't obey the orders. What can we do?"

"You can relieve any commander who won't obey orders, can't you?"

Vandenberg didn't answer. "His lips parted and he looked at me with an expression both puzzled and amazed," Ridgway recounted later. "He walked away then without saying a word and I never afterward had occasion to discuss this with him."

38

MAGGIE HIGGINS HAD heard lots of officers give lots of orders, but she hadn't heard an officer give an order that caused him such anguish as that evinced by a marine colonel in Korea in December 1950. The Chinese counteroffensive had trapped much of the Marine First Division near Chosin Reservoir in the mountains of far North Korea, and Radio Peking was predicting their rapid annihilation. Lieutenant Colonel Ray Murray understood the long odds against his command; the Chinese outnumbered the Americans by several to one and had the Americans surrounded. "The snow lashed hard at the raw faces of a dozen marine officers as they stood in the zero temperature listening to the words of their commander," Higgins recalled of a meeting at Hagaru that Murray allowed her to observe. She knew of the marine tradition of always fighting to the front, of retreating only in extremis. Murray knew the tradition better than she did, and he had great difficulty with the words he was compelled to speak. "At daylight," he said, "we advance to the rear. Those are division orders."

Murray didn't like the orders, so he added a personal sentiment and gloss: "We're going to come out of this as marines, not as stragglers. We're going to bring out our wounded and our equipment. We're coming out, I tell you, as marines or not at all." He thought some more. "This is no retreat," he declared. "This is an assault in another direction. There are more Chinese blocking our path to the sea than there are ahead of us. But we're going to get out of here. Any officer who doesn't think so will kindly go lame and be evacuated. I don't expect any takers."

Higgins knew the marines had been through hell already. She could see it in their faces and their posture. "They had the dazed air of men who have accepted death and then found themselves alive after all. They talked in unfinished phrases. They would start to say something and then stop, as if the meaning was beyond any words at their command."

The marines were bitter. They felt they had been poorly commanded. They had been placed in X Corps and were subject to army orders. They had been ordered to advance, to take the town of Yudamni, even after the Chinese had come dangerously close to their left flank. When the Eighth Army, to their west, was sent reeling, their left flank collapsed and they were surrounded. "Yudamni was the ideal trap," Higgins wrote. "Steep-sided valleys led to it along a narrow, icy road. The Chinese hugged the ridges, and the marines were easy targets." The intensifying winter added to their danger and misery. "The temperature dropped way below zero. Guns and vehicles froze. The marines had to chip ice off the mortars to fire them. Carbines jammed in the cold." Frostbite claimed fingers, toes, ears and noses. The wounded suffered the worst, being unable to move and generate even a little warmth.

Those who had made it out of Yudamni appeared as though they could hardly go farther. "As I looked at the battered men there at Hagaru," Higgins wrote, "I wondered if they could possibly have the strength to make this final punch. The men were ragged, their faces swollen and bleeding from the sting of the icy wind. Mittens were torn and raveled. Some were without hats, their ears blue in the frost. A few walked to the doctor's tent barefoot because they couldn't get their frostbitten feet into their frozen shoepacs. They were drunk with fatigue, and yet they were unable to shrug off the tension that had kept them going five days and nights without sleep and often without food."

But they had no choice. If they were going to get out, they had to keep moving. "It was a battle all the way," Higgins recounted. "The frost and wind, howling through the narrow pass, were almost as deadly as the enemy. Bumper to bumper, trucks, half-tracks, and bulldozers slipped and scraped down the mountain. Half a dozen vehicles skidded and careened off the road. Mortars lobbed in, and sometimes the convoy had to stop for hours while engineers filled the holes. It was a struggle to keep from freezing during these waits."

The cold became a greater enemy than the Chinese. "Most of the marines were so numb and exhausted that they didn't even bother to take cover at sporadic machine-gun and rifle fire," Higgins wrote.

"When someone was killed they would wearily, matter-of-factly pick up the body and throw it in the nearest truck."

One of Higgins's journalist colleagues watched a marine chiseling breakfast out of a frozen tin of beans. His fingers were nearly frozen, too, and he could barely hold his spoon. The journalist asked the marine what he would ask for, if he could have any wish.

"Gimme tomorrow," the marine said, not looking up from his beans.

The marine column got a tomorrow, and then another. After two agonizing weeks they reached the coast at Hamhung. Higgins recounted the relief expressed by one marine captain. "We've really got it made now," he said. "I don't know if I can tell you how the guys feel. It's not having to look for a place to hide. It's being able to sleep without feeling guilty. It's being able to eat something warm. It's not having to spend most of your time just trying not to freeze to death."

39

CLEMENT ATTLEE HAD taken over as British prime minister from Winston Churchill at the moment of victory in World War II. Americans had puzzled at the time as to how such a thing could happen, because most had identified Churchill with the British war effort and couldn't fathom the coalition politics that came unglued as the war ended. Nor did any but a handful of Americans endorse the socialist principles that underwrote Attlee's Labour government. Joseph McCarthy and others on the Republican right branded Attlee as alarmingly pink if not fatally red, but even among American liberals enthusiasm for the mild-mannered Attlee was scarce. Some chuckled at Churchill's characterization of Attlee as a modest man who had much to be modest about.

Yet Truman appreciated Attlee. The president understood what it was like to succeed a great wartime figure, to be destined to be measured against a standard of leadership unachievable during peacetime. More important, Truman valued Attlee as an ally in the Cold War. Attlee's Foreign Office had prompted Truman's State Department to formulate the Truman Doctrine. Attlee's foreign minister, Ernest Bevin, had leaped at George Marshall's suggestion of a recovery plan for Europe. Attlee and Bevin had delivered Britain as an eastern pillar of the North Atlantic alliance. Britain's support in the Security Council had been vital to the first UN decisions to defend South Korea against the communist attack. And Britain led the UN allies in providing arms and men for service under MacArthur.

But Britain's interests, though broadly parallel to America's, were by no means identical. Britain had shed the largest part of its empire—India—yet other parts remained, sometimes devotedly. Hong Kong greatly preferred Britain's embrace to the alternative: absorption by now-communist China. Attlee's Labour party was anti-imperialist, but even most Labour radicals couldn't countenance the abandonment of colonial subjects who didn't want to be abandoned. And his Conservative opponents, led by the arch-imperialist Churchill, would have done to him what the McCarthyists were doing to Truman. Moreover, though India (and Pakistan and Burma) had left the empire, they hadn't left the British Commonwealth, which London fancied as the honorable and influential successor to the empire, and the ex post facto justification for the empire.

Britain's imperial commitments and Commonwealth hopes gave Attlee a decidedly different view of events in Asia. Attlee's government had quickly extended diplomatic recognition to the new government of China. British leaders and diplomats defended the decision on its merits, as acknowledging the obvious fact that Mao's regime now ruled the most populous nation in the world. But London simultaneously reckoned that what it couldn't defend militarily—Hong Kong—it might protect diplomatically. Meanwhile the British cultivated the government of Jawaharlal Nehru in India, believing that whither Nehru and India, thither the Commonwealth.

There was one other thing that separated the British from the Americans in matters relating to Asia. The British, tapping the institutional memory of the empire, judged themselves experts on Asian politics and the Asian mind. They considered the Americans rank novices. Diplomatic politesse, not to mention their country's dependence on American arms and Marshall Plan aid, prompted them to keep their dismal opinion of American understanding of Asia to themselves, for the most part, but undertones of condescension sometimes slipped into conversations with their American counterparts.

Attlee was the soul of tact in his first conversation with Truman. The two men had never met, and Attlee had not been planning a visit to the United States. But Truman's talk of the atom bomb left the prime minister no choice but to invite himself, and Truman consented at once to the meeting. When Attlee arrived in Washington, Truman dispensed with formality and brought him straight to the White House for a conference. He had Omar Bradley give a military briefing, which focused on the fighting retreat being conducted by MacArthur's forces toward beachheads south of the 38th parallel. Attlee's military chief of staff, William Slim, who had fought the Japanese in Burma during World War II while MacArthur was fighting them in the Pacific, asked Bradley if the beachheads were for holding or for evacuating. Bradley responded that this made little difference at the moment but in fact had not been decided. Slim asked if they *could* be held. Bradley said this depended on what shape MacArthur's forces were in when they reached the coast.

Attlee said he understood that it was not possible to hold a line clear across the peninsula. The prime minister gave no indication that he had read MacArthur's recent report making precisely that assertion, but somehow the word had filtered his way.

Bradley acknowledged that this was true. Bradley, of course, had read MacArthur's report, and he had been persuaded by it. At any rate, he decided that if the theater commander thought the line could not be held, then it would not be held.

Attlee asked how the American air cover was faring. Was it as effective as before?

Bradley said the situation was deteriorating. MacArthur had lost control of some airfields in Korea already and was in danger of losing others. If that happened, American planes would have to fly from Japan, as they had early in the fighting, or from aircraft carriers.

George Marshall interjected that American planes were less effective against the Chinese ground troops than they might have been in other situations, because the Chinese excelled at hiding their troop movements and using the mountains for cover.

When Bradley concluded the military briefing, Truman took up the politics of the Korean conflict. "The United States has responsibilities in the East and the West," he said. "We naturally consider European defense primary, but we equally have responsibilities in Korea, Japan and the Philippines, as the British do in Hong Kong and Singapore. It must be clear that we are not going to run out on our obligations even though these are hard to meet." The obligations in Korea had become much more challenging since the entry of China into the fighting. He hoped he and Attlee could reach an accord on what the Chinese intervention signified. He asked for the prime minister's thoughts.

Attlee responded that like the president he deemed it essential to view events in Korea in the broadest perspective. A first concern was the maintenance of the prestige of the United Nations. "The United States is the principal instrument for supporting the United Nations," Attlee said, "and the United Kingdom is giving what help it can. This problem has now become very difficult with the Chinese Communists coming in. It is common to our thinking that we wish the Korean business to be limited to asserting the authority of the United Nations against aggression in Korea. We all realize that other forces might come in and might bring on another world war."

At this point Attlee might have raised the issue of the atom bomb. But it would have been discourteous to mention the unfortunate news conference that had brought him to Washington; his mere presence was reminder enough. Besides, when he spoke of another world war, it went without saying that this one would be waged with nuclear weapons—which was why every effort must be made to prevent it. "We are very eager to avoid extension of the conflict," Attlee said.

Attlee said Britain and the United States must consider Asian opinion. He had been in close touch with the Asian members of the Commonwealth. They did not want to see a war against China. They *did* want the West to try to perceive things from China's point of view. "We ourselves look upon it as a stand by the United Nations against aggression," he said of the effort in Korea. The Chinese interpreted it differently. "The Chinese Communists are not members of the United Nations"—chiefly because the United States insisted they not be, though Attlee didn't say so—"and therefore are not obligated by any of those considerations. They regard it as action by those forces fighting against them, especially the United States." The Chinese feared that the United States, in league with Chiang Kai-shek, would try to reverse their revolution. Attlee added that the Chinese valued their hard-won independence; though allied with the Russians, they would not let themselves become dependent on the Russians.

This opinion provoked a sharp response from Dean Acheson. The secretary of state declared that the Chinese Communists were communists first and Chinese only second. "The Chinese Communists are not looking at the matter as Chinese but as communists who are subservient to Moscow," Acheson said. "All they do is based on the Moscow pattern." Acheson thought the Chinese intervention in Korea demonstrated China's subservience to Moscow. "The Russians are no doubt pleased with the idea that we might be fully engaged in war with the Chinese Communists who are acting as their satellites."

Truman agreed with Acheson. "They are satellites of Russia and will remain satellites so long as the present Peiping regime is in power," he said. "They are complete satellites." There was no room for negotiating with such people. Their aggression had to be resisted lest it spread. "After Korea it would be Indochina, then Hong Kong, then Malaya."

Truman sought to ensure that Attlee understood the lengths to which the United States had gone to avoid war with China. "We have made every possible move to keep out of war with the Chinese Communists," he said. "We do not want such a war and have shown great forbearance so far in withstanding their attacks." The president described his Wake Island meeting with MacArthur. He said he had told the general to take pains not to provoke the Chinese. MacArthur had agreed on the wisdom of this course, Truman said, and had predicted that the Chinese would not intervene. The Chinese had proven him wrong and entered the fighting. They were now attempting to push the United Nations out of Korea. Truman said he was trying to prevent this.

Attlee had not said he distrusted MacArthur, but Truman, distrusting MacArthur himself, supposed he did. In any event, Truman emphasized that MacArthur was on a short leash. "We have never taken a move or given General MacArthur an order unless it came from the United Nations," the president said. The UN connection was crucial, as was America's link to its Atlantic allies. "We do not want to act independently."

THIS WAS PRECISELY the problem, in the minds of MacArthur and the many in America who preferred the five-star general's judgment on war to that of the artillery captain. Attlee's Washington visit was intended to reassure British voters and members of Parliament, besides providing the Americans the benefit of Britain's experience in dealing with troublesome Asians, and it did ease the angst on Attlee's political front. But it sparked a storm in Washington among Truman's Republican critics. Anglophobia had been a staple of American politics during the nineteenth century, when candidates and elected officials routinely blamed the British for designs against the United States, and again after World War I, which many Americans retrospectively deemed a conflict the United States had been suckered into by London. World War II required another suspension of the Anglophobia, which the Truman administration had worked hard to keep in abeyance as the Cold War developed. But critics of the Marshall Plan and the North Atlantic Treaty complained that once more America was acting as London's cat's-paw. And when Attlee came to America, the Anglophobes emerged in force.

Senator William Knowland spoke for many when he warned that Attlee was seeking to undermine American resolve against Asian communism. Attlee, Knowland said, embodied the attitude of the weak-kneed members of the UN coalition who were "vacillating and palavering" over whether the movement of hundreds of thousands of Chinese across the international boundary between Korea and China constituted aggression. "Are we to have one set of rules and one set of penalties for small aggressors and none at all for the large? Are we to continue our moral and material support to an organization"—the UN—"which kowtows to the doctrine that might makes right?" Knowland said he had voted for aid to Britain in the past. But if the British didn't show more spine, he would reconsider. Addressing himself as if to Attlee, Knowland declared, "America has been faced with dark days before. We hoped to meet any future ones with staunch allies in the common cause of freedom, not just regional freedom, Mr. Prime Minister. But if we have to meet them alone, perhaps it is better to find out now. If others want to clasp the hand of the murderer and welcome him into their home, we don't have to stultify ourselves to that extent."

CHIANG KAI-SHEK MONITORED the Truman-Attlee talks from a distance and leveled his own warning. The Chinese Nationalist leader chafed under the continued blockade by the Seventh Fleet, and he hoped that the new crisis between China and the United States would spring him from Formosa. He took the opportunity of Attlee's visit to Washington to throw fuel onto the political fire in America. Branding the Truman-Attlee talks as potentially "another Munich," he reminded all listening that Munich had failed and world war had followed. Appeasement of the Chinese Communists would fail too. "War may break out at any time." Chiang placed his confidence in Douglas MacArthur, not

Harry Truman. He would not let MacArthur down. "If the commander-in-chief of the United Nations forces is given full authority in strategy, and this calls for our military support, we shall certainly give it."

THE TRUMAN-ATTLEE TALKS lasted four days. The president and the prime minister spoke at the White House and aboard the presidential yacht *Williamsburg*. Attlee tried to convince Truman and the Americans that the Sino-Soviet axis was more tenuous than it seemed, that Mao and his colleagues were Chinese first and communists second. "They can be Marxists and yet not bow to Stalin," Attlee said. Diplomatic wisdom lay in cultivating the Chinese, not driving them into utter dependence on Russia.

Truman and his advisers disagreed. "For fifty years we have tried to be friends with the Chinese," Acheson rejoined. But they had denounced America as imperialist and now had attacked the United States in Korea. The prime minister had things backward in saying the West ought to cultivate the Chinese, Acheson said. "Instead of our making an effort to prove that we are their friends, we ask them to prove that they are ours."

Yet the two sides agreed on the necessity of containing the conflict in Korea. "The objectives of our two nations in foreign policy are the same," declared the communiqué issued at the end of the talks. The United States and Britain stood with the United Nations to deter aggression, and they summoned all other countries to do the same. "Lasting peace and the future of the United Nations as an instrument for world peace depend upon strong support for resistance against aggression."

In the conclusion of the communiqué, Truman gave Attlee what the prime minister had come to America to get. "The President stated that it was his hope that world conditions would never call for the use of the atomic bomb."

40

AS HARD AS Truman was working to bolster America's alliance system, the Kremlin was striving to undermine it. Or so said a new CIA analysis that painted an even grimmer picture than the president had seen before. Titled "Probable Soviet Moves to Exploit the Present Situation," the report asserted that Moscow found the current state of affairs most pleasing. "The treatment of developments in Korea by the Soviet Union and the Soviet satellites indicates that they assess their current military and political position as one of great strength in comparison with that of the West." The reverses suffered by American and UN forces in Korea made the Soviets hopeful that American influence could be rolled back from East Asia. The Americans might be forced out of Korea, with damage to their credibility and that of the UN. The American Seventh Fleet might be withdrawn from the waters around Formosa, allowing the emergence of Communist China as the predominant power in the region. In time the United States might be forced out of Japan.

But the larger goal was the weakening of the Western alliance. The CIA report identified Russia's top priorities: "1. Destruction of the unity among the Western countries, thereby isolating the United States. 2. Alienating the Western peoples from their governments so that the efforts of the Western countries to strengthen themselves will be undermined." The report declared that the alliance was most vulnerable in Berlin and West Germany. "So far as Germany is concerned, Moscow has been stepping up at a fast rate its propaganda campaign against rearmament of Germany by the West. The present trend of Soviet activity in Germany suggests that there may soon be drastic action, possibly including a renewal of the Berlin blockade and violence in Western Germany."

The CIA warned that pressure against Germany—complemented perhaps by moves in Indochina, Yugoslavia and Iran—could be the prelude to a broader conflict. "The Soviet Union may seize upon the present crisis to precipitate general war with the United States," the report said. "Soviet propaganda has been stressing the threat of a new world war arising out of the current situation. The Kremlin is continuing preparations for military actions by Soviet troops. Moscow may be hoping, by these steps, to frighten the West and to reduce our will to resist. However, the situation is such that the possibility cannot be disregarded that the Soviet Union has already made a decision for general war and is getting ready for it."

TRUMAN HAD SPOKEN on television before 1950, but few people had seen him. Television receivers were still a curiosity, and television networks lacked the breadth to put a president before the nation as a whole. When he spoke on the evening of December 15, 1950, many more people heard him on radio than saw him on television. Yet the television broadcast caused media executives to see a bright future for the small screen, in that it revealed the natural synergy between television and national crisis.

Truman never mastered a television style, often seeming stiff and cold. On this occasion, however, his demeanor suited his sobering message. "I am talking to you tonight about what our country is up against," he said. "Our homes, our nation, all the things we believe in, are in great danger. This danger has been created by the rulers of the Soviet Union." Not the North Koreans or the Chinese, but the Soviets. Truman reminded his viewers and listeners that the Cold War antedated the Korean conflict. "For five years we have been working for peace and justice among nations. We have helped to bring the free nations of the world together in a great movement to establish a lasting peace."

The work was well begun, but the danger persisted. "Against this movement for peace, the rulers of the Soviet Union have been waging a relentless attack. They have tried to undermine or overwhelm the free nations one by one. They have used threats and treachery and violence." The threat had shifted geographic focus, but its malignant engine was still the same. "In June the forces of Communist imperialism burst out into open warfare in Korea. The United Nations moved to put down this act of aggression, and by October had all but succeeded. Then, in November, the Communists threw their Chinese armies into the battle against the free nations." Here again Truman blamed Moscow: It wasn't the Chinese who had thrown their communist armies into battle but the communists who had deployed their Chinese armies. The world was the prize, not Korea or even Asia. "By this act they have shown that they are now willing to push the world to the brink of a general war to get what they want."

Truman came to the heart of his message. Against the Soviet threat, America must go onto a war footing. "I will issue a proclamation tomorrow morning declaring that a national emergency exists," he said. "This will call upon every citizen to put aside his personal interests for the good of the country. All our energies must be devoted to the tasks ahead of us." The country must build up its defenses as rapidly as possible; military forces needed to double in size and arms production to quadruple. Sacrifice would be required of everyone; all Americans must do their part. "Workers will be called upon to work more hours. More women, and more young people and older workers, will be needed in our plants and factories. Farmers will have to set higher goals of production. Businessmen will have to put all their know-how to work to increase production." Such a rapid buildup would trigger inflation unless the government stepped in. The administration would impose controls on wages and prices. Some would be mandatory, others voluntary. The better the voluntary controls worked, the fewer mandatory ones there would be. But prices would be controlled one way or the other. "The chiselers will not be allowed to get by."

Strikes remained a problem in some parts of the economy; the biggest and most troubling was a rail strike that was slowing economic growth and impeding the transport of troops and war matériel. "This strike is a danger to the security of our nation," Truman declared. "As Commander in Chief, therefore, I call upon the union and its striking members to return to work immediately." Truman still considered himself a friend of labor, but the national interest came first. "I ask you men who are on strike to realize that no matter how serious you believe your grievances are, nothing can excuse the fact that you are adding to your country's danger. I ask you, in the name of our country, to return immediately to your posts of duty." The railroad workers, and all Americans, should take their cue from America's soldiers. "In the days ahead, each of us should measure his own efforts, his own sacrifices, by the standard of our heroic men in Korea."

THE NEXT MORNING Truman signed the proclamation that made the state of emergency official. "His manner was brisk," one of the few reporters allowed into the president's office recounted. "He would not pose for 'one more' for the 'One More Club,' as he calls the photographers. They had to catch him in the act of really signing or lose the picture. Usually he will pose over and over again until each photographer gets a proper 'shot.'"

Briskness pervaded Washington as the significance of the emergency set in. Truman named General Electric president Charles Wilson his mobilization czar, with sweeping powers to place American industry in a war mode. "The director shall on behalf of the President direct, control, and coordinate all mobilization activities of the Government, including but not limited to production, procurement, manpower, stabilization, and transport activities," Truman's executive order decreed. The language of the order prompted speculation that Wilson would exercise powers greater than those wielded by James Byrnes as Roosevelt's World War II mobilization czar. Wilson's powers took hold sooner than at once: the big automakers were ordered to roll back their prices to levels in effect before the current crisis had prompted a preemptive jump.

Truman again brought the leaders of Congress to the White House, this time to discuss the mobilization measures. The Republicans were unusually complaisant. Kenneth Wherry found himself seated opposite Dean Acheson. "Here is your opposition," Wherry said with a smile. When Acheson declined to reply, Wherry added, "I mean your constructive opposition." The session opened with a briefing based on the CIA report that had prompted Truman's emergency declaration. Most of the lawmakers seemed convinced of the reality of the danger confronting the United States, although Robert Taft wanted more time to consider his response. "We shouldn't rush into this," Taft said.

Reactions from beyond Washington varied. The striking railroad workers returned to their jobs. Other workers pledged not to strike. William Green, president of the American Federation of Labor, promised that his union's eight million members would keep working during the state of emergency, as they had done during World War II. Most newspapers endorsed his emergency call. A notable exception was Robert McCormick's *Chicago Tribune,* which wasn't as isolationist as it had been during the 1930s but nonetheless denounced Truman's world-saving schemes. "If there is an emergency, it is Truman himself and his foreign policy," the *Tribune* asserted. "His speech makes it abundantly clear that he intends the country to have more of the same that produced the debacle in Korea." The administration proposed to do for Europe what the Europeans should be doing for themselves, the *Tribune* said. "Do you hear Britain, or France, or Italy, or anybody else proclaiming an emergency? You do not." The projected defense buildup was wrongheaded and unnecessary. "If we can't protect this continent and its outposts after having spent 89 billion dollars on defense in the last five years, and with 45 billion more dedicated to that purpose this coming year, then Mr. Truman and his secretary of defense ought to be impeached and his service chieftains court martialed."

THE *TRIBUNE* WAS equally scathing toward Acheson, as were congressional Republicans, whose modest respect for the state of emergency did not extend to respect for the secretary of state. On the very day of Truman's announcement of the emergency, the Republican caucuses in the Senate and the House of Representatives voted to demand Acheson's removal from office. "It is completely obvious that Secretary Acheson and the State Department under his leadership have lost the confidence of the Congress and the American people and cannot regain it," the Republican motion declared.

The move was mere grandstanding. Congress lacks the power to compel executive resignations, short of impeachment, and in any event the Republicans were a minority in both houses. They would remain minorities, albeit not by much, when the newly elected members were seated. But given the narrowing margins, the motion had political heft, not least because it came on the eve of Acheson's departure for Brussels, where he would meet with the foreign ministers of the other members of the North Atlantic alliance. The Republicans didn't deny intending to hamstring Acheson—and Truman—in the administration's efforts to deepen the American commitment to Europe.

Truman riposted the Republicans with a statement of his own. He charged the Republicans with abetting communist designs by sowing weakness and division in the Western alliance. He would tolerate no such thing. "This meeting in Brussels will show that, contrary to Communist hopes, the peoples of the North Atlantic Community are determined to remain united," the president said. There would be no replacing Acheson, the architect of the alliance. On the contrary: "Secretary Acheson goes to this meeting with my complete confidence."

Truman doubled down by announcing that Dwight Eisenhower would become commander of allied forces in Europe. The hero of the war in Europe would return to the theater of his victory; not even the Republicans could complain at this. "You are undertaking a tremendous responsibility," Truman wrote to Eisenhower in a letter released to the public. "As President and Commander-in-Chief of the Armed Forces of the United States, I know that our entire country is wholeheartedly behind you. Indeed, you carry with you the prayers of all freedom-loving peoples. I send you my warmest personal good wishes for success in the great task which awaits you."

Truman continued his European offensive in a news conference two days later. The usual mimeographed copies of the president's opening statement had not been distributed ahead of time; Truman didn't want leaks. "I will take it real slowly," he said to the reporters, who prepared to write his statement down.

"Mr. President," one asked, "if you get ahead of us, do you mind if we stop you?"

"No, that's all right."

Truman began reading. "There have been new attacks within the past week against the Secretary of State, Mr. Acheson. I have been asked to remove him from office, and the authors of this suggestion claim that this would be good for the country."

"You're ahead of me, sir," a reporter complained.

"You're going to take it all down in longhand?" Truman asked, surprised.

"Worse than that," the reporter answered, "I'm practicing my new shorthand." Truman shared the general laughter.

But he got back to business. "The authors of this suggestion claim that this would be good for the country. How our position in the world would be improved by the retirement of Dean Acheson from public life is beyond me. Mr. Acheson has helped shape and carry out our policy of resistance to Communist imperialism. From the time of our sharing of arms with Greece and Turkey nearly four years ago, and coming down to the recent moment when he advised me to resist the Communist invasion of South Korea, no official in our Government has been more alive to communism's threat to freedom or more forceful in resisting it." Truman noted that Acheson was in Brussels laying the groundwork for a unified defense against communism. Communism had no hardier foe than the secretary of state. "If communism were to prevail in the world—as it shall not prevail—Dean Acheson would be one of the first, if not the first, to be shot by the enemies of liberty and Christianity."

41

MATTHEW RIDGWAY WAS a student of character, besides being an army general, and he had been studying Douglas MacArthur for decades. "My own feeling toward MacArthur was always one of profound respect, developed through a close association dating from the days when he was Superintendent at West Point and I was in charge of the athletic program, reporting directly to him," Ridgway remembered. "Because of his avid interest in sports, I was privileged to see a great deal of him in those years. And while my meetings with him in after years, until I went to Korea, were rather infrequent, I never lost my warm personal interest in his career."

Ridgway found MacArthur fascinating, if at times infuriating. "I came to understand some of the traits of his complex character not generally recognized: the hunger for praise that led him on some occasions to claim or accept credit for deeds he had not performed, or to disclaim responsibility for mistakes that were clearly his own; the love of the limelight that continually prompted him to pose before the public as the actual commander on the spot at every landing and at the launching of every major attack in which his ground troops took part; his tendency to cultivate the isolation that genius seems to require, until it became a sort of insulation (there was no telephone in his personal office in Tokyo) that deprived him of the critical comment and objective appraisals a commander needs from his principal subordinates; the headstrong quality (derived from his success in forcing through many brilliant plans against solid opposition) that sometimes led him to persist in a course in defiance of all seeming logic; a faith in his own judgment that created an aura of infallibility and that finally led him close to insubordination."

Ridgway's remark about MacArthur's penchant for claiming accomplishments not his own reflected Ridgway's experience with MacArthur in Korea. This experience had its genesis in an accident eerily similar to one that had happened five years earlier, almost to the day. In December 1945 George Patton had died after his staff car collided with a truck in occupied Germany. In December 1950 Matthew Ridgway received a call from Joe Collins. "Matt, I'm sorry to tell you that Johnny Walker has been killed in a jeep accident in Korea." It was barely forty-eight hours until Christmas, but Collins had a new assignment for Ridgway. "I want you to get your things together and out there just as soon as you can."

Ridgway departed the next evening. "It was night when we left Washington, night when we landed at Tacoma, still black dark when we took off westward over Puget Sound. Dawn came in a thin, gray light, with no sight of sky or sea. There was nothing to see, nothing to do but think and work." He jotted notes about what he needed to know about the Eighth Army, now his; about the situation in Korea, so perilous; about MacArthur, so complex. "An hour out of Adak the sun broke through, the undercast dissolved, and below me I could see the black crags of the Aleutians—rock-ribbed, snow-capped, and ringed on the Bering side with surf. We landed in brilliant sunshine. A strong salt-tanged wind was blowing and the thermometer was just below freezing." He got a haircut from a navy barber as his plane refueled, and he visited with the commanding officer of the Adak Naval Air Station and his wife. He felt a pang for the Christmas he was missing with his own wife and their small son. He took off once more and, twelve hours later, just before midnight, landed at Tokyo's Haneda Airport.

The next morning he met with MacArthur. "I was again deeply impressed by the force of his personality," he recounted afterward. "To confer with him was an experience that could happen with few others. He was a great actor too, with an actor's instinct for the dramatic—in tone and gesture. Yet so lucid and penetrating were his explanations and his analyses that it was his mind rather than his manner or bodily presence that dominated his listeners." MacArthur evinced recently discovered respect for the Chinese. "They constitute a dangerous foe," he said. "Walker reported that the Chinese avoid roads, using ridges and hills as avenues of approach. They will attack in depth. Their firepower in the hands of their infantry is more extensively used than our own. The enemy moves and fights at night. The entire Chinese military establishment is in this fight." Yet MacArthur urged Ridgway to keep an open mind. "Form your own opinions. Use your own judgment. I will support you. You have my complete confidence."

Ridgway knew the Eighth Army was in retreat. But his was not a retreating spirit. "If I find the situation to my liking," he asked MacArthur, "would you have any objections to my attacking?"

"The Eighth Army is yours, Matt," MacArthur said. "Do what you think best."

MacArthur's vote of confidence in Ridgway was shared by the Truman administration, but Tokyo and Washington agreed on little else at this point. The essence of their dispute, apart from the personal frictions, distilled to a fundamental question about the place of Korea in American strategic planning. Put bluntly: Was saving Korea worth jeopardizing American security elsewhere?

The joint chiefs, following Truman's lead, said no. The chiefs prepared for the possibility that Korea might have to be abandoned. They directed MacArthur to fall back, "inflicting such damage to hostile forces in Korea as is possible, subject to the primary consideration of the safety of your troops." The Eighth Army must survive, for on it depended the defense of Japan. MacArthur must ensure that it did survive. "Since developments may force our withdrawal from Korea, it is important, particularly in view of the continued threat to Japan, to determine, in advance, our last reasonable opportunity for an orderly evacuation."

The chiefs provided closer guidance than previously, and they prepared to provide closer guidance still. "It seems to us that if you are forced back to positions in the vicinity of the Kum River and a line generally eastward therefrom, and if thereafter the Chinese Communists mass large forces against your positions with an evident capability of forcing us out of Korea, it then would be necessary, under these conditions, to direct you to commence a withdrawal to Japan." Yet sensitive to MacArthur's pride, they solicited his response. "Your views are requested as to the above-outlined conditions which should determine a decision to initiate evacuation, particularly in light of your continued primary mission of defense of Japan for which only troops of the Eighth Army are available. Following the receipt of your views you will be given a definite directive as to the conditions under which you should initiate evacuation."

MacArthur disagreed, vehemently. He read the letter in "utter dismay," according to Courtney Whitney. Speaking for his boss, Whitney said of the chiefs' message, "It showed clearly the confusion and contradiction in which Pentagon minds seemed to be weltering." MacArthur was supposed to resist the Chinese but not to fight too hard. "Was it, then, a policy that we would meet Communist aggression in Asia only if we could do it without too much trouble?" Whitney asserted that MacArthur drew two conclusions from the letter: that Truman and the administration "had completely lost the 'will to win' in Korea," and that the joint chiefs were trying to dodge their responsibility for this "shameful decision." Whitney continued, "The implied evacuation of Korea was properly a political decision, not a military one. The thought of defeat in Korea had never been entertained by MacArthur—so long as he would be allowed to use his military might against the enemy's. Indeed, it was his view that, given this authorization, he could not only save Korea but also inflict such a destructive blow upon Red China's capacity to wage aggressive war that it would remove her as a further threat to peace in Asia for generations to come. If, however, the U.N. and the U.S. preferred to multiply this threat by meekly lying down and letting the Juggernaut roll on, it must be a political decision, which must be made in Washington, not Tokyo. Everything in his heart and soul rebelled against such a solution." Speaking for himself, Whitney added, "I have seen MacArthur in moments of great sorrow and distress, but I cannot recall when I have seen heartache etched so vividly on his countenance and in his every attitude."

MacArthur fired back at Washington. He reiterated that the great battle for Asia had already been joined. "It is quite clear now that the entire military resource of the Chinese Nation, with logistic support from the Soviet, is committed to a maximum effort against the United Nations Command," he told the joint chiefs, for Truman's benefit as well. This was a challenge but also an opportunity. "In implementation of this commitment a major concentration of Chinese force in the Korean-Manchurian area will increasingly leave China vulnerable in areas whence troops to support Korean operations have been drawn."

MacArthur proposed a full range of escalatory measures against China. The most important were "(1) Blockade the coast of China; (2) Destroy through naval gun fire and air bombardment China's industrial capacity to wage war; (3) Secure reinforcements from the Nationalist garrison on Formosa to strengthen our position in Korea if we decide to continue the fight for that peninsula; and (4) Release existing restrictions upon the Formosan garrison for diversionary action (possibly leading to counter-invasion) against vulnerable areas of the Chinese Mainland."

MacArthur understood that he was calling for everything short of an invasion of China by American ground forces. But he thought the danger and the opportunity necessitated such bold action. "I believe that by the foregoing measures we could severely cripple and largely neutral-ize China's capability to wage aggressive war and thus save Asia from the engulfment otherwise facing it." He considered the risk manageable, indeed unavoidable. "I am fully conscious of the fact that this course of action has been rejected in past for fear of provoking China to a major war effort, but we must now realistically recognize that China's commit-ment thereto has already been fully unequivocally made and that noth-ing we can do would further aggravate the situation as far as China is concerned."

If the authorities in Washington rejected his advice, if they contin-ued to constrain him, the outcome could be most dire and would include results the administration said it was trying to prevent. "If we are forced to evacuate Korea without taking military measures against China proper as suggested in your message, it would have the most adverse effect upon the peoples of Asia, not excepting the Japanese," MacArthur said. The American position in the island chain off Asia's coast would be placed in jeopardy. "Evacuation of our forces from Korea under any circumstances would at once release the bulk of the Chinese forces now absorbed by that campaign for action elsewhere." Korea once again would become a dagger pointed at the heart of Japan.

MacArthur acknowledged that if his hands continued to be tied, he might have to evacuate. The plan the chiefs had suggested, of retreat toward a beachhead at Pusan, "would seem to be sound." But he was in no hurry. "In the execution of this plan it would not be necessary for you to make an anticipatory decision for evacuation until such time as we may be forced to that beachhead line."

42

H E A L A R M E D U S with his closing sentence," Omar Bradley recalled of MacArthur's response, referring to the general's rebuff of any "anticipatory decision" about evacuating. "That could indicate he was not going to commence evacuation until the Red Chinese were knocking on the gates of Pusan, which could be disastrous."

The chiefs were pondering how to answer MacArthur's latest when the disaster appeared to draw closer. Matthew Ridgway had spent his first days with the Eighth Army gathering information. Commandeering a worn B-17, he undertook a personal reconnaissance of the front lines. "On my orders we flew a roundabout route, covering some sixty miles of rugged mountain country," he recalled. "Peering down from three thousand feet, I traced on a map the ridge lines where later on a reorganized Eighth Army could stand and fight. The sight of this terrain was of little comfort to a soldier commanding a mechanized army. The granite peaks rose to six thousand feet, the ridges were knife-edged, the slopes steep, and the narrow valleys twisted and turned like snakes. The roads were trails, and the lower hills were covered with scrub oaks and stunted pines, fine cover for a single soldier who knew how to conceal himself. It was guerrilla country, an ideal battleground for the walking Chinese rifleman, but a miserable place for our road-bound troops who moved on wheels."

Ridgway received no greater encouragement when he reviewed the troops. "I must say, in all frankness, that the spirit of the Eighth Army as I found it on my arrival there gave me deep concern. There was a definite air of nervousness, of gloomy foreboding, or uncertainty, a spirit of apprehension as to what the future held. There was much 'looking over the shoulder,' as the soldiers say." Ridgway saw an army that had been badly shaken by its recent rough handling. "It was clear to me that our troops had lost confidence. I could sense it the moment I came into a command post. I could read it in their eyes, in their walk. I could read it in the faces of their leaders, from sergeants right on up to the top. They were unresponsive, reluctant to talk. I had to drag information out of them. There was a complete absence of that alertness, that aggressiveness, that you find in troops whose spirit is high."

The dismal spirit showed in the troops' performance. "They were not patrolling as they should. Their knowledge of the enemy's location and his strength was pitifully inadequate." Ridgway believed in fighting by feel. "The first rule in war is to make contact with your enemy at the earliest possible moment. Once you get that physical contact, you never lose it. You hang on to it with a bulldog grip." The Eighth Army had lost the grip. "Here the enemy was leaning right up against us, but we did not know his strength, and we did not have his location pinpointed on a map. All Intelligence could show me was a big red goose egg in front of us, with '174,000' scrawled in the middle of it."

Ridgway embarked on rebuilding morale. He ordered regular patrols along the entire front line; this revealed that the Chinese were preparing another attack, which commenced on the last day of 1950. The ROK forces staggered under the blow, soon abandoning their positions. Ridgway drove toward the front lines, only to encounter the South Koreans racing the other way. "A few miles north of Seoul I ran head-long into that fleeing army," he recounted. "I'd never had such an experience before, and I pray to God I never witness such a spectacle again. They were coming down the road in trucks, the men standing, packed so close together in those carriers another small boy could not have found space among them. They had abandoned their heavy artillery, their machine guns—all their crew-served weapons. Only a few had kept their rifles. Their only thought was to get away, to put miles between them and the fearful enemy that was at their heels."

Ridgway tried to rally them. "I jumped from the jeep and stood in the middle of the road, waving them to a halt. I might as well have tried to stop the flow of the Han. I spoke no Korean, and had no interpreter with me. I could find no officer who spoke English. The only solution was to let them run—and to set up road blocks far enough back where they could be stopped, channeled into bivouac areas, calmed down, refitted, and turned to face the enemy again."

Ridgway turned to Syngman Rhee for help. "I asked him if he would go up to the front with me, find these troops, talk to them and try to put some heart back in them." Rhee agreed. "We flew in bitter cold, in little unheated planes, the battered old canvas-covered Cubs of World War II. The temperature aloft was close to zero, and I nearly froze, though I was bundled in my heavy GI winter gear. President Rhee flew in his native dress, in a long white cotton kimono and low shoes, without even a scarf at the neck. His wrinkled, brown old face seemed to shrivel with the cold, but he never uttered a word of complaint." They met the soldiers where the roadblocks had stopped them. The soldiers had been fed, and the worst of the panic had been stilled. Rhee approached them. "The brave old President addressed them with fiery eloquence," Ridgway said. "I could not understand what he said, but the effect of his words was obvious." After he finished with the soldiers, Rhee turned to Ridgway. He placed his hand on the American general's arm. "Do not be discouraged," he said. "They will fight again."

But not in the same place. Ridgway's aerial reconnaissance had shown him a much better line south of the Han. To retreat there meant yielding Seoul once more to the enemy, but Ridgway saw no alternative. Crossing the river was a daunting challenge. The river was mostly frozen, but shifting floes threatened to wreck the floating bridges American engineers threw across the channel. Ridgway was reminded of paintings of George Washington leading his Revolutionary War troops across the Delaware, but in the present case the army attempting the crossing was vastly larger.

Yet the army was only a small part of the southbound movement. Ridgway informed Rhee that the army was retreating south; word rapidly spread among the civilian population of Seoul. Fearing for their lives, as many as a million men, women and children tried to beat the army across the bridges. Ridgway let them use the bridges until his own columns arrived but then closed the spans to all but military traffic. Yet the refugee surge didn't stop, as Ridgway observed. "Off to the right and left of the bridges was being enacted one of the great human tragedies of our time. In a zero wind that seared the face like a blow torch, hundreds of thousands of Koreans were running, stumbling, falling as they fled across the ice. Women with tiny babies in their arms, men bearing their old, sick, crippled fathers and mothers on their backs, others bent under great bundles of household gear flowed down the northern bank and across the ice toward the frozen plain on the southern shore. Some pushed little two-wheeled carts piled high with goods and little children. Others prodded burdened oxen. Now and then an ox would go down, all four legs asprawl, and the river of humanity would break and flow around him, for in this terrible flight no man stopped to help his neighbor."

Ridgway was one of the last Americans to cross the river. He packed the few personal items he had brought from home, including a photograph of his wife and young son. While gathering his clothing, he noticed that the bottom half of his flannel pajamas had worn through, prospectively baring his posterior to the world. Ridgway's orderly wanted to use it as a shoe rag, but Ridgway had a better idea. "We tacked it up on my office wall—the faded, torn, and worn-out seat flapping derisively in the breeze. Above it, in large block letters, we left this message:

TO THE COMMANDING GENERAL
CHINESE COMMUNIST FORCES—
WITH THE COMPLIMENTS OF
THE COMMANDING GENERAL
EIGHTH ARMY.

43

THE RETREAT FROM the Han saved the Eighth Army. Ridgway directed his troops to the defensive line he had sketched out from the air, and there they turned to face the enemy. But the Chinese didn't attack. The winter was hard on them too, and with each mile they marched south they stretched their supply lines further. They paused to regroup, giving Ridgway time to revive the spirits of his men. He sent them on increasingly aggressive patrols, allowing them to bloody the enemy, be bloodied themselves and rediscover their self-confidence. By mid-January the immediate crisis had passed.

But the larger issue of the war's direction remained. The differences between Truman and MacArthur were as sharp as ever. The president wanted to contain the war, the general to expand it. Of late, with the military situation in Korea highly uncertain, Truman had hesitated to push MacArthur too hard. A political explosion between the president and his theater commander would scarcely help matters. Ridgway's success in stemming the retreat, however, gave Truman confidence to assert his authority. The Eighth Army was holding, at least for now, and MacArthur needed to be dealt with.

At Truman's direction the joint chiefs let MacArthur know he wasn't going to get the wider war he wanted. "The following must be accepted," they wrote. "(1) There is little possibility of policy change or other external eventuality justifying strengthening of our effort in Korea. (2) Blockade of China Coast, if undertaken, must await either stabilization of our position in Korea or our evacuation from Korea." Lest MacArthur get his hopes up, the chiefs added a crucial condition: that a blockade receive British and UN concurrence. "(3) Naval and Air attacks on objectives in Communist China probably can be authorized only if the Chinese Communists attack United States forces outside of Korea." Beyond this, the administration continued to rule out the use of Chinese Nationalist forces.

MacArthur was given more specific orders than before. "You are directed as follows: (1) Defend in successive positions as required by JCS 99935"—the message of December 29 emphasizing the survival of the Eighth Army—"inflicting maximum damage to hostile forces in Korea, subject to primary consideration of the safety of your troops and your basic mission of protecting Japan. (2) Should it become evident in your judgment that evacuation is essential to avoid severe losses of men and materials you will at that time withdraw from Korea to Japan."

"ALL ONE COULD do was smile sadly at such arguments," Courtney Whitney recalled. "It was evidently more important to protect British profits in Hong Kong than to save American—and British—lives in Korea by means of a blockade." Whitney, as usual reflecting MacArthur, called the chiefs' deference to MacArthur on the timing of evacuation a "booby trap"—a "much more obvious attempt to put the onus for evacuation on his shoulders."

MacArthur refused to enter the trap. "Request clarification," he shot back, before launching into a scathing critique of the decisions that had placed him and his command in its current position. "My command as presently constituted is of insufficient strength to hold a position in Korea and simultaneously protect Japan against external assault." Washington had to choose between the two. He could hold on in Korea for a time, but not without losses that would jeopardize Japan. The original mission in Korea had been accomplished, he said. "This command was committed to the Korean campaign to fight the North Korean invasion Army, which in due course was effectively destroyed." The mission had *not* included fighting China. The administration needed to define a new mission. Until it did, his soldiers were bearing the weight of Washington's indecision. "The troops are tired from a long and difficult campaign," MacArthur said. "Their morale will become a serious threat to their battle efficiency unless the political basis upon which they are asked to trade life for time is clearly delineated."

MacArthur complained once more of the restraints imposed on his command and said they made a grim outcome inevitable. "The limitations and conditions—viz., no reinforcements, continued restrictions upon Chinese Nationalist military action, no measures permissible against China's continental military potential and the concentration of China's military force in the Korean-Manchurian sector—eventually will render the military position of the command in Korea untenable." He demanded a straight answer from the president. "Is it the present objective of United States political policy to maintain a military position in Korea—indefinitely, for a limited time, or to minimize losses by evacuation as soon as it can be accomplished?" The decision was the president's, and likewise the moral burden. "Under the extraordinary limitations and conditions imposed upon the command in Korea, its military position is untenable, but it can hold for any length of time up to its complete destruction, if overriding political considerations so dictate."

DEAN ACHESON READ MacArthur's letter with astonishment at its brazenness. "Here was a posterity paper if there ever was one, with the purpose not only of clearing MacArthur of blame if things went wrong but also of putting the maximum pressure on Washington to reverse itself and adopt his proposals for widening the war against China," Acheson wrote. With this letter MacArthur had definitively crossed the line. "Nothing further was needed to convince me that the General was incurably recalcitrant and basically disloyal to the purposes of his Commander in Chief."

Omar Bradley thought MacArthur was blaming his men for his own shortcomings. The joint chiefs chairman recalled a comment he had made in congressional hearings after an admiral had complained about low morale in the navy: "Senior officers decrying the low morale of their forces evidently do not realize that the esprit of the men is but a mirror of their confidence in their leadership." George Marshall drew a similar conclusion: "When a general complains of the morale of his troops, the time has come to look into his own."

Truman bridled at the letter and MacArthur's stunt in sending it. "I was deeply disturbed," he wrote in his memoirs. "The Far Eastern commander was, in effect, reporting that the course of action decided upon by the National Security Council and by the Joint Chiefs of Staff and approved by me was not feasible. He was saying that we would be driven off the peninsula or, at the very least, suffer terrible losses." Truman again was tempted to find another general but concluded that the time wasn't yet ripe.

The president convened the NSC once more. Marshall read aloud MacArthur's message, then commented that the Pentagon wanted to gauge for itself the morale of the troops in Korea. He recommended sending Generals Collins and Vandenberg to Korea and Japan. Truman approved the mission. Discussion turned to the question MacArthur had posed: whether American forces should evacuate Korea. Truman was strongly opposed unless the South Korean forces could be evacuated as well. The note taker at the meeting paraphrased the president: "He was unwilling to abandon the South Koreans to be murdered."

Marshall, Bradley and Acheson urged the president to write to MacArthur directly. The general might argue with the joint chiefs, they explained, but he couldn't argue with the president.

Truman agreed, and he personalized a draft prepared for him by Acheson and the others. As fed up as he was with MacArthur, the president still treated the general considerately. "I want you to know that the situation in Korea is receiving the utmost attention here and that our efforts are concentrated upon finding the right decisions on this matter," Truman said. He took care to explain that he wasn't issuing orders, not at the moment. "This present telegram is not to be taken in any sense as a directive. Its purpose is to give you something of what is in our minds regarding the political factors." Truman outlined the positive purposes that would be served by a successful resistance in Korea. It would demonstrate that aggression did not pay and that the free countries would defend themselves. It would deflate the prestige of China. It would win time for other Asian countries to organize for defense against communism. It would vindicate America's pledge to defend South Korea. It would hearten the Japanese. It would encourage countries around the world to look to the United States rather than the Soviet Union. It would bolster the United Nations.

All this was why the United States must maintain the fight in Korea. "We recognize, of course, that continued resistance might not be militarily possible with the limited forces with which you are being called upon to meet large Chinese armies," Truman granted. "Further, in the present world situation, your forces must be preserved as an effective instrument for the defense of Japan and elsewhere." But the effort must still be made. "In the worst case, it would be important that, if we must withdraw from Korea, it be clear to the world that that course is forced upon us by military necessity." America's allies might forgive defeat; they would never forgive abandonment.

Truman reminded MacArthur—yet again—where the heart of the danger to America lay. "In reaching a final decision about Korea, I shall have to give constant thought to the main threat from the Soviet Union." The president repeated—yet again—why the conflict in Korea must not be widened. "Our course of action at this time should be such as to consolidate the great majority of the United Nations. This majority is not merely part of the organization but is also the nations whom we would desperately need to count on as allies in the event the Soviet Union moves against us."

The president concluded with a generous flourish. "The entire nation is grateful for your splendid leadership in the difficult struggle in Korea and for the superb performance of your forces under the most difficult circumstances."

Acheson thought Truman had done more than any president should have had to do. "It was an imaginatively kind and thoughtful letter for the Chief of State to write his theater commander, admitting him to his private mind," Acheson recalled. "If ever a message should have stirred the loyalty of a commander, this one should have done so."

PART FOUR

THE GENERAL VS. THE PRESIDENT

44

MACARTHUR RESPONDED TO Truman's olive branch with a terse "We shall do our best."

Joe Collins and Hoyt Vandenberg flew west to ensure that he did. Their arrival in Korea coincided with Matthew Ridgway's initial attempt to regain the ground he had yielded in retreating from Seoul. Ridgway ordered a limited attack but one employing infantry, armor and air support. The plan was to hit the enemy hard and then withdraw. The goal was to test the enemy's strength but also the resilience of the Eighth Army. Vandenberg, the air chief, observed the performance of the air wing of the operation; Collins, the army man, watched the ground operations. "I toured the front with Ridgway," Collins recalled later. "I talked to corps and division commanders and a number of junior and noncommissioned officers." He liked what he saw. "I could feel in the Eighth Army the improved spirit that Ridgway had already imparted to his men." Collins remembered the Battle of the Bulge, when he and Ridgway had commanded adjacent corps and strived to convince Bernard Montgomery that no Germans would get past them. Collins didn't need convincing now. "I left Korea fully convinced that the Eighth Army would once again stand and fight," he wrote. Collins quoted Ridgway's words at their parting: "There is no shadow of doubt in my mind that the Eighth Army can take care of itself."

MacArthur elicited less confidence from the visitors. "At our first meeting, Gen. MacArthur read the President's letter, and said it had cleared up questions as to how long and under what conditions the Eighth Army should remain in Korea," Collins wrote to Omar Bradley.

"He said he interpreted the letter as a directive to remain in Korea indefinitely, which the UN forces could do, though in this case he could not assume responsibility for the risk of leaving Japan defenseless."

Collins and Vandenberg pointed out that Truman's letter had expressly declared that it was not a directive. But they went on to say that in their meeting with the president just prior to their departure from Washington the consensus was that any evacuation from Korea should be delayed as long as possible, consistent with the integrity of the Eighth Army and the security of Japan.

MacArthur repeated what he had said, with emphasis. "He declared, with some emotion, that his command could not be held responsible for the defense of Japan while required to hold Korea. Although there were no open indications of Russian moves to attack Japan, they had the capability with forces now in Sakhalin and the Vladivostok area."

Yet MacArthur, like Collins, interpreted Ridgway's recent actions as a good sign. "General MacArthur reviewed the military situation and stated that in his opinion the UN forces could hold a beachhead in Korea indefinitely," Collins told Bradley. "He felt that with our continued domination of the sea and air, Chinese forces would never be able to bring up adequate supplies, over their lengthening lines of communication, to enable them to drive the UN forces from Korea. He reiterated his belief that a decision to evacuate Korea was a political matter and should not be decided on military grounds."

Bradley shared Collins's report with Truman, and when Collins and Vandenberg returned to Washington they briefed the president in person. "The President and his chief advisers, who had access to our reports, were reassured," Collins remembered. For the first time since November, disaster no longer loomed over Korea. Hard fighting remained, but the Eighth Army would hold.

Omar Bradley felt more hopeful than he had in months. "We began to think that the Chinese could not throw us out of Korea, even with the self-imposed limitations under which we were fighting," Bradley remembered. "It was a tremendous relief to all."

But it was no thanks to MacArthur. Collins spoke for the chiefs as a group, and for the administration as a whole, when he pointedly gave credit where he believed it due. "General Ridgway alone was responsible for this dramatic change," Collins said.

45

O N JANUARY 5 Robert Taft of Ohio took the floor of the Senate. Taft had come a long way since his isolationist period, when he had warned, as late as a month before Pearl Harbor, that the United States was sliding into the morass of save-the-world thinking that would doom the country to perpetual war abroad and garrison-state socialism at home. Taft had supported the war effort against Germany and Japan and had even voted in favor of American membership in the United Nations. But he had voted against the North Atlantic Treaty of 1949, arguing that the alliance it created put American security at the risk of reckless actions by any of the other members, that it illegitimately transferred to the president the constitutional power of Congress to declare war, and that by so patently targeting Russia it made a third world war more likely rather than less.

Some Taft watchers thought they heard the Ohio Republican building a platform for another run at the presidency. Taft had tried and failed in 1940 and again in 1948 to win the Republican nomination; each time he had lost to a candidate more tolerant of American engagement in the world. But both candidates—Wendell Willkie and then Thomas Dewey—had lost in the general election. Taft might have inferred that a candidate more clearly different from the Democratic internationalists would have a better chance. Or maybe he was simply speaking his mind.

In any event, when he addressed the Senate in January 1951 he raked the wrong thinking he attributed to Truman, Acheson and the other architects of America's Cold War policies. "In very recent days we have heard appeals for unity from the Administration and from its supporters," Taft said. "I suggest that these appeals are an attempt to cover up the past faults and failures of the Administration and enable it to maintain the secrecy which has largely enveloped our foreign policy since the days of Franklin D. Roosevelt." It was past time to tear the veil. "As I see it, members of Congress, and particularly members of the Senate, have a constitutional obligation to re-examine constantly and discuss the foreign policy of the United States." Taft preemptively deflected charges that he and the Republican minority were being obstructionist. "We have not hesitated to pass a draft law, a law granting extensive powers of economic control, and almost unlimited appropriations for the armed forces." If mobilization moved more slowly than the White House desired, the president should look within his own bureaucracy rather than at the Republicans.

Taft reminded his listeners that the Democrats were the authors of the troubles they now cited to justify the current state of alarm. At wartime conferences at Yalta and Tehran, Roosevelt had signed over to the Soviets large swaths of Central Europe, Taft said. Truman had adopted a policy hostile to the Chinese Nationalists, thereby handing control of the world's most populous nation to the communists. That nation had lately launched a war against the United States in Korea. The two Democratic presidents had done all this without consulting Congress.

Truman now proposed to send large numbers of American troops to Europe as part of a permanent force drawn from the Atlantic alliance members. The president could not avoid Congress in taking such a step, for Congress had to provide the money. But the proposal still reeked of the Democrats' preference for making policy on the sly, Taft said. "The Atlantic Pact may have committed us to send arms to the other members of the pact, but no one ever maintained that it committed us to send many American troops to Europe. A new policy is being formulated without consulting the Congress or the people."

Taft drove to the heart of the matter. "The principal purpose of the foreign policy of the United States is to maintain the liberty of our people. Its purpose is not to reform the entire world or spread sweetness and light and economic prosperity to peoples who have lived and worked out their own salvation for centuries according to the best of their ability. We do have an interest in the economic welfare of other nations and in the military strength of other nations, but only to the extent to which our assistance may reduce the probability of an attack on the freedom of our people."

Taft contended that the Truman administration was exaggerating the threat from the Russians. "I do not myself see any conclusive evidence that they expect to start a war with the United States," he said. "And certainly I see no reason for a general panic on the assumption that they will do so. We have clearly notified them that any attack in Europe upon the United Nations means a third World War, and we are obligated to enter such a war under the terms of the Atlantic Pact." Taft asked his listeners to step back for a moment. "Look at it from any point of view—and, I think, particularly from the Russian point of view—and it is difficult to see how the Russians could reasonably entertain the hope that they can conquer the world by military action. It must seem to their thinkers an extremely difficult undertaking. I believe they are still thinking in terms of a slow but steady advance by the methods which they have used up to this time. Those methods are dangerous enough." And those methods were the ones the United States should focus on, husbanding American strength for the long struggle.

Truman had overreacted in Korea, Taft said. The senator suggested that the Soviet boycott of the Security Council in June 1950, which Acheson and others considered fortuitous with respect to Korea and which enabled the passage of the UN resolution authorizing the defense of South Korea, might have been deliberate. "We took this action"—sponsoring the resolution and acting upon it—"without considering the fact that, if the Chinese Communists attacked and the Russian representative returned to the Security Council, the United Nations could not follow up its action against the Korean Communists by similar action against Chinese Communists. If the Russians had planned it that way, they could not have done better." The administration's misplaced confidence in the UN had proved a dreadful error. "We were sucked into the Korean War by a delusion."

And an unconstitutional one at that. "The President simply usurped authority, in violation of the laws and the Constitution, when he sent troops to Korea to carry out the resolution of the United Nations in an undeclared war," Taft said. Now the president proposed to aggrandize executive power the more by sending American troops to Europe. "Without authority he involved us in the Korean War," Taft said. "Without authority he apparently is now adopting a similar policy in Europe." The lesson of Korea was just the opposite of what Truman adduced. "We must not undertake anything beyond our power as we have in Korea. We must not assume obligations by treaty or otherwise which require any extensive use of American land forces." The president's program must be rejected.

TAFT'S SPEECH WAS the opening salvo in a months-long debate in Congress over America's approach to world affairs. The occasion for the debate was Truman's request for funding for the troops he wanted to send to Europe, but the context, as Taft's speech made evident, was the continuing conflict in Korea. Taft's speech, at ten thousand words, was one of the longest, and it was more carefully reasoned than most. But many other lawmakers weighed in. The Republicans decried the president's handling of foreign affairs, often including the conduct of the war in Korea in their condemnation. Yet few were so bold in declaring the Russian threat overblown. The Democrats were predictably kinder to Truman, even if several in the president's own party wondered where the path he was charting would lead.

All understood that Truman had led the United States to the banks of a Rubicon. On the near side was America's old policy of reacting to aggression after it happened. This had been the country's approach to the two world wars, and it had characterized policy in Korea. On the far side was a new policy of arming in advance of aggression, of having troops in place where the communists might merely think of attacking. The Atlantic alliance was a paper pact thus far; the Atlantic treaty a promissory note. Truman would put steel in the alliance by putting American boots on European ground.

Truman recognized that he had to strike a delicate balance in making the case for his policy. He had to portray the world as sufficiently dangerous that his novel action appeared necessary, yet the world shouldn't seem *so* dangerous that the simple act of sending the troops to Europe would trigger another general war. The administration labored assiduously to coordinate the voices with which it spoke. Dean Acheson at the State Department, George Marshall at the Pentagon, Omar Bradley of the joint chiefs, and their respective seconds and staffs held meeting after meeting to get the message just right.

Matthew Ridgway assisted from Korea. By February 1951 Ridgway's revived Eighth Army had demonstrated that the United Nations would not be driven out of Korea short of a major commitment of new troops and weapons by China. This welcome development allowed the Truman administration to consider options for a ceasefire, presumably leading to political negotiations that would yield a permanent settlement for Korea.

Three months earlier, in the heady aftermath of Inchon, Truman would have judged a ceasefire a distinct disappointment. Victory had appeared within America's grasp. But now a ceasefire—a draw, as it were—was the best he could reasonably hope for. Yet the lowering of expectations in Korea oddly strengthened Truman's argument for sending troops to Europe. Communism wouldn't easily be defeated; consequently it had to be deterred. The United States had held the line in Korea; it must hold the line in Europe. A patient middle course—between the military recklessness of MacArthur and historical heedlessness of Taft—was the surest path to peace.

46

MATTHEW RIDGWAY RECEIVED a February visit from
MacArthur that revealed one of the latter's least attractive
traits as a commander. Ridgway was preparing an offensive
he called Operation Killer. "I had planned this action personally on Sunday evening, February 18, two days before the visit of the Commander
in Chief, and had outlined it to the Commanding Generals of the U.S.
IX and X Corps and of the 1st Marine Division," Ridgway recalled
later. "This resumption of the offensive was the final implementation of
the plan I had nourished from the time of my taking command of the
Eighth Army—and had done so it may be said in the face of a retreat-psychology that seemed to have seized every commander from the Chief
on down. You can imagine my surprise then and even my dismay at
hearing the announcement General MacArthur made to the assembled
press correspondents on February 20, the eve of the target date. Standing before some ten or more correspondents met at the X Corps Tactical
Command Post, with me leaning against a table in the rear, MacArthur
said calmly: 'I have just ordered a resumption of the offensive.'"

Ridgway was more than irked at MacArthur's credit-claiming. "It
was not so much that my own vanity took an unexpected roughing up
by this announcement as that I was given a rather unwelcome reminder
of a MacArthur I had known but had almost forgotten." MacArthur's
grandstanding threatened serious damage to the American war effort,
Ridgway judged. "It had long been MacArthur's habit, whenever a major
offensive was about to jump off, to visit those elements of his command
that were involved and, figuratively, to fire the starting gun. In general

this is an admirable practice. The over-all commander's personal presence has an inspiring effect upon the troops. And invariably the best impressions of the temper of the men under his command are gained through the commander's own eyes and ears." Most commanders made their visits discreetly, with no word reaching the enemy until too late to give anything away. But not MacArthur. "The pattern of MacArthur's flight from Tokyo and appearance at the front every time a major operation was to be initiated had been well established. And the flights themselves were made with such ceremony that knowledge of them was almost certain to reach the enemy." MacArthur, who complained so loudly about being deprived of means to neutralize the enemy, deprived Ridgway and the Eighth Army of the element of surprise. Eventually Ridgway would learn to tell MacArthur to stay in Tokyo. But on this occasion he simply bit his tongue at "another of the Commander in Chief's efforts to keep his public image always glowing."

"I NOW BEGAN to formulate long-range plans for destroying the Chinese forces in Korea," MacArthur wrote later, again slighting Ridgway. "My decisive objective would be their supply lines. By constant, but ubiquitous ground thrusts at widely scattered points with limited objectives, I would regain the Seoul lines for a base of future operations. I would then clear the enemy rear all across the top of North Korea by massive air attacks. If I were still not permitted to attack the massed enemy reinforcements across the Yalu, or to destroy its bridges, I would sever Korea from Manchuria by laying a field of radioactive wastes—the by-products of atomic manufacture—across all the major lines of enemy supply. The destruction in North Korea had left it bereft of supplies. Everything the Chinese used in the way of food or munitions had to come across the border. The Reds had only ten days' supply of food in their North Korean dumps to feed nearly a million troops, and their ammunition was equally limited. Then, reinforced by Chinese Nationalist troops, if I were permitted to use them, and with American reinforcement on the way, I would make simultaneous amphibious and airborne landings at the upper end of both coasts of North Korea, and close a gigantic trap. The Chinese would soon starve or surrender. Without food and ammunition, they would become helpless. It would be something like Inchon, but on a much larger scale."

If MacArthur actually did formulate such plans at the time, he had fairly lost touch with reality in Washington. He had been told again and again that there would be no summons of the Chinese Nationalists. He had been repeatedly ordered not to bomb across the Yalu. And as for sowing radioactive material in North Korea or China, his thinking was delusional.

Unless, of course, something changed in Washington. A general could always hope—and, where necessary, help.

ON FEBRUARY 12, 1951, Joseph Martin celebrated Abraham Lincoln's birthday by speaking to the Kings County Republican Committee of Brooklyn. The Republican leader of the House of Representatives hailed the patron saint of his party for Lincoln's service to freedom in the face of great danger and trial. "Today, after ninety years of political service, the Republican party is still the only party of freedom in these United States," Martin continued. "It is still the only party which steadfastly has refused to accept the alien doctrines of socialism and communism." The Democrats, starting at the top, formed a sorry contrast, putting politics above policy, and party above country. "It is the great tragedy of our day that in a period of crisis we have an administration in Washington which is so bankrupt in leadership that its first measurement of every undertaking is whether it will help perpetuate those in power. Votes have become the yardstick of their policies."

The problem was especially acute in foreign policy, Martin said. The administration had acquiesced in Russian control of half of Europe. Although the Republican Eightieth Congress had voted support for Chiang Kai-shek in China, the Truman White House had blocked its delivery. Meanwhile the Russians had built a nuclear arsenal, with American help. "Because we had fuzzy-minded, pinko officials in our security setup, the Soviet Union was able to steal the secrets of the atomic and the hydrogen bombs." The Korean war was simply the most recent exhibit of communist malignity and Democratic incompetence. The war had caught the administration by unforgivable surprise and had exacted a fearful cost. The administration's war-fighting strategy was criminally perverse. American troops were fighting greater numbers of Chinese Communist troops, but the administration refused to employ an army of Chinese Nationalists eager to confront the Communists. Truman had gone so far as to order the American Seventh Fleet to prevent any move by Chiang against the Chinese mainland. What could be more counterproductive than that?

The heart of the problem, Martin said, was the administration's obsession with Europe. "Everyone knows that we must have an effective aid program for Europe," he conceded. "Everyone knows that we must not, if we can possibly prevent it, allow the resources and productive capacity of the free European nations to fall into Communist control." But Truman and his minions had carried things entirely too far. "I protest with every resource at my command the formulation of any over-all strategy which virtually ignores the focal point of our trouble today—Asia."

Martin cited several distinguished soldiers and statesmen who had protested the short shrift given Asia. None was more distinguished than Douglas MacArthur. "How many people recall that General MacArthur declared that our failure to help the Republic of China may be 'the single greatest blunder in the history of the United States'?" he asked rhetorically. Yet the blunder persisted. "If we really want to take the pressure off our forces in Korea, and if we want to diminish the threat of a Soviet sweep across Europe, why, may I ask, do we not employ the 800,000 anti-Communist Chinese troops on Formosa?" General MacArthur had frequently advocated such action, and Martin was happy to add his voice to that of the general. "What could be sounder logic, both strategically and militarily, than to allow the anti-Communist forces of the generalissimo on Formosa to participate in the war against the Chinese Reds? Why not let them open a second front in Asia? . . . If it is right for American boys to fight Chinese Reds in Korea, what can be wrong with American help to the anti-Communist Chinese fighting the Reds on their own soil? What are we in Korea for, to win or to lose?"

MARTIN'S SPEECH WAS unremarkable in itself. Republicans had long used Lincoln's birthday as an occasion to applaud themselves and castigate their opponents; Democrats did much the same at their annual celebrations of Jefferson and Jackson. Martin's insults against Truman said nothing Joseph McCarthy and other Republicans hadn't been saying for months and years about the president. To be sure, Martin as House leader held a higher post than McCarthy and most of the other Truman baiters, but still his remarks could easily have gone unnoticed.

And so they did until they received the endorsement of Douglas MacArthur. Martin might have been hoping to draw MacArthur into the 1952 presidential campaign; he might have been trying to cause mischief for the Democrats. He doubtless believed what he said about a change in America's Asia policy being necessary. In any case, having cited MacArthur in his remarks, he made sure the general received a copy of the speech. "In the current discussions on foreign policy and overall strategy," Martin wrote to MacArthur in early March, "many of us have been distressed that although the European aspects have been heavily emphasized, we have been without the views of yourself as Commander-in-Chief of the Far Eastern Command." Martin reiterated that American security and the peace of the world required that America not weaken its position in Asia. "Enclosed is a copy of an address I delivered in Brooklyn, N.Y., February 12, stressing this vital point and suggesting that the forces of Generalissimo Chiang Kai-shek on Formosa might be employed in the opening of a second Asiatic front to relieve the pressure on our forces in Korea." Martin solicited MacArthur's response. "I would deem it a great help if I could have your views on this point, either on a confidential basis or otherwise."

MacArthur later said he had no choice but to answer. "I have always felt duty-bound to reply frankly to every Congressional inquiry into matters connected with my official responsibility," he wrote. "This has been a prescribed practice since the very beginning of our nation, and is now the law. Only in this way, and by personal appearance, can the country's law-makers cope intelligently with national problems." Yet his response went considerably further than any duty demanded.

"Dear Congressman Martin," he wrote on March 20. "I am most grateful for your note of the eighth forwarding me a copy of your address of February 12. The latter I have read with much interest, and find that with the passage of years you have certainly lost none of your old time punch." Addressing the congressman's question, MacArthur continued, "My views and recommendations with respect to the situation created by Red China's entry into the war against us in Korea have been submitted to Washington in most complete detail. Generally these views are well known and clearly understood, as they follow the conventional pattern of meeting force with maximum counter force as we have never failed to do in the past." MacArthur endorsed Martin's call for employing Chinese Nationalist troops. "Your view with respect to the utilization of the Chinese forces on Formosa is in conflict with neither logic nor this tradition"—the American tradition of meeting force with maximum counterforce. The general lamented the wrongheadedness of the president's policy toward communism. "It seems strangely difficult for some to realize that here in Asia is where the Communist conspirators have elected to make their play for global conquest, and that we have joined the issue thus raised on the battlefield; that here we fight Europe's war with arms while the diplomats there still fight it with words; that if we lose the war to communism in Asia the fall of Europe is inevitable; win it and Europe most probably would avoid war and yet preserve freedom." The war for the world had begun, despite what the president might think. And America must prevail. "There is no substitute for victory."

47

I F MacArthur realized that his letter to Martin was a tick- ing time bomb, he gave no sign. "I attached little importance to the exchange of letters, which on my part was intended to be merely a polite response couched in such general terms as to convey only a normal patriotic desire for victory," he wrote afterward.

In the moment, he placed much greater significance on an exchange with the joint chiefs and the White House. The State Department had been discussing with America's allies possible terms of a ceasefire offer to the Chinese and the North Koreans. Sufficient progress had been made that the joint chiefs felt obliged to inform and consult MacArthur. "State planning Presidential announcement shortly that, with clearing of bulk of South Korea of aggressors, United Nations now prepared to discuss conditions of settlement in Korea," the chiefs cabled MacArthur on March 20. "Strong UN feeling persists that further diplomatic effort towards settlement should be made before any advance with major forces north of 38th parallel." In other words, MacArthur should sit still for the present. Yet the administration didn't want to leave his troops vulnerable. "State has asked JCS what authority you should have to permit sufficient freedom of action for next few weeks to provide security for UN forces and maintain contact with enemy. Your recommendations desired."

MacArthur responded at once, rejecting the State proposal and, in effect, any ceasefire. "Recommend that no further military restrictions be imposed upon the United Nations Command in Korea," he cabled. "The inhibitions which already exist should not be increased. The mili- tary disadvantages arising from restrictions upon the scope of our Air and Naval operations coupled with the disparity between the size of our command and the enemy ground potential renders it completely impracticable to attempt to clear North Korea or make any appreciable effort to that end."

Omar Bradley read the response and shook his head. "I do not know what went on in MacArthur's mind at this time," the joint chiefs chairman recalled. MacArthur understood perfectly well that the clearing of North Korea had long since been ruled out. The president wanted an end to the fighting, not an escalation of it. But MacArthur couldn't resist reminding the chiefs—on the record—of the "military disadvantages" under which he was compelled to labor.

Bradley considered two explanations for MacArthur's intransigence. The first was personal. "He had been made a fool of by the Chinese communist armies; now, as all the world had seen, Ridgway's brilliant leadership had bailed him out," Bradley wrote. MacArthur's constant agitation for greater authority to attack the Chinese signaled his hope to regain the limelight. The chiefs' new message shattered that hope. "There would be no all-out war with China directed from Tokyo. Perhaps this realization snapped his brilliant but brittle mind. What lay ahead now was merely a diplomatic search for the status quo and unrestricted praise for his subordinate, Ridgway."

The other explanation was political. "Perhaps at this time MacArthur decided that he would come home and run for the presidency in 1952," Bradley wrote. "He still had considerable popularity and substantial support among right-wing politicians on the Hill and in some state houses. Perhaps he believed that a sharp break with Truman, whose popularity was slipping badly, would redound to his credit and build such a massive groundswell of support that he could knock Republican front runner Bob Taft aside." Bradley was still scratching his head years later. "I don't know; I can only speculate. However, it is noteworthy that the events that were to transpire would fit this scenario."

POSSIBLY FEELING ECLIPSED by his subordinate, definitely convinced he would be a better president than his commander-in-chief, MacArthur set off a new explosion that rattled Washington and several other capitals. On the eve of Truman's announcement of ceasefire terms, the general issued his own call for a cessation of hostilities. "We have now substantially cleared South Korea of organized Communist forces," he declared on March 24. The tide of battle had indisputably turned. "The enemy's human wave tactics definitely failed him as our own forces become seasoned in this form of warfare; his tactics of infiltration are but contributing to his piecemeal losses, and he is showing less stamina than our own troops under rigors of climate, terrain and battle."

MacArthur's statement acquired a taunting tone. "Of even greater significance than our tactical success has been the clear revelation that this new enemy, Red China, of such exaggerated and vaunted military power, lacks the industrial capacity to provide adequately many critical items essential to the conduct of modern war. He lacks manufacturing bases and those raw materials needed to produce, maintain and operate even moderate air and naval power, and he cannot provide the essentials for successful ground operations, such as tanks, heavy artillery and other refinements science has introduced into the conduct of military campaigns." In former days, the massive numbers of the Chinese might have offset their technical deficiency. But no longer; the American advantage was too great. "The resulting disparity is such that it cannot be overcome by bravery, however fanatical, or the most gross indifference to human loss."

If the enemy was not blind to all reality, he must give up his aggression. If he failed to do so, much worse might befall him. "A decision of the United Nations to depart from its tolerant effort to contain the war to the area of Korea through expansion of our military operations to his coastal areas and interior bases would doom Red China to the risk of imminent military collapse." MacArthur called for an end to hostilities. "There should be no insuperable difficulty arriving at decisions on the Korean problem if the issues are resolved on their own merits without being burdened by extraneous matters not directly related to Korea, such as Formosa and China's seat in the United Nations." The decision was up to the Chinese. "I stand ready at any time to confer in the field with the Commander-in-Chief of the enemy forces in an earnest effort to find any military means whereby the realization of the political objectives of the United Nations in Korea, to which no nation may justly take exception, might be accomplished without further bloodshed."

48

MacArthur's "pronunciamento"—Dean Acheson's word for it—triggered fresh outrage in Washington. For the general to threaten full war against China, at the moment when the president was trying to coax the Chinese to the peace table, egregiously exceeded his authority, impugned the integrity of the president, and once more threatened to shatter the unity of the American alliance system and the UN coalition.

The deputy secretary of defense, Robert Lovett, visited Acheson at eleven o'clock that night bearing a copy of MacArthur's words. "Bob, usually imperturbable and given to ironic humor under pressure, was angrier than I had ever seen him," Acheson recalled. "The General, he said, must be removed and removed at once." Acheson shared Lovett's anger as soon as he read MacArthur's statement. "It can be described only as defiance of the Chiefs of Staff, sabotage of an operation of which he had been informed, and insubordination of the grossest sort to his Commander in Chief."

Acheson discussed the matter with Lovett and some of Acheson's State Department lieutenants until well after midnight, then resumed the discussion the next morning at the office. Lovett consulted with the joint chiefs at the Pentagon. He called Acheson to summarize their views. They had divided the MacArthur problem into three parts, according to the notes of the call. "The first related to the embarrassment with the 13 countries occasioned by MacArthur's statement at the time this Government was negotiating with the 13 countries to agree on a proposed statement by President Truman." Beyond the embarrassment, MacArthur's statement nullified weeks of work with all those UN allies and made a future agreement harder. The second problem was the complication it threw in the path of future proposals. "It brought up the question again of how many negotiators there are; i.e., whether the State Department, the United Nations or MacArthur was the negotiator." In the Chinese system, no general would spout off unauthorized; the Chinese would assume MacArthur spoke with authority, perhaps as part of some double game by the Americans. The third problem touched the matter of military discipline. The joint chiefs proposed to deal with this one first, because it was most clearly in their ambit. "They were considering it in the light of the directive of December 5"—transmitted on December 6—"which had been sent to MacArthur, among others. That directive specifically requires the Commander in the field to clear any statements, speeches, or anything else relating to political matters with Washington."

The record was plain to the chiefs, Lovett told Acheson, even if the conclusion was not. "It would be perfectly obvious if it were anybody else who had made the statement which MacArthur made yesterday, he would be relieved of his command at once. However, the JCS recognized that the consequences of relieving MacArthur are startling. It would have its effect at once in the field and it would probably prejudice the success of the Japanese treaty negotiations." All the same, the chiefs had to act. "They do not feel they can just let this slide by." Yet they were willing to go only so far. "Their thinking at the present moment is that they will try to work out a reprimand rather than a relief."

Lovett had said he thought this a good solution. He pointed out that the situation was complicated by the fact that MacArthur held four separate commands: supreme commander for the Allied powers in Japan, commander-in-chief of UN forces, U.S. commander-in-chief in the Far East, and commanding general of U.S. Army forces in the Far East. Recalling MacArthur could cause serious administrative problems.

The politics were even trickier. The press had carried MacArthur's statement, and it was playing quite well. "It is very clever," Lovett said. "It offers peace and holds out the hope of getting out of Korea. If the President challenged it, he would be in the position at once of being on the side of sin. MacArthur has gotten us in Washington in a tight box from which there seems to be no escape."

Lovett recommended that the president not respond. "The best thing would be to have as much silence about it as possible." Behind the scenes the State Department could assure other governments that MacArthur's words did not represent U.S. government policy—"that this was another statement made by the field commander and that it is really not very important." Lovett understood that this approach would not be easy; he acknowledged the "really great difficulties" it entailed.

Acheson replied that the State Department had analyzed the MacArthur problem similarly. He was willing to leave the disciplining of the general to the Defense Department; for him the important question was how to keep the problem from recurring. "If this statement can be straightened out, that will not do much good if the same thing is apt to happen next week." As for the line the State Department should take with other governments, Acheson proposed to bring in the thirteen ambassadors and tell them "that the MacArthur statement was unauthorized, unexpected, and that steps had been taken to deal with it."

Acheson and Lovett—the latter sitting in for George Marshall, again ailing—met with Truman later that morning. "The President, although perfectly calm, appeared to be in a state of mind that combined disbelief with controlled fury," Acheson recalled. Truman asked Acheson and Lovett if his directive of the previous December 6, the one requiring statements to be approved by the White House, was clear. They assured him it was. Truman nodded. Still calm but not less angry, the president turned to his secretary. "He dictated a message to MacArthur which laid so plainly the foundation for a court-martial as to give pause even to General MacArthur," Acheson recalled. Speaking in the third person, Truman said, "The President has directed that your attention be called to his order as transmitted 6 December 1950. In view of the information given you 20 March 1951"—about the president's imminent ceasefire offer—"any further statements by you must be coordinated as prescribed in the order of 6 December." Referring specifically to MacArthur's unauthorized offer, Truman continued, "The President has also directed that in the event the Communist military leaders request an armistice in the field, you immediately report that fact to the JCS for instructions." Truman ordered the message sent to Tokyo at once.

MacArthur later professed to have been taken aback when he read Truman's message. He gathered that his truce offer was what had provoked the president's response. "The argument was made that I had disrupted some magic formula for peace on which the United States had already secured international agreement and which it was about to announce," he recalled sarcastically. "This was utter nonsense. No such plan was even in draft form. And what I said would entirely support any peace effort that might be made. Under any interpretation, it was only the local voice of a theater commander." MacArthur noted that he had twice before called on the enemy to surrender and halt further bloodshed—once after Inchon and again after the capture of Pyongyang. "In neither instance had there been the slightest whisper of remonstrance from any source—indeed, quite the contrary." His offer had been entirely in keeping with military tradition. "From the beginning of warfare, it has not only been a right, but a duty for a field commander to take any steps within his power to minimize bloodshed of the soldiers committed to his command." As to his aspersions on China's military prowess, this was a psychological ploy. "My statement was not only factual, but intended to present to the enemy the basic reason why he should agree to stop the war."

Courtney Whitney perceived a deeper meaning in Washington's response—a perception MacArthur certainly shared, since Whitney never diverged from his chief in such matters, though MacArthur commonly hewed to a higher road in public. "Far from MacArthur's ken, a sinister element in the last act of the tragedy had been taking place," Whitney wrote a few years later, in typically dark tones. "It seems reasonable to assume that in some parts of the U.N. and the U.S. State Department, and in some very high places elsewhere in Washington"—the White House was the only place that qualified as "very high" compared with the State Department—"men were scheming to change the status of Formosa and the Nationalists' seat in the United Nations." Whitney cited no evidence of such scheming on Truman's part, for there was none. Yet he credited the general with spiking such a conspiracy all the same. "What had happened was that by sheer accident, in his statement and in its reference to settling the war without reference to Formosa or the United Nations seat, MacArthur had cut right across one of the most disgraceful plots in American history. Or was it not accident, but intuition? This I do know: had MacArthur fully realized the hornets' nest he would stir up, he still would not have been deterred."

49

OMAR BRADLEY REMEMBERED the first week of April 1951 as the time when the administration felt more fearful than ever about the possibility of the outbreak of World War III. "We had recently received alarming intelligence information (from a classified source) that the Soviet Union was preparing for a major military move; where, we did not know," Bradley wrote. "One suggestion, taken with utmost seriousness, was that they would intervene in Korea. Another was that they might attempt to overrun Western Europe."

This was the nightmare scenario of the administration: that the Soviets would exploit America's involvement in Korea by launching a general war. Bradley and the chiefs huddled with their intelligence officers and produced a plan for responding to a Soviet thrust. "If the USSR precipitates a general war, United Nations forces should be withdrawn from Korea as rapidly as possible and deployed for service elsewhere," the plan declared. Korea, in other words, was expendable. But MacArthur might yet get what he wanted, for if things escalated, the United States had to be ready to hit the communists where they would feel it. "Preparations should be made immediately for action by naval and air forces against the mainland of China," the chiefs said.

Bradley and the chiefs followed up with a proposal for new orders to MacArthur. "The Joint Chiefs of Staff recommend that you obtain Presidential approval now for them to send the following message to General MacArthur if and when the enemy launches from outside Korea a major air attack against our forces in the Korean area," the chiefs wrote to George Marshall: "'You are authorized with the U.S. forces assigned to the Far East Command to attack enemy air bases and aircraft in Manchuria and the Shantung peninsula in the immediate vicinity of Weihaiwei.'"

It was a measure of Truman's alarm at the possibility of general war that he approved the proposed order. But it was a measure of Bradley's distrust of MacArthur that the joint chiefs chairman declined to send the order. "Ordinarily we would have sent this letter to MacArthur for contingency planning," Bradley explained later. "However, I was now so wary of MacArthur that I deliberately withheld the message and all knowledge of its existence from him." Bradley didn't want MacArthur to see anything that even prospectively authorized the escalation he had been agitating for. MacArthur had interpreted orders expansively in the past. With World War III apparently closer than ever, Bradley wasn't going to give him a chance to do so again.

REPORTERS SENSED THE rising tension in the administration. A reporter at the president's regular news conference on April 5 asked him about a recent comment by Sam Rayburn, the speaker of the House of Representatives. The administration had shared some recent intelligence with Rayburn, who, out of the best intentions toward the administration's defense bill, had told his House colleagues that large numbers of troops were massing in Manchuria. The reporter sought Truman's reaction.

"I have no comment on Speaker Rayburn's statement," Truman said. "But the Speaker is a truthful man."

The reporter went on to say that Rayburn had offered the opinion that World War III might be beginning.

"I have no further comment to make on Speaker Rayburn's comment," Truman said.

"I wonder if your statement covered the whole of the—"

"No further comment."

Another reporter took a slightly different tack. "Mr. President, aside from your statement, do you think there is a danger of a major world war greater today than at any time, say, since the end of World War II?"

"It is just as great as it ever has been," Truman said. "We were faced with that in the Berlin airlift. We were faced with it in Greece and Turkey. We were faced with it in Iran, when the troops of the Allies and

Russia moved out of Iran. We were faced with it in Korea as an actual fact on June 25th. That situation has been a dangerous one for the last five years—last four years, I will say."

A reporter offered Truman a chance to reassure the American people. "Mr. President, do you agree with Senator Connally's belief that there won't be a third world war this year?"

"I hope there never will be a third world war. That is what we are trying to prevent. That is the reason for all this preparation."

The questioning moved to other topics before a reporter drew the discussion back. "Mr. President, this massing of troops in Manchuria, are you—"

"I can't comment on that, and I don't intend to answer any further questions on it at all."

Yet the reporters persisted. The question of one of them suggested he might have sources in the upper echelons of the Pentagon. Or perhaps it was a lucky guess, for at just the moment when the joint chiefs were writing the order that would have given MacArthur provisional authority to bomb China, the reporter asked, "Mr. President, has General MacArthur been authorized to bomb bases in Manchuria?"

Truman hadn't yet seen the chiefs' recommendation, so his refusal to comment likely came more easily than some of his other deflections. "That is a question that cannot be answered because it is a military strategy question, and it is not a question that I can answer."

Another reporter either hadn't heard the question or hoped to lure Truman into a fuller answer. "I wonder if we could have that question—"

"He asked me if General MacArthur had been authorized to bomb bases in Manchuria," Truman said. "And I said that is a military strategy question that I cannot answer."

JOSEPH MARTIN CHOSE just this moment to read MacArthur's letter to him into the public record. MacArthur had not said that his remarks were confidential, though Martin had invited him to do so if he thought appropriate. Martin concluded that MacArthur wanted the letter aired. Almost certainly MacArthur did. And he must have realized how it would provoke Truman further. The friendly tone of MacArthur's letter seemed to endorse Martin's bitterly partisan attack on the administration. MacArthur's assertion that Martin's demand that the administration unleash Chiang and the Chinese Nationalists was in conflict with neither logic nor tradition placed the general again at odds with Truman on this crucial issue. His dismissal of the administration's global strategy—"It seems strangely difficult for some to realize that here in Asia is where the Communist conspirators have elected to make their play for global conquest, and that we have joined the issue thus raised on the battlefield; that here we fight Europe's war with arms while the diplomats there still fight it with words"—was not simply provocative but insulting. And his stirring summation—"There is no substitute for victory"—could only complicate the president's desire to limit the war in Korea.

Doubtless MacArthur sought to increase the pressure on Truman to shift American policy in the direction MacArthur thought it should go. Possibly he thought the pressure would produce the desired policy change in the near term; conceivably he thought it wouldn't but would thereby position him for the 1952 presidential race, after which he might effect the change himself, as commander-in-chief.

Joseph Martin might have reckoned things similarly. Or perhaps he merely wanted to vex the administration. The Republicans had made no secret, since their come-from-ahead defeat in 1948, of their determination to reclaim the White House in 1952 by almost any means necessary. Another MacArthur salvo against Truman would certainly benefit the campaign.

"RANK INSUBORDINATION," a furious Truman wrote in his diary. "This looks like the last straw." The president's pen gouged the paper as he recounted MacArthur's most recent offenses, and several earlier ones. "The situation with regard to the Far Eastern General has become a political one. MacArthur has made himself a center of controversy, publicly and privately. He has always been a controversial figure. He has had two wives—one a social light he married at 42, the other a Tennessee girl he married in his middle fifties after No. 1 had divorced him. He was chief of staff in the Hoover regime, made the front pages in the bonus affair. . . . Last summer he sent a long statement to the Vets of Foreign Wars—not through the high command back home, but directly! He sent copies to newspapers and magazines particularly hostile to me.

I was furnished a copy from the press room of the White House which had been accidentally sent there. I ordered the release suppressed and then sent him a very carefully prepared directive dated Dec. 5 1950 setting out Far Eastern policy after I'd flown 14404 miles to Wake Island to see him and reach an understanding face to face. He told me the war in Korea was over, that we could transfer a regular division to Germany Jan 1st. He was positive Red China would not come in. He expected to support our Far Eastern policy."

From the past Truman switched to the present. "MacArthur shoots another political bomb through Joe Martin, leader of the Republican minority in the House." This final affront left the president no recourse. "I call in Gen. Marshall, Dean Acheson, Mr. Harriman and Gen. Bradley. I've come to the conclusion that our Big General in the Far East must be recalled." But the president kept this conclusion to himself. "I don't express any opinion or make known my decision."

DEAN ACHESON CAUGHT a whiff of coup d'état in MacArthur's collaboration with Joseph Martin. At the meeting with Truman, George Marshall suggested bringing MacArthur home for a talk. Acheson thought this a terrible idea. The Republicans he called primitives had been gunning for Truman, with Joseph McCarthy and others branding him unfit to be president. Acheson distrusted them deeply. "Their attachment to constitutional procedures was a veneer at best," he wrote afterward. Bringing MacArthur home would play into their unprincipled hands and invite the worst kind of adventurism. "The effect of MacArthur's histrionic abilities on civilians and of his prestige upon the military had been often enough demonstrated. To get him back in Washington in the full panoply of his commands and with his future the issue of the day would not only gravely impair the President's freedom of decision but might well imperil his own future." Marshall accepted the criticism and withdrew his suggestion.

No notes were taken at this meeting. Truman didn't want anything in writing until he was prepared to announce his decision. Recollections of what was said at the meeting differed. Truman said that Averell Harriman remarked that MacArthur should have been fired two years earlier when the general had refused to return to Washington for consultation on Japan. Harriman later denied this, saying instead that he had merely remarked that MacArthur had been trouble since the summer of 1950. Truman also remembered that Marshall had counseled caution, with the defense secretary asserting that a row over MacArthur would complicate passage of the defense bill then before Congress.

Truman recollected that Omar Bradley considered the MacArthur question from the perspective of military discipline. "As he saw it, there was a clear case of insubordination and the general deserved to be relieved of command." Bradley later said the president remembered things inaccurately. Bradley said he hadn't said what Truman claimed he said, because he didn't believe what Truman said he believed. "There was considerable doubt in my mind that MacArthur had committed a clear-cut case of military insubordination as defined in Army Regulations," Bradley wrote. Bradley was painfully aware that the joint chiefs had been sufficiently vague with MacArthur that an insubordination charge—of willful violation of a direct order—might be impossible to prove. Bradley, like Marshall, wanted time to think things over.

Truman adjourned the meeting without revealing his own thoughts. He asked Marshall to review the Pentagon's communications with MacArthur during the previous two years. Marshall did so that evening, and when the president reconvened the group on Saturday morning, April 7, the defense secretary—according to Truman's version—delivered his verdict. "General Marshall stated that he had read the messages and that he had now concluded that MacArthur should have been fired two years ago," Truman wrote.

"That is not true either," Bradley retrospectively rejoined. Bradley had argued that any recommendation should await a full meeting of the joint chiefs, which couldn't take place until Joe Collins returned Saturday night from a trip. Marshall had agreed, Bradley said. "As planned, we merely advised the President to postpone any action until Monday, giving us all another two full days to cogitate and me time to meet with the full JCS." Truman accepted the delay.

Bradley wanted all the time he and Marshall could get. Truman seemed to be leaning toward dismissal of MacArthur, even if the president hadn't said so directly. Acheson wasn't merely leaning. "Acheson clearly favored firing MacArthur," Bradley recalled. "He did not attempt to disguise his position." Yet Acheson understood that the decision would be filled with peril. "If you relieve MacArthur, you will have the biggest fight of your administration," the secretary told the president.

Marshall and Bradley didn't want the military to be in the middle of that fight. They sought an alternative to dismissal. "Marshall and I were not certain that it was the wisest course, for a number of reasons—certainly not on a charge of military insubordination, as defined in Army Regulations," Bradley recalled. "That could lead to myriad legal entanglements, perhaps even—God forbid!—a Billy Mitchell–type court-martial." Bradley suggested to Marshall that they send a letter "in effect telling MacArthur to shut up." They began drafting it. "But this grew too complicated and we tore it up."

Bradley and Marshall had personal reasons for avoiding an uproar. Marshall's health remained uncertain, and he had agreed to fill the position of defense secretary for a year only. He had five months left. "Firing MacArthur was certain to cause an unprecedented furor and provoke yet another savage right-wing political attack on Marshall personally, hardly a pleasant way to wind up his long and distinguished public career," Bradley wrote. "Moreover, although untrue, there was a widespread belief in military circles (and some media) that Marshall had long had it in for MacArthur, and a recommendation to fire him might be construed as an act of revenge."

Bradley felt something similar for himself. His term as chairman of the joint chiefs would end in four months, and he expected to retire from the army soon thereafter. He had managed to avoid becoming a political target so far. Firing MacArthur would change that. "It might provoke the primitives and subject me to the kind of savage mauling they were giving Acheson and Marshall."

This might have larger ramifications, Bradley said. "If the JCS endorsed Truman's decision to fire MacArthur and if the firing was construed as mainly political, this could have the effect of 'politicizing' the JCS. This, in turn, could lead to a drastic erosion in the standing of the JCS as objective advisers to any and all presidents, whatever the party."

"That night I thought long and hard," Bradley wrote of the hours from Saturday to Sunday. He finally reached a conclusion he could support. "Truman, as President and Commander in Chief, had established our policy for the conduct of the Korean War. MacArthur was clearly opposed to that policy and had openly and defiantly challenged it to the point where there was serious question that he could carry out that policy. It was not a question of who was right or wrong. As the ultimate in civilian control over the military, Commander in Chief Truman had every right to replace a general who defied his policy and in whom he had lost confidence."

Bradley summoned the chiefs the next day. He said the president wanted their views on MacArthur from a military standpoint. "We discussed every conceivable aspect," Bradley recalled. "We even considered proposing that MacArthur be left in his Tokyo post with no direct control over Ridgway and the Eighth Army." But given the connections between the defense of Korea and the defense of Japan, this seemed likely to produce impossible headaches. "In the end the JCS agreed unanimously that MacArthur should be relieved."

Yet they stopped short of asserting insubordination. "Because of the legal complexities that could arise, we avoided the term 'insubordination' as a reason. In point of fact, MacArthur had stretched but not legally violated any JCS directives. He had violated the President's December 6 directive, relayed to him by the JCS, but this did not constitute violation of a direct JCS order." In other words, MacArthur had disobeyed the president but not the joint chiefs.

This was hairsplitting, even from a narrowly military perspective. The president was, after all, commander-in-chief. Bradley implicitly acknowledged as much in a memo he wrote a short while later summarizing the reasons MacArthur should be relieved. First: "By his public statements and by his official communications to us, he had indicated that he was not in sympathy with the decision to try to limit the conflict to Korea. This would make it difficult for him to carry out Joint Chiefs of Staff directives. Since we had decided to try to confine the conflict to Korea and avoid a third world war, it was necessary to have a commander more responsive to control from Washington." Second: "General MacArthur had failed to comply with the Presidential directive to clear statements on policy before making such statements public. He had also taken independent action in proposing to negotiate directly with the enemy field commander and had made that statement public, despite the fact that he knew the President had such a proposal under consideration from a governmental level." Third: "The Joint Chiefs of Staff have felt, and feel now, that the military must be controlled by civilian authority in this country. (The Congress itself was very careful to emphasize this point in the National Security Act of 1947 and in its amendment in 1949.) They have always adhered to this principle and they felt that General MacArthur's actions were continuing to jeopardize the civilian control over the military authorities."

Bradley and the chiefs took their decision to Marshall on Sunday afternoon. "It was a sad and sober group," Joe Collins remarked later. "It was not easy to be a party to the dismissal of a distinguished soldier." Marshall withheld his own view but asked Bradley to relate the chiefs' verdict to the president the next day.

ON SUNDAY TRUMAN met with Acheson again and separately with John Snyder, the secretary of the treasury. Snyder had no formal link to the MacArthur question, but he and Truman had served together in World War I and Truman valued his political opinion. The president also met with Chief Justice Fred Vinson, another old friend, and with Sam Rayburn. Vice President Barkley was in the hospital, but Truman spoke to him by phone. "The situation in Far East is discussed but I do not disclose my intentions," Truman wrote in his diary.

Acheson endorsed the president's discretion. "Whatever his action," Acheson explained later, "all of us would be examined and questioned. On one matter we should all be clear and under no necessity to plead privilege: the President had never intimated to any of us his opinion and intended action until, having heard the recommendations of all the responsible civilian and military officers, he announced his decision."

The critical meeting occurred on Monday morning, April 9. Truman asked for recommendations. Bradley reported that the joint chiefs had concluded unanimously that MacArthur should be relieved of all his commands. Marshall said he concurred in the recommendation. Acheson and Averell Harriman likewise concurred.

Truman listened silently. He nodded. Then he finally delivered his own verdict, the only one that truly mattered. MacArthur had to go. Truman added, according to his own account, that he had come to this conclusion two weeks earlier, after MacArthur's preemption of the UN truce negotiations.

Truman asked Bradley whom the chiefs recommended as MacArthur's replacement. Bradley replied that Matthew Ridgway was their first choice. Truman nodded again.

Truman dismissed the group with instructions to draw up the necessary orders. It went without saying that no one should discuss the decision until the president made it public.

50

Likely no one *did* discuss the decision—no one of the principals, that is. But the Martin-MacArthur exchange had every reporter in Washington on high alert, and the flurry of meetings of the president with his most senior military and diplomatic advisers suggested that this manifestation of the long-running tension between Truman and MacArthur might not blow over.

Truman appreciated the desirability of treating MacArthur with all the dignity possible, given the circumstances of his being fired. MacArthur's many supporters would be outraged by his dismissal, and there was no reason to add avoidable disrespect to their list of indictments against the administration.

A plan was laid to have Frank Pace, who happened to be in Korea, travel to Tokyo and personally deliver a letter from Truman to MacArthur. The general deserved to hear the news from the president, via the secretary of the army. But the logistics of the plan were daunting. Pace had to be alerted without any of the reporters who were accompanying him catching on. And the content of the president's letter had to be transmitted without any of those involved in the transmission being tempted beyond resistance to share what they had sent.

Moreover, reporters weren't above manufacturing rumors and asking for an official response. Under the present circumstances, a "no comment" rather than a ringing endorsement of MacArthur would be tantamount to confirmation of his firing.

In the event, the chain of secrecy didn't hold. A *Chicago Tribune* radio reporter covering MacArthur heard something that caused him to tell the home office that the general might be fired soon. The *Tribune* put its Washington men on the trail. One of them, Walter Trohan, cornered Joe Short, Truman's new press secretary. "I got a double talk," Trohan recalled later, "so I knew there must be something to it." Another *Tribune* man, Lloyd Norman, buttonholed Omar Bradley's press aide, Ted Clifton, and, as Norman said afterward, "could not get a denial."

Ironically, the *Tribune's* radio man called back to say that he had concluded that his hunch was wrong. He couldn't find corroborating evidence. The *Tribune's* managing editor decided to pull the story. Trohan complained, to no avail. "It was a stupid decision," he said later. "Although Norman and I did not have a solid confirmation, by that time we thought we had enough to go with a speculative story."

Joe Short and Ted Clifton didn't know that the story had been killed. They took Trohan's and Norman's queries as evidence that the *Tribune* was going to publish. "This fear—groundless, as it developed—led to a tremendous flap," Omar Bradley recalled. *Tribune* owner Robert McCormick loathed Truman and loved MacArthur. He would certainly play the story to the benefit of the latter and the detriment of the former. He might even pass the word along to MacArthur, thereby prompting MacArthur to resign before he could be fired.

Bradley called Truman. "Said there had been a leak," Truman wrote in his diary. The president immediately met with Bradley and the other advisers he could find on a moment's notice. "Discussed the situation and I ordered messages sent at once and directly to MacArthur."

Theodore Tannenwald remembered the train of events from the perspective of the White House staff. Tannenwald worked for Averell Harriman, who came back from the Monday meeting with the president's decision. "He got hold of me and said, 'Go over to Charlie Murphy's office this afternoon,'" Tannenwald recounted. "'The president is going to fire MacArthur and he wants to start working on a speech.'" Murphy was special counsel to the president, and he, Tannenwald and others spent the next several hours working on what Truman should say. "About 5 o'clock, the president called Murphy in," Tannenwald continued. "Murphy came back and said, 'The speech is off for the time being. We're going to write a press release. The president is going to fire MacArthur tonight.'" Tannenwald heard secondhand about the story the *Chicago Tribune* was investigating. He wasn't surprised at Truman's reaction. "The president inferred that MacArthur had gotten wind of what was going on and was going to try and beat him to the punch by making a statement in advance of the president's statement and the president was damned if he was going to let MacArthur beat him to the punch."

Tannenwald and the others redoubled their efforts. "We worked on a press statement from about five in the afternoon until about ten at night," Tannenwald recounted. "I remember this so vividly, because I had a great argument with Charlie Murphy throughout the period, because I wanted the press statement to include the fact that the president was doing this on the unanimous advice of the principal civilian and military advisers. And Murphy wouldn't put it in, and never convinced me that he was right in not putting it in. So at ten o'clock we assembled in the Cabinet Room, the president, Harriman, Acheson, Marshall was away and Lovett was there, Bradley was there, as chairman of the joint chiefs, and what I will call us 'Indians' who had worked on this statement, and Joe Short, the press secretary. And just like in every other major speech, the president went through this line by line, and various comments and suggestions were made. And when he finished, also as part of the regular pattern, before he handed it to Joe Short, he turned to the assembled group and said, 'Does anybody have anything to say?' And the rule of the house was that you could be the lowest man on the totem pole, and if you thought there was something that ought to be said, you could do it. And Truman was the kind of guy you could do this with. I said, 'Yes, Mr. President, I think there's something missing. I think this statement ought to say that you're doing this on the unanimous advice of your principal civilian and military advisers.'"

Truman listened politely before rejecting Tannenwald's advice. "I will never forget this night as long as I live," Tannenwald related. "He turned to me with a twinkle in his eye and he said, 'Not tonight, son. Tonight I am taking this decision on my own responsibility as president of the United States, and I want nobody to think that I am trying to share it with anybody else. This will come out in forty-eight or seventy-two hours, but as of tonight, this is my decision, and my decision alone.'"

JOE SHORT ABRUPTLY announced a press conference, to begin at the unusual hour of 1:00 a.m. The presidential statement and a presidential order were released to the sleepy correspondents. "With deep regret I have concluded that General of the Army Douglas MacArthur is unable to give his wholehearted support to the policies of the United States Government and of the United Nations in matters pertaining to his official duties," the president's statement read. "In view of the specific responsibilities imposed upon me by the Constitution of the United States and the added responsibility which has been entrusted to me by the United Nations, I have decided that I must make a change of command in the Far East. I have, therefore, relieved General MacArthur of his commands and have designated Lt. Gen. Matthew B. Ridgway as his successor. Full and vigorous debate on matters of national policy is a vital element in the constitutional system of our free democracy. It is fundamental, however, that military commanders must be governed by the policies and directives issued to them in the manner provided by our laws and Constitution. In time of crisis, this consideration is particularly compelling. General MacArthur's place in history as one of our greatest commanders is fully established. The Nation owes him a debt of gratitude for the distinguished and exceptional service which he has rendered his country in posts of great responsibility. For that reason I repeat my regret at the necessity for the action I feel compelled to take in his case."

The separate presidential order was addressed to MacArthur. "I deeply regret that it becomes my duty as President and Commander in Chief of the United States military forces to replace you as Supreme Commander, Allied Powers; Commander in Chief, United Nations Command; Commander in Chief, Far East; and Commanding General, U.S. Army, Far East," the president said. "You will turn over your commands, effective at once, to Lt. Gen. Matthew B. Ridgway. You are authorized to have issued such orders as are necessary to complete desired travel to such place as you select. My reasons for your replacement will be made public concurrently with the delivery to you of the foregoing order, and are contained in the next following message." The referenced message was the presidential statement just issued.

51

WEDNESDAY, APRIL 11, 1951, dawned in New Japan with the breath of early spring in the air," Courtney Whitney remembered. "The sun rose, as it had since time immemorial, upon this land of the chrysanthemum with its deep shadows and brilliant hues, with its majestic peaks and low-lying valleys, its winding streams and inland seas, its cities and towns and rolling plateaus, all with their natural beauty enhanced by man-made lacquer-red bridges and with customary calm and industry."

But then things changed. "Suddenly this atmosphere of calm and serenity and progress was rent as though by a thunderclap," Whitney wrote. "The radios all over Japan brought upon the land a hushed silence as a special bulletin from Washington broke through all programs." MacArthur was having lunch with Jean and two visitors: Senator Warren Magnuson of Washington and William Stern of Northwest Airlines. MacArthur's aide Colonel Sidney Huff got the attention of Jean without alerting MacArthur. She rose from the table and went out of the room, where Huff told her what the radios were saying. She returned quietly. "The General was laughing heartily at a remark made by one of his guests when she walked into the room behind him and touched his shoulder," Whitney wrote. "He turned and she bent down and told him the news in a voice so low that it was not heard across the table. . . . MacArthur's face froze. Not a flicker of emotion crossed it. For a moment, while his luncheon guests puzzled on what was happening, he was stonily silent. Then he looked up at his wife, who still stood with her hand on his shoulder. In a gentle voice, audible to all present, he said: 'Jeannie, we're going home at last.'"

MATTHEW RIDGWAY GOT the news at the front without realizing what he was getting. Spring had arrived in the mountains of Korea, which meant that hail was mixed with the driving snow. Ridgway was showing Frank Pace around when a reporter from Pace's detail approached him.

"Well, General, I guess congratulations are in order," the reporter said.

Ridgway was puzzled. "What for?" he said.

"You mean you don't know?"

"Don't know what?" Ridgway demanded. "What's this all about?"

The reporter said no more. He walked away, perhaps wondering if *he* had heard things right. Not until that night back at his command post did Ridgway learn, via an urgent message over his radio, that MacArthur had been fired and that he—Ridgway—had succeeded to all his commands.

He flew to Tokyo as soon as he could. In the same office where MacArthur had willingly handed him the Eighth Army, the senior general now unwillingly turned over the entire Far Eastern theater. MacArthur angrily denounced Truman, questioning his mental stability and telling Ridgway—as Ridgway recorded in a private memorandum—that a physician who knew Truman's doctor declared "that the President was suffering from malignant hypertension; that his affliction was characterized by bewilderment and confusion of thought." MacArthur suggested that Truman had but months to live. Meanwhile he—MacArthur— would return to America and "raise hell" against the president's misguided policies.

Ridgway let MacArthur rage, and when he published his memoir five years later he tactfully reported a much calmer conversation. "He was entirely himself—composed, quiet, temperate, friendly, and helpful to the man who was to succeed him," Ridgway wrote of MacArthur. "He made some allusions to the fact that he had been summarily relieved, but there was no trace of bitterness or anger in his tone. I thought it was a fine tribute to the resilience of this great man that he could accept so calmly, with no outward sign of shock, what must have been a devastating blow to a professional soldier standing at the peak of a great career."

WILLIAM SEBALD HAD watched the last days of MacArthur's command convinced that the general had got in over his head. "I am afraid that the General underestimates the difficulties involved in the world situation or, for that matter, in political circles in Washington," Sebald wrote in his diary. "What appears easy here is magnified many times in complexity when viewed in the light of the broad world picture. Should the matter come to a showdown, I think the General would lose: he could not stand the searchlight and shafts of public criticism."

Yet Sebald was as shocked as anyone when the ax fell. He learned the news from someone who had heard it on the radio. "Refused to believe it at first," he wrote. The State Department instructed him to visit Shigeru Yoshida, the Japanese prime minister, and assure him that the change in command connoted no change in American policy. "He was visibly shaken but grateful for my message and its assurance," Sebald recorded. A short while later Sebald went to headquarters. "Called on General MacArthur who met me with a smile—unfortunately, I was so keyed up that tears came into my eyes. The General handed me, and lit, a cigarette. We sat down; I said, 'General, you are a better soldier in this than I am.' The General was very bitter about the *method* employed in sending him home, 'publicly humiliated after 52 years of service in the Army.' He said that if the President had indicated that he wished him to retire, he would have done so without difficulty." MacArthur read deep significance into his dismissal. "He intimated that his removal was a plot in Washington; that Formosa would be handed over to Red China; that the Philippines would fall next; Japan would be isolated and fall too; that our whole position in the Far East would crumble." MacArthur considered his successor. "On General Ridgway, he said he is an excellent soldier; whether he is also a good administrator remains to be seen, but he doubted it. He wondered whether Gen. Ridgway had 'sold his soul'; he hoped not. These were, of course, bitter words, which may, perhaps, excuse them. Under the circumstances, they are understandable." MacArthur defended his conduct. "The General denied that he has violated any orders from Washington. When the letter to Rep. Joseph Martin was first mentioned, the General said that he didn't even remember it and had to fish it out of his files; in any event, it was a personal letter."

Sebald, wiping the tears from his eyes, said MacArthur still had his support. The general responded gravely, "Bill, your weakness is that you have probably been too loyal to me. You may have to pay for that loyalty."

52

ON WEDNESDAY EVENING, April 11, eighteen hours after the news conference announcing MacArthur's dismissal, Truman offered his explanation to the American people, except that he hardly touched on the matter they all wanted to know about. He spoke by radio from his office. The lengthiest part of the speech was a reiteration of the administration's argument that Korea was but one theater in the struggle against world communism. "The question we have had to face is whether the communist plan of conquest can be stopped without a general war," he said. Until now the United States had been successful. "So far, we have prevented World War III. So far, by fighting a limited war in Korea, we have prevented aggression from succeeding." America's allies had been heartened by the resolute stand of American and UN forces. But the enemy remained determined. New intelligence suggested that a major offensive was coming. Yet Truman wasn't overly worried. "If a new attack comes, I feel confident it will be turned back. The United Nations fighting forces are tough and able and well equipped." He placed the burden of decision on the enemy. "They may take further action which will spread the conflict. They have that choice, and with it the awful responsibility for what may follow." He hoped they would choose another course. "We do not want to see the conflict in Korea extended. We are trying to prevent a world war, not to start one."

Astute listeners sensed Truman was approaching the topic that kept them all tuned in. "You may ask why can't we take other steps to punish the aggressor," he said. "Why don't we bomb Manchuria and China itself? Why don't we assist the Chinese Nationalist troops to land on the mainland of China?" He answered his own questions. "If we were to do these things we would be running a very grave risk of starting a general war. If that were to happen, we would have brought about the exact situation we are trying to prevent. If we were to do these things, we would become entangled in a vast conflict on the continent of Asia and our task would become immeasurably more difficult all over the world. What would suit the ambitions of the Kremlin better than for our military forces to be committed to a full-scale war with Red China?" The United States must avoid this trap, for three reasons: "to make sure that the precious lives of our fighting men are not wasted; to see that the security of our country and the free world is not needlessly jeopardized; and to prevent a third world war."

Finally he reached the issue of the hour. "A number of events have made it evident that General MacArthur did not agree with that policy," Truman said. "I have therefore considered it essential to relieve General MacArthur so that there would be no doubt or confusion as to the real purpose and aim of our policy." The decision did not come easily. "It was with the deepest personal regret that I found myself compelled to take this action. General MacArthur is one of our greatest military commanders." But a president had larger interests to consider. "The cause of world peace is much more important than any individual."

53

Q UITE AN EXPLOSION," Truman wrote in his diary, summarizing the public response to the firing. "Was expected but I had to act. Telegrams and letters of abuse by the dozens."

He sampled the correspondence. "Your action toward MacArthur is completely unwarranted in my opinion," a New Jersey writer declared. "I hope history will bear out the soundness of your action, for if you are wrong the consequences will be a great blood bath for all free people." The writer supplied a bit of biography and a promise. "I voted for you in 1948 and have regretted it ever since. The way things look now I not only will *not* vote for you or the democratic party in 1952 but will actively work *for* republican candidates—even if he be Taft whose isolationism I consider almost as dangerous as your appeasement." The writer signed off: "A loyal but alarmed American."

A San Antonio woman said she had written to her senators and representative urging Truman's impeachment. "You have sold us out, just as your noble predecessor sold us out at Yalta, and the Kremlin should give you a 21-gun salute," she wrote. "They probably will—aimed right at our bewildered forces in Korea. . . . You have kicked out, with insults, the most brilliant, courageous and successful man representing our country abroad. . . . You have fired a man whose first and whole devotion has been to the best interest of our country. (He didn't have to think about the Democratic vote in Missouri.) He has done a top job, but he couldn't be red-taped. So he got fired, and the hell with U.S.A. Harry is top-boy, and he has to prove it. Why stop with Formosa? Let's give them Japan, and Hawaii, and Alaska—and why not the Panama Canal?"

A Washington, D.C., woman said she had never voted for Truman and never would. But she thought he had outdone himself in incompetence this time and was undoing America. "General MacArthur has probably forgotten more about the Far East than those advising you in Washington have ever known. As a good American, I am ashamed of my President! . . . You have committed the worst blunder of your administration."

The attacks mounted. By the afternoon of April 12 the White House had received more than 5,000 telegrams, with three-quarters of them, by staff estimates, opposing the president. At the Capitol the count was even more strongly against the president. The Republican Congressional Committee reported that the forty-seven Republican senators and two hundred Republican representatives had received 5,986 letters supporting MacArthur and only 32 siding with Truman. The telegrams for MacArthur were 42,024 compared with 334 for Truman. Telephone calls for MacArthur were 1,776 against 13 for Truman. The correspondence received by the Democrats in Congress didn't come close to offsetting this negative tide.

Editorial opinion was mixed. The *Columbus Dispatch* asserted, "It is no secret that MacArthur's dismissal from Japan was more deeply desired by the forces of communism than any number of Korean victories. With MacArthur out of authority in Tokyo, the Communist conquest of Asia becomes a softer assignment." But the *Cleveland Plain Dealer* declared, "General MacArthur overstepped the prerogatives of a military officer in the issuance of political statements, and, therefore, President Truman exercised his right and followed his duty in relieving him of his command." Yet the *Plain Dealer* immediately qualified its approval, saying, "The President may have set off a thorough exposure of the bankruptcy of his own administration." The *Boston Globe* allowed that Truman had the right "to remove a subordinate commander who was unwilling to follow orders with which he did not agree." But the *Globe* wanted to hear the other side of the story. "General MacArthur's ideas are entitled to a full hearing, and he is obviously the best man to present them." The *Boston Herald* likewise opined that a thorough airing was in order. "One of the principal difficulties in this whole situation is that most Americans, like General MacArthur himself, are not clear as to what the United Nations policy is in Korea," the *Herald* said. "The coming debate ought to clear that up." The *Chicago Daily News* put the burden on Truman to straighten things out: "Having taken full responsibility in the MacArthur case, President Truman cannot escape the greater responsibility of defining, in company with other members of the United Nations, what further course of action is to be followed."

But the *Chicago Tribune* wanted to hear nothing more from this president. "President Truman must be impeached and convicted," the *Tribune* asserted. "His hasty and vindictive removal of General MacArthur is the culmination of a series of acts which have shown that he is unfit, morally and mentally, for his high office. Mr. Truman can be impeached for usurping the power of Congress when he ordered American troops to the Korean front without a declaration of war. He can be impeached, also, for surrounding himself with grafters and incompetents. The American nation has never been in greater danger. It is led by a fool who is surrounded by knaves."

54

C OURT, PLEASE ARRANGE the trip so that we will arrive in San Francisco and New York after dark to enable us to slip into a hotel without being noticed."

So said MacArthur, according to Courtney Whitney's recollection. Speaking in his own voice, Whitney went on, "I looked with astonishment at MacArthur as he gave me these instructions, and suddenly for the first time realized the humiliation that seared his soul as a result of the foul and shocking blow by which his long and devoted service to the nation had been so abruptly terminated. So deep was this humiliation that it deprived him of a true understanding of public reaction at home. For he had only a general idea of the thousands of supporting cables which had accumulated from world-wide sources. He had read none of the press accounts of the popular indignation aroused by the President's curt order. He knew nothing of the great pressure on the telephone circuits from people trying to get through to Tokyo to register their personal resentments and extend expressions of sympathy and understanding."

Whitney, responsible for arranging MacArthur's travel, took particular umbrage at a sentence in the dismissal decree overlooked by most others: "You are authorized to have issued such orders as are necessary to complete desired travel to such place as you select." Whitney resentfully remarked, "This was the treatment accorded to the one great World War leader who had not taken time off from duty to return home to receive a hero's welcome and the nation's tribute for his World War victories, to the 'principal architect' of the Pacific victory as Stimson had so aptly described him, to a soldier after fifty years of devoted service, half on foreign soil, to the recipient of all the nation's highest honors. No other American soldier had ever received such a list, and none had served abroad so long. I have never seen the order committing Napoleon to exile, but I dare say it exuded greater warmth and was couched in terms reflecting higher honor than that which authorized MacArthur to spend the public funds necessary to take him to an oblivion of his own selection."

THE JAPANESE WERE stunned by the news. Most were astonished at the idea that a general could be fired by a civilian official; in recent Japanese history power had typically run in the opposite direction. When the truth sank in—that MacArthur was leaving—they turned out in immense numbers to bid farewell to the one who had conquered and then resurrected them. MacArthur, accompanied by Jean and Arthur, left their residence in the American embassy at 6:30 in the morning on Monday, April 16. A thirty-man honor guard comprising members of each of the armed services stood at attention. MacArthur snapped a salute and entered his limousine. The car drove through the still-rutted streets of Tokyo, past crowds estimated at up to one million men, women and children. Ten thousand police turned out, most not for crowd control but in their own tribute to their de facto emperor. The nominal emperor, Hirohito, did not appear; he had paid a final visit—his first social call on MacArthur, or any other mortal—the previous day.

A nineteen-gun salute, the maximum allowed a five-star general, greeted MacArthur at Haneda Airport. The diplomatic corps was present, besides the senior American military officers and ranking Japanese officials. A military band played "Auld Lang Syne." Jet fighters screamed above the field. MacArthur had previously changed the name of his plane from *Bataan* to *SCAP;* now that he was no longer Supreme Commander for the Allied Powers, the old name had been repainted onto the fuselage.

MacArthur followed Jean and Arthur up the ramp to the plane's door. Jean openly wept. The general's eyes were dry and his jaw set. Someone yelled, "Job well done." The crowd cheered. Matthew Ridgway stepped forward and saluted. MacArthur returned the salute. He lifted his famous campaign cap to the crowd. He ducked his head and entered the plane.

It taxied down the runway and lifted off at 7:20. All eyes continued to follow it as it climbed into the eastern sky.

Courtney Whitney sat beside MacArthur in the plane. "As I looked down," Whitney wrote later, "I saw the upturned faces of those thousands of Japanese who jammed the airbase. They were still waving farewell, and I could feel rather than see that their lips still formed the traditional Japanese expression at parting: 'Sayonara, Sayonara'— good-by and Godspeed." Whitney looked to the horizon. "There stood Mount Fuji, still snow covered, rising majestically into the sky as if to claim the right over mortal man to bespeak the final farewell." Whitney noticed that MacArthur was looking toward Fuji, too. "It will be a long, long time, Court, before we see her again," MacArthur said.

55

THE CROWDS IN San Francisco began gathering hours before MacArthur's plane came into view. The afternoon sun dipped toward the Pacific; a half-moon floated upward over the bay; high clouds parted like curtains on the stage of history. The most eager of the watchers headed for the airport, south of the city; others lined the highway and streets from the airport to Union Square at San Francisco's heart. All took their cue from the radio reports of the airplane's progress. Air traffic controllers put the *Bataan* at the 138th meridian, altitude seventeen thousand feet, at 4:22 p.m. The plane's speed of two hundred sixty knots would bring it into sight a bit after eight o'clock.

People in the city saw the plane first, its white and red running lights winking against the blue-black of the late evening sky. The rumble of the aircraft's four engines sent a frisson through the growing throng. An amplified voice boomed across the runway and aprons at the airport: "The *Bataan* is making her final approach." The crowd roared.

The plane's landing lights suddenly came on, like kliegs in a theater. The crowd roared again. The official greeters inched closer to the spot where the plane would taxi to a halt. The unofficial throng pressed harder against the fence that ringed the airfield; police warned them back lest the barrier crumple and they be crushed.

At 8:29 the wheels of the plane scuffed the asphalt. "He's down! He's down!" a hundred voices shouted to the thousands around them.

From the airport tower a searchlight panned the field before locking onto the slowing plane. The silver hull gleamed back the light. The cheering rose to a new level and remained there for minutes. A bystander might have wondered when the cheerers took a breath. A cacophony of other sounds—car horns, kitchenware, whistles—intensified the pandemonium.

The plane trundled to a stop. The engines shut off, allowing the propellers to spin down. Airport workers hustled rolling stairs to the side of the plane. The door opened inward. Now the cheerers did catch their breath, preparing a greater yell.

But they had to hold themselves a moment longer. The first face to appear in the door was that of Jean MacArthur. Almost no one knew what she looked like, so carefully had she kept in the background of her famous husband. But it had to be her, as no other woman was thought to be on the plane. And she looked the part of the hero's wife: composed, neatly elegant, able to bear good news and bad without a flutter. Her jacket was navy or black; the searchlight's brilliance erased the distinction. An orchid corsage lent freshness after the long flight from Hawaii, where the general's party had stopped and spent a night.

Close behind her came the great man himself. He had said he didn't want a fuss. He could see at once that his words had been ignored; the city had never greeted anyone more effusively. He wasn't sure what to do. He had never dealt with an audience as large as this. Generals in ancient times had spoken to entire armies on the eve of battle; this general addressed much smaller groups. Nor had he often spoken to civilian audiences. He knew the mind of soldiers; of civilians he was less sure.

He preferred not to speak on this occasion. He would save his words for Washington. He stepped through the airplane door and was blinded by the flash of camera bulbs and the glare of television floodlights.

The mayor of San Francisco and the governor of California greeted him on behalf of the city and the state. A battery of guns thundered its welcome. A company of red-scarved troops from an engineer battalion presented arms. An army band rolled ruffles and flourishes and pitched into "The General's March." The engineers' captain invited him to review the troops; he did so with practiced efficiency.

A podium draped in bunting and bristling with microphones loomed before him. He had to say something. "I can't tell you how good it is to be home," he obliged. Observers close to the podium thought they saw a tremble in the famous jaw; emotion briefly roughened his voice. "Mrs. MacArthur and I have thought long about this moment. Now that the moment has come, the wonderful hospitality of this city has made it all the more enjoyable. Thank you so much. We won't forget it."

He said no more. He looked for the car assigned to take him and Jean and Arthur to the hotel. But before he could reach the vehicle he was swarmed by cameramen who wanted the perfect photo and well-wishers who sought to shake his hand or simply touch the sleeve of his trench coat. Lesser army brass crowded to be in the frame with the most decorated senior officer of the age. Military and civilian police pushed back against the crowd, to partial avail. Jean MacArthur's mouth kept smiling, but fear flitted into her eyes as the crowd closed in. The general's jaw muscles clenched. Arthur thought the excitement marvelous.

The special five-star flag of his rank was carried to the head of the motorcade, and the MacArthurs found their car. The army band struck up "California, Here I Come" as the vehicles pulled away. The crowd scarcely thinned along the road from the airport toward the city. Fathers and mothers lofted their small children, many in pajamas, to see the hero and share the stirring moment. Hand-lettered signs said, "Welcome home, Doug!" and "Mac is back." Many without signs waved American flags.

Bayshore Boulevard took the motorcade through South San Francisco and Daly City; north of the Mission District the column turned onto Market Street. A tide of cheering and applause surged forward with the motorcade: swelling, climaxing and gradually falling as the general's vehicle passed. But the general remained in the wave's crest, all but overwhelmed by sound the entire way.

Management had cleared the furniture from the first floor of the St. Francis Hotel lest the shorter members of the anticipated mob stand on the sofas and tables. Another five-star flag adorned the entrance. The Presidential Suite had been renamed Apartment M for the general's visit. The St. Francis professed no politics in the name change, but more than a few of the visitors, reflecting on the cause of the general's homecoming, smiled approval. With difficulty the police parted the crowd at the curb and in the lobby, and the MacArthurs reached the elevator, which took them to their rooms. Patrolmen secured the hallway outside the apartment door, keeping the bedlam at a distance. Yet they were helpless against the general's supporters outside the hotel, who continued to shout for their hero. A friendly reporter noted approvingly MacArthur's request to hold the formalities to a minimum. "But he could not control the hearts of Americans who surrendered unconditionally to him here," the reporter said.

SAN FRANCISCO SET the tone for the general's triumphal progress east. Church bells pealed beneath the *Bataan* as the aircraft crossed the country. Cities and towns voted resolutions of gratitude and congratulations. Parents named sons for the general. Truman, Texas, debated whether to rechristen itself MacArthur, Texas.

Washington turned out in greater force than for any figure in the history of the nation's capital. Half a million men, women and children swarmed the slopes around the Washington Monument and spilled out across the National Mall. An army band provided music. Every veterans' group in America showed up: the American Legion, the Veterans of Foreign Wars, the Disabled American Veterans, the Catholic War Veterans, the Jewish War Veterans, the Irish War Veterans and several more. Each brought its auxiliary of wives and mothers. The secretaries of defense and of the separate services were there, with the joint chiefs. Another seventeen guns saluted, their concussion giving way to fighter jets streaking overhead. Longtime Washington residents remarked that the only previous celebration that approached MacArthur's in size and intensity was Dwight Eisenhower's after V-E Day. "But there was one thing noted yesterday that was absent in the case of Ike: a look of awe," said a local who had seen them both. "Some men and women just stood there and stared, a little pop-eyed, and neither yelled nor clapped their hands."

THE CELEBRATIONS THAT greeted MacArthur on his return from Asia were unlike anything ever seen in America, and unlike anything ever imagined almost anywhere. Rome had lavished public triumphs on its victorious generals, and America had done the same after the Civil War and the two world wars, but to save the greatest celebration for a general who had just been fired, amid a war that was far from won, suggested that something larger was afoot. The parades for MacArthur were celebrations, but they were also protests: against the president who fired him, against the ambiguous policies the president pursued, against the constraining circumstances that kept America from smiting its enemies as decisively as it had done in those earlier, more satisfying wars. The millions of Americans cheering and shouting for MacArthur wanted the general to lead them, like a modern Moses, out of the wilderness of uncertainty that seemed to be Americans' lot in the contemporary struggle against communism. MacArthur was the last general to return home from World War II; if anyone could restore the certainty—the moral certainty, the civic certainty, the political certainty—that had characterized American life during that earlier struggle, against fascism, MacArthur could.

All ears and many eyes turned to MacArthur as he mounted the biggest stage in American politics. The majority Democrats and minority Republicans wrangled on nearly everything else, but the two parties agreed that MacArthur must speak to a joint session of Congress. The invitation was proffered and accepted, and the preparations were made. The national radio networks wired the chamber of the House of Representatives for what promised to be the most listened-to speech in history; the still emerging medium of television broadcast the event on a more limited basis.

MacArthur gave his congressional hosts and the media companies all they desired. No one had ever heard anything like the speech MacArthur delivered that day. It combined pathos with passion, experience with erudition, strategy with philosophy. MacArthur was not a practiced public speaker; many lawmakers in the room had delivered more public speeches in a single election campaign than MacArthur had delivered in his entire career. But he was an intuitive performer, and he understood how to play on the emotions of his audience.

He began with a suitable compliment to his hosts. "I stand on this rostrum with a sense of deep humility and great pride: humility in the wake of those great architects who have stood here before me, pride in the reflection that this home of legislative debate represents human liberty in the purest form yet devised," he said.

One sentence into his speech, he was interrupted by rousing bipartisan applause.

"I do not stand here as advocate for any partisan cause," he continued when the tumult diminished, "for the issues are fundamental and reach quite beyond the realm of partisan considerations. They must be resolved on the highest plane of national interest if our course is to prove sound and our future protected. I trust, therefore, that you will do me the justice of receiving that which I have to say as solely expressing the considered viewpoint of a fellow American."

More applause, louder and longer than before, at this touch of self-deprecation, which by its implausibility reminded the listeners that this was no ordinary American but one of the most distinguished military officers of his generation. Those present and the people watching on television took note of MacArthur's posture: almost as straight and tall as when he had donned the uniform of a cadet at West Point more than half a century earlier. Radio listeners had only his voice to go by. His diction was clear; his phrasing slow and deliberate. Few Americans had ever heard MacArthur's voice, even on radio; those who didn't know his biography might have wondered where he got his accent, in which the Virginia drawl of his mother slightly softened the Wisconsin twang of his father. There was, in addition, a care with enunciation that could sound a little affected, as though the army brat wanted to mingle with Ivy Leaguers and those to the manner born.

His hair was thinner than at the last time he had been in Washington, and slickly combed over to conceal a receding hairline. It was surprisingly dark for a seventy-one-year-old, though no one could tell, and none had the effrontery to ask, if he colored it. His features were sharper as age thinned the face; his aquiline nose looked in profile more hawk-like than ever.

"I address you with neither rancor nor bitterness in the fading twilight of life," he said in his closest approach to the cause of his appearing there that day. He professed but one purpose: "to serve my country."

He turned to strategy and to the dangers that confronted America. "The issues are global, and so interlocked that to consider the problems of one sector oblivious to those of another is to court disaster for the whole. While Asia is commonly referred to as the gateway to Europe, it is no less true that Europe is the gateway to Asia, and the broad influence of the one cannot fail to have its impact upon the other. There are those who claim our strength is inadequate to protect on both fronts, that we cannot divide our effort." A dramatic pause. "I can think of no greater expression of defeatism."

Louder applause still, but chiefly from the Republican side of the chamber. These remarks were what the Asia advocates had wanted to hear, and they responded enthusiastically.

"The Communist threat is a global one. Its successful advance in one sector threatens the destruction of every other sector. You cannot appease or otherwise surrender to communism in Asia without simultaneously undermining our efforts to halt its advance in Europe."

More applause, with nearly all the Republicans and many conservative Democrats nodding hearty approval.

MacArthur launched into a detailed, nuanced and surprisingly pragmatic interpretation of the last half century of Asian history. Revolutions in Asia had almost nothing to do with the ideologies that had roiled the rest of the globe, he said. "World ideologies play little part in Asian thinking and are little understood. What the people strive for is the opportunity for a little more food in their stomach, a little better clothing on their backs, a little firmer roof over their heads, and the realization of the normal nationalist urge for political freedom." The Chinese in particular were largely immune to the appeals of either communism or democracy. "There is little of the ideological concept either one way or another in the Chinese make-up. The standard of living is so low and the capital accumulation has been so thoroughly dissipated by war that the masses are desperate and eager to follow any leadership which seems to promise the alleviation of woeful stringencies."

This was abstruse stuff for most of the lawmakers; even MacArthur's enthusiasts sat on their hands, wondering where he was headed. Fortunately for them, he turned to the firmer ground of military strategy. He defined America's western military perimeter as Dean Acheson had done fifteen months earlier, with one important difference. MacArthur's perimeter ran along the Pacific island chain from the Aleutians to the Philippines. It did not include Korea, as Acheson's version had not. But it most definitely included Formosa. "Under no circumstances must Formosa fall under Communist control," the general said.

The Republicans and the conservative Democrats erupted in their loudest ovation so far. MacArthur let the applause roll around the chamber.

"Such an eventuality would at once threaten the freedom of the Philippines and the loss of Japan and might well force our western frontier back to the coast of California, Oregon and Washington."

More applause, tempered shortly by the realization that MacArthur had just described what would be a grave reversal for the United States.

MacArthur got to the heart of his argument, and the crux of his difference with Truman. The general asserted that the North Korean invasion of South Korea had been the work of the Chinese rather than the Russians. "I have from the beginning believed that the Chinese Communists' support of the North Koreans was the dominant one." China's interests paralleled those of Russia for the moment, but China had its own agenda and its own expansionist urge, one that owed next to nothing to the teachings of Marx and Lenin. "The aggressiveness recently displayed not only in Korea but also in Indo-China and Tibet and pointing potentially toward the south reflects predominantly the same lust for the expansion of power which has animated every would-be conqueror since the beginning of time."

This was why China had to be confronted and stopped, MacArthur said. He offered a capsule history of the Korean fighting. "While I was not consulted prior to the President's decision to intervene in support of the Republic of Korea, that decision, from a military standpoint, proved a sound one, as we hurled back the invader and decimated his forces. Our victory was complete, and our objectives within reach, when Red China intervened with numerically superior ground forces." MacArthur declined to mention that the action of the Chinese contradicted his prediction that they would not enter the war. "This created a new war and an entirely new situation, a situation not contemplated when our forces were committed against the North Korean invaders; a situation which called for new decisions in the diplomatic sphere to permit the realistic adjustment of military strategy." MacArthur paused, before adding ominously, "Such decisions have not been forthcoming."

Loud agreement from the lawmakers with MacArthur's criticism.

"While no man in his right mind would advocate sending our ground forces into continental China, and such was never given a thought, the new situation did urgently demand a drastic revision of strategic planning if our political aim was to defeat this new enemy as we had defeated the old."

MacArthur's admirers knew where he was going; even as they applauded, many edged forward in their seats.

"Apart from the military need, as I saw it, to neutralize the sanctuary protection given the enemy north of the Yalu, I felt that military necessity in the conduct of the war made necessary, first, the intensification of our economic blockade of China; two, the imposition of a naval blockade against the China coast; three, removal of restrictions on air reconnaissance of China's coastal area and of Manchuria; four, removal of restrictions on the forces of the Republic of China on Formosa, with logistical support to contribute to their effective operations against the common enemy."

The cheering began after item three and rose through item four. If the volume was an indicator of how a voice vote taken at that moment would have gone, Congress was eager to unleash both MacArthur against the Chinese across the Yalu and Chiang Kai-shek against the Chinese across the Formosa Strait.

MacArthur interrupted the clamor. His voice darkened further. "For entertaining these views, all professionally designed to support our forces committed to Korea and to bring hostilities to an end with the least possible delay and at a saving of countless American and Allied lives, I have been severely criticized in lay circles, principally abroad, despite my understanding that from a military standpoint the above views have been fully shared in the past by practically every military concerned with the Korean campaign, including our own Joint Chiefs of Staff."

The applause and cheering this time went on and on, surging around the chamber and seeming to make MacArthur into a modern Cato, standing resolutely against the weakness and corruption of those who ignored his stern counsel. The cheerers might have missed the artfulness of his phrasing. He attributed to foreigners the criticism he had suffered, while everyone knew that his most important critic was the president of the United States. He thereby dodged any additional charge of insubordination while allowing sympathetic listeners to conclude that Truman had more in common with those appeasing foreigners than with a true patriot like MacArthur. He meanwhile summoned the joint chiefs to his side on the military aspects of his advice while ignoring the central criticism of his behavior: that he had crossed the boundary that was supposed to separate military advice from politics.

His lament grew sharper. "I called for reinforcements but was informed that reinforcements were not available. I made clear that if not permitted to destroy the enemy built-up bases north of the Yalu, if not permitted to utilize the friendly Chinese force of some 600,000 on Formosa, if not permitted to blockade the China coast to prevent the Chinese Reds from getting succor from without, and if there were to be no hope of major reinforcements, the position of the command from the military standpoint forbade victory." There would be only endless bloodletting. He had urged a change in policy. But the response had been attacks on him personally. "Efforts have been made to distort my position. It has been said in effect that I was a war monger. Nothing could be further from the truth."

Loud applause.

"I know war as few other men now living know it, and nothing to me is more revolting." He quoted himself, speaking on the day of the Japanese surrender in 1945, from the deck of the battleship *Missouri*, declaring that war must be abolished as an instrument of international affairs. "We have had our last chance," he had said, and now said again. "If we will not devise some greater and more equitable system, then our Armageddon will be at our door." But war's replacement had not yet emerged, as the conflict in Korea demonstrated. And that conflict revealed a stubborn truth of armed conflict. "Once war is forced upon us, there is no other alternative than to apply every available means to bring it to a swift end. War's very object is victory, not prolonged indecision."

More applause.

"In war there is no substitute for victory."

Still more applause.

"There are some who for varying reasons would appease Red China. They are blind to history's clear lesson, for history teaches with unmistakable emphasis that appeasement but begets new and bloodier war." Appeasement was akin to blackmail. "Like blackmail it lays the basis for new and successively greater demands until, as in blackmail, violence becomes the only other alternative."

The general assumed the role of father to his troops. "Why, my soldiers asked of me, surrender military advantages to an enemy in the field?" He lowered his voice in sorrow. "I could not answer."

The room erupted once more.

"I have just left your fighting sons in Korea," MacArthur continued. "They have met all tests there, and I can report to you without reservation that they are splendid in every way."

Enthusiastic applause.

"It was my constant effort to preserve them and end this savage conflict honorably and with the least loss of time and a minimum sacrifice of life. Its growing bloodshed has caused me the deepest anguish and anxiety." He paused, his voice breaking. He proceeded slowly: "Those gallant men will remain often in my thoughts and in my prayers always."

Loud applause for such men and such a leader.

"I am closing my fifty-two years of military service. When I joined the Army, even before the turn of the century, it was the fulfillment of all my boyish hopes and dreams. The world has turned over many times since I took the oath on the plain at West Point, and the hopes and dreams have long since vanished. But I still remember the refrain of one of the most popular barrack ballads of that day, which proclaimed most proudly that old soldiers never die; they just fade away. And like the old soldier of that ballad, I now close my military career and just fade away, an old soldier who tried to do his duty as God gave him the light to see that duty. Good bye."

Huge, prolonged applause, with the entire body of senators and representatives, Republicans and Democrats, rising to their feet.

56

FROM THE 1600 block of Pennsylvania Avenue, Truman could almost hear the roars at the Capitol, and he wondered if MacArthur's farewell would be his own political requiem. The president's staff let the media know he hadn't watched or listened to the general's speech on television or radio. The business of the country required his full attention. But Truman realized that his hold on the presidency and, what he deemed more important, the policies he had labored to put in place since the start of his presidency were in serious trouble. Whether or not MacArthur ran for president himself—and Truman deeply doubted that MacArthur's grandiloquent good-bye foreclosed a political career—the outpouring of support for the general signaled broad unhappiness with the actions of his commander-in-chief.

The outpouring continued. From Washington, MacArthur went to New York. Since Thomas Edison had popularized stock tickers in the nineteenth century, no triumph in America had been complete without a ticker-tape parade up the canyons of Manhattan. But New York had never produced an extravaganza like the one given MacArthur. Seven and a half million people shouted themselves hoarse for the general; from the buildings that lined the parade route nearly three thousand *tons* of torn paper rained down upon the hero. The route had to be lengthened to nineteen miles to accommodate everyone who wanted to catch a view. "Welcome home, Mac!" they cried. The local worthies elbowed to be photographed with MacArthur: the mayor, the aldermen, Cardinal Spellman. A blimp took pictures from overhead; ship whistles and tugboat blasts rose in rude chorus from the East River; fireboats shot celebratory fountains hundreds of feet into the air. High school students held up a banner with a rhyming benediction: "Welcome back—God bless you, Mac." Demands for photos, waves and salutes set the parade back an hour; not until after three did the general's car arrive for the luncheon in his honor at the Waldorf Astoria. Speaker after speaker lavished praise on the city's esteemed guest, who appeared exhausted by the time the midday meal ended at five thirty. Only then did the grip of adulation ease long enough for MacArthur to escape to his suite in the hotel.

Truman watched, without appearing to. And the more he saw, the more determined he became to counter the pro-MacArthur tide. He revealed to the world, through a carefully orchestrated leak to *New York Times* reporter Anthony Leviero, that the crucial meeting at Wake Island, in which MacArthur had dismissed the prospect that the Chinese would enter the war and had proclaimed they would be annihilated if they did, had been transcribed. The *Times* thereupon interrupted its coverage of MacArthur's New York triumph to relate how the general's forecast of the war's development had been egregiously wrong. "Today The New York Times gained access to documented sources on the meeting of President Truman, the Commander in Chief, and the United Nations Commander on the mid-Pacific atoll," Leviero wrote. The article provided a nine-point summary of the meeting transcript, starting with MacArthur's prediction that by January 1950 the victory would be so complete he would be able to send his best division of troops from Korea to Europe. The ground rules of the leak forbade Leviero to quote from the document, and his paraphrase of MacArthur's estimate of the prospects of a larger war was more than kind to the general. "The possibilities that Red China and Russia would intervene were discussed, and General MacArthur said that he did not believe either country would do so."

The article, as Truman intended, took some of the shine off MacArthur. Reporters inquired about it at Truman's next news conference. "Are you in a position to confirm or deny the report in the *New York Times* of your Wake Island conference with General MacArthur?" one asked.

"I have no comment," Truman said.

Another correspondent complained of Leviero's favored treatment. "A number of reporters have asked for the record on that Wake Island meeting, and had been told that they could not get it as the record was with you and could only be given out with your consent," he said. "And then Mr. Leviero, who is a very fine reporter, asked for it and got it. I was hoping that if in the future there was anything to be given out—scoops like that—we could all have a chance at it."

Truman deflected the question. "I remember a certain turmoil that was created by an interview I had with Arthur Krock," he said. "And some of your people wept and cried, and I finally made a statement that I would talk to anybody I pleased any time I pleased. I didn't talk to Mr. Leviero, however."

A reporter didn't catch Truman's last sentence. "Mr. President, you say you did or did not?"

"Did not!"

Truman was ready to move on, but the reporters wanted to hear more. This was a big story—in fact it would win Leviero a Pulitzer Prize—and they sought the details. "Would you have any objection to the publication of that Wake Island document now?" Merriman Smith of United Press asked.

"I am not in a position to answer that question, Smitty," Truman said.

The reason Truman didn't answer was that he had decided to release the document at a moment better timed to embarrass MacArthur. A week later, just as the general was about to testify before a Senate committee, the administration published the whole Wake Island document and explained its provenance. Thereupon Vernice Anderson, the State Department secretary whose walk on the beach had been foiled by the marine MPs, became famous, and the world read of MacArthur telling Truman that there was "very little" chance of Chinese intervention, and that if the Chinese were so foolish as to enter the war, "there would be the greatest slaughter."

57

THE NEXT DAY MacArthur had a chance to explain himself when he addressed a combined session of the Senate Armed Services and Foreign Relations Committees. The meeting took place in the Caucus Room of the Senate Office Building, which was jammed with committee members, staff, reporters, photographers and others eager to have a seat—or a standing place—where history was about to be made. Or at least revisited: the committees had not publicized what they intended to ask MacArthur, but informed observers expected a searching review of American policy in Korea. The general had been deeply involved in the implementation of that policy, though he was known to disagree with crucial aspects of it. The members of the committee were certain to ask him about those disagreements and how they had shaped the war effort.

Republican critics of Truman's war policy had compelled their Democratic colleagues to consent to the hearings, but the Democrats, being the majority party, would control the proceedings. Richard Russell of Georgia, chairman of the Armed Services Committee and chairman of the hearings, was as conservative as many Republicans, but he was still a Democrat, with a Democratic president to defend. Tom Connally of Texas, chairman of the Foreign Relations Committee and de facto second-in-command of the hearings, had views and objectives similar to Russell's. Neither Russell nor Connally felt a personal bond to Truman; other things being equal, they might have found MacArthur, who had climbed the military ladder through his own efforts and talents, a more appealing figure than Truman, who had been plucked from the Senate by Franklin Roosevelt and become president by the accident of Roosevelt's death. Yet Russell and Connally were not about to let MacArthur stampede the hearings. He would be permitted to air his views but must respond to questions.

Russell brought the session to order at 10:30 a.m. "We are opening hearings on momentous questions," he said. "These questions affect not only the lives of every citizen, but they are vital to the security of our country and the maintenance of our institutions of free government." Russell presented the first witness as one who needed no introduction. "On the permanent pages of our history are inscribed his achievements as one of the great captains of history through three armed conflicts. But he is not only a great military leader. His broad understanding and knowledge of the science of politics has enabled him to restore and stabilize a conquered country and to win for himself and for his country the respect and affection of a people who were once our bitterest enemies."

Russell quoted from MacArthur's speech to Congress the general's assertion that the issues before the country transcended partisanship and must be addressed on the highest plane of national interest. He hoped the hearings would be conducted in just that spirit. He explained that he and the other committee members had weighed whether the hearings should be public or confidential. The sensitivity of certain issues argued for the latter, but the stake of the public in discovering what was being done in its name suggested the former. Russell explained that a compromise had been chosen. The hearings would be closed to reporters and the public, but transcripts would be released daily. If a response risked endangering American troops or the broader national security, that response would be deleted from the transcript before release. Russell asked MacArthur to indicate when he was about to venture into the risky realm, so that the transcribers would know what to keep confidential.

Russell thereupon turned the floor over to MacArthur, only to have Senator Wayne Morse of Oregon interject, "Mr. Chairman, are you going to swear the witness?"

Russell caught himself. "Thank you for reminding me of that," he said. Turning to MacArthur, he explained almost apologetically that the committee had decided to swear the witnesses, of whom there might be many. Russell's words and tone indicated that the other witnesses were the ones the committee thought needed swearing, not the general. MacArthur nodded congenially and took the oath.

Russell asked MacArthur if he wished to make an opening statement. MacArthur surprised the committee by saying he did not. His speech to Congress would suffice.

Russell consulted his question list. He asked MacArthur about the performance of American military. How were the troops doing?

"I would rate it as 100 percent," MacArthur replied. "And the only reason I do not rate it higher is because I believe the mathematicians say 100 percent is all there is."

Russell asked about the South Korean army.

"In courage and in determination, and in resolution, they are very fine troops," MacArthur replied. They had been badly outnumbered at times but had performed admirably.

Broadening the inquiry, Russell asked MacArthur about his assessment of Soviet intentions and capabilities.

MacArthur replied that he could answer only for himself, not for the army or the administration. "Everything I say, Senator, is on my own personal authority, and represents nothing but my own views."

"A great many people are interested in your views," Russell replied.

MacArthur reiterated what he had said on various occasions: that the Kremlin's timetable for world conquest was independent of what happened in Korea. Personifying the Russian enemy, MacArthur said, "I do not believe that anything that happens in Korea, or Asia, for that matter, would affect his basic decision."

Russell inquired into two of the issues that had caused so much controversy between the general and Washington: the restraints on his use of air and naval power against China, and the possible employment of Chinese Nationalist troops. Had the general requested that those restraints be lifted and the Chinese Nationalist troops employed? What form had his requests taken?

"I very definitely recommended that the Chinese Nationalist troops be employed," MacArthur answered. He had done so in writing and in discussions with the army chief of staff. He couldn't remember what form his recommendation to remove the restraints on his use of air and naval power had taken, but he had made the case very forcefully. "In my discussions with General Collins I pointed out how extraordinarily necessary it was to lift those inhibitions."

Russell pushed back for the first time. "But you did not formally request that through channels—that those interdictions be removed?" he asked.

MacArthur offered nothing more specific. The restrictions had been imposed at the beginning and were never lifted, he said. "When General Collins came out there on these various things, I pointed out the grave effects of not lifting them."

"Yes, I understood that," Russell said. But the committee wanted to know what form his objections took. "Every member of the committee wishes to develop just how the controversy arose, whether it was through a formal request or through discussion with General Collins."

MacArthur asserted that his problem was not with the joint chiefs. "The position of the Joint Chiefs of Staff and my own so far as I know were practically identical," MacArthur said. As evidence he cited a study produced by the joint chiefs for the secretary of defense, dated January 12, 1951, which he had brought with him. He read portions of its conclusions, including recommendations to intensify the economic blockade of China, to prepare a naval blockade of China, to remove restrictions on air reconnaissance of Manchuria and the China coast, and to facilitate operations of the Chinese Nationalist army against the Chinese Communists. MacArthur said he had been happy to learn of the joint chiefs' recommendations. "I was in full agreement with them and am now." He added, "As far as I know, the Joint Chiefs of Staff have never changed those recommendations. If they have, I have never been informed of it."

Russell inquired if the study MacArthur cited had been sent to him as commander of American and UN forces.

"I beg your pardon, Senator?"

"Was that message, that document from which you have just read, transmitted to you as part of your instructions?"

"No, sir. This was the recommendation, the study made by the Joint Chiefs of Staff which was submitted to the secretary of defense. A copy of it was furnished to me."

"But it was furnished to you as a recommendation to the secretary of defense and you, of course, awaited a decision from that source before proceeding along—"

"A decision putting this into effect never arrived."

"Did you get any instructions it was not to be put into effect?"

"No, sir."

Russell was puzzled. "So if that was a recommendation of the joint chiefs, it encountered a veto somewhere along the line, either from the secretary of defense or the commander in chief, the president of the United States."

"I would assume so, sir."

"Did the joint chiefs ever advise you formally or informally as to what happened to their recommendations?"

"No, sir."

"You did not discuss it with them on subsequent visits to your command?"

"I discussed, every time any of them ever came out there, I discussed all these subjects."

"And they did not tell you what had happened to their recommendations?"

"Nothing. I have no knowledge of what happened to this study after it reached the secretary of defense."

RUSSELL OFFERED TO relinquish the questioning to Tom Connally, but the Texas senator deferred. MacArthur took the pause that ensued to offer a recommendation to the members of the committee. "If you can get three or four days off, go over to Korea," he said. "You will learn more in forty-eight hours in that atmosphere than you will learn in forty-eight weeks at this distance. They would give you the heartiest of welcome, and you would have an indelible impression."

Russell was not going to be told his business. "I do not want to go to Korea right now, General, because I am trying to be objective in this matter, and I know that any man that gets over there with troops and under fire would immediately go to shouting for airplanes, more troops, blockade the coast, bomb the Chinese. Because when a man is under fire in the Pacific area, that is the most important thing in the world."

Russell turned the discussion in a new direction. "General, did your intelligence have any previous knowledge of the fact that the Chinese were crossing the boundaries in any considerable force, prior to the attack and our reversal in North Korea, last December?"

MacArthur was expecting the question. "We had knowledge that the Chinese Communists had collected large forces along the Yalu River," he said. "My own reconnaissance, you understand, was limited entirely to Korea; but the general information, which was available from China and other places, indicated large accumulations of troops. The Red Chinese, at that time, were putting out, almost daily, statements that they were not intervening, that these were volunteers only. About the middle of September our secretary of state announced that he thought there was little chance, and no logic, in Chinese intervention. In November our Central Intelligence Agency here had said that they felt there was little chance of any major intervention on the part of the Chinese forces. Now, we ourselves on the front realized that the North Korean forces were being stiffened, and our intelligence, made just before General Walker launched his attacks, indicated they thought from 40,000 to 60,000 men might be down there. Now you must understand that the intelligence that a nation is going to launch war is not an intelligence that is available to a commander limited to a small area of combat. That intelligence should have been given to me."

"So," Russell asked, "the disposition of the forces in the field, then, were based upon the assumption that there would be no intervention by a considerable number of Chinese?"

"No, sir. You are not correct in that statement."

"I asked a question. I did not make a statement."

"The disposition of the forces was made upon the basis of the enemy that existed, and the orders that I had to defeat them," MacArthur said. "That enemy was the North Korean group, and our forces had practically destroyed them. We would have completely destroyed them if the Chinese had not intervened." The disposition of his forces was dictated by his mission—to liberate and pacify North Korea—and by the comparatively small size of his force. And yet, that disposition proved optimal for dealing with the Chinese. "The disposition of those troops, in my opinion, could not have been improved upon had I known the Chinese were going to attack."

In response to the questioning looks of the committee members, MacArthur continued, "The difficulty that arose was not the disposition of the troops, but the overwhelming number of the enemy forces and the extraordinary limitations that were placed upon me in the use of my air." The latter restriction was the most harmful. "Had I been permitted to use my air, when those Chinese forces came in there, I haven't the faintest doubt we would have thrown them back." MacArthur said his air officers shared this opinion. His inability to use his airpower against the Chinese was fatal. "Thousands and hundreds of thousands of troops were permitted to concentrate on the Yalu at that time, only two nights' march down to the front lines."

Russell wanted clarification. "Of course, I do not know anything about the military part of it," he said. "But it does not seem to me that we would have bombed them before they came in. That is the thing I did not understand about it."

"What is that, Senator?"

"You said if you had been permitted to bomb them before they crossed the Yalu, but the Chinese army—"

"If I had been permitted to bomb them before they crossed the Yalu, Senator, they never would have crossed."

"I can understand that."

"Correct. If I had been permitted to bomb back of their bases, when they crossed the Yalu they would have been—their logistical supply would have been cut off so rapidly that they would not have been able to advance with any degree of force or strength against the Eighth Army."

"I see. Of course, I can see the handicap you were under in not bombing them before they crossed. But it would have been a rather dangerous thing to have bombed them before they crossed."

"As soon as we realized that the Chinese were moving across the Yalu in force as a national—as national entities—I ordered the bridges across the Yalu bombed from the Korean side, halfway to the stream. That order was countermanded from Washington, and it was only when I protested violently that I was allowed to continue my original directive."

Russell returned to what MacArthur had said a few moments before about troop disposition. "Did I understand you correctly, General, when you said you, had you known the Red Chinese were coming in in great force, that you would have had exactly the same disposition of troops that you did have?"

MacArthur was glad for the chance to elaborate, to rebut the impression that the Chinese had caught him off guard. "I don't see how I could have done anything else, Senator," he said. "You understand, it was a calculated risk from the day we entered in Korea on June 27. The calculated risk was whether China or the Soviet would intervene. In the face of that risk, which I had nothing to do with, you understand, I was ordered with these forces I had to clear North Korea. I understood the dangers every day as nobody else, perhaps, understood them, but I had my directives, and I was implementing, to the best of my ability." He understood the dangers and yet he went ahead. He had no choice. "There was no other way, when we had to clear the Pyongyang-Wonsan line, to clear North Korea, but to go north." He nonetheless was ready for what might happen. "When we moved forward I had already prepared and the troops had in their hands the order for retreat if we found the enemy in force. What we did was really a reconnaissance in force. It was the only way we had to find out what the enemy had and what his intentions were. When we moved forward we struck him in tremendous force—or he struck us—and we withdrew." They withdrew in good fashion. "The concept that our forces withdrew in disorder or were badly defeated is one of the most violent prevarications of truth that ever was made. Those forces withdrew in magnificent order and shape." MacArthur repeated for emphasis: "It was a planned withdrawal from the beginning."

Russell thanked MacArthur for this explanation. He offered the general an opportunity to clarify something else. "Well, now, going back to the concentration on the other side of the Yalu—of course, you would not have advised that they be bombed until they had disclosed their hand, that they were coming into the war and thereby precipitate a contest between Red China and ourselves, would you, General?"

"Senator, you ask me what I would do. I will tell you."

"Yes, sir."

"When that formation of troops, that extraordinary groupment of troops—those are the troops that threatened Formosa. When they were withdrawn up there, I would have warned China that if they intervened, we would have regarded it as war and we would have bombed her and taken every possible step to prevent it. That is what I would have done, and it seems to me that is what common sense would have dictated should have been done."

"Do you know whether or not any such warning was given to the Red Chinese?"

"None that I know of."

Russell wanted to hear more about the Chinese Nationalist troops.

MacArthur went back to the first days of the war. "When I received the orders that I was to prevent, with the Seventh Fleet and my air, any invasion of Formosa, and reciprocally prevent the Nationalist Chinese troops from leaving Formosa to attack the mainland, there was a concentration of Red Chinese troops on the mainland which threatened

Formosa seriously. Those troops were the Fourth and the Third Field Armies which afterward showed up in North Korea."

Russell interrupted. "In other words, you think the inhibition imposed on the Nationalists by the president, of the Seventh Fleet, and the order to prevent any movement either way in between Formosa and China was responsible for unleashing, or at least making available, these Third and Fourth Armies."

"No, Senator, I didn't say any such thing. If you will let me finish—"

"Pardon me, General, I thought you had completed—"

"I said that these troops down there threatened Formosa at that time. At that time, Formosa—it was necessary for the Generalissimo's troops to be held in Formosa for its defense. As these troops were moved north and the threat to Formosa disappeared, it became quite evident there was no necessity to keep the Generalissimo's troops tied up on Formosa. As soon as it became known these troops had been moved up north and were attacking me—the Third and Fourth Field Armies—I recommended to Washington that the wraps be taken off the Generalissimo, that he be furnished such logistical support as would put those troops in fighting trim, and that he be permitted to use his own judgment as to their use. The slightest use that was made of those troops would have taken the pressure off my troops. It would have saved me thousands of lives up there—even a threat of that. We were at that time with the Seventh Fleet supporting my fighting line and doing everything else in Korea that was possible, bombarding and everything else; at the same time with the other hand they were holding back these troops which, if they had been used, or even threatened to be used, would have taken the pressure off my front. It was at that time that I made the recommendation that the Generalissimo's troops be brought into play against the common enemy."

"Did you get any reply to that request, or was it vetoed?"

"I don't think I received any reply, as far as I know."

"There was never any expression of approval or disapproval from the Defense Establishment, even though your forces were under terrific pressure?"

"As far as I recall there was nothing, no reply. I certainly didn't receive any affirmative reply. It was after that, or about the same time, that the Joint Chiefs of Staff made this similar, made exactly the same recommendation, on January 12."

RICHARD RUSSELL HAD been content to ask about military strategy; Styles Bridges wanted to talk about the politics of the general's firing. "General, you questioned the right of the President of the United States to dismiss you?" the New Hampshire Republican asked. "Did you or do you now?"

"You mean, to recall me?"

"Yes."

"Not in the slightest," MacArthur said. "The authority of the president to assign officers or to reassign them is complete and absolute. He does not have to give any reasons therefor or anything else. That is inherent in our system."

"How did you first receive word of your recall?" Bridges queried.

"I received it from my wife. One of my aides had heard the broadcast and instantly told her, and she informed me."

"You received it via the radio before you had any official notice?" Bridges obviously disapproved of such cavalier treatment of a hero.

"Yes, sir," MacArthur said.

When had he received the official notice?

"Oh, I should say within thirty minutes, perhaps, or an hour. I couldn't tell you."

"Were you recalled with the action to take effect summarily, immediately?"

"The order relieved me of the command upon receipt."

"Is that a customary procedure?"

"I have never known it in the American Army, and I know of no precedents in any place," MacArthur said. "Being summarily relieved in that way made it impossible to carry out directives that I was working on at that moment. I had to turn them over to my successor, an admirable officer in every respect, General Ridgway, who was 350 miles away on the Korean front."

"General, when you—"

"I don't think there is any question that the interest of the United States was jeopardized in such a summary mode of turning over great responsibilities which involve the security of the country."

Bridges asked MacArthur about his respect for the chain of command. "Have you ever, to your knowledge, refused to carry out a military order given you?"

"Senator, I have been a soldier fifty-two years," MacArthur replied. "I have in that time, to the best of my ability, carried out every order that was ever given me. No more subordinate soldier has ever worn the American uniform. I would repudiate any concept that I wouldn't carry out any order that was given me. If you mean to say that the orders I have carried out I was in agreement with, that is a different matter. Many of the orders that I have received, I have disagreed with them, both their wisdom and their judgment. But that did not affect in the slightest degree my implementing them to the very best and maximum of my ability. Any insinuation by anyone, however high his office, that I have ever in any way failed, to the level of my ability, to carry out my instructions, is completely unworthy and unwarranted."

Bridges, nodding satisfaction, jumped back in time to the Wake Island conference. He invited MacArthur to impeach the veracity of the conference transcript the administration had just released. "Was there a stenographic report made of that conference?" he asked.

"There was no official stenographic report," MacArthur replied. "I asked Mr. Ross, who was in charge of public relations, whether there should be stenographic notes taken, because I wished to take them myself, but he told me that no notes would be taken, and there was no stenographer present. I have heard within the last forty-eight hours that apparently a stenographer in an adjacent room took down some notes, but I have no knowledge of it."

Bridges suggested a conspiracy, a trap. "And you were not aware that a stenographer was secreted in another room?" he asked.

"No, sir."

"When the conference was held in the room, were the voices normal voices, or were you engaged in discussion that reached a high level, a high pitch at the time?"

"No, sir. I think it was a small table and a dozen men were around it—the ordinary conversational tone of voice. There would have to have been a lot of eavesdropping to get any report by anyone that wasn't in that room."

Richard Russell cut into the questioning. Omar Bradley's office had made public that it had delivered to MacArthur copies—five, to be exact—of the Wake Island transcript. Russell asked MacArthur if he had received them.

MacArthur's tone lost some of its assurance. He acknowledged that he had gotten something from Bradley's office. "I don't know whether there were five copies. . . . If I remember correctly, I filed the copies; I didn't even check them."

"I beg pardon?" Russell asked.

"I said I did not read the copies—the copy that was sent to me. I merely put it in the file. I have no idea whether it was authentic or whether it represented it or not. By that time, Senator, that incident was about as dead as the dodo bird. They had no bearing on what was taking place in Korea then."

Russell was skeptical. "General Bradley's letter, as I recall, stated that it was forwarded to you in October 1950, and was receipted for by some member of your staff a few days later, well within October," he said.

Democrat John Sparkman of Alabama supplied the date: "October 27th."

"October 27th," Russell continued. "Do you remember whether or not those documents that General Bradley forwarded were received?"

"It could have been in October," MacArthur granted. "I have no doubt they are the documents that are referred to."

Russell stated for the record that he himself had recently sent MacArthur a copy of the transcript, as released by the administration. "I hope you received that," he said.

"Thank you very much, Senator. I got the copy just as I was stepping into the plane, so have not had a chance to read it."

So he didn't know whether the transcript was accurate?

"I don't know, sir. I had no stenographic notes myself, and I have explained the circumstances under which they were composed."

"So you are not in position to state whether or not there are inaccuracies in that report or whether it is a reasonably accurate statement of what transpired on Wake Island?"

"No, sir. I have no way of telling you that. I have no doubt that in general they are an accurate report of what took place."

REPUBLICAN ALEXANDER WILEY opened a new front against the administration. "You mentioned in your testimony that the inhibitions that were given you were without precedent. Do you want to amplify that?"

"I think, Senator, they are so well known that unless somebody wishes me to, I have no desire to amplify them."

Wiley pitched MacArthur a softball. "Have you ever advocated the invasion of the Chinese mainland by U.S. ground forces?"

"Senator, you know that is ridiculous. No man in his proper senses would advocate throwing our troops in on the Chinese mainland. I have never heard that advocated by anybody at any time. That is, any military man."

So what *would* the general have done?

"As soon as it became apparent that Red China was throwing the full might of its military force against our troops in Korea, I would have served warning on her that if she did not within a reasonable time discuss a cease-fire order, that the entire force of the United Nations would be utilized to bring to an end the predatory attack of her forces on ours. In other words, I would have supplied her with an ultimatum that she would either come and talk terms of a cease-fire within a reasonable period of time or her actions in Korea would be regarded as a declaration of war against the nations engaged there, and that those nations would take such steps as they felt necessary to bring the thing to a conclusion. That is what I would have done, and I would still do it, Senator."

Wayne Morse of Oregon, who was rethinking his Republicanism en route to converting to Democracy, noted that some in the administration had said that the war in Korea was a holding action: that by fighting in Korea the United States bought time to rearm in preparation for a showdown with the Russians. Morse asked what MacArthur made of this argument.

"The great trouble, Senator, is when you try to buy time in Korea, you are doing it at the tremendous expense of American blood," MacArthur replied. "That does not seem to be buying time. It seems to me to be sacrificing our youth."

But was it not possible, as the administration suggested, that *more* lives would be lost in a premature war against Russia?

"I have never accepted the theory that underlies your question, that the bringing of the Korean problem to a close would necessitate bringing the Soviet into war against us," MacArthur said. "I believe that there is an excellent chance that if you apply the power against the Chinese, that that would not necessarily involve the Soviet into taking action against us."

Morse sought a stronger statement. "I am to understand, from your testimony, that you discount the danger of Russia coming into the war, either with a bombing operation or on a full-scale basis, including manpower, if we should bomb bases in Manchuria?"

MacArthur took a step backward. "That is stating it a little different way than I stated it, Senator. I stated that under the present conditions, the losses we are sustaining, of Americans in Korea, cannot go on indefinitely, without bleeding this country white. I say that if you are trying to buy time, you are doing it the worst way you can. You are buying time at the expense of American blood. I think that is too expensive. There is no certainty that Russia will come in. There is no certainty that she will not come in. There is no certainty that anything that happens in Korea will influence her. That is speculative. You have to take a certain risk on these things, one way or another. All I know is that our men are going by the thousands over there, every month, and if you keep this thing on indefinitely, nothing could happen that would be worse than that. Therefore, I suggest that some plan be carried out that will bring this dreadful slaughter to a definite end."

MacArthur's words became more impassioned. "War, never before in the history of the world, has been applied in a piece-meal way, that you make half-war, and not whole war. Now, that China is using the maximum of her force against us is quite evident. And we are not using the maximum of ours against her, in reply. We do not even use, to the maximum, the forces at our disposal, the scientific methods. And the result is that for every percentage you take away in the use of the Air and the Navy, you add a percentage to the dead American infantrymen. It may seem emotional for me to say that, but I happen to be the man that had to send them into it. The blood, to some extent, would rest on me."

MacArthur grew warmer still. "The inertia that exists! There is no policy—there is nothing, I tell you, no plan or anything." The enemy knew what he was doing, but America did not. "He attacks today. We resist it. We fall back. We form a new line, and we surge back. Then he is right back, within a week maybe, up to the battlefront with his inexhaustible supply of manpower. He brings in another hundred thousand, or another half-million men, and tosses them at these troops constantly." MacArthur shook his head darkly. "That is not war. That is appeasement."

58

I T WAS A good day for MacArthur, and it should have been an exhausting one, for his testimony filled the entire session. But his stamina belied his years, and he bounced out of the room convinced he had done well. He was not used to such questioning; his subordinates were notorious for not questioning him, and he rarely held press conferences. But his natural eloquence and his moral self-confidence carried him over the few rough spots, and his stirring peroration moved even the skeptics on the committee.

Yet he wasn't finished, or, rather, the committee wasn't finished with him. He was invited back for the following day. Overnight the position of the parties firmed. The Republicans grew more determined to make the hearings an indictment of Truman and the administration's policies; the Democrats sought to parry the Republicans' thrust by tangling MacArthur in contradictions.

Brien McMahon, Democrat of Connecticut, asked about MacArthur's characterization the previous day of the November advance as a reconnaissance in force. "As I recollect it, General, last November you issued a communiqué in which you said that this was the end-of-the-war offensive which would bring the boys home by Christmas."

"That was my hope," MacArthur said.

"Did you anticipate that you could get them home by Christmas with a reconnaissance in force?" McMahon asked.

"The reconnaissance would have developed the strength of the enemy. If it was not sufficient to resist us, it would have been an all-out assault and, as I explained in my communiqué, it would have undoubtedly destroyed the last remnants of the North Korean force."

MacArthur considered his response a moment and decided he needed to do better. "Where a reconnaissance in force—the line between a reconnaissance in force and an assault attack is a rather nebulous one and depends upon circumstances. What starts out as a reconnaissance in force might well result in a full-scale assault so far as your forces are concerned."

"Was there any difference in opinion between you and the joint chiefs relative to how far you would go toward the Yalu in that advance?" McMahon asked.

"The Joint Chiefs of Staff believed that it would be probably advisable, based upon the considerations at that time, to occupy the north of Korea with South Korean forces. They were adverse to having other nationals there. But the tactical conditions were such that South Koreans were not able to do so."

McMahon shifted his line of questioning. He quoted from MacArthur's speech to Congress, where the general said of the questions facing American foreign policy planners, "The issues are global and so interlocked that to consider the problems of one sector oblivious to those of another is to court disaster for the whole." McMahon continued, "Now, General, you are aware, I am sure, of the mechanics that this government has set up for carrying out this business of weighing these interlocking factors—in other words, our global defense as a whole." The senator cited the National Security Act of 1947, which established the National Security Council. "That is the body that has been set up by this Congress to coordinate our total global strategy." McMahon noted that the membership included the secretary of defense and the chairman of the Joint Chiefs of Staff. "Now, General, assuming for the sake of discussion that subsequent testimony brings real differences between you and the joint chiefs on how far our Eastern strategy can best promote our global security, and assuming this difference of viewpoint, would you then be prepared to admit that the joint chiefs' judgment is better than yours and that the American people would be well advised to follow the judgment of the joint chiefs?"

MacArthur dodged the question. "The authorities and responsibilities of the joint chiefs are laid down and prescribed by law," he said. "Their position in the niche of American governmental procedure is entirely in accordance with the statutes. Whether I should agree with it or should not agree with it is not pertinent to the actions of the government of the United States." As a theater commander he would not pass judgment on the policies of higher authorities. "That is a matter for public opinion. I therefore would not attempt to answer such a hypothetical question as you put up."

McMahon tried another tack. "General, there are some fundamental basic differences between the government and yourself as to the wisdom of the best course to pursue in the East; that is true?"

"Naturally."

"Do you consider, General, that it comes within the province of a theater commander to register publicly with persons in political life, or out of it, for that matter, his differences of opinion while he is still in active charge of the theater?"

"I believe the theater commander has the responsibility of registering his views as he might see fit, if they are honest views and not in contradiction to any implementing directives that he may have received," MacArthur said. He allowed himself to bristle slightly as he riposted: "I do not believe the implication of your question, that any segment of American society shall be so gagged that the truth and the full truth shall not be brought out. I believe it is in the interest, the public interest, that diverse opinions on any controversial issue shall be fully aired." MacArthur had never joined the chorus that called Truman soft on communism, but now he likened the administration to the Kremlin on one critical matter. "The totalitarian and the Soviet method is entirely in contradiction to that"—the airing of differences of opinion. "They do muzzle certain segments of society." The U.S. government should not. "I do not believe that is the American way. And if your question is intended to mean that I would be subservient to and not register within the proper processes my opinions, I would refute it at once. Otherwise you do not get what is the foundation of the very liberty that we breathe, that the people are entitled to have the facts, that the judgment of the government itself is subject to their opinion and to their control, and in order to exercise that, they are entitled to the truth, the whole truth and nothing but the truth, Senator."

McMahon asked if MacArthur would allow one of his brigadier generals to air opinions that differed from his.

"I wouldn't have a brigadier general or anyone else on my staff that didn't freely and frankly give me his opinion in contradiction to my own," MacArthur said emphatically. "The very value of a subordinate is the freedom with which he expresses his initiative."

"Now, General, we are not talking about the same thing, I don't think," McMahon rejoined. "You see, General, what I was raising was the question of the advisability, if not the propriety, of any subordinate military officer to take his differences of opinion, on a governmental policy, when he is in the military command, and chain of command, to people in political life."

"I do not know what you mean by 'people in political life,' Senator," MacArthur said.

MacArthur should have seen it coming. "We have your answer, General, in the letter to Mr. Martin," McMahon said.

MacArthur threw the challenge back at McMahon. "It seems to me that the American people are entitled to certain basic facts when it involves the lives of their sons and, perhaps, the future of our country."

McMahon again shifted approach. "Who is overwhelmingly the main enemy, in your opinion?" he asked.

"Communism, in my opinion," MacArthur said.

"When you talk about communism, do you mean as evidenced in Red China, or the Kremlin?"

"I mean all over the world, including the interior of many of the fine democratic countries of the world."

"General, where is the source and brains of this conspiracy?"

MacArthur sensed trouble. "How would I know?" he offered.

"Would you think that the Kremlin was the place that might be the loci?"

"I might say that it is one of the loci."

"Would you say it was one of the main loci, the main place?"

"I think the world public opinion would so locate it."

"Pardon me?"

"I say, I should think that the world public opinion would so locate it."

"You would not differ from that opinion, General?" Before MacArthur could answer, McMahon pushed further: "General, if we were to fight a victorious war with China, will you tell this committee how the strength of the Soviet Union, the armed strength of the Soviet Union, would be impaired—that is, assuming she does not come into the war?"

MacArthur declined to venture an opinion. "As I have said so frequently, Senator, our purpose, as I see it, in the Korean war, is to force China to stop her aggression in North Korea. It does not necessarily mean the overwhelming of China. It simply means that sufficient pressure be brought upon her to make her stop killing our boys by the thousands in Korea. Just how that might impinge with reference to the Soviet forces is purely speculative."

HENRY CABOT LODGE offered MacArthur a respite. The Massachusetts Republican praised the clarity of the general's description of recent past policy before inviting him to prescribe policy for the immediate future. "There is only one point that I would like to have elucidated: whether you still advocate bombing or any aerial reconnaissance of the enemy bases on the northern bank of the Yalu."

MacArthur was happy to oblige. "I would advocate that the Chinese, the Red Chinese government, be served notice that if they continued this type of predatory attack in North Korea and refused to consider terms of an armistice and ceasefire, that after a reasonable period of time we should exercise such military sanctions and economic sanctions as would be necessary to force him to stop. That would unquestionably involve bombing of the bases on the other side of the Yalu."

"But that proposition has not been approved or disapproved by the joint chiefs, has it?"

"I have basic directives that we shall not bomb beyond the Yalu."

"Do you think that our Air Force today is big enough to undertake bombing missions in the Far East and at the same time retain enough power to act as a deterrent to the Kremlin?" Lodge asked.

"I think that it is big enough to handle the situation in the Far East without serious detriment to any other program we have."

J. WILLIAM FULBRIGHT resumed the Democratic cross-examination. "You said in answer to a question by the senator from Connecticut"—McMahon—"that the enemy, and it is important, I think, that we try to identify the enemy, is communism," the Arkansas senator said.

"That is correct," MacArthur replied.

"What is your concept of communism? I mean is this the communism of Marx and Engels, or is it the communism as practiced by the Kremlin. Or just what do you mean?"

"Communism has many various factors," MacArthur said. "The great threat in what is called present communism is the imperialistic tendency or the lust of power beyond their own geographical combines. It is their effort to enslave the individual to the concepts of the state. It is the establishment of autocracy that squeezes out every one of the freedoms which we value so greatly."

Fulbright asked whether a country like China, ruled by communists, could ever be dissociated from the control of the Kremlin.

"I have never said the Chinese were under the control of the Kremlin," MacArthur disclaimed.

"You don't believe they are?"

"I believe there is an interlocking of interests between Communist China and the Kremlin. The degree of control and influence that the Kremlin may have is quite problematical."

"Well, do you think—"

"The main issues in Asia are the ones that I put forth in my speech." And the foremost issue was bringing the war in Korea to a successful close. "The great question is how you are going to end it. Are you going to let it go on indefinitely, destroying the fabric of society, or are you going to make an effort to end it? Are you going to let it go on indefinitely, on the plea that a still greater calamity might follow? You certainly have a tremendous calamity on your hands right now. You may avoid a future calamity. It is my belief that if you bring the Korean war to a successful conclusion, you will put off and diminish the possibility of a third world war. It is my own belief, if you continue this thing indefinitely, it will eventually overtake you. It will spread. I believe that the plan and the policy I have offers the greatest hope for not having a third world war."

MacArthur then qualified his statement. "Those are my opinions. I am not trying to force their acceptance." He acknowledged his limitations and evinced some resentment at being questioned on matters beyond his expertise. "I have a vast experience in the Orient. I have been there the last fourteen years, and I am glad indeed to place my views before you. But to attempt to have me pose here as an expert on things that I have had no direct connection with places me in a very false position."

"Well, I do not think you are posing as one," Fulbright responded.

"But most of us regard you as an expert whether you pose as one or not. But you can't help that."

"Well, Senator, if you do, you are wrong."

BY THE AFTERNOON of the second day, MacArthur was repeating himself for the third and fourth times, responding to the questions of senators who chiefly wanted to get themselves on the record as interlocutors of the celebrated soldier. The Associated Press tallied the words MacArthur spoke during his two days with the committees: more than ninety thousand, enough to fill a respectable novel. When MacArthur announced that he was going to fly to New York that evening to rest at his suite in the Waldorf, none of the committee members objected. Some doubtless wished they could do the same.

And yet there was still another day of testimony. MacArthur flew back the next morning and resumed his seat. For several hours more he answered the same questions put by different senators. He added new chapters to the growing tome of verbiage. The senators could come and go, claiming business on the Senate floor; MacArthur recessed only for a brief lunch. His voice occasionally rose to make a point, but his patience never failed.

Finally the end came. Richard Russell conveyed the thanks of the committees. "General MacArthur, I wish to state to you that the three days you have been here with us are without parallel in my legislative experience," the chairman said. "I have never seen a man subjected to such a barrage of questions in so many fields and on so many varied topics. I marvel at your physical endurance. More than that, I have been profoundly impressed by the vastness of your patience and the thoroughness and the frankness with which you have answered all of the questions that have been propounded."

MacArthur accepted the thanks and prepared to leave. As he did, Russell casually reminded the members that the general would not have the final word. "We have only commenced the hearings," Russell said. "We will have next week other great and distinguished military leaders, as well as civilian witnesses."

59

THE HEARINGS RIVETED the attention of America, but in an oddly time-lagged manner. The major papers devoted several entire pages each day to the testimony, and the volume of the testimony challenged even the most assiduous readers to keep up. More significantly, because the committee refused to allow reporters into the room, what pundits and the public learned of the testimony was always a day behind the testimony itself. Opinionators paused, knowing that their commentary might already have been overtaken by subsequent testimony. Perhaps better to hold the strong reactions until all was said.

George Marshall followed MacArthur to the witness chair. He began with a personal comment. "It is a very distressing necessity, a very distressing occasion, that compels me to appear here this morning and in effect in almost direct opposition to a great many of the views and actions of General MacArthur. He is a brother Army officer, a man for whom I have tremendous respect as to his military capabilities and military performances and, from all I can learn, as to his administration of Japan."

Marshall proceeded to the substance of the matter. He corrected an impression given by MacArthur. "From the very beginning of the Korean conflict down to the present moment, there has been no disagreement between the president, the secretary of defense and the Joint Chiefs of Staff that I am aware of," Marshall said. He continued, "There have been, however, and continued to be basic differences of judgment between General MacArthur, on the one hand, and the president, the secretary of defense and the Joint Chiefs of Staff, on the other. In his testimony last week, General MacArthur indicated that, in his understanding, there had been at least two instances in which the Joint Chiefs of Staff had been overruled by the secretary of defense or by higher authority."

One of these instances involved the status of Formosa and of China in the United Nations. "General MacArthur suggested that I, as secretary of defense, had overruled the Joint Chiefs of Staff in their opposition to turning Formosa over to Communist China and to seating Communist China in the United Nations." This was flatly wrong, Marshall said. "At the time I became Secretary of Defense last September, the established policy of the United States was to deny Formosa to Communist China and to oppose the seating of the Communist Chinese in the United Nations. There has been no deviation from that policy whatsoever. At no time have I entertained the opinion that there should be any deviation."

The second instance related to the January 12 memorandum MacArthur had cited as evidence that the joint chiefs agreed with him on the need for stronger measures against China. Marshall read back MacArthur's testimony, which identified four measures in particular. Marshall then said that MacArthur had selectively quoted from the document and omitted crucial context. "At the time this memorandum was prepared, we were faced with the very real possibility of having to evacuate our forces from Korea. The proposals advanced by the Joint Chiefs of Staff, which I have just quoted, were put forward as tentative courses of action to be pursued if and when this possibility came closer to reality." The possibility never got closer to reality; within a very short while the Eighth Army found its footing and turned the tide. The tentative recommendations were rendered moot. Marshall emphasized, "None of these proposed courses of action were vetoed or disapproved by me or by any higher authority. Action with respect to most of them was considered inadvisable in view of the radical change in the situation which originally had given rise to them."

He addressed the broader issue of MacArthur's differences with the joint chiefs, himself and the president. "Our objective in Korea continues to be the defeat of the aggression and the restoration of peace," Marshall said of the joint chiefs and the Truman administration. "We have persistently sought to confine the conflict to Korea and to prevent its spreading into a third world war. In this effort, we stand allied with the great majority of our fellow members of the United Nations. Our efforts have succeeded in thwarting the aggressions in Korea, and in stemming the tide of aggression in Southeast Asia and elsewhere throughout the world. Our efforts in Korea have given us some sorely needed time and impetus to accelerate the building of our defenses and those of our allies against the threatened onslaught of Soviet imperialism."

Marshall paused, then went on. "General MacArthur, on the other hand, would have us, on our own initiative, carry the conflict beyond Korea against the mainland of Communist China, both from the sea and from the air. He would have us accept the risk of involvement not only in an extension of the war with Red China but in an all-out war with the Soviet Union. He would have us do this even at the expense of losing our allies and wrecking the coalition of free peoples throughout the world. He would have us do this even though the effect of such action might expose Western Europe to attack by the millions of Soviet troops poised in Middle and Eastern Europe."

Marshall had encountered comparable differences of opinion—with MacArthur among others—during World War II, and he appreciated their origins. "This divergence arises from the difference between the position of a field commander, whose mission is limited to a particular area and a particular antagonist, and the position of the joint chiefs of staff, the secretary of defense and the president, who are responsible for the total security of the United States, and who, to achieve and maintain this security, must weigh our interests and objectives in one part of the globe with those in other areas of the world so as to obtain the best over-all balance." The difference in perspectives was wholly unsurprising. "There is nothing new about this sort of thing in our military history."

"What *is* new," Marshall continued, "and what has brought about the necessity for General MacArthur's removal, is the wholly unprecedented situation of a local theater commander publicly expressing his displeasure at and his disagreement with the foreign and military policy of the United States. It became apparent that General MacArthur had grown so far out of sympathy with the established policies of the United States that there was grave doubt as to whether he could any longer be permitted to exercise the authority in making decisions that normal command functions would assign to a theater commander. In this situation, there was no other recourse but to relieve him."

THE MEMBERS OF the committee put numerous questions to Marshall. Richard Russell's were friendly, affording Marshall the chance to augment the case against MacArthur. Russell asked about particular instances in which MacArthur's outspokenness had undermined American policy. Marshall cited MacArthur's proclamation of March 24, the one that preempted efforts by the White House and the State Department to arrange peace talks. "At the time the foregoing statement"—MacArthur's of March 24—"was issued, the clearance of the proposed presidential declaration with the thirteen other nations having forces in Korea had very nearly been completed," Marshall said. "In view of the serious impact of General MacArthur's statement on the negotiations with these nations, it became necessary to abandon the effort, thus losing whatever chance there may have been at that time to negotiate a settlement of the Korean conflict."

Russell sought Marshall's judgment on the threat of Russian intervention in a widened war.

"I think it is a very real possibility," Marshall responded. "And like all other matters pertaining to the Soviet government, the decision is that of a few men and can be an instant decision whenever they choose to make it."

What might Soviet intervention entail?

"It would be a very serious matter," Marshall said, "because they have, according to estimates that I have seen, a considerable force—I have forgotten exactly how many thousands—in the vicinity of Vladivostok, Dairen, Port Arthur, Harbin. I don't know whether there are any plane concentrations in relation to Sakhalin, but there have been reports of troop concentrations."

Styles Bridges commenced the cross-examination. The Republican senator chided Marshall for the ungracious manner of MacArthur's relief, then chastised the Truman administration for its overall Far Eastern policy. "Do we have anyone in political life who has a wider knowledge and experience in the Far East than General MacArthur?" he asked.

"In political life?" Marshall rejoined.

"Yes, in public life."

"When you say Far East, you mean the whole Far East?"

"Yes."

"Well, there might be some difference about that. I don't think of them at the moment."

"Do you know of any military man on the side of the Free World that has a greater experience in the Far East than General MacArthur?"

"Any military man?" Marshall countered.

"In the service of the free nations, our allies in other words."

"Offhand, I do not know of any."

Bridges sallied backward into the Chinese civil war, blaming the Truman administration for failing to assist Chiang Kai-shek at the pivotal moment. He returned to the topic at hand—Korea—by suggesting Soviet deviousness in the outbreak of the fighting there. "Do you think, General Marshall, that there was any ulterior motive, or was there any planned procedure by the Soviet in having the Korean attack take place when they were absent from the Security Council?" Did the Soviets sucker the United States into Korea via the UN?

Marshall thought not. "The general reaction at the moment was that it was rather fortunate they were not present on the Security Council at that time," he said. As soon as the Soviets returned, they sabotaged the UN effort in Korea. "They did everything in the world to obstruct what we were doing."

Bridges jumped to MacArthur's letter to Joseph Martin. "Don't you think that if a United States senator or a congressman of the United States writes a letter to a military policy-making man in authority, whether it is here or in some area of the world, that he is entitled to get a frank reply?"

"No, sir, I don't think from the senior commander when he knows he is advocating something to the leader of the opposition party to the administration that he, as the commander, is in total disagreement with his own people."

What was the rule, then, for a military commander answering a letter from a member of Congress?

"He has to exercise considerable discretion," Marshall said. "I have had to write a good many thousand, and it depends on the back and forth, but I don't think I would ever be involved myself in a criticism of the commander in chief to any congressman of either party."

Alexander Wiley grilled Marshall on just where MacArthur had sinned. "I want to know what policies he can't support wholeheartedly and didn't support," the Republican senator demanded.

"The policies involved here related to the conduct of the operations in Korea, our relations with the United Nations in the responsibility of the chief executive of this country as the commander of those units, the resolution of the United Nations in relation to the matters in Korea, over which General MacArthur was the United Nations commander."

Wiley grew snide. "Do you mean to say that a man in General MacArthur's position, who was the chief of staff when you were a colonel, had no right to discuss or advise or recommend to you leaders in Washington? Is that what you mean in violation of policy?"

"There was no limit whatever on his representations of his views to the officials in Washington. There is a great difference between that and public announcements."

Wiley pressed on. "Now, someone said 'no' to his suggestions. How did he violate that 'no'?"

"By his public statements, or statements that were made public in the ordinary press, he set up a very serious reaction among our allies, which threatened our collective action with them, and which threatened our position in the world in relation to this great crisis, and which threatened to leave us in a situation of going it alone."

Wiley didn't like Marshall's answer and supplied his own. "The answer is that MacArthur, on the ground, 10,000 miles away, had a very different idea as to how the battle should be carried on, that when he gave those different ideas to his superiors here in Washington, and they must have given them to the allies, that they disagreed with MacArthur's ideas, and you people came to the conclusion that he was violating a directive of some kind, which justified his removal."

"I'll say this, Senator," Marshall replied. "He was creating a feeling of uncertainty with our allies as to who was directing these affairs— our chief executive, as the executive agent for those allies, or otherwise. When he proposed the utilization of the Chinese Nationalist troops from Formosa he was setting up a very serious consideration."

DEAN ACHESON GOT less respect than Marshall, and infinitely less than MacArthur. Richard Russell inquired, "Do you have a prepared statement, Mr. Secretary?" But before Acheson could answer, the Republicans and the Democrats on the committee got into a four-hour wrangle whether to admit into the record a 1949 State Department policy paper on the future of Formosa.

Civility diminished from there. MacArthur was forgotten in

Republican recriminations at the Truman administration for having lost China to the communists. Acheson's National Press Club speech of January 1950 was thrown back at him for inviting the aggression in Korea. Chairman Russell let the Republicans largely have their say, feeling little affection himself for Acheson and acknowledging the secretary's status as the administration's most polarizing figure. The highlight of the day came after the session ended when Acheson bumped into Joseph McCarthy in the elevator of the Senate Office Building. Evidently the two hadn't actually met before, and they introduced themselves and shook hands. When the elevator door opened, photographers snapped McCarthy looking quite pleased with himself, beside Acheson, who was visibly pained at his proximity to the most Neanderthal of the Republican primitives.

Acheson spent thirty-eight hours with the committee, spread over eight days. The ordeal produced a silver lining for himself and the administration, in that it gave the Republicans ample opportunity to vent their accumulated spleen; afterward the calls for Acheson's impeachment declined substantially.

OMAR BRADLEY PROVED to be the most important witness for the administration. Marshall and Acheson were known quantities, having been in Republican crosshairs for years, while Bradley was comparatively unfamiliar. As chairman of the joint chiefs, he had testified to Congress before, but never in such fraught circumstances. His words carried the weight of a military reputation only slightly inferior to that of MacArthur, for his field command of the American army that invaded Germany in World War II had made him a hero of the first rank, and his fifth star, awarded in 1950, put him in the highest constellation of military luminaries.

Bradley began with a prepared statement. "At the very outset I want to make it clear that I would not say anything to discredit the long and illustrious career of General Douglas MacArthur," he said. "We may have different views on certain aspects of our government's military policy, but that is not unusual. Certainly there have been no personal considerations in our differences of opinion. In matters of such great scope and of such importance many people have different ideas and might consequently recommend different courses of action." Bradley reminded the members of the committee what the Joint Chiefs of Staff did: they advised the president on matters of national security, from a military point of view. They understood that the military view was not the only perspective. Sometimes it was decisive, but at other times it might take second place to political or diplomatic judgments. "When all of these aspects are considered, the government's policy is determined," Bradley said. "As military men we then abide by the decision."

Segueing from procedure to substance, Bradley posed a question to the committee members: "What is the great issue at stake in this hearing?" He supplied his own answer: "Principally I would say that you are trying to determine the course we should follow as the best road to peace." It was crucial to hold this objective in mind, though it wasn't always easy. "At present the issue is obscured by many details which do not relate to the task of keeping the peace and making America secure." Getting down to specifics, Bradley continued, "The fundamental military issue that has arisen is whether to increase the risk of a global war by taking additional measures that are open to the United States and its allies. We now have a localized conflict in Korea. Some of the military measures under discussion might well place the United States in the position of responsibility for broadening the war and at the same time losing most if not all of our allies."

This was the bone of contention. "General MacArthur has stated that there are certain additional measures which can and should be taken, and that by doing so no unacceptable increased risk of global war will result." Moreover, MacArthur had said or strongly implied that the joint chiefs agreed with him. Bradley denied it. "The Joint Chiefs of Staff believe that these same measures *do* increase the risk of global war and that such a risk should not be taken unnecessarily." Bradley didn't dispute that the measures MacArthur recommended would benefit the American position in Korea and perhaps in the Far East generally. Bradley explained that it was appropriate for MacArthur to think in these terms. "A field commander very properly estimates his needs from the viewpoint of operations in his own theater or sphere of action." But the joint chiefs had to look at the larger picture. "Those responsible for higher direction must necessarily base their actions on broader aspects, and on the needs, actual or prospective, of several theaters. The Joint Chiefs of Staff, in view of their global responsibilities and their perspective with respect to the world-wide strategic situation, are in a better position than is any single theater commander to assess the risk of general war."

Bradley judged it absolutely crucial for the committee—and Congress and the American people—to correctly identify the central struggle of the present era. "One of the great power potentials of this world is the United States of America and her allies. The other great power in this world is Soviet Russia and her satellites. As much as we desire peace, we must realize that we have two centers of power supporting opposing ideologies." The bipolar division of world power dictated America's broad strategy. "From a global viewpoint—and with the security of our nation of prime importance—our military mission is to support a policy of preventing communism from gaining the manpower, the resources, the raw material and the industrial capacity essential to world domination. If Soviet Russia ever controls the entire Eurasian land mass, then the Soviet-satellite imperialism may have the broad base upon which to build the military power to rule the world." Bradley reminded the members that three times in the past five years the United States had taken action to thwart Soviet imperialism. In Greece in 1947, in Berlin in 1948 and in Korea since the summer of 1950, America and its allies had responded to communist aggression. "Each incident has cost us money, resources and some lives. But in each instance we have prevented the domination of one more area and the absorption of another source of manpower, raw material and resources." The conflict in Korea must be viewed in the context of this continuing global effort. "It is just one engagement, just one phase of this battle that we are having with the other power center in the world which opposes us and all we stand for." American actions had not been without peril. "In each of the actions in which we have participated to oppose this gangster conduct, we have risked World War III. But each time we have used methods short of total war. As costly as Berlin and Greece and Korea may be, they are less expensive than the vast destruction which would be inflicted upon all sides if a total war were to be precipitated."

MacArthur had said that Russia's timetable of aggression had an internal logic not tied to events in Korea. Bradley didn't disagree. "I am under no illusion that our present strategy of using means short of total war to achieve our ends and oppose communism is a guarantee that a world war will not be thrust upon us. But a policy of patience and determination without provoking world war, while we improve our military power, is one which we believe we must continue to follow. As long as we keep the conflict within its present scope, we are holding to a minimum the forces we must commit and tie down."

Bradley invited his listeners to consider the issue from the Soviet point of view. "The strategic alternative, enlargement of the war in Korea to include Red China, would probably delight the Kremlin more than anything else we could do. It would necessarily tie down additional forces, especially our sea power and our air power, while the Soviet Union would not be obliged to put a single man into the conflict."

Bradley reiterated how this shaped the recommendations the joint chiefs gave the president. "Under present circumstances, we have recommended against enlarging the war. The course of action often described as a 'limited war' with Red China would increase the risk we are taking by engaging too much of our power in an area that is not the strategic prize. Red China is not the powerful nation seeking to dominate the world. Frankly, in the opinion of the Joint Chiefs of Staff, this strategy would involve us in the wrong war, in the wrong place, at the wrong time and with the wrong enemy."

60

BRADLEY'S CATEGORICAL CONCLUSION proved the most compelling public statement by either side at the committee hearings. For a soldier of Bradley's stature, with no history of politics, to contradict MacArthur so completely caused even the most ardent of MacArthur's supporters to pause and reconsider.

Yet it was the statements that were *not* made public that did the real damage to MacArthur. The rule of excision in the hearings was to delete testimony that might compromise American security. Such testimony included remarks related to American knowledge of Chinese and especially Soviet arms and war readiness; revealing *what* the American side knew might tip the communists as to *how* the Americans knew it. Democrat Harry Byrd asked Omar Bradley about Russian strength in the vicinity of Manchuria and North Korea. Bradley responded forthrightly, "There are 35 Russian divisions in the Far East. Nine of them are in the Vladivostok area; four in the Port Arthur-Dairen area; three in Sakhalin; two in the Kurile Islands; one near Kamchatka; and sixteen others scattered along the railway from Lake Baikal on east."

"About 500,000 in all?" asked Byrd.

"Thirty-five divisions, plus supporting troops, run probably something like 500,000 or more," Bradley replied.

Bradley's comments were deleted when the transcript was released.

Another category of excisions revealed American vulnerabilities in a larger war. Harry Byrd's questioning continued: "What would happen to the United Nations forces in Korea should these 500,000 trained troops be thrown into action with enemy submarine attacks to prevent the evacuation of our troops should they be badly outnumbered and have to evacuate?"

Bradley answered: "Should Russia come in with this army strength, her naval strength, which is quite strong in submarines, and her air power, which is quite strong in the Far East—if she should come in with all of those, we might have a hard time supplying our troops in Korea and would even, under certain circumstances, have difficulty evacuating them."

How many submarines did the Russians have in the vicinity of Korea? asked Byrd.

"Approximately 85," Bradley said.

"If they went into action, could we then still evacuate our troops?"

"Yes, to a certain extent because we have considerable naval forces there who could help us."

But it wouldn't be easy, Byrd sensed. "It would be a very serious situation?"

"It would be a very serious situation," Bradley confirmed.

Byrd asked about the broader consequences of Russian intervention. "What other areas in Asia is Russia likely to take over if there is war in Asia?"

"Through the use of the Chinese they have the possibility of and even capability of taking over Indochina, Siam, Burma and maybe eventually India," Bradley said. "In addition to that, they could take over Hong Kong and Malaya."

Bradley knew that this alarming estimate might sound defeatist, but he thought the senators needed to hear it. He insisted on the deletion of the exchange before the hearing transcript was released to the newspapers and published the next day.

OTHER EXCISED TESTIMONY revealed a fundamental reason for the administration's reluctance to escalate in Korea: There was precious little for the United States to escalate *with*. American airpower, in particular, was stretched very thin. Hoyt Vandenberg told the committee that Korea was already claiming a large part of America's available air strength. "The Air Force part that is engaged in Korea is roughly 85 percent—80 to 85 percent—of the tactical capacity of the United States," he said. "The strategic portion, which is used tactically, is roughly between one-fourth and one-fifth. The air defense forces are, I would judge, about 20 percent."

Many Americans, and much of the world, imagined the United States had boundless military capacity. MacArthur had suggested as much, regarding airpower, in answering Henry Cabot Lodge that the U.S. air force could take on China without diminishing America's capacity to check the Soviets. Vandenberg wasn't going to disabuse America's enemies of such notions, but he needed for the senators to hear, behind closed doors, that this was far from the case. "I am sure Admiral Davis will take this off the record," Vandenberg said, referring to the officer overseeing the excisions, who did indeed take his remarks off the record. "The air force of the United States, as I have said, is really a shoestring air force." Vandenberg had used the phrase in open testimony; now he provided the details. One small, intrinsically insignificant country—Korea—was absorbing an alarming portion of America's air resources. "These groups that we have over there now doing this tactical job are really about a fourth of our total effort that we could muster today." To escalate against China, even if only from the air, would be reckless in the extreme. "Four times that amount of groups in that area over that vast expanse of China would be a drop in the bucket."

OTHER REMARKS CONTRADICTED MacArthur's recurrent complaint about the advantage the Chinese derived from the administration's refusal to grant him permission to bomb beyond the Yalu. Democrat Walter George of Georgia, echoing MacArthur's assertion that "China is using the maximum of her force against us," said it was unfair that MacArthur had to fight a limited war while the Chinese fought all out.

Omar Bradley responded that George was quite mistaken—and, by implication, that MacArthur was quite misleading. The Chinese were not fighting all out, not by a great deal. "They have not used air against our front line troops, against our lines of communication in Korea, our ports; they have not used air against our bases in Japan or against our naval air forces." China's restraint in these areas had been crucial to the survival of American and UN forces in Korea. On balance, Bradley said, the limited nature of the war benefited the United States at least as much as it did the Chinese. "We are fighting under rather favorable rules for ourselves."

Hoyt Vandenberg amplified this point. "You made the statement, as I recall it, that we were operating against the Chinese in a limited fashion, and that the Chinese were operating against us in an unlimited fashion," the air chief said to Republican Harry Cain of Washington.

"Yes, sir," Cain replied.

"I would like to point out that that operates just as much a limitation, so far, for the Chinese as it has for the United Nations troops in that our main base of supply is the Japanese islands. The port of Pusan is very important to us."

"It is indeed."

"Our naval forces are operating on the flanks allowing us naval gunfire support, carrier aircraft strikes, and the landing of such formations as the Inchon landing, all without the Chinese air force projecting itself into the area," Vandenberg said. "Therefore, the sanctuary business, as it is called, is operating on both sides, and is not completely a limited war on our part."

George Marshall made the same argument. Marshall proceeded with the greatest concern for confidentiality in addressing the limitations on the war. "The next thing I would like to say, I wish to be certain it will be eliminated from the record," he said. "In your questions yesterday, there was a debate between us as to how much advantage the Chinese Communists were getting out of our not bombing their supply bases in Manchuria, and what the possible result of that was in casualties to our troops." Marshall said he had raised the issue with the joint chiefs just hours before, asking them, "What happens to the Army if we do bomb, and what happens to our Army if we don't bomb in that way." The chiefs had been quite clear. "Their general view was that the loss of advantage with our troops on the ground was actually more than equaled by the advantages which we were deriving from not exposing our vulnerability to air attacks."

In other words—and this was Marshall's crucial point, as it had been Vandenberg's—the limitations on the fighting in Korea, so loudly assailed by MacArthur and his supporters, in fact favored the *American* side.

Marshall elaborated. "I am referring to the air fields, which we have very few of with the length of runway required, and wing-tip to wing-tip of planes, which are very vulnerable. I am referring to the fact that our transportation runs without regard to visibility, whereas theirs"—China's—"has to be handled only at night, and if the weather is fair, that is illuminated and is subject to destruction." China's decision to yield the air was what allowed America to remain in Korea. "We can move reserves with practically no restriction at all, and they have the greatest difficulty in relation to that. If bombing starts, we have a great many conditions that will be far less advantageous to us."

Joe Collins supplied another example of American vulnerability, and he explained how communist restraint had prevented an utter American debacle. Referring to the moment MacArthur had initially sought permission to bomb into China, the army chief said, "When the first recommendations came in to bomb across the frontier, our troops were separated in Korea. The Tenth Corps was operating from the base at Hungnam, and our other forces were operating from bases at Pusan and Inchon. As soon as the Chinese attack began we were very much concerned about the fact that we would have to get that Tenth Corps out; and had we permitted the bombing north of the Yalu, we were dreadfully afraid that that might be the thing that would release the Russian planes, and additionally, have them give additional assistance to the Chinese, and might well have subjected the Tenth Corps to bombardment and possibly submarine attack during the perilous evacuation from Hungnam. Troops evacuating from a port of that character, in commercial ships, are terribly subject to air and underwater attack; and in my judgment, it would be a much too risky procedure." Collins wasn't quite so brutal as to say it, but his message was unequivocal: Far from complaining about the limited nature of the war, MacArthur should have been grateful for it.

THE COMMITTEE MEMBERS were sobered, if not stunned, by the chiefs' and Marshall's descriptions of the actual condition of the American military vis-à-vis America's enemies. Americans tended to believe that having won World War II, the American military could dispatch China with one hand and whack Russia with the other. The secret testimony of Marshall and the chiefs made patent that America's military had its hands full already.

Other testimony deleted from the published transcript severely undercut the idea that Chiang Kai-shek and the Chinese Nationalists would be anything but a burden in a larger war. Chiang's forces had proven inept in their fight against the Chinese Communists, and several of the senators wanted to know if they could be expected to improve. Democrat Russell Long of Louisiana put the question directly to Marshall: "Do you have any indication that the Chinese Nationalist troops on Formosa could be depended upon to fight more fiercely than they did when they were fighting on the Chinese mainland?"

"Well, whatever reply I would make to that I would want off the record," Marshall answered.

"I would like my question also to be off the record," Long added.

Marshall explained that the Pentagon had sent a reconnaissance team to Formosa to determine the readiness and improvability of the Chinese Nationalists, and it had yet to report back. But he wasn't at all hopeful. He particularly worried about Chinese infiltration of the Nationalists. "What we have feared all the time was a boring from within," he said. Marshall noted that similar infiltration by German agents and sympathizers had debilitated the French army in 1940; in the present case the possibility of infiltration rendered any reliance on the Nationalists extremely dubious. The Nationalists had abandoned a great deal of American weaponry in losing the mainland to the Communists; Marshall couldn't see risking more.

Joe Collins again spoke more pungently. "We were highly skeptical that we would get anything more out of these Chinese"—the Nationalists—"than we were getting out of the South Koreans, because these were the same people that were run off China in the first place," the army chief said.

The problem with the Nationalists started at the top, Marshall and the chiefs declared confidentially. "The trouble of it is Chiang is not accepted by a large part of the Chinese," Omar Bradley declared. "Chiang has had a big chance to win in China and he did not do it." There was little reason to think he would do better if given a second chance. "From a military point of view, in my own opinion I don't think he would have too much success in leading the Chinese now. It is true some of them are getting tired of the Communists and might be more loyal to him now than they were before, but in my opinion he is not in position to rally the Chinese against the Communists even if we could get him ashore." Talk of restoring Chiang and the Nationalists to power in China was idle or dangerous. "We do not feel they have the capability," Bradley said. A turn to Chiang's army, as MacArthur and others recommended, would not bolster American security but weaken it. "Their leadership is poor, their equipment is poor, and their training is poor."

61

THE SECRET TESTIMONY damaged MacArthur in ways he never understood. Veteran observers of Washington expected the Senate committee to draw formal conclusions; the tenor of the hearings, the predilections of the questioners and the partisanship of the moment suggested that there would be a majority report, a minority report and possibly separate statements by individual members.

But the co-chairmen of the committee, Russell of Georgia and Connally of Texas, guided the process in a different direction. Though Democrats, they felt no obligation to make a hero of Truman, and so they reckoned that a report by the majority Democrats was unnecessary. This calculation simultaneously spiked the efforts of the minority Republicans to issue a formal condemnation of Truman. Meanwhile in Korea, the Eighth Army, which had retaken Seoul and established a defensible line that crisscrossed the 38th parallel, turned back a new communist offensive, with heavy losses to the Chinese. The Chinese failure prompted a suggestion from Moscow, during the last days of the hearings, that an armistice in Korea would contribute to world peace. This raised hopes of an end to the fighting and complemented the chairmen's desire to put the controversy over the war's conduct behind them.

The result was an anodyne assertion of national unity. "For the past seven weeks the Senate Committees on Armed Services and Foreign Relations have assiduously examined into the facts and circumstances bearing on the relief of Gen. Douglas MacArthur and on American policy in the Far East," the committee statement declared. Significantly, this was the sole mention of MacArthur's name, and the statement said nothing more about his firing. It acknowledged differences of opinion among the witnesses and among the examiners, yet it hailed these differences as a sign of strength rather than weakness. It assured America's allies that the country's commitment to freedom hadn't wavered. And it warned enemies not to misunderstand the workings of democracy. "The issues which might divide our people are far transcended by the things which unite them. If threatened danger becomes war, the aggressor would find at one stroke arrayed against him the united energies, the united resources, and the united devotion of all the American people."

The statement was silent, of course, on the secret testimony of Marshall, Bradley, Vandenberg and Collins. MacArthur thereby escaped the public injury the testimony would have done his reputation, but he nonetheless suffered grievous harm, for the secrets badly eroded his support among those who should have been loudest on his behalf. Alexander Wiley, Styles Bridges and the other Republicans were compelled by the revelations about America's vulnerability to rethink their endorsement of MacArthur and the belligerent course he favored. They didn't recant in public; they wouldn't give Truman that satisfaction. But they no longer looked to MacArthur as a credible alternative to Truman on military strategy or in politics. They eased away from the general, and because the testimony was sealed, they never said why.

And MacArthur never found out.

62

F RANK PACE HAD a theory about the MacArthur firing. The by-
then-former army secretary admitted it was only conjecture—
"purely a Pace thought," he called it. But he advanced it anyway,
in an interview some years after the fact. "I believe that General MacArthur really created the basis for his firing. I felt that the crowds around
the Dai Ichi Building were getting to be very small; I felt that his period
of glory there had passed; he was a great student of history; I felt he
felt Mr. Truman would be easily defeated and that if he could be fired
under dramatic circumstances he could return and get the Republican
nomination for president and run for president against Mr. Truman. I
felt he engineered his own dismissal. The kind of letters that he wrote, a
man steeped in military and national tradition knew very well was out
of order. I can't believe that he would undertake such an action without
realizing what the consequences would have to be."

"Conscious acts on his part?" the interviewer paraphrased.

"That was my feeling," Pace answered. "I never heard anyone else
advance that theory, but I always felt that way."

In fact Harry Truman advanced the same argument, according to his
press aide Roger Tubby. Tubby remembered Truman saying MacArthur
had "double-crossed" him by going behind his back to Joseph Martin.
MacArthur was being deliberately provocative, Truman judged. "I'm
sure MacArthur wanted to be fired," he said.

If these were really Truman's words, they at least partly contradicted
an earlier remark Tubby attributed to the president. "Everybody seems
to think I don't have courage enough to do it," Truman said of firing the

general. Presumably Truman included MacArthur among those who doubted his courage. "Well, let 'em think so," Truman continued. "Then we'll announce it."

WHETHER OR NOT MacArthur intended his own dismissal, he certainly seemed to have his eye on the presidency. The Senate committee was still hearing testimony when MacArthur embarked on a campaign of appearances and speeches that closely resembled what could be expected of a Republican presidential candidate looking toward 1952. He attended a New York Giants baseball game at the Polo Grounds, where he threw the ceremonial opening pitch and pronounced himself "happy to witness the great American game of baseball that has done so much to build the American character." He was guest of honor at a celebration of the 122nd anniversary of the founding of the Brooklyn Sunday School Union. He reviewed the event's parade and heard the New York Police Department Band play "Old Soldiers Never Die." He hailed America's Sunday schools for their contribution to American foreign policy, asserting, "One of the greatest influences in the Far East is the Christian religion."

He journeyed with Jean and Arthur to her hometown of Murfreesboro, Tennessee. He laid a wreath at a monument to the dead of World War II and reaffirmed his own Southern roots. "I am no stranger to the South," he said. "Indeed, I may be called part of it. I was born in Arkansas of a Virginia mother. I grew up with the sound of 'Dixie' and the Rebel yell ringing in my ears. Dad was on the other side, but he had the good sense to surrender to my mother." The crowd laughed and applauded. "Therefore it brings a warm feeling to my heart to be once again in this atmosphere of friendliness in this land I have known so long and these people I have loved so well. And I shall return!" More laughs, applause and admiration for the hero.

He traveled to Texas to revisit scenes of his own youth. His speeches grew more overtly political. A parade in Dallas drew hundreds of thousands of supporters, showers of confetti and even whole telephone books tossed out of office windows. At the Cotton Bowl he pronounced a parting of the ways: "Some, with me, would achieve peace through a prompt and decisive victory at a saving of human life, others through appeasement and compromise of moral principle, with less regard for human life." He didn't have to mention Truman and the administration by name for his audience to know his referent when he said, "How fantastically unrealistic it is for them to refuse to accept the factuality that we are already at war—a bitter, savage and costly war. If all other evidence were ignored, our mounting dead would alone stand as mute evidence that it is war in which we are now actually engaged. Yet, despite this, they seek to avoid the grave responsibility inherent in the fact of war—seek to divert public thought from the basic issue which war creates: how may victory be achieved with a minimum of human sacrifice."

In San Antonio he stood in front of the Alamo and blasted the State Department for a 1949 policy paper declaring Formosa to be of little military significance. "Propaganda of this type closely parallels the Soviet system which we so bitterly condemn," he said. Summoning the "spirit of the Alamo," he decried the "counsels of timidity and fear" that currently guided American policy.

In Houston he proclaimed that America was strong but its leaders were weak. "It is not from threat of external attack that we have reason for fear. It is from those insidious forces working from within. It is they that create the basis for fear by spreading false propaganda designed to destroy those moral precepts to which we have clung for direction since the immutable Declaration of Independence became the great charter of our liberty."

In Austin he stood on the steps of the Texas state capitol and compared communism to a cancer. "Like a cancer, the only cure is by major operation," he said. "Failure to take such decisive action, as in cancer, is but to invite infection of the entire blood stream." Yet the president entirely failed to see this, as his policy in Korea—"the existing policy of appeasement"—revealed. "The present plan of passive defense envisages the indefinite continuance of the indecisive stalemate with its compounding losses, in the vain hope that the enemy will ultimately tire and end his aggression." Such thinking was the epitome of dangerous folly. "Could anything be more naïve, more unrealistic, more callous of our mounting dead?"

MacArthur's Texas tour was funded by a small group of conservatives from the Lone Star State who dreamed that he might become president one day soon. Their Democratic heritage didn't prevent them from despising Truman, who was far too liberal for their taste, and from working for his ouster. MacArthur appeared a promising vehicle.

MacArthur obliged them and other followers by becoming shriller each time he spoke. From Texas he ventured to the Northeast, arriving in Boston in late July. He cast himself as tribune of received American values. "I shall raise my voice as loud and as often as I believe it to be in the interest of the American people," he said. "I shall dedicate all of my energies to restoring to American life those immutable principles and ideals which your forebears and mine handed down to us in sacred trust." Sounding more than ever like a Republican candidate, he condemned the New Deal and the high taxes he charged to its account. "More and more we work not for ourselves but for the state," he said. "In time, if permitted to continue, this trend cannot fail to be destructive. For no nation may survive in freedom once its people become the servants of the state, a condition to which we are now pointed with dreadful certainty."

Then, in obvious reference to his own case, he uttered a statement that flummoxed even his strongest supporters. Portraying himself once more as the courageous speaker of hard but necessary truths, he declared, "Men of significant stature in national affairs appear to cower before the threat of reprisal if the truth be expressed in criticism of those in higher public authority. For example, I find in existence a new and heretofore unknown and dangerous concept that the members of our armed forces owe primary allegiance and loyalty to those who temporarily exercise the authority of the executive branch of government, rather than to the country and its Constitution which they are sworn to defend. No proposition could be more dangerous. None could cast greater doubt upon the integrity of the armed services. For its application would at once convert them from their traditional and constitutional role as the instrument for the defense of the republic into something partaking of the nature of a praetorian guard, owing sole allegiance to the political master of the hour."

Sympathetic listeners understood MacArthur's point: that the armed forces defended the country rather than an administration. But his ill-concealed condescension toward those who "temporarily" exercised the authority of the executive made him sound dismissive of democracy. He appeared to be saying that generals were more legitimate judges of the national interest than presidents. Not many Americans knew that Franklin Roosevelt had once called MacArthur the most dangerous man in America. But more than a few began wondering if there wasn't some Caesarism lurking behind those five stars.

63

HARRY TRUMAN KNEW what Marshall and the chiefs had told the Senate committee, for he had heard it from them—and from the intelligence briefers on whom they relied—during the previous several months. He wasn't surprised that MacArthur's campaign gained little traction, though he couldn't tell how much the slippage owed to the distancing of the Republican stalwarts and how much to MacArthur's lack of anything like a common touch. The shriller the general's message grew, the less attractive he seemed, and the more pleasure the president took.

Truman held a press conference in the wake of the committee statement and the Russian peace feelers. "Mr. President," he was asked, "do you think that the Russian overtures are a sign that the stand taken by your administration in the MacArthur controversy was justified?"

"Yes," Truman replied.

"Didn't hear that," a reporter shouted.

"Yes."

"Didn't hear the question," the reporter clarified.

"He wanted to know if I thought that the stand taken in the MacArthur controversy by the administration was the right one," Truman said. "I said yes. I thought so when I took it, and I think so now."

"Mr. President," another reporter volunteered, "if I may raise this question, I didn't understand it that way. I thought the question was: Do you think the Russian overtures are a sign that the stand taken by the administration is the right one?"

"Yes to that too," Truman said.

During the ensuing months the president said very little about MacArthur. A reporter at a news conference in July mentioned the general's vitriolic Boston speech against the president. Before the reporter could ask his question, Truman declared, "No comment." A short while later the same reporter observed that MacArthur, in the Boston speech, had hinted that the administration was preparing a reprisal against him. "Still no comment," Truman interrupted, again ahead of the question.

"May I finish the question, sir?" the reporter pleaded.

"I know what you are going to say," Truman said, before adding, "Go ahead and finish it so it will be for the record."

"Has any additional disciplinary action against General MacArthur been considered?"

"No. No. I will say no to that."

Truman named MacArthur in a speech in San Francisco opening a conference called to draft the final Japanese peace treaty; the president paired MacArthur and Matthew Ridgway as the occupation leaders who had brought Japan to the point where a treaty was possible and desirable. And he responded, in the autumn of 1951, to an assertion by MacArthur that the general had foiled an administration plot to turn Formosa over to the Red Chinese. "Not based on fact," Truman said tersely. "The general knew it."

THAT WAS HIS last public word on MacArthur for a long time. He didn't ignore the general; members of his administration closely monitored the response to MacArthur's continued campaigning. The State Department surveyed the published opinions of influential newspapers and columnists. The *Chicago Tribune* and the Scripps-Howard chain of papers were strongly pro-MacArthur, expressing a willingness to widen the Korean war in the interests of defeating communism definitively, but the *New York Times* and the *Washington Post* favored the more cautious policy of the president. On balance the president appeared to be winning the battle for the nation's editorial pages. The White House staff tallied incoming correspondence—letters, cards, telegrams—and reported a substantial shift in the balance of criticism and commendation. In the week following MacArthur's firing, the messages had run two to one against the president. Since then support for the general had weakened and that for the president grown stronger. Of late the president ran ahead of MacArthur by a margin of three to one, albeit on much smaller volume.

Yet the White House refused to grow complacent. "I don't like to be a kill-joy, but I wonder if we aren't a little too optimistic about the way things are going on the MacArthur row," George Elsey wrote to Averell Harriman and Charles Murphy. "I think we may be over-optimistic about the extent to which the public understands the President's position and sympathizes with the Administration in the firing of MacArthur." Elsey cited a recent survey showing that approval of the president's action was directly correlated with formal education. Put otherwise, the educated elite agreed with the president, but the masses did not. In this poll two-thirds of the general public thought the president was wrong. The administration needed to keep making its case, Elsey said. "We cannot afford to slack off in our constant emphasis and reiteration that MacArthur stood for war and the President stands for peace. This and this alone will sink in with the general public, while technical arguments about 'civilian control' won't mean a thing to the people at large."

All the same, Elsey and the others in the White House took comfort from anecdotal evidence that the president was gaining ground. A Texas attorney wrote to Truman from Fort Worth describing sentiment among his associates. "Thirteen men gather bi-weekly for luncheon and discussion," he said. "None of these men are in any way connected with politics of any kind. Their meeting is informal and frequently informative." Right after MacArthur's address to Congress, the group had strongly favored MacArthur, with several predicting happily that he would be the next president. But the general's subsequent speeches had raised doubts among the group, as a recent gathering revealed. One declared, "Even if MacArthur is correct in everything he says, he is doing the country a disservice by spreading such seeds of discord." Others were equally critical. "If this change is any index," Truman's correspondent concluded, "it would appear that the General will talk himself into disrepute."

Letters like this might be straws in the wind, but Truman judged that time was on his side. For all the homage he paid to straight talk, he understood the value of silence. And he concluded that the less he said about MacArthur, the better.

64

Truman had an additional reason for reticence on MacArthur. He had decided not to seek another term as president. He was old enough and sufficiently historically minded to appreciate the cyclical nature of reform and reaction in American politics. The generation of reform that had started with Theodore Roosevelt and culminated in Woodrow Wilson had been followed by the conservative reaction of the 1920s. The generation of reform that began with Franklin Roosevelt and included himself seemed similarly to have run its course; Americans again appeared poised for a turn to the right.

Further, Truman understood the meaning of the Twenty-Second Amendment, ratified just weeks before the MacArthur controversy blew up. The amendment's ban on third terms exempted him, as the current officeholder, but the nation had clearly indicated its belief that eight years in the White House sufficed for anyone. Truman didn't lack self-confidence—his handling of the MacArthur affair being the most recent illustration—but he wasn't so egotistical as to think himself above the spirit of the new ban.

Eighteen months earlier, weeks before the Korean War commenced, Truman had confided to his diary words he intended to publish in the spring of 1952. "I am not a candidate for nomination by the Democratic Convention," he wrote. He cited history as his guide. "Washington, Jefferson, Monroe, Madison, Andrew Jackson and Woodrow Wilson as well as Calvin Coolidge stood by the precedent of two terms. Only Grant, Theodore Roosevelt and F.D.R. made the attempt to break that precedent. F.D.R. succeeded. In my opinion eight years as President is enough and sometimes too much for any man to serve in that capacity." By the end of his current term, Truman would have been president just two months shy of eight years. "There is a lure in power. It can get into a man's blood just as gambling and lust for money have been known to do. This is a Republic. The greatest in the history of the world. I want this country to continue as a Republic. Cincinnatus and Washington pointed the way. When Rome forgot Cincinnatus its downfall began. When we forget the examples of such men as Washington, Jefferson and Andrew Jackson, all of whom could have had a continuation in the office, then we will start down the road to dictatorship and ruin. I know I could be elected again and continue to break the old precedent as it was broken by F.D.R. It should not be done. That precedent should continue—not by a Constitutional amendment but by custom based on the honor of the man in the office. Therefore to reestablish that custom, although by a quibble I could say I've only had one term, I am not a candidate and will not accept the nomination for another term."

A year and a half later some things had changed. The Twenty-Second Amendment had been ratified, and its definition of a presidential term as one lasting more than two years precluded Truman's quibble, though the amendment grandfathered him in. More important, the furor around the Korean War and the MacArthur firing had undercut the basis of Truman's confidence that he could be elected again. Truman's job approval rating had been declining since his reinauguration in January 1949. It blipped upward after his decisive response to the outbreak of fighting in Korea, but it had fallen by nearly half since then, heading toward a low of 22 percent. Truman's firing of MacArthur sealed his demise; those roars in the Capitol had indeed been his requiem. He had become a liability for the Democrats, and he wouldn't harm the party by trying for a reelection he could never win.

And so in November 1951, Truman read his declaration of non-candidacy to a small group of his closest advisers. He swore them all to secrecy until the following spring; he wasn't going to make himself a lame duck any sooner than necessary.

PART FIVE

FADE AWAY

65

DWIGHT EISENHOWER HAD a wonderfully expressive face. His grin could light up a room or an arena; his glower sent aides scurrying to remedy whatever had provoked his wrath. But the most wonderful thing about his face was that it was impossible to read the expressions with any specificity. Those who knew him well understood that *he* understood the power of his expressions; he could employ his face at will. His smile might beam brilliantly even as his blue eyes coolly calculated his next step. He didn't lose his temper so much as *use* his temper to get the attention of those who needed to be frightened into better behavior.

Eisenhower's face was never more expressive than when he learned that Douglas MacArthur had been relieved. Eisenhower was stationed in Paris as the newly appointed commander of North Atlantic alliance forces in Europe; his job was to create the integrated military structure that would form the backbone of the North Atlantic Treaty Organization. Eisenhower watched the growing tension between Truman and MacArthur but left the commentary to others. A Midwesterner, Eisenhower knew about the Pendergast political machine, and he shared the view common among Midwesterners that little good came out of Kansas City politics. Truman's actions bolstering Europe pleased Eisenhower without much changing Eisenhower's view of their author. The general had still less respect for MacArthur, whom he considered brilliant but woefully deficient in everyday sense.

Yet when Eisenhower got the news of the firing, his face spoke volumes his words didn't. A journalist caught up with Eisenhower on the banks of the Rhine, where he was observing French troops in field exercises, and relayed the startling report. A photographer snapped a picture a split second later. The photo showed Eisenhower's brows raised in surprise, his lips pursed as if to say he didn't think Truman had the nerve, and his gaze turned aside lest he give away more than he intended.

But he knew he had to say something. After a long moment, he offered, "When you put on a uniform there are certain inhibitions you accept." He added, "I hope there will not be acrimony."

HE HEARD FROM Truman a short while later. "I was sorry to have to reach a parting of the way with the big man in Asia, but he asked for it and I had to give it to him," the president wrote.

Eisenhower realized what he had to do. Or rather he figured it out with the help of others. Eisenhower watched the MacArthur political balloon rise and then sink as many of MacArthur's supporters grew tepid. That left the field for 1952, as far as Eisenhower could tell, to Truman and Robert Taft. Truman wanted bigger government and tolerated deficit spending; Eisenhower distrusted the former and loathed the latter. Taft was sounder domestically but anathema in foreign policy; Eisenhower feared that a Taft presidency would unleash the isolationism that had nearly undone democracy in the 1930s.

All the same, Eisenhower had to be convinced that he was the one to save America. He had consistently eschewed politics as corrosive of the soldier's calling. He took as his negative example none other than Douglas MacArthur, his interwar superior. "Most of the senior officers I had known always drew a clean-cut line between the military and the political," Eisenhower wrote later. "Off duty, among themselves and close civilian friends, they might explosively denounce everything they thought was wrong in Washington and the world, and propose their own cure for its evils. On duty, nothing could induce them to cross the line they, and old Army tradition, had established. But if General MacArthur ever recognized the existence of that line, he usually chose to ignore it."

MacArthur had crossed the line once again, and the transgression strengthened Eisenhower's conviction that soldiers ought to stay out of politics. But he couldn't make the conviction stick, not as it applied to himself. Republican admirers importuned him to consider a run. Truman was hopeless, they said, and unelectable besides, given his abysmal approval ratings. This meant that Eisenhower was the only person who could save America from Taft and from a disastrous retreat from responsibility for world order. Did Eisenhower really want to lose at the polls what had been won at such cost on the battlefields of Europe?

The Ike fans staged a rally at Madison Square Garden in February 1952. Fifteen thousand turned out on a cold night to plead with the general, still in Europe, to come home and run for president. The organizers of the rally rushed a film of the event to Paris, where Eisenhower watched and listened. He was deeply moved. "I've not been so upset in years," he wrote in his diary. "Clearly to be seen is the mass longing of America for some kind of reasonable solution for her nagging, persistent, and almost terrifying problems. It's a real experience to realize that one could become a symbol for many thousands of the hope they have."

He let himself be persuaded. He returned home and tossed his general's cap into the ring for the Republican nomination.

MacArthur had never stopped campaigning, though he declined to say what he was campaigning for. He was patently campaigning *against* Truman and everything Truman represented. Numerous audiences were pleased to hear the message, which grew sharper and more alarmist with each iteration. His autumn of 1951 culminated in an address to the annual convention of the American Legion, meeting in Miami. He again alleged that Truman intended to betray Chiang Kai-shek and turn Formosa over to the Communist Chinese; he claimed that the fell deed would have happened already if not for his own timely protest, which, "with the overwhelming support it received from the American people, unquestionably wrecked the secret plan." He once more lambasted the administration for preventing American soldiers in Korea from defending themselves with the full power of America's arsenal. "We have deprived them of supporting military power already on hand and available which would blunt the enemy's blows against them, save countless American lives, fulfill our commitment to the tragic people of Korea and lead to the victorious end of a war which has already left so many thousands of American soldiers maimed or dead." He didn't quite call Truman a communist, but he declared that the thinking of some of America's leaders was "more in line with Marxian philosophy than animated by a desire to preserve freedom." This philosophy tolerated socialism among America's allies in Europe, and its final result "would be to reduce our own standard of life to a level of universal mediocrity."

The legionnaires loved him, bouncing to their feet several times and interrupting him with applause at dozens of points. But not every audience was so enthusiastic. MacArthur mistook what had been planned as a nonpolitical celebration of Seattle's centennial for an occasion to assail the Truman administration yet again; some in attendance were offended and walked out. The flap emboldened certain of Truman's allies to come to the president's defense, albeit obliquely. John McCormack, the Democratic majority leader in the House of Representatives, declared, "It is about time General MacArthur took off his Army uniform when he is making Republican political speeches."

As the presidential primary season unfolded in the late winter and the spring of 1952, MacArthur kept speaking. He disavowed political ambitions, pleading only the welfare of the country. Yet he didn't contradict a supporter, the head of a group called Fighters for MacArthur, who asserted that only MacArthur could rescue America from "the pro-Soviet forces behind Truman and Eisenhower." Time was of the essence, this supporter declared. "He must become a candidate or he must be drafted. If not, America is lost and Soviet Russia will be dominating the world, including America, within ten years."

MacArthur declined to declare himself a candidate, but he left open the possibility of a draft at the convention. Eisenhower ran ahead of Taft in the primaries, yet the outcome was uncertain as the Republicans gathered in Chicago in July. Though MacArthur kept mum, his supporters hoped for a deadlock between Eisenhower and Taft that would cause the convention to turn to MacArthur. With this in mind, they floated the idea that MacArthur should deliver the convention's keynote. Eisenhower's handlers didn't favor putting another general before the delegates, but they didn't want to give the MacArthur camp a grievance and so acquiesced. The Taftites hoped MacArthur would steal votes from Eisenhower and thereby strengthen their own candidate.

MACARTHUR FLEW FROM New York to Chicago aboard a regular United Airlines flight, accompanied by Courtney Whitney and a New York police detective. The plane landed just past five in the afternoon at Midway Airport, where passengers awaiting other flights gazed out the windows and thought the man in the double-breasted blue suit descending into the crowd of reporters looked familiar. But many couldn't place him, which wasn't surprising, in that almost no one had ever seen

MacArthur out of uniform. The reporters shouted questions. Would he be a compromise candidate? Would he accept the vice presidential nomination? MacArthur smiled but declined to comment.

He was hustled toward his motorcade. Just before he got to his car, a man in shirtsleeves stepped from the curb and reached into a brown cloth bag. None of the police on the ground or on the motorcycles that were to escort MacArthur's car seemed to notice the man; neither did MacArthur. Those who did notice didn't move, from uncertainty or fear; none shouted or said anything audible at all. The man's hand abruptly emerged from the bag—and threw confetti at the general. Most of it missed and fell harmlessly to the ground.

MacArthur was whisked to the Stock Yard Inn, within sight of the convention hall. But he was kept behind closed doors and curtains, surrounded by police detectives in plain clothes who held onlookers and reporters at bay. He entered the arena just in time for his speech.

His appearance stirred the delegates into a frenzy. They leaped to their feet as he took the podium and they stamped, clapped and howled for what seemed an eternity, defying efforts by the convention chairman to gavel them into silence. A "California for MacArthur" sign bobbed frantically up and down; other delegations made similar shows of support. MacArthur let the tumult swell and echo, occasionally waving but otherwise soaking up the adulation.

Finally he was allowed to speak. And when he did, he demonstrated once and for all that he wasn't cut out for elective politics. Unthinking observers had expected a reprise of his speech to Congress the previous year. He gave them much of that. But what neither they nor he appreciated was the difference between a joint session of Congress and a national nominating convention. He had spoken to Congress with the authority of a five-star general fresh from the fighting front, and he had framed his speech as a farewell address. The senators and representatives applauded the uniform and the past accomplishments of the man who wore it. Their applause committed them to nothing in the future. The Republican convention had a very different aim. The delegates cared about the past only for what it promised for the future. And what they saw, once the euphoria of the initial greeting faded, was an old man in mufti who couldn't find the rhythm of his audience. MacArthur was seventy-two at the convention; he would be within a week of his seventy-third birthday on inauguration day. He would be nearly five years older than the oldest inauguree to date, William Henry Harrison, whose death just weeks after the oath-taking didn't speak well for elderly executives. In his fifteen months of speech-giving, MacArthur had never been out of uniform; now, in the dress of every other man in the hall, he seemed diminished. His words, always ponderous, suddenly sounded leaden. The delegates wanted to like him, but they also wanted to be inspired. When they discovered that they weren't inspired, they grew restive. Their response to his applause lines grew fainter; they began speaking among themselves. Amid the uproar that greeted his entrance, a commentator for NBC News had remarked, "It is a trick to stampede a convention like this without having said a word, but that's what the general seems to be doing." By the end of his speech, the only stampede that threatened was of the delegates to get on to the real business of the convention, to nominate a candidate who could lead them to victory.

67

T HAT CANDIDATE WAS Eisenhower, who beat Taft on the first ballot and rolled into the autumn campaign against Illinois governor Adlai Stevenson, the Democratic nominee. Stevenson suffered from the accumulation of two decades' worth of grievances against Democrats, most strikingly manifested in the unpopularity of Truman. Stevenson would likely have lost anyway, but Eisenhower sealed the result by announcing that if elected, he would devote himself to achieving peace in Korea. "That job requires a personal trip to Korea," Eisenhower said. "I shall make that trip. . . . I shall go to Korea."

He was elected and he went to Korea. In the eighteen months since MacArthur's relief, the fighting had continued inconclusively. Truce talks begun in July 1951 got nowhere, leaving the armies in the field to battle forward and back over this hill and that ridge, to little lasting effect. Casualties mounted and with them the frustration of stalemate from which, among Americans, Eisenhower's journey to the front promised relief. The president-elect visited the troops and spoke with them and their officers. He conferred with South Korean president Rhee. His mere presence raised hopes of an end to the conflict, but he boarded his plane for America without giving away any secrets about a new strategy for bringing peace to the suffering and scarred peninsula.

En route home he heard that MacArthur had been in the news again. MacArthur hadn't exactly sulked in his tent after Eisenhower's nomination, but he declined to campaign for his old protégé. He took a job as chairman of the board of Remington Rand, a corporation that made business machines, including new electronic computers, and had manufactured weapons for the U.S. Army during World War II. The company valued MacArthur for the visibility he brought it; he appreciated the pay and perks of the chairmanship, which he collected on top of his lifetime salary as a five-star general. In his debut for Remington Rand, at a meeting at the Waldorf in New York, conveniently downstairs from the suite where he and Jean had taken residence, he announced that he had a plan to end the war in Korea. Perhaps he didn't like Eisenhower getting credit for winning the war that he—MacArthur—still considered his own; perhaps he thought a Republican president, his former adjutant, would be more sympathetic to his opinions than Truman had been. MacArthur said he couldn't make his plan public without spoiling its chance of success, but he would be happy to share it with those in position to put it into effect.

THE APPROACHING END of his presidency liberated Truman from his unspoken pledge not to mention MacArthur's name in public. "Mr. President," a reporter asked, following MacArthur's announcement of his secret plan for Korea, "do you intend to invite General MacArthur to come to Washington?"

"I do not," Truman said. "General MacArthur is in the Army, and on active duty, and if he has anything that is of use to the Defense Department, he ought to tell them so they can make use of it."

"You feel that it is any Army man's duty to come forward if he has—"

"Certainly it is. Certainly it is. He is on active duty and will be the rest of his life. The law provides for that."

"Mr. President, General MacArthur said that nobody has listened to his counsels since he came back. It seems to me the MacArthur investigating committee went over his war plans pretty thoroughly."

"They went over them completely and thoroughly," Truman said. "And I read every word of the testimony up there. And the committee did not come up with any suggestions or any advice to me or to the Defense Department."

"Mr. President, have you talked to General MacArthur since Wake Island?"

"No."

"Have you seen him since then?"

"I made a 14,400-mile trip to get a lot of misinformation. He didn't even do the courtesy, which he should have done, of reporting to the President when he came back here. I have never seen him, and I don't want to see him."

"Mr. President, if it is General MacArthur's duty to report any plan he may have to you, and if he does not fulfill his duty by reporting, what follows then? What steps do you take?"

"I wouldn't take any, now. It's a little late."

EISENHOWER AGREED TO meet MacArthur. John Foster Dulles, who had worked with MacArthur on the Japanese peace treaty and who would become Eisenhower's secretary of state, hosted the generals at his New York apartment. After minimal pleasantries, MacArthur handed Eisenhower a document titled "Memorandum on Ending the Korean War." In it MacArthur briefly recapitulated the history of the Korean fighting, then offered a detailed several-part policy recommendation that went far beyond Korea. Eisenhower should invite Stalin to a parley, at which Eisenhower should insist on the reunification of Korea and Germany under popularly elected governments. Subsequently the United States and the Soviet Union should guarantee the neutrality of Korea and Germany, as well as of Japan and Austria, with the removal of all foreign troops from those countries. Eisenhower should urge Stalin to agree that the United States and the Soviet Union ought to incorporate into their constitutions provisions outlawing war as an instrument of public policy.

Then came MacArthur's concluding recommendations: "That at such conference, the Soviet be informed that should an agreement not be reached, it would be our intention to clear North Korea of enemy forces. (This could be accomplished through the atomic bombing of enemy military concentrations and installations in North Korea and the sowing of fields of suitable radio-active materials, the by-product of atomic manufacture, to close major lines of enemy supply and communication leading south from the Yalu, with simultaneous amphibious landings on both coasts of North Korea.)"

Followed by: "That the Soviet should be further informed that, in such eventuality, it would probably become necessary to neutralize Red China's capability to wage modern war. (This could be accomplished by the destruction of Red China's limited airfields and industrial and supply bases, the cutting of her tenuous supply lines from the Soviet and the landing of China's Nationalist forces in Manchuria near the mouth of the Yalu, with limited continuing logistical support until such time as the communist government of China has fallen.)"

MacArthur had made sure the media knew of the meeting, and reporters were ready when he and Eisenhower emerged from Dulles's apartment. Eisenhower had replied noncommittally to MacArthur indoors; outside he was equally evasive. "We had a very enjoyable lunch and a very fine conversation on the general subject of peace, not only in Korea but throughout the world, with particular reference to the world situation in which, of course, such a Korean peace would have to be determined." Eisenhower turned to MacArthur. "I hope my old commander will have a word to say."

MacArthur understood that he mustn't put Eisenhower on the spot if his grand scheme were to have a chance of adoption. So he reciprocated the banalities. "I had a very pleasant reunion with the president-elect," he said. "It was a resumption of an old friendship and comradeship of thirty-five years' standing. The subject was peace in Korea and the world in general."

The two men posed for photographs; the newsreel and television cameras whirred. Then Eisenhower got in his car and prepared to be driven off. A reporter asked him if he intended to speak with MacArthur again soon. "I certainly hope it isn't another six years before we meet again," Eisenhower said, alluding to a Tokyo meeting in 1946. "Surely we'll see each other."

MACARTHUR WAITED FOR Eisenhower to call. But Eisenhower never did. Neither did Omar Bradley, who knew about the meeting and the memo. "From that day to this," MacArthur wrote in his memoirs more than a decade later, "I have never been further approached on the matter from any source."

He shouldn't have been surprised. Eisenhower understood the implications of MacArthur's plan. At the very least it would shatter the alliance system America had been building since 1945; at worst it would trigger World War III. Eisenhower knew how stubbornly the Soviets insisted on their rights in Germany; Stalin would never abide a popularly elected all-Germany government, which would certainly be anti-Soviet. Nor would the Kremlin stand idle while the United States used nuclear weapons against Chinese forces in Korea and probably against China itself. Like the United States, Russia had a reputation to uphold, and its alliance with China obligated it to defend that country. MacArthur's recommendation for laying radioactive materials in North Korea was lunacy; how would the Koreans live there, even after a victory? In any case, Eisenhower could never allow himself, at the outset of his presidency, at the moment when he was clearly and definitively stepping out of MacArthur's shadow, to be seen as adopting the MacArthur program for dealing with the communists.

Yet if MacArthur shouldn't have been surprised, he nonetheless was galled at being ignored by his former subordinate. "The trouble with Eisenhower," MacArthur muttered to some close supporters after his meeting with the president-elect, "is that he doesn't have the guts to make a policy decision. He never did have the guts and he never will."

The Korean fighting ended without further assistance from MacArthur. The apparently interminable truce talks and the accompanying bloodletting continued into early 1953, when Stalin's death caused a change in leadership in the Kremlin. The new men reconsidered their backing for a conflict that aggravated tension with the West to no observable Russian advantage. Meanwhile Eisenhower, in an effort to balance the federal budget, sought to diminish the drain Korea had become on American resources. Syngman Rhee required persuasion; the South Korean president still dreamed of ruling a unified country. But finally, in the summer of 1953, the two sides consented to an armistice. No peace treaty followed, yet the cessation of shooting allowed all parties to begin to move on.

A decade later Eisenhower asserted in his memoir that he had broken the deadlock in the peace negotiations by quietly threatening to use nuclear weapons against the Chinese. "We dropped the word, discreetly," he wrote. "We felt quite sure it would reach Soviet and Chinese Communist ears." Whether the threat was decisive was impossible to know. No one on the communist side said it was—not that they would. Anyway, the last big obstacle to an armistice was Rhee, not the communists.

Such risk as Eisenhower was taking in threatening to escalate in 1953 was less than that MacArthur had courted in 1951, for the bolstering of NATO begun by Truman had proceeded sufficiently that a Soviet countermove against Western Europe appeared unlikely. All the same, if things did transpire as Eisenhower said in his memoir, MacArthur could have felt a certain vindication at the disclosure. Perhaps his aggressive advice to his erstwhile adjutant hadn't been entirely without effect.

68

Y ET MACARTHUR HAD little time left for vindication, or for anything else. The old soldier had retired to his aerie in the Waldorf; he ventured out occasionally to give speeches and receive the plaudits of those who remembered his role in World War II. The Korean chapter of his career slowly faded into the background of American memory as the Korean War itself receded from view, overshadowed by the great victorious war that preceded it and the vexingly protracted conflict in Vietnam that followed. MacArthur wrote a memoir that was excerpted in *Life* magazine, whose publisher, Henry Luce, wished that the nation had followed MacArthur's counsel regarding Korea and China. MacArthur treated Truman more politely in the memoir than he had on the campaign trail, but the general was as convinced as ever of the wisdom of the course he had recommended. And as the war in Vietnam labored on, he pronounced himself as certain as ever that America should have had things out with the Asian communists more than a decade before.

MacArthur's death in 1964 elicited respect but little warmth. He and Eisenhower were the remaining giants from World War II, George Marshall having died in 1959. Eisenhower was almost as popular as he had been when he vaulted past MacArthur into the White House, and MacArthur still suffered by comparison. Ike had the common touch MacArthur lacked, and postwar America demanded the common touch. At almost the two-thirds mark of the twentieth century, MacArthur seemed a figure from the nineteenth century, ever more the son of the hero of Missionary Ridge.

HARRY TRUMAN LIKEWISE suffered by comparison with Eisenhower. Truman was annoyed that Eisenhower, on the campaign trail in 1952, had lent his prestige and sometimes his voice to the Republican assaults on Truman's foreign policy. Truman responded by lashing back, albeit in private. He told friends Eisenhower would be lost in politics. "He'll sit here, and he'll say, 'Do this! Do that!' *And nothing will happen.* Poor Ike! It won't be a bit like the Army. He'll find it very frustrating." Yet Eisenhower proved adept at politics, navigating between the Democrats on his left and the McCarthyists on his right, ending the war in Korea and avoiding other conflicts. Truman looked small and clumsy by comparison.

But if Truman's presidency seemed nothing to boast about, Truman's personality caught the American imagination. While MacArthur retired to the Waldorf, Truman returned to his roots in Independence. He walked each day to the library that housed his presidential records, and he engaged the neighbors and visitors in conversation. He was as unassuming as always and more plainspoken than the presidency had allowed. His candor appealed to screenwriter and novelist Merle Miller, who in the early 1960s proposed a television series recounting Truman's life and career. Miller conducted numerous interviews with Truman, giving Truman opportunity to display his characteristic pungency of expression. The television series never materialized, as the networks decided Truman wasn't sufficiently popular to draw viewers. But after Truman's 1972 death, Miller published transcripts of the interviews as a book, *Plain Speaking.* The volume delighted readers, who kept it on the best-seller lists for months, and sparked a renewal of interest in Truman. In the wake of the Pentagon Papers and amid the Watergate scandal, as Americans discovered how often they had been lied to by presidents, straight-talking Harry Truman provided a bracing antidote.

The book was not without controversy. Truman scholars alleged that Miller embellished, if not fabricated, some of the stories and phrases he ascribed to Truman. Miller asked Truman why he fired MacArthur, and gave as Truman's response: "I fired him because he wouldn't respect the authority of the President. That's the answer to that. I didn't fire him because he was a dumb son of a bitch, although he was, but that's not against the law for generals. If it was, half to three-quarters of them would be in jail." Perhaps Truman had spoken these words; perhaps not. Yet they sounded like what he would say. And with generals in low repute after a decade in Vietnam, such words were what Americans were ready to hear. Moreover, the stalemate of the Korean War, which had evoked such dissatisfaction in the 1950s, when the American measure of war was the unqualified victory of World War II, began to look good as the American misadventure in Vietnam spiraled to defeat. Truman had held the line against communism in Korea; by the early 1970s most Americans would have been thrilled at a similar outcome in Vietnam.

Yet it was the American victory in the Cold War that made Truman a genuine folk hero. Americans concluded, after all, that the everyman-president, in crafting the policy of containment, had known better than his critics what defeating communism required: firmness and patience, in balanced measure. Truman hadn't yielded to communist aggression in Korea, but neither had he panicked and let himself be stampeded into World War III, by Douglas MacArthur or others. The collapse of the Soviet Union and the Chinese abandonment of communism in all but name confirmed Truman's belief that democracy would endure if Americans kept their faith and their heads. A clutch of respectful academic studies lifted Truman to the rank of presidents just below the triumvirate of Washington, Lincoln and Franklin Roosevelt, while such celebratory popular works as David McCullough's hugely successful biography secured Truman's place in the hearts of ordinary Americans.

Six decades after the general and the president, standing at the brink of nuclear war, wrestled over Korea and China; six decades after their contest brought to a head the issue of whether the president or a general determines American policy; six decades after MacArthur received a hero's reception from Congress and ticker-tape parades from an adoring public while Truman was castigated as an appeaser and howled into retirement, it was hard to find any knowledgeable person who didn't feel relief that the president, and not the general, had been the one with the final say in their fateful struggle. Truman's bold stroke in firing MacArthur ended his own career as surely as it terminated MacArthur's, but it sustained hope that humanity might survive the nuclear age. The courage of Truman's decision had never been in question; six decades later, its wisdom was apparent as well.

ACKNOWLEDGMENTS

The author would like to thank the staffs of the Harry S. Truman Library and the MacArthur Memorial Archives and Library, as well as those of the National Archives, the United States Naval Academy, and the library of the University of Texas at Austin. He additionally thanks Kristine Puopolo, William Thomas and Daniel Meyer at Doubleday, and his students and colleagues at the University of Texas at Austin.

PHOTO CREDITS

Maggie Higgins: Syracuse University Libraries

MacArthur with binoculars: U.S. Army, Robert W. Porter, courtesy of Harry S. Truman Library

MacArthur at a briefing: U.S. Army, Robert W. Porter, courtesy of Harry S. Truman Library

MacArthur with North Korean prisoners: U.S. Army, Robert W. Porter, courtesy of Harry S. Truman Library

Eighth Army forces on village road: Courtesy of Harry S. Truman Library

Crossing the Han River: U.S. Army, courtesy of Harry S. Truman Library

Reinstallation of Syngman Rhee: Courtesy of Harry S. Truman Library

MacArthur and Walton "Johnnie" Walker: Courtesy of Harry S. Truman Library

MacArthur and Omar Bradley: Courtesy of Harry S. Truman Library

Truman and MacArthur in a car: Courtesy of Harry S. Truman Library

Wake Island conference building: Courtesy of Harry S. Truman Library

Vernice Anderson: Courtesy of Harry S. Truman Library

Truman and MacArthur at airport: U.S. Army Signal Corps, courtesy of Harry S. Truman Library

Troops with fallen power lines: Courtesy of Harry S. Truman Library

U.S. troops retreat in snow: Courtesy of Harry S. Truman Library

Tanks: Courtesy of Harry S. Truman Library

Frank Pace with MacArthur in Tokyo: U.S. Army, courtesy of Harry S. Truman Library

Matthew Ridgway and Frank Pace: Courtesy of Harry S. Truman Library

MacArthur and family: U.S. Army Signal Corps, Art Marasco, courtesy of Harry S. Truman Library

MacArthur heading into Senate hearings: AP Photo

Truman holding his hat: Courtesy of Harry S. Truman Library

SOURCES

The events related here took place in the public view, but not entirely in the public view. The actions and words of Harry Truman and Douglas MacArthur were reported in the major newspapers of the day, of which the *New York Times* and the *Washington Post* have been the most useful in preparing the present account. Truman's public statements and news conferences are readily available in the Public Papers of the Presidents, a database compiled and maintained by the American Presidency Project (http://www.presidency.ucsb.edu).

What the public did *not* see and read were the confidential deliberations and communications within the Truman administration, the comparable conversations and correspondence of MacArthur and his aides and interlocutors, and the communications between the two camps. The papers of Truman are at the Harry S. Truman Library in Independence, Missouri. Many were originally classified for reasons of national security; nearly all are now available to researchers. Selections from the papers have been published on the Internet and in various edited collections. The Truman Library also houses papers of Dean Acheson, George Elsey and others close to the president, as well as oral histories of those who worked with him. The papers of MacArthur are at the MacArthur Memorial Archives and Library in Norfolk, Virginia. Many of these papers are available on microfilm.

What was intended, at its origin in the 1860s, to be the definitive account of American foreign relations is *Foreign Relations of the United States*, compiled and edited by the Department of State. By the 1950s, U.S. foreign policy had become too extensive and complicated for the series to be considered definitive, but the volumes of the series that cover the Korean War contain many pertinent memoranda, reports, cables and letters. The Department of Defense produces nothing like the *Foreign Relations* series, but for the present account two works have been very helpful: *The History of the Joint Chiefs of Staff* and *United States Army in the Korean War.*

Transcripts of the Senate hearings on the MacArthur dismissal were published almost in their entirety within hours of the testimony. The crucial portions that were withheld then—the portions that silently torpedoed MacArthur's political ambitions—were released only a quarter century later. They are in the National Archives.

Most of the principal actors in the Truman-MacArthur drama wrote memoirs; these give voice to their authors' strong opinions. Truman's memoir tends to be dry; MacArthur's melodramatic. Dean Acheson is admiring toward Truman and condescending toward many others; Courtney Whitney is fawning toward MacArthur and conspiratorial toward the world at large. Omar Bradley and Matthew Ridgway take pride in their professionalism as soldiers.

Of the biographies of Truman, David McCullough's stands out. Alonzo Hamby's is excellent too. Of the lives of MacArthur, D. Clayton James's is the most thorough and William Manchester's the most entertaining.

Accounts of the Korean War are numerous. Marguerite Higgins was the best of the contemporary correspondents; her reporting won her a Pulitzer Prize. Many other journalists covered aspects of the war; their reporting, like Higgins's, often appeared first in the press and subsequently in book form. Histories of the war range from the popular to the academic. David Rees, *Korea: The Limited War* (1964), is an early retrospective. William Stueck, *The Korean War* (1995), places the conflict in international context. David Halberstam, *The Coldest Winter* (2007), is history as journalism. Bruce Cumings, *The Korean War* (2010), distills a career of close study. Other histories examine the different facets and phases of the war.

NOTES

PROLOGUE
3   "Is it World War III?": *New York Times,* Dec. 3, 1950.
3   "on the basis": *New York Times,* Dec. 1, 1950.
3   "We would veritably be playing": *Los Angeles Times,* Dec. 1, 1950.
5   "We will take whatever steps": Truman news conference, Nov. 30, 1950, Public Papers of the Presidents.

CHAPTER 1
11   "Of all the amazing deeds": D. Clayton James, *The Years of MacArthur* (1970–85), 2:785.
12   "Years of overseas duty": Douglas MacArthur, *Reminiscences* (1964), 270.
12   "We circled the field": Courtney Whitney, *MacArthur* (1956), 270.
12   "Bob, this is the payoff": James, *MacArthur,* 2:785.
12   "The turning away of faces": Ibid., 786.
13   "Our first wave": Ibid., 785.
13   Toonerville Trolley: Whitney, *MacArthur,* 215.
13   "He is a man of light": William Manchester, *American Caesar* (1978), 457.
14   "Look at Mac": Ibid., 450–52.
14   "I was on my own": MacArthur, *Reminiscences,* 272.
14   "We are gathered here": *New York Times,* Sept. 2, 1945.
14   "For me, who expected": Manchester, *American Caesar,* 452.
15   "His white hands": William M. Leary, ed., *MacArthur and the American Century* (2001), 244–46.
16   "I shall wait": MacArthur, *Reminiscences,* 287.
17   "I offered him an American cigarette": Ibid., 288.
18   "Destroy the military power": Ibid., 282–83.
18   "I don't think": Manchester, *American Caesar,* 507.
18   "It is undoubtedly": Ibid., 499.
19   "I regret to say": MacArthur, *Reminiscences,* 305.
20   "I am the humble Japanese carpenter": Manchester, *American Caesar,* 475–76, 518–20.

CHAPTER 2

23   "Dear Margie": Truman to Margaret Truman, March 3, 1948, in *Letters from Father*, ed. Margaret Truman (1981), 103–8.

25   "Boys, if you ever pray": Harry S. Truman, *Memoirs* (1965), 1:31.

26   "General, there is nothing": David McCullough, *Truman* (1992), 430.

26   "Great White Jail": Truman diary, Aug. 3, 1948, in *Off the Record: The Private Papers of Harry S. Truman*, ed. Robert H. Ferrell (1980), 146.

27   "The main difficulty": Truman to Ernest W. Roberts, Aug. 18, 1948, in ibid., 146–47.

28   "double-crossers all": McCullough, *Truman*, 634–36.

29   "Senator Barkley and I": Truman acceptance speech, July 15, 1948, Public Papers.

30   "We'll stay in Berlin": Truman diary, July 19, 1948, in Ferrell, *Off the Record*, 145.

30   "We had to face the possibility": Truman, *Memoirs*, 2:149.

31   "Absolutely impossible": Richard Reeves, *Daring Young Men: The Heroism and Triumph of the Berlin Airlift, June 1948–May 1949* (2010), 34.

32   "I have a terrible feeling": Truman diary, Sept. 13, 1948, in Ferrell, *Off the Record*, 148–49.

33   "It will be the greatest campaign": Truman to Mary Jane Truman, Oct. 5, 1948, in ibid., 149–50.

33   "I don't have to give 'em hell": Truman remarks, Oct. 22, 1952, Public Papers.

33   "It wasn't, in my opinion": McCulloch, *Truman*, 717–18.

34   "The Soviets had declared": Willy Brandt, *My Road to Berlin* (1960), 197.

CHAPTER 3

35   "If this system": *New York Times*, April 14, 1944.

36   "I request that no action": *New York Times*, April 30, 1944.

36   "The humiliation": James, *MacArthur*, 2:527.

36   "One officer was conspicuously absent": H. W. Brands, *Traitor to His Class: The Privileged Life and Radical Presidency of Franklin Delano Roosevelt* (2008), 773–74.

37   Gallup poll: James, *MacArthur*, 3:197–98.

37   "The need is not" and "We must DRAFT": Manchester, *American Caesar*, 521.

38   "Your career": James, *MacArthur*, 3:201.

38   "No man could fail": Manchester, *American Caesar*, 521–22.

38   "MacArthur sentiment": Ibid., 522.

CHAPTER 4

40   "I believe the American people": Truman statement, Sept. 23, 1949, Public Papers.

42   "It is part of my responsibility": Truman statement, Jan. 31, 1950, Public Papers.

42   "The atom's power": Truman, *Memoirs*, 2:356.

43   "M'Carthy Charges Reds Hold U.S. Jobs": *Wheeling Intelligencer*, Feb. 10, 1950.

43   "We know of no Communist members": *Washington Post*, Feb. 12, 1950.

43   "In a Lincoln Day speech": McCarthy to Truman, Feb. 11, 1950, Truman Papers, Harry S. Truman Library.

44   "This is the first time": Undated draft of Truman to McCarthy, Truman Papers.

CHAPTER 5

45   "There is not the slightest doubt": *New York Times*, Jan. 12, 1950.

46   "Secretary Johnson also strongly pointed": *New York Times*, Jan. 14 and 15, 1950.

46   "General Bradley said": *New York Times*, Jan. 27, 1950.

46   "The decision to withdraw": MacArthur, *Reminiscences*, 320–22.

48   "After the war": *New York Times,* Jan. 13, 1950; *Washington Post,* Jan. 13, 1950;
      "Secretary Acheson and the Defense of Korea," undated memo, George Elsey
      Papers, Truman Library.
49   "The Ambassador expressed": Memo of conversation, Jan. 28, 1950, Dean Acheson
      Papers, Truman Library.

CHAPTER 6
50   "President Truman is a rather simple": Oliver Franks oral history, Truman Library.
51   "You all start": Dean Acheson oral history, Truman Library.
52   "I look at that fellow": Eric Goldman, *The Crucial Decade* (1956), 124.
52   "I had a long meeting": Dean Acheson, *Present at the Creation* (1969), 104.
53   "I do not intend to turn my back": *New York Times,* Jan. 26, 1950.
53   "turn his back": *Washington Post,* Jan. 26, 1950.
53   "screen out a Dr. Fuchs": *New York Times,* Feb. 14, 1950.
54   "worth a tinker's damn": *New York Times,* Feb. 23, 1950.

CHAPTER 7
56   "better than a Rembrandt": Manchester, *American Caesar,* 515–17.
56   "No one seems to know": MacArthur, *Reminiscences,* 8–9.
57   "Handsome as a prince": Manchester, *American Caesar,* 50–51.
58   "I met all the great Japanese commanders": Ibid., 30.
58   "Here lived almost half": Ibid., 32.
59   "My whole world changed": Ibid., 36.
59   "I had never before met": James, *MacArthur,* 1:254.
60   "He has no superior": MacArthur, *Reminiscences,* 70n.
61   "Marriage of Mars": Manchester, *American Caesar,* 130.
61   "It's all damn poppycock": Ibid.
61   "incompetency, criminal negligence": Alfred F. Hurley, *Billy Mitchell* (1975), 101.
61   "one of the most distasteful orders": MacArthur, *Reminiscences,* 85–86.

CHAPTER 8
63   "It's a very lonely thing": McCullough, *Truman,* 45.
64   "If I succeeded": Ibid., 49.
64   "Politics is the sure ruination": Truman to Bess Wallace, date illegible, in *Dear Bess:
      The Letters from Harry to Bess Truman, 1910–1959,* ed. Robert H. Ferrell (1998), 132.
65   "Have only seen one": Truman to Bess Wallace, April 17, 1918, in ibid., 259.
65   "I could just see my hide": *The Autobiography of Harry S. Truman,* ed. Robert H.
      Ferrell (1980), 46.
65   "Never on the front": McCullough, *Truman,* 117–18.
66   "It isn't as bad": Truman to Bess Wallace, Oct. 8, 1918, in Ferrell, *Dear Bess,* 274.
66   "It made me feel": McCullough, *Truman,* 134.
67   "The Boss wanted me": Ibid., 184–85.
68   "Work hard": Ibid., 213.
68   "I was a New Dealer": Truman, *Memoirs,* 1:171.
69   "I am hoping": Truman to Bess Truman, June 28, 1935, in Ferrell, *Dear Bess,* 365.
70   "Mr. President": Truman, *Memoirs,* 2:377–78; McCullough, *Truman,* 773–75.

CHAPTER 9

73 "None of us got much sleep": Margaret Truman, *Harry S. Truman* (1973), 455.
74 "It would appear": Muccio to State Department, June 25, 1950, in *Foreign Relations of the United States* (1950), vol. 7, *Korea*, 125–26.
74 "Don't make it alarmist": *New York Times*, June 26, 1950.
75 "During the afternoon": Acheson, *Present at the Creation*, 405.
75 Acheson now made this last case: Memo of conversation, June 25, 1950, Acheson Papers.
77 "The three of us": Omar N. Bradley and Clay Blair, *A General's Life* (1983), 429, 444, 523, 534.
79 "We must draw the line somewhere": Memo of conversation, June 25, 1950, Acheson Papers.
81 "unprovoked aggression": Truman statement, June 26, 1950, Public Papers.
81 "I stayed behind": Elsey memo for the record, June 26, 1950, Elsey Papers.

CHAPTER 10

83 "in pretty good shape": Memo of telephone conversation, June 26, 1950, Acheson Papers.
83 In another conversation: Memo of telephone conversation, June 26, 1950, Acheson Papers.
83 "The President said": Memo of conversation, June 26, 1950, Acheson Papers.
84 "offer the fullest possible support": Memo of conversation, June 26, 1950, Acheson Papers.
86 "In these circumstances": Truman statement, June 27, 1950, Public Papers.
86 "This act": Memo of conversation, n.d. (June 27, 1950), Elsey Papers; memo of conversation, June 27, 1950, Acheson Papers.
87 Stalin's approval: William Stueck, *The Korean War: An International History* (1995), 31–41.
87 "vitally essential": Memo of conversation, n.d. (June 27, 1950), Elsey Papers; memo of conversation, June 27, 1950, Acheson Papers.

CHAPTER 11

89 "The strategic interests": MacArthur memo, June 14, 1950, in *Foreign Relations of the United States* (1950), vol. 7, *Korea*, 161–64.
90 "Not more than one in ten": Ibid., 94.
90 "incipient revolution": James, *MacArthur*, 1:399.
90 "He said he was too busy": Dwight D. Eisenhower, *At Ease* (1967), 217.
91 "Had he waited": Manchester, *American Caesar*, 152.
91 "Well, Felix": Brands, *Traitor to His Class*, 259.
91 "Douglas MacArthur": Ibid., 259–61.
91 "General, you have been": Stephen Ambrose, *Eisenhower* (1983), 1:107.
92 "The time is ripe": H. W. Brands, *Bound to Empire: The United States and the Philippines* (1992), 191–92.
93 "disastrous debacle": Ibid., 193–94.
93 "losing his nerve": Ambrose, *Eisenhower*, 1:139.
93 "American forces will continue": Brands, *Bound to Empire*, 194–95.
93 "These people are depending on me": Ibid., 196–97.
94 "I came through": James, *MacArthur*, 2:109.
95 "It is a strange thing": Ibid., 3:426.
95 "The moment I reach Tokyo": Marguerite Higgins, *War in Korea* (1951), 33–34.

95 "The Korean army and coastal forces": MacArthur to Joint Chiefs of Staff, June 30, 1950, Truman Papers.

CHAPTER 12

96 "Mr. President": Truman news conference, June 29, 1950, Public Papers.

97 "Even then": MacArthur, *Reminiscences*, 330.

98 "I do not want": Notes of meeting, June 29, 1950, Elsey Papers; Kirk to Acheson, June 29, 1950, Elsey Papers.

CHAPTER 13

101 "Your authorization": Memo of Teletype conference, June 30, 1950, in *Foreign Relations of the United States* (1950), vol. 7, *Korea*, 251.

102 "Time was all-important": Truman, *Memoirs*, 2:390.

102 "The net result": Acheson, *Present at the Creation*, 412.

103 "The President announced": *Washington Post*, July 1, 1950.

103 "the boss": Memo of meeting, June 30, 1950, Elsey Papers.

106 "Move the 24th Division": MacArthur to Walker, June 30, 1950, Elsey Papers.

106 "I don't understand this order": Truman note, n.d., Elsey Papers.

106 "I was already up and shaved": Truman memo, June 30, 1950, Elsey Papers.

CHAPTER 14

108 "The Red invasion": Higgins, *War in Korea*, 15–49.

CHAPTER 15

114 "At long last": *New York Times*, July 1, 1950.

114 "We are now actually engaged": *New York Times*, June 29, 1950.

114 "When you are in": *New York Times*, July 1, 1950.

115 "whitewash": *New York Times*, June 29, 1950.

115 "There is in Washington": *New York Times*, June 28, 1950.

115 "As the American people": *New York Times*, June 29, 1950.

115 "When orders to attack": Higgins, *War in Korea*, 61–70, 82–89.

118 "I recall so vividly": MacArthur to Truman, July 11, 1950, Douglas MacArthur Papers, MacArthur Memorial Library and Archives.

118 "I deeply appreciate": Truman to MacArthur, July 11, 1950, Truman Papers.

118 "This chance he has now lost": MacArthur to Truman, July 19, 1950, Truman Papers.

119 "The issue of battle": Truman radio address, July 19, 1950, Public Papers.

119 "To meet the situation": Truman message, July 19, 1950, Public Papers.

119 "It is a great state paper": MacArthur to Truman, July 19, 1950, Truman Papers.

CHAPTER 16

120 "General Douglas MacArthur": *New York Times*, July 9, 1950.

121 "An agreement was reached": *New York Times*, Aug. 2, 1950.

122 "Harriman and I": MacArthur, *Reminiscences*, 341.

122 "General MacArthur met me": Harriman report, in Truman, *Memoirs*, 2:397–402.

125 "If he has horns": Sebald diary, July 24, 1950, William J. Sebald Papers, U.S. Naval Academy.

CHAPTER 17

126 "Walker, you can make": Geoffrey Perret, *Old Soldiers Never Die: The Life of Douglas MacArthur* (1996), 544–45.

126 "General MacArthur was over here": Roy E. Appleman, *South to the Naktong, North to the Yalu* (1961), 207–8.

127 "We hope you can talk": Higgins, *War in Korea,* 101, 107, 117, 120–21, 130.

CHAPTER 18

129 "General burst": Sebald diary, July 26 and Sept. 4, 1950, Sebald Papers.

130 "This visit": *New York Times,* Aug. 10, 1950.

130 "General MacArthur says": Truman news conference, Aug. 10, 1950, Public Papers.

131 "Look at him now": *New York Times,* Aug. 20, 1950.

132 "From senior commanders": MacArthur to Clyde A. Lewis, Aug. 20, 1950, MacArthur Papers.

CHAPTER 19

136 "When we filed": Acheson, *Present at the Creation,* 423.

137 "In obvious consternation": Memo for file, Aug. 26, 1950, Elsey Papers; memo for the record, Aug. 26, 1950, Acheson Papers.

140 "The President of the United States": Johnson to MacArthur, Aug. 26, 1950, Truman Papers.

CHAPTER 20

141 "My message": MacArthur to Johnson, Aug. 27, 1950, Truman Papers.

142 "complete confidence": *New York Times,* Aug. 29, 1950.

143 "That's the day": Merle Miller, *Plain Speaking: An Oral Biography of Harry S. Truman* (1974), 291–92.

CHAPTER 21

144 "We have no choice": *New York Times,* Aug. 26, 1950.

145 "For the first time": Truman radio and television address, Sept. 1, 1950, Public Papers.

147 "The political objective": NSC 81, Sept. 1, 1950, Truman Papers.

CHAPTER 22

151 "A big 250-pound bear": Bradley and Blair, *General's Life,* 501–2.

151 "Louis began to show": Truman diary, Sept. 14, 1950, in Ferrell, *Off the Record,* 191–93.

152 "Tomorrow I have to break": Truman to Bess Truman, Sept. 7, 1950, in Ferrell, *Dear Bess,* 563.

CHAPTER 23

153 "I was now finally ready": MacArthur, *Reminiscences,* 346.

154 "For your information": Truman to Gordon McDonough, Aug. 29, 1950, published with Truman to Commandant of the Marine Corps League and Commandant of the Marine Corps, Sept. 6, 1950, Public Papers.

154 "General, I have not been asked": James, *MacArthur,* 3:468.

154 "I could feel the tension": MacArthur, *Reminiscences,* 349–50.

157 "It was at this eleventh hour": Ibid., 351–52.

158 "A majority of MacArthur's staff": Bradley and Blair, *General's Life,* 556.

CHAPTER 24

159   "Our assault": Higgins, *War in Korea,* 139–46.

CHAPTER 25

162   "Today, as on eleven previous landings": *New York Times,* Sept. 16, 1950.
163   "If that can be accomplished": Ibid.
163   "As far as we are concerned": *Washington Post,* Sept. 30, 1950.
163   "While mopping-up fighting": MacArthur communiqué, Sept. 27, 1950, *Los Angeles Times,* Sept. 27, 1950.
163   "But at this juncture": MacArthur, *Reminiscences,* 354–55.
164   "By the grace of merciful Providence": *New York Times,* Sept. 29, 1950.
165   "'We admire you'": MacArthur, *Reminiscences,* 356.
165   "Inchon proved to be": Bradley and Blair, *General's Life,* 556–57.
165   "Accept my personal tribute": Marshall to MacArthur, Oct. 1, 1950, MacArthur Papers.
165   "Thanks, George": MacArthur to Marshall, Oct. 1, 1950, MacArthur Papers.
166   "I know that I speak": Truman to MacArthur, Sept. 29, 1950, Public Papers.

CHAPTER 26

167   "Mr. President, have you decided": Truman news conference, Sept. 21, 1950, Public Papers.
167   "Mr. President, has this government": Truman news conference, Sept. 28, 1950, Public Papers.
169   "The early and total defeat": MacArthur surrender demand, Oct. 1, 1950, Public Papers.
170   "Your military objective": Directive to Commander of the United Nations Forces in Korea, attached to Marshall to Truman, Sept. 27, 1950, Truman Papers.
171   "There is no indication": MacArthur to Joint Chiefs of Staff, Sept. 28, 1950, Truman Papers.
171   "We want you to feel": Joint Chiefs of Staff to MacArthur, Sept. 29, 1950, Truman Papers.
171   "Parallel 38": MacArthur to Joint Chiefs of Staff, Sept. 30, 1950, Truman Papers.

CHAPTER 27

172   "We had never had any personal contacts": Truman, *Memoirs,* 2:413–14.
172   "The President did not wish": Meeting notes, Oct. 9, 1950, Acheson Papers.
173   "Japan, Philippines": Notes on the Wake Conferences, Oct. 13, 1950, Acheson Papers.
174   "General MacArthur and I": Truman statement, Oct. 10, 1950, Public Papers.
174   "political junket": Sebald diary, Oct. 12, 1950, Sebald Papers.
175   "In view of the number": MacArthur, *Reminiscences,* 360–61.
175   "The idea of the General": Sebald diary, Oct. 11, 1950, Sebald Papers.
175   "For heaven's sake": Swigart (no first name given) to MacArthur, Oct. 12, 1950, MacArthur Papers.
175   "We urge you": Mr. and Mrs. George Leary to MacArthur, Oct. 12, 1950, MacArthur Papers.
175   "Do not give in": Carl S. Carlson to MacArthur, Oct. 13, 1950, MacArthur Papers.
175   "He read me": Sebald diary, Oct. 12, 1950, Sebald Papers.
175   "MacArthur sat down": John Muccio oral history, Truman Library.
175   "It is an eight-hour flight": Whitney, *MacArthur,* 385–86.

176 "I've a whale of a job": Truman to Nellie Noland, Oct. 13, 1950, in Ferrell, *Off the Record*, 195–96.

176 "It was still dark": Truman, *Memoirs*, 2:415–16.

177 "General MacArthur was at the airport": Truman memo, Nov. 25, 1950, Truman Papers.

177 "I have been a long time": Log of trip to Wake Island, Oct. 11–18, 1950, Truman Papers.

177 "I had been warned": MacArthur, *Reminiscences*, 361.

177 "The general seemed": Truman, *Memoirs*, 2:416–17.

178 "The General assured the President": Truman memo, Nov. 25, 1950, Truman Papers.

178 "The building where the conference": Vernice Anderson oral history, Truman Library.

179 "I believe that formal resistance": "Substance of Statements Made at Wake Island Conference," compiled by Omar Bradley, Oct. 15, 1950, Elsey Papers.

183 "None whatsoever": Whitney, *MacArthur*, 389.

183 "The very complete unanimity": Truman statement, Oct. 15, 1950, Public Papers.

CHAPTER 28

185 "I have just returned": Truman address in San Francisco, Oct. 17, 1950, Public Papers.

186 "I am glad he went": *New York Times*, Oct. 17, 1950.

186 "Mr. President, are you now": Truman news conference, Oct. 19, 1950, Public Papers.

188 "Rarely has the President": *New York Times*, Oct. 20, 1950.

188 "very angry": *Washington Post*, Oct. 20, 1950.

188 "the establishment of a unified": UN General Assembly Resolution 377, Oct. 7, 1950.

189 "I didn't see any opposition": James, *MacArthur*, 3:496.

189 "The enemy is thoroughly shattered": MacArthur to U.S. mission to UN, Oct. 20, 1950, Truman Papers.

189 "The progress the forces": Truman to MacArthur, Oct. 24, 1950, Truman Papers.

189 "I left the Wake Island conference": MacArthur to Truman, Oct. 30, 1950, Truman Papers.

CHAPTER 29

193 "They may even drop atom bombs": K. M. Panikkar, *In Two Chinas* (1955), 108.

194 "They will not be afraid": *New York Times*, Oct. 2, 1950.

194 "He was emphatic": Panikkar, *In Two Chinas*, 110.

194 "Why didn't they": *New York Times*, Oct. 2, 1950.

194 "The Chinese Communists undoubtedly fear": CIA memo, Oct. 12, 1950, in *Foreign Relations of the United States* (1950), vol. 7, *Korea*, 933–34.

194 "It was obvious": Acheson, *Present at the Creation*, 452.

195 "Mr. Panikkar": Truman, *Memoirs*, 2:413.

195 "In light of the possible intervention": Joint Chiefs of Staff to MacArthur, Oct. 8, 1950 (sent Oct. 9), Truman Papers.

195 "The conference at Wake Island": MacArthur, *Reminiscences*, 363.

196 "to drive forward": MacArthur to Walker et al., Oct. 24, 1950, quoted in James F. Schnabel and Robert J. Watson, *The History of the Joint Chiefs of Staff: The Joint Chiefs of Staff and National Policy*, vol. 3, *The Korean War* (1979), pt. 1, 274.

196 "Up to this point": Bradley and Blair, *General's Life,* 578.

196 "a matter of some concern": Joint Chiefs of Staff to MacArthur, Oct. 24, 1940, in Schnabel and Watson, *History of the Joint Chiefs of Staff,* 275.

196 "as a matter of policy": MacArthur to Joint Chiefs of Staff, Oct. 24, 1950, in ibid., 275–76.

CHAPTER 30

198 "On 26 October": Walker to MacArthur, Nov. 6, 1950, in James F. Schnabel, *United States Army in the Korean War,* vol. 3, *Policy and Direction: The First Year* (1972), 235.

198 "Chinese Communist hordes": *New York Times,* Nov. 3, 1950.

199 "Prisoners averaged": MacArthur to Joint Chiefs of Staff, Oct. 31, 1950, Truman Papers.

200 "Various possibilities exist": MacArthur to Joint Chiefs of Staff, Nov. 4, 1950, Truman Papers.

201 "We came here": *Washington Post,* Nov. 2, 1950.

CHAPTER 31

203 "The President said": Memo of conference, Nov. 6, 1950, Acheson Papers.

203 "The President recognizes": Summary of telephone conversation with the President, Nov. 6, 1950, Acheson Papers.

204 "Men and material": MacArthur to Joint Chiefs of Staff, Nov. 6, 1950, Truman Papers.

205 "Neither I nor anyone else": Bradley and Blair, *General's Life,* 588.

205 "General Bradley read me this message": Truman, *Memoirs,* 2:428.

205 "considerably changed": Joint Chiefs of Staff to MacArthur, Nov. 6, 1950, Truman Papers.

CHAPTER 32

207 "very cheerful" and "The President is taking": *Washington Post,* Nov. 9, 1950.

208 "This new situation": Joint Chiefs of Staff to MacArthur, Nov. 8, 1950, in *Foreign Relations of the United States* (1950), vol. 7, *Korea,* 1097–98.

208 "I cannot agree": MacArthur to Joint Chiefs of Staff, Nov. 9, 1950, in ibid., 1107–10.

209 "The forces that had struck": Acheson, *Present at the Creation,* 465–66.

209 "By violation of territory": Schnabel, *United States Army in the Korean War,* 3:246.

210 "One of those bomber pilots": MacArthur, *Reminiscences,* 365–71.

CHAPTER 33

212 "The United Nations massive compression": MacArthur communiqué, Nov. 24, 1950, MacArthur Papers.

212 "I hope to keep my promise": *New York Times,* Nov. 24, 1950.

212 "His exact words": John Muccio oral history, Truman Library.

213 "The giant U. N. pincer": MacArthur communiqué, Nov. 24, 1950, MacArthur Papers.

213 "The developments resulting": MacArthur to Joint Chiefs of Staff, Nov. 28, 1950, in *Foreign Relations of the United States* (1950), vol. 7, *Korea,* 1237–38.

214 "No new directive": Notes of NSC meeting, Nov. 28, 1950, Truman Papers; memo of conversation of NSC meeting, Nov. 28, 1950, Acheson Papers.

CHAPTER 34

220 "Recent developments": Truman news conference, Nov. 30, 1950, Public Papers.

223 "The President wants": Truman statement, Nov. 30, 1950, Public Papers.

CHAPTER 35

226 "Undoubtedly General MacArthur": Minutes of meeting with congressional leaders, Dec. 1, 1950, Truman Papers.

CHAPTER 36

228 "Outwardly there is a new unity": *New York Times,* Nov. 30, 1950.

229 "Were there any warnings": Interview with MacArthur, *U.S. News & World Report,* released by the magazine and published in *New York Times,* Dec. 1, 1950; "Categorical Replies to Mr. Lawrence's Questions," n.d., MacArthur Papers.

CHAPTER 37

232 "Tell General MacArthur": LCB (unidentified) to MacArthur, Dec. 2, 1950, MacArthur Papers.

232 "I should have relieved": Truman, *Memoirs,* 2:437.

233 "The attitude": CIA memo, Dec. 2, 1950, in *Foreign Relations of the United States* (1950), vol. 7, *Korea,* 1308–10.

234 "The X Corps": MacArthur to Joint Chiefs of Staff, Dec. 3, 1950, in ibid., 1320–22.

237 "Why don't the chiefs": David Halberstam, *The Coldest Winter: America and the Korean War* (2007), 483.

CHAPTER 38

238 "The snow lashed hard": Higgins, *War in Korea,* 181–97.

CHAPTER 39

243 "The United States has responsibilities": Minutes of Truman-Acheson meeting, Dec. 4, 1950, in *Foreign Relations of the United States* (1950), vol. 7, *Korea,* 1361–74.

246 "vacillating and palavering": *New York Times,* Dec. 5, 1950.

246 "another Munich": *New York Times,* Dec. 6, 1950.

247 "They can be Marxists": Minutes of Truman-Attlee meeting, Dec. 5, 1950, in *Foreign Relations of the United States* (1950), vol. 7, *Korea,* 1392–408.

247 "The objectives of our two nations": Joint statement by Truman and Attlee, Dec. 8, 1950, Public Papers.

CHAPTER 40

248 "Probable Soviet Moves to Exploit the Present Situation": Summary of CIA report, Dec. 13, 1950, Elsey Papers.

249 "I am talking to you tonight": Truman address, Dec. 15, 1950, Public Papers.

251 "His manner was brisk": *New York Times,* Dec. 17, 1950.

251 "Here is your opposition": *Washington Post,* Dec. 18, 1950.

252 "If there is an emergency": *Chicago Tribune,* Dec. 17, 1950.

252 "It is completely obvious": *New York Times,* Dec. 16, 1950.

253 "This meeting in Brussels": Truman statement, Dec. 17, 1950, Public Papers.

253 "You are undertaking": Truman to Eisenhower, Dec. 19, 1950, Public Papers.

253 "I will take it real slowly": Truman news conference, Dec. 19, 1950, Public Papers.

CHAPTER 41

255 "My own feeling": Matthew B. Ridgway, *The Korean War* (1967), 142.

256 "Matt, I'm sorry": Matthew B. Ridgway, *Soldier* (1956), 195–201.

256 "I was again deeply impressed": Ridgway, *Korean War,* 81–83.

257 "inflicting such damage": Joint Chiefs of Staff to MacArthur, Dec. 29, 1950, in *Foreign Relations of the United States* (1950), vol. 7, *Korea,* 1625.

258 "utter dismay": Whitney, *MacArthur,* 430–31.

258 "It is quite clear now": MacArthur to Joint Chiefs of Staff, Dec. 30, 1950, in *Foreign Relations of the United States* (1950), vol. 7, *Korea,* 1631.

CHAPTER 42

260 "He alarmed us": Bradley and Blair, *General's Life,* 617.

260 "On my orders": Ridgway, *Soldier,* 203–14.

CHAPTER 43

264 "The following must be accepted": Joint Chiefs of Staff to MacArthur, Jan. 9, 1951, in *Foreign Relations of the United States* (1951), vol. 7, *Korea and China,* pt. 1, 41–42.

265 "All one could do": Whitney, *MacArthur,* 435.

265 "Request clarification": MacArthur to Joint Chiefs of Staff, Jan. 10, 1951, in *Foreign Relations of the United States* (1951), vol. 7, *Korea and China,* pt. 1, 55–56.

266 "Here was a posterity paper": Acheson, *Present at the Creation,* 515.

266 "Senior officers decrying": Bradley and Blair, *General's Life,* 619.

266 "When a general complains": Acheson, *Present at the Creation,* 515.

266 "I was deeply disturbed": Truman, *Memoirs,* 2:492.

267 "He was unwilling": Memo of conversation, Jan. 12, 1951, in *Foreign Relations of the United States* (1951), vol. 7, *Korea and China,* pt. 1, 68–70.

267 "I want you to know": Truman to MacArthur, Jan. 13, 1951, Truman Papers.

268 "It was an imaginatively kind": Acheson, *Present at the Creation,* 516.

CHAPTER 44

271 "We shall do our best": MacArthur to Joint Chiefs of Staff, Jan. 14, 1951, in *Foreign Relations of the United States* (1951), vol. 7, *Korea and China,* pt. 1, 79n.

271 "I toured the front": J. Lawton Collins, *War in Peacetime* (1969), 253–55.

272 "We began to think": Bradley and Blair, *General's Life,* 622.

272 "General Ridgway alone": Collins, *War in Peacetime,* 255.

CHAPTER 45

273 "In very recent days": *New York Times,* Jan. 6, 1951.

CHAPTER 46

278 "I had planned": Ridgway, *Korean War,* 108–10.

279 "I now began": MacArthur, *Reminiscences,* 384.

280 "Today, after ninety years": Martin press release of speech, Feb. 12, 1951, Truman Papers.

282 "In the current discussions": Martin to MacArthur, March 8, 1951, in MacArthur, *Reminiscences,* 385–86.

282 "I have always felt": MacArthur, *Reminiscences,* 386.

282 "Dear Congressman Martin": MacArthur to Martin, March 20, 1951, MacArthur Papers.

CHAPTER 47

284 "I attached little importance": MacArthur, *Reminiscences*, 386.

284 "State planning": Joint Chiefs of Staff to MacArthur, March 20, 1951, in *Foreign Relations of the United States* (1951), vol. 7, *Korea and China*, pt. 1, 251.

284 "Recommend that no further military restrictions": MacArthur to Joint Chiefs of Staff, March 21, 1951, in ibid., 255–56.

285 "I do not know what went on": Bradley and Blair, *General's Life*, 626–27.

285 "We have now substantially cleared": MacArthur press release, March 24, 1951, MacArthur Papers.

CHAPTER 48

287 "pronunciamento": Acheson, *Present at the Creation*, 518–19.

287 "The first related": Memo of telephone conversation, March 24, 1951, Acheson Papers.

289 "The President, although perfectly calm": Acheson, *Present at the Creation*, 519.

289 "The President has directed": Joint Chiefs of Staff to MacArthur, March 24, 1951, Truman Papers.

290 "The argument was made": MacArthur, *Reminiscences*, 388–89.

290 "Far from MacArthur's ken": Whitney, *MacArthur*, 467–68.

CHAPTER 49

291 "We had recently received": Bradley and Blair, *General's Life*, 629–30.

291 "If the USSR": Bradley to Marshall, April 5, 1951, in *Foreign Relations of the United States* (1951), vol. 7, *Korea and China*, pt. 1, 295–96.

291 "The Joint Chiefs of Staff": Bradley to Marshall, April 6, 1951, in ibid., 309.

292 "Ordinarily we would have sent": Bradley and Blair, *General's Life*, 630.

292 "I have no comment": Truman news conference, April 5, 1951, Public Papers.

294 "Rank insubordination": Truman diary, April 6, 1951, Truman Papers.

295 "Their attachment": Acheson, *Present at the Creation*, 521–22; Truman, *Memoirs*, 2:507–8; W. Averell Harriman, "Mr. Truman's Way with Crises," in *The Korean War: A 25-Year Perspective*, ed. Francis P. Heller (1977), 235; Bradley and Blair, *General's Life*, 631–33.

297 "Marshall and I": Bradley and Blair, *General's Life*, 633–35; Collins, *War in Peacetime*, 283–84.

299 "The situation in Far East": Truman diary, April 8, 1951, Truman Papers.

299 "Whatever his action": Acheson, *Present at the Creation*, 522; Truman, *Memoirs*, 2:508.

299 The critical meeting occurred: Truman, *Memoirs*, 2:508; Acheson, *Present at the Creation*, 522; Bradley and Blair, *General's Life*, 635.

CHAPTER 50

302 "I got a double talk": Bradley and Blair, *General's Life*, 636.

302 "Said there had been a leak": Truman diary, on page dated April 9 but referring to events of April 10, 1951, Truman Papers.

302 "He got hold of me": Theodore Tannenwald oral history, Truman Library.

303 "With deep regret": Truman statement and order, April 11, 1951, Public Papers.

CHAPTER 51

305 "Wednesday, April 11": Whitney, *MacArthur*, 470.

306 "Well, General": Ridgway, *Soldier*, 220.

306   "that the President": Michael Schaller, *Douglas MacArthur: The Far Eastern General* (1989), 239–40.

306   "He was entirely himself": Ridgway, *Soldier,* 223.

307   "I am afraid": Sebald diary, April 8, 1951, Sebald Papers.

307   "Refused to believe it at first": Ibid., April 11, 1951.

CHAPTER 52

309   "The question we have had to face": Truman radio address, April 11, 1951, Public Papers.

CHAPTER 53

311   "Quite an explosion": Truman diary, on page dated April 10 but referring to events of April 11, 1951, Truman Papers.

311   "Your action toward MacArthur": Lindsey Williams to Truman, April 11, 1951, Truman Papers.

311   "You have sold us out": Elisabeth Wood to Truman, April 12, 1951, Truman Papers.

312   "General MacArthur has probably forgotten": Dorothy Weir to Truman, April 11, 1951, Truman Papers.

312   5,000 telegrams: *New York Times,* April 13, 1951.

312   Editorial opinion was mixed: Sampling of editorials, *New York Times,* April 12, 1951.

CHAPTER 54

314   "Court, please arrange": Whitney, *MacArthur,* 479–80.

315   MacArthur, accompanied by Jean and Arthur: *Los Angeles Times,* April 16, 1951; *New York Times,* April 16, 1951.

316   "As I looked down": Whitney, *MacArthur,* 480.

CHAPTER 55

317   "The *Bataan* is making": *Los Angeles Times,* April 18, 1951; *New York Times,* April 18, 1951.

320   "But there was one thing": *Washington Post,* April 20, 1951.

321   "I stand on this rostrum": MacArthur address to joint session of Congress, April 19, 1951, transcript in *New York Times,* April 20, 1951, and *Washington Post,* April 20, 1951; radio recording on YouTube.

CHAPTER 56

328   "Welcome home, Mac!": *New York Times,* April 21, 1951; *Washington Post,* April 21, 1951.

329   "Today The New York Times": *New York Times,* April 21, 1951.

329   "Are you in a position": Truman news conference, April 26, 1951, Public Papers.

330   "very little": *New York Times,* May 3, 1951.

CHAPTER 57

332   "We are opening hearings": *New York Times,* May 4, 1951; *Washington Post,* May 4, 1951; *Los Angeles Times,* May 4, 1951.

CHAPTER 58

346 "As I recollect it": *New York Times*, May 5, 1951; *Washington Post*, May 5, 1951; *Los Angeles Times*, May 5, 1951.

352 "General MacArthur, I wish to state": *New York Times*, May 6, 1951.

CHAPTER 59

353 "It is a very distressing necessity": *New York Times*, May 8, 1951.

356 "At the time the foregoing statement": *New York Times, Washington Post* and *Los Angeles Times*, May 9–10, 1951.

358 "Do you have a prepared statement": *New York Times*, June 2, 1951.

359 "At the very outset": *New York Times*, May 16, 1951; *Washington Post*, May 16, 1951.

CHAPTER 60

363 "There are 35 Russian divisions": Declassified transcript of MacArthur hearings, 2579, Record Group 46, National Archives.

363 "What would happen": Ibid., 2580–83.

364 "The Air Force part": Ibid., 3948–52.

365 "They have not used air": Ibid., 2311.

365 "We are fighting": Ibid., 2436.

366 "You made the statement": Ibid., 3945–46.

366 "The next thing": Ibid., 1300–1302.

367 "When the first recommendations": Ibid., 3124.

368 "Do you have any indication": Ibid., 1732–33.

368 "We were highly skeptical": Ibid., 3217.

368 "The trouble of it is": Ibid., 2506–7.

369 "We do not feel": Ibid., 2341.

CHAPTER 61

370 "For the past seven weeks": *New York Times*, June 28, 1951.

371 And MacArthur never found out: The redacted portions of the transcript of the hearings were not released until more than a decade after MacArthur's death.

CHAPTER 62

372 "purely a Pace thought": Frank Pace oral history, Truman Library.

372 "double-crossed": Robert J. Donovan, *Tumultuous Years: The Presidency of Harry S. Truman, 1949–1953* (1982), 355.

373 "happy to witness": *New York Times*, May 13, 1951.

373 "One of the greatest influences": *New York Times*, June 8, 1951.

373 "I am no stranger": *New York Times*, May 1, 1951.

373 "Some, with me": *New York Times*, June 14, 15 and 16, 1951.

375 "I shall raise my voice": *General MacArthur: Speeches and Reports, 1908–1964*, comp. Edward T. Imparato (2000), 179–81.

CHAPTER 63

376 "Mr. President": Truman news conference, June 28, 1951, Public Papers.

377 "No comment": Truman news conference, July 26, 1951, Public Papers.

377 Truman named MacArthur: Truman address, Sept. 4, 1951, Public Papers.

377 "Not based on fact": Truman news conference, Oct. 18, 1951, Public Papers.

377 The State Department surveyed: Daily Opinion Summary, Department of State, May 7, 1951, Elsey Papers.

377 The White House staff tallied: Memo for the President by William J. Hopkins, May 8, 1951, Truman Papers.

378 "I don't like to be": Elsey to Harriman and Murphy, May 29, 1951, Elsey Papers.

378 "Thirteen men gather": W. V. Myers to Truman, June 15, 1951, Truman Papers.

CHAPTER 64

379 "I am not a candidate": Truman diary, April 16, 1950, in Ferrell, *Off the Record*, 177–78.

380 22 percent: "Presidential Approval Ratings—Gallup Historical Statistics and Trends," www.gallup.com.

CHAPTER 65

384 "When you put on a uniform": *New York Times*, April 12, 1951.

384 "I was sorry": Donovan, *Tumultuous Years*, 361.

384 "Most of the senior officers": Eisenhower, *At Ease*, 213.

385 "I've not been so upset": Robert H. Ferrell, ed., *The Eisenhower Diaries* (1981), 214.

CHAPTER 66

386 "with the overwhelming support": *New York Times*, Oct. 18, 1951.

387 "It is about time": James, *MacArthur*, 3:645.

387 "the pro-Soviet forces": *New York Times*, March 20, 1952.

387 The plane landed just past five: *Washington Post*, July 8, 1952.

389 "It is a trick": Video of NBC News coverage of MacArthur address, July 7, 1952, C-SPAN, www.c-span.org.

CHAPTER 67

390 "That job requires": *New York Times*, Oct. 25, 1952.

391 "Mr. President": Truman news conference, Dec. 11, 1952, Public Papers.

392 "That at such conference": "Memorandum on Ending the Korean War," in MacArthur, *Reminiscences*, 411; James, *MacArthur*, 3:653–54.

393 "We had a very enjoyable lunch": *New York Times*, Dec. 18, 1952.

393 "From that day to this": MacArthur, *Reminiscences*, 414.

394 "The trouble with Eisenhower": Peter Lyon, *Eisenhower* (1974), 500.

394 "We dropped the word": Dwight D. Eisenhower, *The White House Years: Mandate for Change, 1953–1956* (1963), 181.

CHAPTER 68

397 "He'll sit here": Robert H. Ferrell, *Harry S. Truman: A Life* (1994), 379.

397 "I fired him": Miller, *Plain Speaking*, 287.

INDEX

ABOUT THE AUTHOR

H. W. Brands holds the Jack S. Blanton Sr. Chair in History at the University of Texas at Austin. A *New York Times* best-selling author, he was a finalist for the Pulitzer Prize in biography for *The First American* and *Traitor to His Class*.

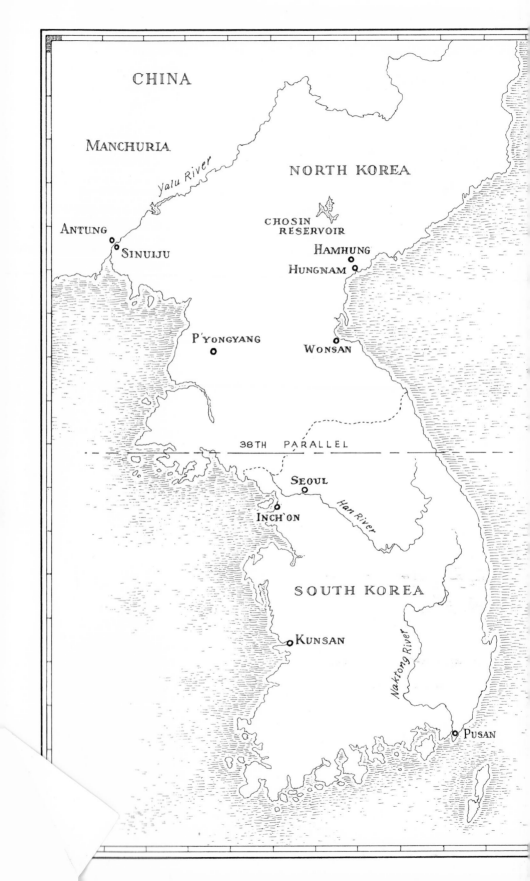